Swamp, Strand, & Steamboat

Voices of Horry County, South Carolina
1732-1954

Randall A. Wells

50th Anniversary of Coastal Carolina University

Horry County Historical Society

Text and cover designer: Paul Olsen, Coastal Carolina University

Printed by: Sheriar Press

Please visit our website at http://www.hchsonline.org

ISBN 0-9763387-0-X

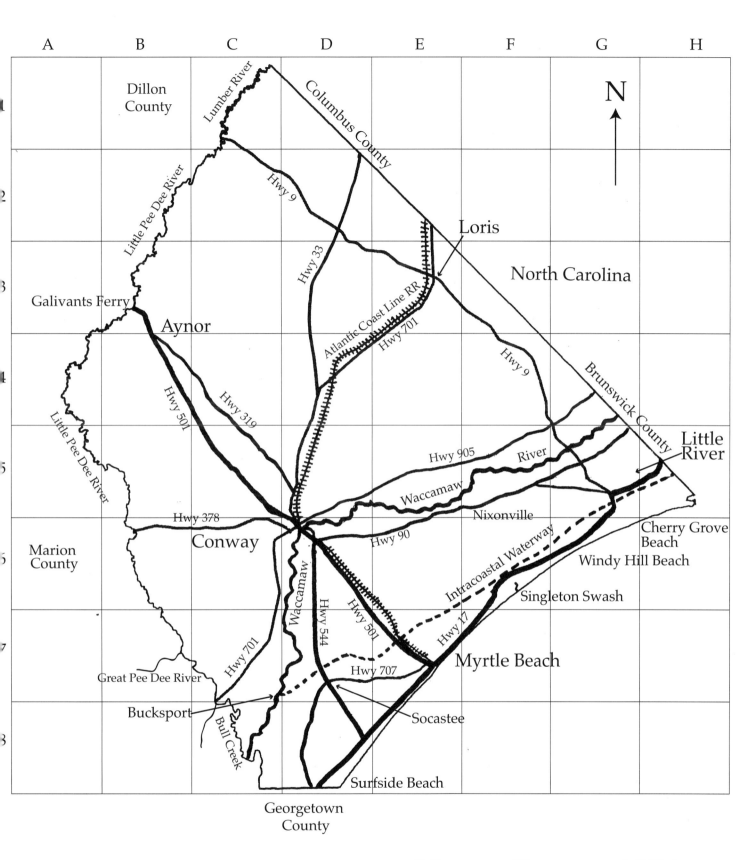

A B C D E F G H

N

Dillon County

Lumber River

Columbus County

Little Pee Dee River

Hwy 9

Hwy 33

Loris

North Carolina

Galivants Ferry

Aynor

Atlantic Coast Line RR

Hwy 701

Hwy 9

Brunswick County

Little River

Hwy 501

Hwy 319

Little Pee Dee River

Hwy 905

River

Waccamaw

Nixonville

Hwy 378

Conway

Hwy 90

Intracoastal Waterway

Cherry Grove Beach

Windy Hill Beach

Singleton Swash

Marion County

Waccamaw

Hwy 544

Hwy 501

Hwy 17

Hwy 701

Myrtle Beach

Great Pee Dee River

Hwy 707

Bucksport

Bull Creek

Socastee

Surfside Beach

Georgetown County

Horry County 1954

Contents

Foreword..i

List of Plates...iv

1. THE LAND...1

2. THE ROAD..19

3. THE BOAT..35

4. THE GUM...49

5. THE LOG..61

6. THE WEED...77

7. THE BEACH...93

8. THE FISH...107

9. THE DANCE...119

10. THE STORM...133

Afterword...141

Works Cited...145

Index...159

Dedicated to LaVerne and the late Sidney Bernard

Chinese junk came into Conway
tied up at the old warehouse
before 1941, before the war

They wore red in my mind's eye
Almost a carnival almost, go on boat, trinkets for sale,
tin, paper, don't remember anything else but that
Was at least one family of Chinese
it seems that my father told me more than one

They told my father that was the blackest water they'd
    ever seen,
on the darkest night you felt like you were out at sea
They had been all around the world.

Several others remember it coming.

Boat I think was red with lanterns

A "found poem" based on notes taken during a
telephone interview with Mrs. Belle Miller Spivey Hood, 2000.

FOREWORD

A volcano, dotted with palmetto trees and shrubbery, juts skyward. Its vertical sweep continues as the top meets the sloping back of a creature: three times higher than a human being, the animal has a perpendicular neck even longer than its white-gaitered forelegs, which are muscularly shouldered, stiffly planted, and taller than the hind legs. Its white hide, brilliant in the sun, is covered by tan polygonal spots and fringed by a dark mane. Its equine head has a small mouth, stubby horns between erect ears, and eyes, shadowed like those of ancient Egyptians, that focus on the nearby Atlantic, whose breeze wafts toward land.

Below this apparition a young fellow wearing sunglasses, Bermuda shorts, and a muscle shirt taps an orange ball with a club. When it rolls down a carpeted chute but misses the hole, he sighs "Oh-h" as the loudspeaker croons about "Shagging in the daytime." Automobiles whiz past the grass huts, the waterfall, and the elephant whose tail is patched with duct tape.

In Old Horry, by contrast, animals were about the only things not made by hand. "It was rough as an old boot!" declared Mrs. Catherine Heniford Lewis with a generous laugh. She had been raised in Loris and served for decades as the County Librarian. A boot—leather, scuffed, workaday–is the perfect simile for the era before manmade jungles.

Suppose this giraffe had been a sentinel for the past two or three hundred years. Its bulging eyes would have seen an evangelist who admired God's porpoises as they frolicked near shore; a chariot drawn by four horses and decorated with the Washington coat of arms (the Grand Strand's first out-of-state license plate); an ox that "snaked" logs out of the woods for a man with skin the color of their bark; a covered wagon trundling up to Windy Hill on a camping trip; a lantern swinging along the dunes to guide lost fishermen; campers abandoning their sand-swallowed car; a vacationer marking out a golf course in the sand; couples smooching on blankets near a boardwalk; and a storm hurling a tree inside a bowling alley.

This book records memories about what would become a major ocean resort, and about the vast inland area behind it. Both make up the northeastern corner of South Carolina known after 1801 as Horry District–even though Peter Horry (1743-1815), who was celebrated for his role in the Revolutionary War, actually lived in what would become Georgetown County. His Huguenot family would have pronounced their name "Oh-Ree," the French way, in equally stressed syllables, rather than "OAR-y."

Where did these recollections come from? The author did a lot of fishing by telephone wire, postage stamp, e-mail, and face-to-face conversation, but the two main sources are a project and a journal.

"Sounds just like her": The Horry County Oral History Project

It began as a spin-off from the author's first book, *Along the Waccamaw: A Yankee Discovers a Home by the River* (Algonquin, 1990). What became the Horry County Oral History Project (1989-2004) sponsored about a hundred interviews, videotaped or audiotaped, generally conducted in people's homes. The two main interviewers got help from a dozen others who conducted one-time sessions. The Project also salvaged about thirty earlier interviews, some on audiotape, some on videotape, some already transcribed. The Project transcribed the tapes, corrected and edited the transcriptions, and secured releases for depositing the materials in Kimbel Library, Coastal Carolina College/University. Besides their more obvious value to historiography, these primary sources, according to Prof. Stephen J. Nagle, make up a treasury of data on local varieties of speech.

In the early 1990s the Project flourished with the help of Catherine Lewis, later the author of *Horry County, South Carolina 1730-1993*. (See Fig. F.1.) With the expertise of Catherine as well as David Parker, and with funding from the South Carolina Humanities Council, the Director produced several video-tape programs from interview footage: *Horry Stories, Wood & Water*, and *"No Match for Our Dad."* Eventually his account of the whole project appeared in the *Oral History Review* ("Let's Call It" in the Works Cited). For a brief chronicle, see the Afterword, which also acknowledges the many people who helped with this book.

Fig. F.1. Catherine Lewis (left) interviews Rebecca Graham Page of Loris, 1990. From videotape filmed by David Parker.

"Just got in it—'n couldn't get out!"–*The Independent Republic Quarterly*

The other main source for this book is the journal of Horry County Historical Society, first published in 1967. (See Fig. F.2.) E.R. McIver, Jr., an early president and editor, recounted the origin of the *Independent Republic Quarterly*. After the Society printed numerous copies of the 1880 Census, the only way it could pay the $13,000 bill was to sell subscriptions to a journal: "Just got in it," he chuckled, "'n couldn't get out!" At the age of 92, Rick is pictured on the back cover as he and Charles E. Johnson (b. 1926) make crown moldings on a 1960 Yates American.

The *IRQ* itself includes a number of interviews. These and many other items can themselves be thought of as "oral sources"–broadly defined as "all materials derived ultimately from memory." Allen and Montell explain:

> "While primary materials consist of the spoken word, a good deal of written material is drawn from memory or oral communication and can be used as orally communicated secondary data. The written materials include letters…, autobiographies…, family histories, diaries, travel accounts, and newspaper columns." (*From Memory to History: Using Oral Sources in Local Historical Research*, 22)

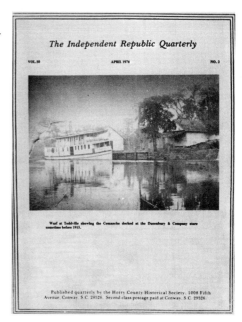

Fig. F.2. Cover of *IRQ,* vol. 10, number 3 (1976). Steamboat *Comanche* docks at Toddville on the Waccamaw River.

So by this definition "voices" can use ink.

In the narrower sense, as spoken, oral history often recognizes those who by temperament or circumstance are unlikely to record their memories. Partly because the Oral History Project interviewed folks of diverse locales, backgrounds, and colors, *Swamp* can present a wealth of information about common people—even while gently subverting this notion with details as to their language, personalities, and experiences. African Americans especially. In the year 2000, blacks made up between 15 and 16 percent of Horry County–about 31,000 out of 196,629 (U.S. Bureau of Census, DP-1). But in 1950 non-whites (mostly black) made up 27 percent of the 59,820 citizens (U.S. Bureau, "Table"). And going back to the 1810 census, those of African descent made up about a third of the 4349 people in Horry District. *Swamp* pays tribute to these under-recorded Africans and descendants of Africans.[1]

For a sharper focus, this book doubly narrows its scope as to when and what.

Time. *Swamp* covers a 222-year span that begins in 1732. Surveyors working for the royal governor make a report about the swampy Waccamaw–the first printed mention of the area, about the time that the Waccamaw Indians disappear from official records. The period ends in 1954, when several winds of change reached the county. Hurricane Hazel turned cottages into houseboats. The passenger train to Myrtle Beach eked out its last full year of service. And the federal government reactivated the old Myrtle Beach Army Air Field used in World War II: according to James D. Sanders (b. 1925), who retired as chief engineer, the contracts specified the year 1954,

> "So Christmas Eve, we started Myrtle Beach Air Force Base. We had pictures taken of the mayor, knocked down a bunch of trees, cleared a big area and then celebrated." (Int. 9)

This facility would serve as the headquarters for the 354th Tactical Fighter Wing from 1956 to 1993.

The most enduring change, however, took place in Conway High School, where Coastal Carolina Junior College began to offer a few classes, introducing higher education to the area and eventually rendering unnecessary the parallel institution for Negroes.[2] For whites and blacks, vowed J.M. Vaught, Jr., this change was a blessing "second to electricity" (Int. J. & E. Vaught: 8). Five of Coastal's original founders enrich this book: Mr. Thurman Anderson, Mr. James P. Blanton, Mr. E. E. Burroughs, Mr. William F. Davis, and Dr. R. Cathcart Smith. *Swamp, Strand & Steamboat* has been published by Horry County Historical Society to commemorate that event.

Theme. These memories support the idea that water permeated everyday life in Horry. *Swamp* devotes only a few syllables to politics, and when it touches upon education, religion, and agriculture, look for water.

Apart from the book's scope, what about the nature of its "I remembers"? Here are a few hints for appreciating an earthly richness that would make Plato himself turn another page:

Notice the diversity of viewpoints. The writers or speakers are male and female, black and white, town and country, insider and outsider, educated and uneducated, genteel and plain, situated on the upper and lower decks of life's steamboat. Their memories come from childhood and adulthood.

At the same time, look for circumstantial details. These include names (of a person, a horse, a boat, brand of fertilizer), dialogue ("As long as I can make $50 per acre…"), numbers (a hundred or more barrels of pears), and countless other particulars (ballast rock, an apple still on the table). How many species of animals are mentioned–wild or domestic, winged, scaled, or hairy, literal or metaphorical?

What physical processes did people rely on to wrest a living from wood, soil, or water? What were the pleasures of life, and what were the dangers in an era when the words "public health" were mutually exclusive?

Physical sensations are rare in other historical sources like business records, legal documents, and news articles. But memories register sights, sounds, tastes, smells, textures, temperatures, weights, hunger, exhaustion, even kinesthesia (e.g., swaying). Don't let old black-and-white photographs fool you into thinking that people lived in a colorless world. (Photographs in *Swamp* are credited unless taken by the author.)

Emotions, too, emerge from decades of dust: pleasure, fear, tedium, excitement, exhaustion, security, love, loneliness, faith, surprise, nostalgia, grief, anger, cheerfulness….

The more dramatic the story, the more unhurried and detailed: "As the boat docked, the preacher doffed his hat…." By contrast, the more summarized, the more telescoped: "We had a tobacco hand the other day cropping tobacco and he got sick on tobacco." A third kind of narration, generalized, tells of a recurrent event: "Storekeepers would meet the steamers," "But I got so I took me a short-handled shovel…."

The language used by these many people heightens the personal quality of their information. As writers they range in style from the plain to the artful; the author has usually corrected errors of spelling or grammar and sometimes tightened the style with no change in meaning. He preserves the unsophisticated grammar and phonetic spelling, however, of early documents, along with the original punctuation. As speakers, these informants use a looser style (like everyone), and some use a folk grammar, vocabulary, and pronunciation as pungent as cured tobacco. Although the author has often crossed out some redundancy in the transcripts, you will still enjoy audible Horry: "Sounds just like her," declared one grandson.

"Even if all that has come down to us by report from the past should be true and known by someone," declared Montaigne, "it would be less than nothing compared with what is unknown" (692). Indeed, of the many thousands of people who have lived or sojourned in Horry, few have left accounts. Yet this very scarcity makes them all the more precious. They are like the shells dredged onto the beach by Hurricane Hazel and plucked up by little Susan Hoffer—the tornado-shaped whelks and the fifty-one heart urchins–tokens of countless others buried forever in the deep.

As you read these memories, chapter by chapter, they might evoke a question. How could this sprinkling of isolated farms and communities, this headquarters of hardscrabble, this domain of *Anopheles* (Queen of Mosquitoes), this spongy wilderness edged by a great arc of useless sand, draw millions of outsiders who sweat from leisure?

Notes

[1] The concept of "race" is a social one rather than genetic, for all humans come from the same stock. "The major stereotypes, all based on skin color, hair color and form, and facial traits," date from recent evolution mostly under the effect of climate" (Cavalli-Sforza et al., 19). Although *Swamp* uses the word "race," it considers African Americans, whites, and Native Americans as ethnic or cultural groups. One sign of racism is the "n-word." Now used covertly, it was used freely by both blacks and whites in the era covered by this book. *Swamp* quotes the word not to endorse it but to record it as another fact of life, like malaria.

[2] See Dozier, "Eastern Carolina Junior College." *IRQ* 7.2/3 (1973): 30-31

PLATES

Between pages 18 and 19

1. Sweetbay prevails over winter

2. Dave Carr, World War I, c. 1918

3. "Colored Cafe" painted on brick wall

4. Donnie Grant, ex-ferryman

5. Turpentine gum salvaged from Waccamaw River

6. Andrew Stanley on his backup tractor

7. Robert Bellamy at his kitchen table

8. Janie Johnson tidies up the grounds

9. "Miss Flossie" Morris with salt-boiling cauldron

10. Map of Kings Highway, 1930

11. "Reflections from the East"—ocean seining

12. Henry Small in his 90s

13. Young Marion Moore and shadow

14. Undercarriage of 1930s log-loader

15. Author of *Berry's Blue Book*

16. "The morning after," Myrtle Beach

17. A Sunday stroll, Ocean Drive

18. Virginia B. Marshall above Waccamaw River

CHAPTER 1
THE LAND

"Yessir, I cleared this place here when I was 21 years old…. It was solid wood and there was 63 acres to it. It goes on down—I got a ditch on each line—goes down to the swamp."
John Fowler (b. 1881), Int: 3.

Fig. 1.1. The Waccamaw River flows past the swamp that feeds it, 1920's, while a tugboat converts coal to steam, smoke, and motion. Courtesy Col. Thomas W. Rich, Jr.

Rivers and swamps nearly isolate it from the rest of South Carolina, while salty waves divide it from Morocco. Upon geology and geography depends each memory in this book.[1]

The largest county in South Carolina, Horry encompasses 1,134 square miles, an area equal to about three New York Cities plus one Chicago. The county helps to make up the almost-two-thirds of South Carolina known as the Low Country.

From the beginning, farmers had to reckon with this reluctantly-draining land. In the Cedar Branch area, for example, floods would inundate crops: "Asparagus, collards, potatoes and stuff would just rot out in the fields because we couldn't get it out" (Interview Hemmingway: 5). Growers might skirt or even drain the apparently useless lowlands. In 1977 ditches cut by slaves remained in the woods near Cool Spring—"They're just rounded-out places now" (Int. W. Jones, undated 1977: 40-41). According to S. F. Horton (b. 1911) of Loris:

> "The first year that I worked tobacco on land that had been tile drained [i.e., by pipes], I believe I made $500 to the acre more than anybody within a mile of me. Good land, and I had it on high beds and had it tiled; the water could get into it and work its way into the tile. Where a lot of tobacco just drowned, mine fared good…. They won't let you drain it now." (Int. 15 May: 12)

What geological forces ultimately made the collards rot and the 'baccer drown?

The coastal plain lies seaward of the Fall Line, a low cliff that parallels the Atlantic shore from New Jersey to the Carolinas, and that "separates the metamorphic rocks of Appalachia from the sedimentary rocks of the Coastal Plain" (Taylor 7). This line marks the westernmost boundary of the ancient ocean. The plain was laid down by eroding mountains and sinking marine sediment. Horry County, which has geographical and geological features common to the lower reaches of this coastal plain (Thom iii), remains a patchwork of former barrier islands and their mainland-side troughs. For a map, see Fig. 1.2.

For over a hundred million years the Atlantic receded and returned any number of times. For one reason, during glacial periods some of the earth's water shifted from salt-water to ice; when the glaciers melted, their water caused the oceans to rise. As the sea level dropped, it left ridges of sand, along with swales behind them that were incised by rivers. As the sea level rose it created another shoreline.

Around 40 million years ago, when the Atlantic would have flooded the tenth floor of a motel on the present strand, it lapped the present Marion County. Starting about two and a half million years ago, its wind, waves, currents, and tides impeded sediment transported from mountains at the west; from this ongoing collision grew a beach-barrier island called the Horry Barrier. That land now makes up most of northwestern Horry County and extends from Loris through Aynor.

Toward the mainland from this deposited matter, organic sediments were deposited in lagoons near the future Little Pee Dee River. The barrier itself, a plane surface ridged by dunes, was gradually eroded by many small streams.

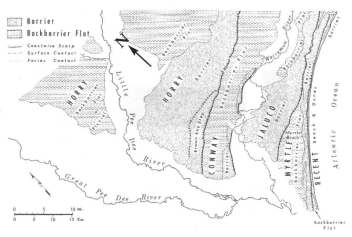

Fig. 1.2. Coastal depositional surfaces. Modified from Thom with permission, p. 10.

Around 650,000 years ago the ocean level dropped further and another such island made of dune sand and beach ridges developed offshore. Upon this rise settlers built a town that eventually gave its name to the Conway Barrier. A resident can stand in the shade of the live oaks that flourish on the sandy edge of this formation, look east-ward down a steep incline, and see the former beachfront, now the city marina and flood-plain of the Waccamaw River. To the northeast out of town, Highway 905 follows this ridge. West of this barrier the shovel-shattering, wheel-slithering gumbo clay marks an ancient lagoon of five miles in width.

Fig. 1.3. Deer tracks in sand, Lewis Ocean Bay Preserve, 2003.

Likely prior to 450,000 years ago, another barrier system developed, the Jaluco. This sandy plain seems to have been named after a spot on the Atlantic Coast Line between Conway and Pine Island.[2] The Jaluco barrier extends from Red Hill, east of Conway, to North Carolina. A sandy plain, it is home to shrub bogs, swamps, and creeks, along with old beach ridges that run parallel to the ocean. Note the microenvironment in Figure 1.3: this area could be the top of a small dune either left from the original beach formation or built in the last 25,000 years.

Then prior to 120,000 years ago, another such island developed offshore. The Myrtle Barrier eventually supported Kings Highway and the town of Myrtle Beach.

Then east of the Myrtle Barrier accrued yet another one, the long stretch of shoreline called Recent. "About 5,000 years ago a new thin barrier was plastered against the pre-existing barriers," explains Professor Nelson. "It is best seen where marshes separate it from the older deposits" as at Cherry Grove and (in Georgetown County) Murrells Inlet, Pawleys Island, and North Island ("Geology" 8). To this latest for-mation human beings would take salt-boiling kettles, hors-es, rowboats, hooks, seining nets, woolen swimsuits, and plastic shovels.

Boulder, rock, cobblestone, gravel, sand, silt: these are phases whereby mountains erode into foothills, plains and beaches. The sand of Long Bay is made up of pulver-ized feldspar and quartz, as well as pebbles of quartzite so thin that you can see through them. On the shore, relics turn up from before Time, a concept of humans. One is the obsolete oyster of Fig. 1.4. (dollar bill for scale). Scalloped, whorled, and pocked, it weighs the hand down like the stone it has become. A precursor to the modern version, which has lost the coil markings, it lived in shallow water near a beach. Then it disappeared under sandy deposits–not for seven years, like the Citadel ring found in the dunes nearby, but for more than 63 million.

However amazing, this object may seem less exotic

Fig. 1.4. Beach relics. A: Petrified half of a bivalve, genus *Exogyra*. B: Spheroidal rock. C: Smooth stone, 2.5 inches long. Photo by Bill Edmonds.

than the squat ball in Fig. 1.4, also picked up from Surfside Beach. Non-sedimentary rocks seem foreign to Horry County and need to be hauled in for a railroad bed, a jetty, or a retaining wall for a volcano-golf course. This one, gray-sand in color, weighs two and a half pounds. A few experts inferred that it had been worked by humans and served as a tool, but the majority concluded that it had come from either the Piedmont-Blue Ridge area or a similar terrain, and that its shape had resulted from mechanical weathering caused by transport of some type.

And on the same beach among shell fragments lay a reddish-brown chunk of stone (Fig. 1.4, C). It is quartzite, one of the materials most resistant to chemical and mechanical weathering. It rolled, slid, and floated from the Piedmont-Blue Ridge. Prof. Douglas Nelson estimates its age as between 500 million to one-and-a-half billion years, and he suggests that it had been deposited by an ancient river that slowed as it met interference from the ocean.

Inland, too, relics turn up from the Old Ocean. Near the Waccamaw River Fred McNeill (b. 1894) found a petri-fied fragment that came from the snout of a porpoise, and while excavating a pond he discovered a whalebone (W. Thomas, "Family's"). In the riverbed itself one scuba diver shone his light on several 2-3-inch-high triangular shark's teeth, original location unknowable after eons of erosion and transport (Sasser).

In the older barriers, where organic material has had many thousands of years to accumulate, sand tends to include more soil. Other inland legacies of the ocean are marl (a mixture of clay, carbonates, and shells) and coquina (fragments of shells and coral that form porous limestone). The ocean has even left underground limestone caverns filled with water.

Behind the former sedimentary islands are the vestiges of backbarrier-flats. These are now tidal marshes, stretch-es of level ground, or channels composed of "fine-textured sediments, usually silty clays" (Thom 9). For example, near the junction of the Inland Waterway and Highway 501, at Pine Island, a lagoon left clay that was later shaped and baked into bricks. "From what I understand," said Cad Holmes (b. 1945),

> "there's a big bed of gumbo in this area [Burgess] runs from Murrells Inlet to Waccamaw
> Pottery. Even now, if you travel the woods enough, you can see some of the holes where they'd
> dig it out of the ground…. The same gumbo they would make the tobacco-barn flue with they
> would make chimneys with." (Int. Peterkin: 12)

Added Nellie Johnson (b. 1918): "They'd get clay out and slap it on the sticks [*illustrating*] inside and outside" (Int. Peterkin: 12).

"Must be nature for sand hill to move"

In outline, ocean-bestowed Horry resembles a scalloped fan or a diamond. A tour around it – a map is furnished opposite the copyright page – will help you locate the memories to come. (See Index for coordinates of many places.)

Its northwest facet begins with the Lumber River, also called Drowning Creek. Shared by Dillon County in South Carolina, this stream runs southwest to merge with the Little Pee Dee, shared by Marion County. At Galivants Ferry, according to Carrie Doyle (b. 1901), people filled barrels "to water the cattle with. They would have to haul a lot of times…" (Int. 8 Sept: 18). The river then turns 90 degrees at Dog Bluff to make up Horry's southwest facet.

Eventually the twisting Little Pee Dee widens into a lake from which, as the wondering canoist discovers, pro-trude unearthly islets, stubby of trunk and lacy of foliage. This expanse then drains into the Great Pee Dee River, which soon hooks a right into Georgetown County, leaving most of its gallons to rush ahead to form Bull Creek near the bot-tom tip of Horry. On its left Bull Creek slices a 35-foot-high cake, a gift of the receding and returning ocean. The bottom layer is peat and organic clay (visible at low water); the next is a dune sheet; the next is a layer of soil; the next is another dune sheet (Thom 26-27).

Also on its left the Creek passes the tree-sheltered cove of Eddy Lake, once a lumbering village. Then, instead of flowing straight to the ocean like its precursor, the ancient Pee Dee, it encounters a long spit of land along the coast, so it veers southward to flow with the Waccamaw past the former rice plantations along Waccamaw Neck. This narrow peninsula stretches from Horry into Georgetown County as a continuation of the Myrtle Barrier, and it keeps rivers from severing Horry completely from the rest of the state.

The southeast facet of Horry is the Atlantic. As the tide rises and falls, the county narrows and widens. Long Bay arcs gently from the Santee River in Georgetown County to the mouth of the Cape Fear River in North Carolina, in Horry curving past Garden City Beach, Withers Swash, Singleton Swash, White Point Swash, and Cherry Grove Inlet. (A swash is a creek that widens with the tide.) Just above Hog Inlet at the border with North Carolina lies the final piece of land, Waties Island. There, partly excavated shell mounds revealed a harpoon point; a pottery-smoothing tool; evidence of fireplaces and post-holes; animal bones; and shells from oysters, clams, periwinkles, and sea snails (Wiegand 21).[3]

The marine border of Horry changes not only over the day but over the decade and eon. About 20,000 years ago the coast itself extended 60 miles farther, to the edge of the continental shelf. "Reckon you wouldn't blieve it," declared a former slave, "but I ken cummember…when all that beach [later Surfside] been cultivate field. Must be nature for sand hill to move" (Chandler, "Uncle Sabe Rutledge," 60). In about 1886, Dr. John D. Bellamy (b. 1817) affirmed that the

Cherry Grove Inlet "changed to the east-southeast, several hundred yards while I was familiar with it" (Berry, "Great," 23; see also 20, 21).[4] Human beings have assisted nature in such changes. Cherry Grove was once an island (see Fig. 10.3); but in 1950, the opening between marsh and sea was filled in by two mountains of sand (Berry, "Bulldozers").

The last edge of the county is not fluid but fixed. Established by legislators and surveyors, it extends northwest at a 44 degree angle for as many miles, connecting Little River Inlet to the Lumber River, defining the borders of Brunswick and Columbus Counties in North Carolina, and keeping Horry from being a peninsula of that state.

"There are swamps on both sides of the river"

What might be called the Waterland has generally low elevation, its highest point rising about 113 feet above sea level (*Soil Survey* 1). The result of minimal relief is what humans call poor drainage: in 1991, 45 percent of the county was wetlands. Saltwater wetlands include marshes as well as ever-widening and narrowing swashes. Riverine include rivers, streams, and areas that drain directly into them. Isolated wetlands are low areas that, unconnected to a means of drainage, collect water and keep it (Greene 9-A). These last can resemble ponds ringed by hardwood forests or deep swamps where trees and other vegetation thrive in the wet soil (Fretwell 4-C). Isolated wetlands could be used to grow upland rice, as Henry Small (b. 1897) testifies:

> "I worked in rice ditches, not in the rice field. I raised rice myself. I raked…. I plant in a low place; and I worked that rice, and harvest 'em, et 'em off the stalk they grow on. And then take a mortar and a pestle and beat that rice…." (Int: 17)

A creek runs through a riverine swamp, however imperceptibly, but not through an isolated one.

Creeks or "branches" were ubiquitous in the Waterland, among them Honey Camp, Long, Little Long, Cross, Cages, Jernigan Mill, Chicken Coop, Spring, Holly, Rooty, Boggy, Mullet, Swannish, Schoolhouse, Savannah, Wasp, Cypress, Simpson, Gum & Reedy, Buck, Hell, Rattlesnake, and Seven. Across the branch at night, Fred W. Hucks (b. 1883) used to hear Robert T. Nichols beat his drum, a souvenir of the drum and bugle corps during the Civil War (Epps, "Mr. Hucks," 18). The farming village of Socastee was established around Socastee Creek (Mrs. J. Cooper 137).

Rice planters at the bottom of the county took advantage of the rising and falling tide on the Waccamaw River to soak the fields and then drain them. There were oxbows (isolated bends left from earlier courses of a river), bottomlands that flooded, and elongated swamps that drained into other swamps, creeks, or rivers. (See Fig. 1.5.) This topography was noted by surveyors in the reign of George II, when they made the earliest extant first-person report of Horry, dated 1732:

> "The Township on Wacamaw River hath been mark'd out & named Kings Town, & the Courses of the River duly taken…. We are Sencible that there are Swamps on both Sides of the River, and Shall make it our Endeavours to lay out the Town & Township the most comodi-ously in such a Manner, as it may be beneficial to the whole Province." (Middleton)

Laid out on a sandy bluff to the northwest, Kingston would become Conwayborough, then Conway. Such townships were part of the royal governor's strategy of developing the frontier economically and protecting the colony from the Spanish and Indians.

Swamps are named frequently in plat books of land-grants, beginning in 1809: Hell Hole, Pleasant Meadow, White Oak, Play Card, Mitchells, Hunting, Spring, Pometto, Johnson's, Gapway, Oxbow, Camp, Maple, and Kingston Lake. With a population density of five persons per square mile in 1820 (Lewis, "Little River," 10), the area figuratively had a swamp for each resident. William Norton, Sr., was granted a triply aqueous tract, surveyed in 1802, that was bounded by Mitchells Swamp, Iron Spring Branch, and Buck Creek ("South Carolina").

Fig. 1.5. Swamp drains Lewis Ocean Bay Preserve, 2003.

These riverine swamps can extend for miles, as you can see in Figure 1.6. The prongs extend through a large area between Highways 90 and 501, and its creek flows into the Waccamaw. Maple Swamp twists from the Adrian area

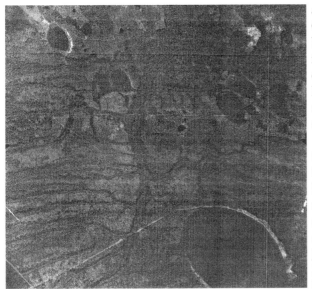

Fig. 1.6. 1949 aerial view of Sterritt Swamp, which extends on both sides of Highway 90 and drains into the Waccamaw. Courtesy Sanford D. Cox, Jr., family.

and drains into the narrow beginning of Kingston Lake far above Conway. Lake Swamp traces the line between the ancient Horry Barrier island and its backbarrier flat (Thom 41) before it empties into the Little Pee Dee. This wetland could differentiate an extended family, as explained by Mary W. Hardee (b. 1907): "Up there at Noah Edwards', he's my daddy's first cousin, he stayed on one side and we stayed on the other side, but we was farther up the swamp" (Int: 5).

Brown Swamp (named after a person) once arbitrated the distinction between races. *When Southern Hospitality Was in Flower*, by Charles Mack Todd, is a memoir with pseudonyms published in Dallas (1959). According to oral history preserved by the book, after the Civil War Old Joe Hammer kept a beautiful Negro woman and had children by her. Society ostracized them on the north side of the swamp, yet on the south side people accepted Little Negro John Brewton, the dark-skinned son of the popular Aunt Jane Hilton by a mulatto handyman. This child "showed as much Negro blood as they" and even married a blond woman (6).

A temporarily dry swamp could mean good hunting. After their coon dog treed a few possums, W. Irving Jones (b. 1895) and his father-in-law spotted a mink that disappeared into a hollow log; they ran a pole into one end and forced the animal out between two fires. "We got $22 for him," more than a dollar per shotgun pellet (Int. Aug. 18: 31).

For domesticated fowl, a swamp could provide a hazardous refuge. Georgia Smalls Lance (b. 1926) remembers that as a child in the Freewoods (an area between Socastee and Georgetown County that was appropriated by former slaves), she minded the turkeys and guinea fowl, pheasant-like natives of Africa. If she fell asleep, they would roost in the swamps or woods at night and be eaten by foxes. During the day she would have to call them back with an imitated gobble or endure her mother's scolding (Int. Peterkin: 39-40).

More than animals could be concealed in swamps. Slaves, for example, could forfeit a roof to escape a harsh driver. Before the Civil War, according to a Burroughs family story, a relative killed a black man and fled southward. "Anybody who got in trouble with the law in North Carolina came to Horry County," said Virginia B. Marshall, "because you had so many swamps and rivers to get to us that it was too much trouble for the law to follow them" (Int: 3). This same man was the initial contact for F.G. Burroughs, the future timber-and-turpentine magnate, when he left Williamston, North Carolina.

Riverine wetlands could also give temporary sanctuary to cannon-fodder. After the Civil War, Nathaniel Bishop talked with Mr. Wilson Edge, who raised pigs near the Waccamaw and nursed a grudge against those who had owned slaves:

> "After all they dragged off my boy to Chambersburg, Pennsylvania, and killed him a fighting for what? Why, for rich nigger owners. Our young men hid in the swamps, but they were hunted up and forced into the army." (235)

Possessions, too, could be hidden among cypress knees and frog legs. When F. G. Burroughs was a prisoner of war in the North (according to another oral heirloom), one of the colored families that worked for him hid his rosin and turpentine down in the swamp (Int. Marshall: 4). After the war, barrels of corn and pork also disappeared into a swamp near Cool Spring, as well as a large box packed with dishes, goblets, and dry goods that had been buried under a smokehouse floor. Lawmen flushed out these items along with Confederate deserters who had been raiding the Cool Spring area (E. Johnson 16). Decades later, swamps even rendered up steam when locomotives pumped water from them to the boilers (Fetters 61).

"Those bays used to be full of water"

One type of wetland is the "bay," named for the range of bay trees that flourish there. (The tree itself derived its name from the Latin word for "berry.") (See Plate 1.) Like the swamps, this ubiquitous shrub bog impeded farming and mobility, except for bears. In a map of Horry District, a mass of foliage between Conwayborough and the beach is called "Impassable Bay," less a name than a warning (Fig. 1.7). "Those bays used to be full of water," remembered Turner Chestnut (b. 1896), "but since they cut the Waterway through, it drained it all out" (W. Thomas, "Turner," 13-4). "You couldn't get across [one bay] with a mule and plow, hardly," reported J. Harry Lee (b. 1908); "had a little opening to get into this field" (18). Low even for the Low Country, a bay supports bushes or small trees, primarily evergreens.[5]

Plat books of the early 1800s list these bays: Little Cowpen, Green Sea, Sandhill, Big, "Aligator," Cow Bog, Brown, Roberts. The boundaries of Mt. Olive alone enclose five bays: Pole Cat, Cart Wheel, Little Cart Wheel, Wolf, and Cypress (Ayers 14). Juniper Bay is named for the Atlantic white cedars that resemble the juniper group (Pinson).

The generic "bay" includes the Carolina species. Thick and tangled, it forms an elliptical depression--a shape not understood until the early 1930s when it was discovered from the air, along with its northwest-south-east alignment. (See Fig. 1.8.) Typically the Carolina bay drains slowly to groundwater, and one edge is raised and sandy. See the aerial view in Fig. 1.6, where the largest bay is Cotton Patch, lower right corner. (Note also the sand ridges aligned parallel to the ocean.) An opening slowly drains the pool, and sometimes the horseshoe shapes overlap. By one reckoning there are thousands of these depressions scattered from southern New Jersey to northern Florida (Eyton and Parkhurst 1). In South

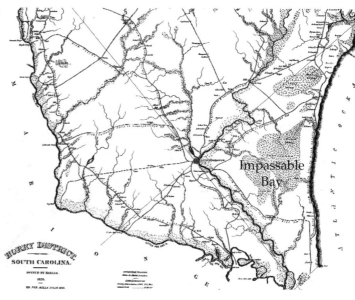

Fig. 1.7. Harlee map, 1820. Robert Mills.

Carolina they occur only in the southeastern parts, and in 1991 only about 200 of the state's original 2600 existed without human modification (Greene 9-A).

Fig. 1.8. Author's bald head almost invisible just inside a Carolina bay, Lewis Ocean Bay Heritage Preserve. Photo by Reginald Daves.

Carolina bays range in length from 200 feet to 7 miles (Eyton and Parkhurst 3). According to Sharitz and Gibbons, they include the 3-by-5-mile Lake Waccamaw itself. Many of the smaller and more shallow bays may remain dry; many of the larger and deeper may hold water permanently; the majority, however, "are essentially intermittent lakes" that become wet or dry depending on precipitation (8, 22). These wetlands sponge up excess water and purify it. Their boundaries support the rare Venus flytrap and several pitcher plants (the yellow cobra or cobra lily) that catch their own winged fertilizer. (See Fig. 1.9.) Complex fire history produces different vegetation in bays. Carolina bays are frequently surrounded by savanna wiregrass and trees that have adapted to such an environment: longleaf pines (a main source of turpentine) and "running oaks" with their underground stems that give rise to multiple shrubby stems bearing acorns.

Mysterious of origin, these ellipses may result from forces terrestrial (such as wind on ancient ponds) or extraterrestrial (such as an exploding comet). Surprisingly, no one has thought to link them with the "air ship" that flew over Wilmington one night in April 1897 and seemed to point a searchlight earthward ("Wonderful").

One way to appreciate the barrier that swamps and shrub bogs presented to mobility is to imagine them as upward protrusions—like the mountains that separate hollows in West Virginia. A person might envision Brown Mountain, White Oak Mountain, Mt. Impassable, Alligator Knob, Juniper Ridge, Old River Peak, Maple Ridge.

"The Hermit County"

Writing in 1890, John I. Green noted that some years earlier, a correspondent for the Charleston *News and Courier* had labeled Horry "The Hermit County." How appropriate, Green judged, not only as to its isolation but as to its rectitude: "To-day one may find…many houses whose welcoming doors are never barred by locks, and many barns without any doors

Fig. 1.9. Pitcher plants in winter.

at all" (31). This same area of widely-separated homesteads displayed a self-reliance which Catherine Lewis admires in *Horry County*.

Mainly because of the area's remoteness, it played host to only a couple of skirmishes in the Revolutionary and Civil Wars, all of them associated with water. In 1832 Josias Sessions (1764-1837) gave the following testimony as part of his effort to secure a veteran's pension:

> "He was in the company of Cap't. Daniel Murrell in a severe battle with the Tories at a place called Bear Bluff in All Saints Parish the Tories were commanded by Joshua Long, after a very sharp conflict our company was under the necissity of capitulation but rather than be taken he and eight others swam the Waccamaw River and effected their escape." ("Josias" 10)

Transportation meant determination. On the day his granddaughter Kathryne was born, William A. Smith (b. 1849) wrote her a letter "so she will no us Smiths love our fokes and our land when she is old enuf to no":

> "Some of our fokes staid hear but some never done that. My pa sed that his pa ware James [b. 1793] but nevr left over past the old sand road. they never had no way to travel mutch. We live hear but Tom Smith staid over akros the river…. [A cousin] come cross the river one time to see us all. he staid most a month I nevr did see him no more yet." (Hurt 11)

(If you listen to this phonetic writing, sounds just like him.) In 1899, at the age of twelve, J. Robert Carter, Sr. (b. 1887) made his first trip to Conway from his home in Longs, covering the eighteen miles in six hours ("Horry Old-Timer" 6). Barney Dawsey (b. 1912) was eight or ten years old before he crossed the Little Pee Dee into Marion County (Int: 26).

One sojourner called Horry "the Dark Corner" in a book by that name published in 1908 (McGhee). Darkness aside, the place was certainly remote and the inhabitant often rooted to family land. "They didn't never get far away from where their family was," recalled Claudia Allen Brown (b. 1901), "like a lot of people does now" (Int. 24 June: 6). In the earliest days, an extended family might provide a spouse, perhaps with occasionally tragic results. An old white man from Loris, who was interviewed by Genevieve Willcox Chandler in 1938, reports:

> "Isba, my old Grand Daddy Joe married her. That way our race come on. Old lady Isba. After they come over from Ireland. Warn't nobody much to marry them days and here people'll say it's a sin to marry your cousin! They was first cousin and two of the children here dif (deaf) and dumb. Didn't have but one girl—Zilphy. She can't talk but like a cat a–meowlin. Uncle Sam and Aunt Zilphy was first cousin. Everyone died but one and she married two second cousins. She went jam out of my remembrance." (Chandler, "An Old Man," 2).

Unlike hermits, people tended to have large families, so Horry folks were often "cousin" to one degree or another. High and low were connected by blood, as were many whites, blacks, and native Americans. (See S. Smith.)

Ignorance of the outside world can be seen at its most extreme in the following anecdote. During World War I a young conscript from Socastee used to sell vegetables from his mule-and-wagon, driving through the thick sand in front of the Epps cottage at Myrtle Beach:

> "I recall his slight frame, weathered face, and trousers well shrunk as he stood in our front door, tears streaming down his face, saying to my mother: 'Mis' Epps, dey tell me I got to cross dat water. And dey ain't no bridge dere.'" (Epps, "Have," *IRQ* 1.3: 14)

Any number of Horry County males learned geography the hard way. As one prominent example, Capt. Henry L. Buck II fought in the Battle of the Crater. (For a stunning account of that disaster written by an Horryite–the captain of Company K, 26th Regiment, S.C. Volunteer Infantry–see B. L. Beaty.) How many Confederate soldiers buried a limb like a pet dog? How many ghosts of their never-begotten descendants still wander the upper world?

During World War I, white and black men served in the military. David Carr (b. 1887), who grew up in the Freewoods–Burgess Community, was logging near Dunn, N.C., in about 1916. "I went to the mailbox and see a letter in there for me and I take it out. Uncle Sam, he got his finger on the letter like that [*pointing*]. Say 'I Want You.'" In France, Carr put his rural expertise to work: "Some of the men didn't even know how to put a bridle on the mule, and they bog down and they'd come get me and all rushin' back. Fifteen-twenty minutes after I'd have a gun on the hill. Horse and all. They pick me up, tote me there. I'd say 'Put me down, I ain't no baby'" (Int: 10). See Plate 2 for soldier Carr.

During World War II, many a young man received a ticket (sometimes one-way) to Europe, North Africa, or unheard-of places. Olin I. Blanton of the Mt. Olive area posthumously sent five sons. In the early 1950s, men whose ancestors had fought for the Confederacy rode a bus across the Little Pee Dee and sailed across the Pacific to fight in Korea.

Yet this was a corner, not a crossroads. After the Civil War one woman continued to call her son-in-law "Johnson" because he was from Vermont, even after he had lost a leg fighting for the South (Godfrey, "Some," 8). Outsiders can almost be listed. In the twentieth century the mother of the Epps sisters was a New Yorker and Jewish. In Conway, toward the end of the period covered by this book, the Banners and other Jewish families "had a visiting Rabbi and met once per month in the library in Conway and, later, in Myrtle Beach" (Mishoe 7). The mother of Roberta Rust was from Chicago, having traveled down with hopeful farmers of the Sunny South Colony. On the northern strand the Tilghmans were a rather suspect group as Catholics (Int. Rust: 14). During World War II, one soldier's bride was shunned at the dinner table of the hotel because she came from the North (Bell 16).[6]

The hermit clung to his retreat. When the state's highway system was inaugurated in 1925, Horry seems to have been the only county that did not request any new or improved roads above the minimum suggested by the chief engineer. When the state offered to pave roads if the counties borrowed the money to foot the bill, Horry's senator objected because of the extra tax (Lewis, "Cordie Page," 26-28).

The school served the neighborhood and was pretty much run by local trustees. In 1941, when Thurman Anderson was elected Superintendent, there were about 92 white schools and 40 black (Int: 9). Churches, too, were neighborhood centers, as were post offices before rural free delivery was established. In 1968, John P. Cartrette (b. 1898) could name 30 post offices from the sparsely-populated bygone days (Epps, "Post"). Banks were often mistrusted. According to Alice Floyd (b. 1922), the father of her student played barber by fitting a bowl on his head and shaving the hair up to the rim. Dr. Archie Sasser told her that the old man had paid the physician for a house call by digging up a tin can full of money. In 1940 or '41, while she was speaking to a politician in Columbia, a man walked up to them "barefoot, dirty, bib overalls":

> "He had tobacco hanging out—scraggly looking beard and matted hair.... Years later I found
> out this was the guy that had the $60,000 cash buried in the ground." (Int. G. Floyd: 61-2)

"The first Saturday I was in Conway," remembers Jose (Mrs. James) Holbert, a native of England, "I went downtown and the men were in overalls, no shirt under them.... And in Jerry Cox [store] there was a row of chairs across there and the women were nursing their babies" (Int. G. Floyd: 64). In 1953, when Stanton L. Collins (b. 1919) arrived in Conway, some people had never heard of an obstetrician-gynecologist. After learning the definition, one person asked, "Does your mother know what you do for a living?"

As a census worker in 1950, Harriette Scoggins Stogner (b. 1921) was fording branches in the outback when a man assured her that the area was safe: "The men don't work. Their wives do. It's kind of like the Indian tribes: they work their women."

> "Sure enough, I drove up and the fellow was sitting under the tree with his hat down over his
> face, asleep, and his wife was out hoeing in the field." Waking up, the man said he couldn't read
> or write, and invited Harriette in. His wife sat in a rocking chair, chewing tobacco and spitting.
> "I think there were five or six adults living in this one big room." They asked her to sit down:
> "I could have sat on the bed and there was a chair with coils of wire coming out" [laughter].

She later saw this man vote at a meeting called to fire the superintendent of schools (Int. G. Floyd: 60-1).

Ironically, this Southeastern frontier was always tethered to the North. Agents for naval stores lived in New York City and prominent Horryites came from the upper East Coast. The original Henry L. Buck (b. 1828) apparently bid farewell to one family in Maine and started a new one along the Waccamaw. Mary Brookman (b. 1824), from Maine, worked as a schoolmarm for Buck's children and married Thomas Beaty. T. C. Dunn, formerly a captain in the Union Navy, blockaded the port of Little River and then settled there with plenty of capital ("Waccamaw," qtd. in C. Lewis, "Little River," 1990). Capt. Thomas Randall, born in Massachusetts, owned thousands of acres in the Little River area and had one of the largest slaveholdings, sixty-one. In 1911 the Burroughs family was able to marry land with cash, thanks to a partnership with Simeon B. Chapin from Chicago (near where their father had been imprisoned).

The federal government also made its presence known legally, economically, and militarily.

During Prohibition (1920-33), alcoholic beverages could not legally be manufactured or sold. Tobacco regulation attempted to protect the farmer from market extremes (see Prince, *Long Green*). The Depression saw numerous attempts to get dollars in wallets and food in stomachs: members of the Civilian Conservation Corps built Myrtle Beach State Park on land donated by Myrtle Beach Farms, the Intracoastal Waterway yielded construction jobs, and the Federal Writers' Project sponsored the priceless interviews conducted by Genevieve Willcox Chandler. In 1940 the Work Progress Administration began to upgrade runways so as to integrate the Myrtle Beach Municipal Airport into the national defense system, and soon the Army Air Corps was firing at targets on the beaches at Singleton Swash.[7]

Public electricity for the countryside was first generated in 1940, when the Horry Electric Cooperative was formed. Then in 1952, after the Rural Electrification Administration offered telephone loans, the Horry Telephone Cooperative was formed. "There was no fire service in the rural areas, no doctors or drug stores," said Henry McNeil, one of the founders. "People felt like they had moved to town." Horry Tel became the largest of 253 members belonging to the National Telecommunications Cooperative Association (Dayton D-3).

"You don't want to go in there"

Unlike the typical hermit, Horry tended to be violent. Chandler's unidentified "old man" of 1938 tells this story about Uncle Pitman's sister:

"A man run up with her, knocked her down, roll her up in leaves and went to get a shovel to bury her. And warn't long 'fore old Jack Lane was a huntin' him with his gun and when he caught him he took him and had Aunt Louise to put the rope round his neck, chained him in the kitchen and kept him chained a week and made a box. (Warn't no church! Didn't think there was ever goin' to be no church! Thought they'd make a nigger buryin' ground of it!) Hung him to the tree where the church sits now. Right to the Lake Swamp." (Chandler, "An Old Man," 2).

The county itself had its own outlands. One was Gunters Island, a large enclave west of Aynor, where the Horry Barrier slopes down to the Little Pee Dee. There a car could have its tires shot off and a tobacco barn could hide bootleg liquor (Int. G. Floyd: 58). According to Mrs. G.W. Collier, this place was the home of the Dimery clan, people of "mixed blood" (i.e., of partial American Indian ancestry). In a preview of integration, the Gunters Island children transferred from their school to the one in Aynor, and some parents made threats, but no violence occurred (4). While working for a food survey in 1948, Alice Floyd tried the north entrance to this place when the mailman stopped her:

"'Ma'am, what are you doing?' I explained what I was doing and he said, 'You don't want to go in there.' And I said, 'Well, I see these dwellings on the map.' 'No ma'am, you don't want to go in there.' I said, 'A school and a church?' He said, 'No ma'am. You don't *want* to go in there.'" (Int. G. Floyd: 57)

"The Jam" or "Jamb" was "a corner along the line of the two states" that lay between Green Sea and Tabor City ("Robber"). There, people said "yander" for "yonder" (Int. Grainger: 15 Sept.). James P. Blanton (b. 1915) tells this story about his father, Olin Isaac Blanton (b. 1892):

In the early '20s, Sen. Hal Buck [Henry III, b. 1872] created a three-man rural police force. Blanton's father was one of the members, along with Kirby King (Finklea) and Ben Owens (Bucksport). Although Blanton had quit the force, agents of the Federal Alcohol and Drugs asked him to accompany them on a raid because he knew the very northern area of the county. He led a sheriff's party on an expedition to destroy the still and caught a 30-30 rifle bullet.

Even after a month in the hospital he never recovered his health from being wounded. Back home, he advised an agent of the Federal Bureau not to go in again until he could lead them by another route. "I can still see how the chief from Columbia put his arms on the mantle and said 'I'm going to go in today.'" This man was killed along with a bootlegger, while another agent and a bootlegger were wounded. Olin I. Blanton himself died at the age of 40, leaving six sons and three daughters.

James magnanimously added that the distillers were good people trying to survive and that most of their offspring turned out pretty well.

In the late 1940s a surveyor's level dueled with a shotgun. The woman pointing it eventually offered a glass of bootleg wine to Robert Winfield and his crew, who were working on the new Highway 501 northwest of Conway (Int. 5). An editorial from the Loris newspaper in 1954, supplied by Catherine Lewis, inveighs against "Lawlessness in Old Horry," which "is almost as much a part of this county as the tobacco along the highways":

"They tell us that, a few years ago, one could witness stabbing and shooting and drunkenness on the main streets of town; that a man either had to carry a gun or watch his step whenever he ventured outside at night. Even now, although the town of Loris has been cleaned up tremendously…, although a lady is safe on the streets long after dark, the back-woods areas and the State Line area are known for their complete disregard for the law.

"Men who run afoul of the law many times have no difficulty in getting permits to carry and use deadly weapons. A bottle of tax-paid liquor, or bottle of corn whiskey, can be bought with the greatest of ease in Horry County at any time of the day or night. In one place we stopped, on the way to the beach, the owner of a combination motel and filling station was mixing drinks for three youthful customers." (Powledge)

The odor of anarchy helped to revive the Ku Klux Klan in the early 1950s. Many people approved of its moral policing, examples of which were recalled by Stanley Coleman (b. 1915):

"They'd catch a man running around and leaving his family—they would just take him out and work him over good and that was it. You didn't have to worry about him anymore. And if you would hear of a girl running around too. They usually put them on a log, it was about that big around, and take a belt and wear her out." Prostitutes were also disciplined. (Int. 13 Oct: 30-31)

J.D. Gilland (b. 1914), a general surgeon, arrived in Conway in 1948. Once in 1950 he was called to the emergency room at 2 a.m. to find a dead man in what he thought was a white sheet:

"When I removed it I recognized it as a uniform of the KKK—and the deceased man was wearing the uniform of the Conway City Police. He'd been shot one time in the back." About fifty men milled around the hall "sort of lookin' around." Word was, the man had been part of a caravan that had driven to Myrtle Beach to shoot up a Negro night club, but had been shot by a fellow Klan-member who wanted to settle a feud. There was no autopsy performed or coroner's report.

Dr. Gilland made hundreds of other calls to the emergency room for knife wounds to whites and blacks, many of them made or received by notorious characters. One ruffian scared the nurse so much that she wouldn't enter the examination room, and one family shot itself out of existence. "A bunch of people took out life insurance on a certain man—and collected." "In my desk drawer now," he adds, is a 6-inch switchblade that he once had to pull out of one man's back: "I *shook* him off." Usually, however, the knifer's purpose was to cut, not kill, by holding the blade itself and slashing with the exposed inch. Despite all this unoffical surgery, Gilland affirms that "It's been a good place to live, with all its faults."

"The old Granny (Mrs. Todd)"

For two centuries many who tilled the Land of Horry would have been considered poor by later standards, especially before the advent of Bright Leaf tobacco. Yet they expected little in the way of material comfort, relished what they did have in the realm of the senses, and enjoyed the companionship of kin and neighbors: "we shur workd hard," wrote Katherene McCormick Smith in 1850, "en foks heped bak then" (Hurt 7).

During the Civil War, Elizabeth Collins, from England, visited the Plowden C. J. Weston family of Hagley Plantation in Georgetown County. With Mr. Weston a captain in the army, it seemed prudent for the women to look for a refuge inland from Yankee gunboats, so they bought Snow Hill farm on Kingston Lake. There she overheard this tart comment by a slave, Prince: "Conwayboro," he said to the cook, "must have been the last place God made." And there she met "the old Granny (Mrs. Todd)":

"I ought not to call her old, for I was quite surprised when she told me her age (46!). I never saw an English person at 70 look so old and miserable, and to make the worst of herself, she always had the pipe in her mouth, or a thick handkerchief about her head."

Collins qualifies her judgment: "I used to think them a rough lot of people, but their manner showed that they were very kind…" (9-10). For a photograph of a latter-day Granny Todd, see Figure 1.10.

In 1890 John I. Green quoted the *Horry Herald* on the life of subsistence before the railroad arrived in 1887: "Only a few years ago we were completely isolated from the world…. We were content to live as our fathers before us had lived, struggling along in darkness and eking out an existence of a precarious and uncertain kind" (35). In an article entitled "Building Up Waste Places in the South," which appeared in *The Southern Workman* (1905), Zach McGhee lauds the impact of colonists from a dozen Northern states on a hurting area:

"There is no city there and the people have no intention of building one. Neither is there even a cotton mill or other manufacturing concern or anywhere in that vicinity. People have lived there for nearly two hundred years, and tilled the soil, and that is what they are doing now."

McGhee describes the typical farmer:

"He had one mule and a cart, which with a few worn out and antiquated farming tools constituted his outfit. When he sold his cotton at the end of the year it came just near enough to paying his debts to enable

Fig. 1.10. Resident of Aynor area, 1940s? Horry County Museum.

him to get credit on a lien on his crop for the next year. He and his family would, therefore, not exactly starve; so he was happy." (Lewis, "Homewood," 27)

"When I was a boy," explains one man born in 1884, there were not a great many buggies over the county. Many people rode in an ox cart and wagon" (Lewis, "Cordie Page," 29). Dave Carr, whose parents had been slaves, was interviewed after reaching his one-hundredth birthday. How did his parents earn a living?

"They farm and pick cotton and hoe cotton and plow and ditch. We didn't had no tractor, nothing—[a] few people, big shot, had mule and buggy. No road chair. [?] After a while the buggy came out and most of the colored people then and a few whites didn't had anything but an ox and a cart. And the crippled people or couldn't walk, they have a big goat with a little wagon and git in there and drive or ride, go where they want." (Int: 2)

"Whenever it come field time," stated Mary Hardee (b. 1907), "it was just like you had to go and go to war" (Int: 6). Schools depended on the annual rhythms of agriculture for their pupils. In a rate that varied according to era, location, and race, school-terms progressed from the rare to the haphazard, then to the regular but with short sessions and generally primitive buildings. Although taxes were modest, a landowner might sell acreage to pay the taxes due on them, like someone who burns the house to heat it. Many a citizen had to leave the area for the North, West, or other areas for lack of economic opportunity. Blacks no doubt hoped, too, for a more congenial racial climate, and many of them must have taken the *Chickenbone Special*, the composite nickname for two trains that ran through South Carolina to points north (Walls 82).

Writing in 1909, J. W. Ogilvie believed that the *Shoo-Fly* had chugged into the county to rescue it from economic isolation. He described the people before that turning point as:

"bound as so many slaves at work in the treadmill doing the bidding of the taskmasters to eke out a bare subsistence for themselves and their loved ones." (24)

Although a potato, a chunk of smoked pig, and a slice of cornbread were familiar, rare was an olive, a grapefruit, even a strawberry. "Fresh fruit was not available every day as it is now," remembers Kelly Paul Joyner (b. 1915), "and the smell of apples and oranges still reminds me of Christmas long ago" ("Priceless" 9). As a boy John Dawsey (b. 1930) was asked to hand out a shipment of grapefruit that his school had received: "everybody thought they were overgrown oranges" (Int: 4).

"We have come for Brookie"

The life span of Old Horry inclined toward that of a horse. In the federal census of 1810 a theme recurs among heads of families: Widow Vaught, Widow Mcalroy, Widow Nicolson, Widow Murdock, Widow Singleton, Widow Burges, Widow Potter…(*Federal*). The incidence of widowers among the handwritten flourishes can only be guessed. According to the *1850 Mortality Schedule for Horry District* (Woodall), the average person eked out thirty-one years. The schedule lists fever as the most frequent cause of death, while others include childbirth, accidents, sickness, and murder. During the Civil War, although vaccination was available for smallpox, this disease was brought from Virginia to an area between Wampee and Stephens Crossroads: "a good many has died with it" (Montgomery 36).

In the Port Harrelson graveyard, where the earliest birth noted is 1835 and the latest death 1908, the average lifespan for the eight markers showing both dates is 20 years. In the Negro cemetery at St. Paul Missionary Baptist Church, Homewood, catalogued by Etrulia Dozier ("Cemetery"), the average is about 51 years for the 88 people whose life span can be determined. (For Zion Cemetery, see Fig. 1.11). The author of this book made calculations based on the birth and death dates recorded by Lewis, et al., for Lakeside Cemetery in Conway ("Lakeside"). The average lifespan of the 981 people buried between 1869 and 1974 was about 51 years. If the 62 babies who had no life span are omitted, the average is about 54 years. Twenty-five people were not counted for lack of full information.

Perhaps the single most valuable memoir in the *Independent Republic Quarterly* was written by Lucille B. Godfrey, a daughter of Franklin G. and Adeline Cooper Burroughs. Three of her siblings died as infants–one from complications of pregnancy, and two in accidents; the remaining five lived to

Fig. 1.11. Tombstone of Minta Lewis, Zion Cemetery, Pee Dee Highway.

an average of over 80 years. For a partial family tree, see Fig. 1.12. Lucille's aunt was Lucy Burroughs Mayo, the sister of F. G.; of Lucy's ten children, only five lived. One of these Mayo Sisters became the mother of Miss Evelyn Snider. Evelyn, known as Conway's First Lady for her lively personality and for her influence both as a teacher and as a member of the First Baptist Church, outlived her two infant brothers by nine decades.

Franklin Gorham Burroughs, 1834-1897, m. Adeline Cooper, 1846-1919.

Effie Tolar [Egerton], b. 1867.

Franklin Augustus (F.A.), b. 1872, m. Iola Buck.
Son **Edward E. Burroughs**, b. 1900.
Daughter **Virginia B. [Marshall]**, b. 1914.

Ruth Adeline, b. 1875.

Edith Ella [Buck], b. 1877.

Arthur Manigault, b. 1881, m. **Frances Coles.**
Son **Franklin G.**, b. 1908, m. **Geraldine Bryan.**
Grandson Franklin, b. 1942.

Sarah Best [Sherwood], b. 1884.

Donald McNeil, b. 1887.

Lucille Norton [Godfrey], b. 1891.

Fig. 1.12. F. G. & Addie Burroughs and their Eight Children

Boldface = Person quoted in *Swamp, Strand, & Steamboat*
[Brackets] = Married name

Before 1910, pneumonia was a major killer in Horry County; it took four children in one family (Skipper). The most dangerous animal was not the cottonmouth moccasin or the wildcat, but the *Anopheles* mosquito. The female bites a person infected with malaria, then transfers the causative organism, *Plasmodium*, to another victim. At the outset, the victim suffers recurrent chills and fever. If the disease is not treated, the person can die. James Saye Dusenbury (b. 1881) notes that the remedy for malaria in each family was a mixture of whiskey and quinine (6). Every spring in Little River, the father of Carl Bessent would prepare a preventative tonic of quinine and coffee for the family and for all the Negroes in the area. He would also run a torch made of tar around the house to control mosquitoes ("About" 6). "Hood's Sarsaparilla Makes Pure Blood and Cures Malaria," declared an advertisement in the *Horry Herald*, 1894, but like many patent medicines it was probably a compound of lies and alcohol ("Impure").

Mary Brookman Beaty, the Yankee schoolmarm, died in 1901 as a lonely old woman, according to Marjory Q. Langston (b. 1891). Langston's father, Colonel C. P. Quattlebaum, came to Conway in 1874, boarded at Mary's place, and handed down these stories:

> In 1870 [the Beatys'] daughter Cora was on her honeymoon down the Waccamaw River when the steamboat became grounded on a sandbar (a frequent occurrence). "For days and nights, while the boat was disabled, the passengers were devoured by mosquitoes from the surrounding swamps." Her husband contracted a fever and died. Shortly after returning to Conway, Cora saw a maid trying to prevent her little sister from drowning in Kingston Lake behind their house; all three died [the maid and the sisters]. Then one afternoon their son Brookie seemed

unwell: Mrs. Beaty laid him down and that evening heard sweet music: among the angels was Cora, who declared, "We have come for Brookie." (Langston 13)

The other two Beaty children had already died from diphtheria (Warwick).

For one group of would-be immigrants, hailing the ferryman was like summoning Charon to cross the River Styx. Tom Livingston (b. 1875) heard about a mystery settlement from Mrs. Spicey Ann Edge (1815-1895):

When she was a girl living in the Red Bluff Section, a group of 40 or 50 families crossed the Waccamaw in covered wagons, came down the river bank, camped overnight beside her house, and played fiddles and danced past midnight. They told her they planned to settle near the ocean. Daylight saw them heading down a wagon road toward the beach.

On her way to visit relatives in Socastee, she noticed a settlement in Big Swamp, an area extending from Spivey's [Withers] Swash to Singleton Swash, and from the Waccamaw to the Atlantic. To her surprise, she recognized the same group of settlers. Telling her that there had been much sickness and many deaths, they blamed the water. Eventually the remaining few came back by her house and told her they were crossing the river and heading back for North Carolina.

It was said (Livingston added) that no white man could live in Big Swamp. There was no drainage at all so that insects could breed easily. Many people may have died from yellow fever and malaria. Remembering Edge's report of seeing 30 to 40 log cabins with adobe chimneys in the settlement, he saw graves and the remains of houses while rounding up his father's cows and horses in about 1886. (D. Micheaux 17-8)

The farther back in the period covered in this book, the likelier that doctors were absent, rare, and respected more than effective. They even had difficulty getting to the patient. Mary Kate Benjamin remembers a contraption powered by Dr. Homer Hope Burroughs (b. 1874): "The bicycle had a high, large front wheel and two small rear wheels joined together by an axle that fit the railroad tracks" (32). Non-medical people acted as midwives and dispensed home remedies, for example, the esteemed Mary Elizabeth Causey Martin (1864-1930), who lived in the Mineral Springs area near Bucksport (Eulee Thomas). Medicine was often a home remedy. One expert used tea made from fresh-run pine resin or parched crickets. According to Frances C. Coleman (b. 1911), one boy, handed an aspirin after being hit by another student, put it in his ear (Int. 13 Oct: 9).

Until electricity heated bathwater, personal hygiene was a challenge. John P. Cartrette (b. 1898) writes:

Woolen underwear was donned at the first cold spell in October and removed after the last cold spell (sheep shearing time) in May. As late as the 1920s some children from poor families were sewed into their suits during this period. The teacher put the worst offenders near a window to air them out. ("To Bathe")

In his novel provoked by Horry County in the 1890s, Zach McGhee describes the pupils of a school in "Washmore Swamp" as if they were the offspring of Poverty and Disease:

"Seated in rows on crude, backless benches set irregularly in different parts of the room, were some fifteen or twenty sallow-faced, dull-eyed, lifeless-looking children, ranging in age from six to sixteen. The benches were all of the same height, and made to seat the larger children, so that the smaller ones sat with their little scrawny legs, all clothed in dirty white stockings, suspended in air. The boys were clothed in suits of coarse, home-made jeans, the breeches of most of them patched at various points along the anatomy fore and aft. The girls each wore the usual coarse homespun one-piece dress; now and then there was a crude attempt at adornment with a bit of faded ribbon at the neck or a fancy-colored comb in the crudely dressed hair....

"There was a lifeless, stupid air about everything and everybody. The children all looked up blankly at the newcomers...." (*The Dark Corner* 123-4. Qtd. in Lewis, "Education," 26)

In 1913, everyone at Cool Spring schoolhouse drank from the same gourd: "no one had ever heard of a germ nor the need for vaccination" (R. Jones, "Vicissitudes," 43). In 1920, sand fleas invaded one school in Little River, where hogs and pigs lived beneath the floor before being fenced in by law. Lice, ticks, pinworms and bedbugs had the run of the county. The first toothbrush held by Roberta Rust (b. 1909) was sent by her grandmother in Chicago (Int: 25).

Polio, an unnamed disease, forced a leg brace upon Mitchelle Collins, whose father was the business partner of F.G. Burroughs, and who had until then climbed a mulberry tree for its fruit. Measles damaged the eyesight of William J. Rowe, b. 1886 ("Memories" 10), who as a boy had lost his mother. Mary W. Hardee, interviewed at a nursing home in 1990, recalled: "My daughter was born in January and died in June of 1936. She was just big enough to love and hold

14

[*clasping her arms together as if rocking a baby*]. She lacked three days of being five months old" (Int: 6).

A "revolution" occurred in about 1920 when the Red Cross sent the sister of Ruby Sasser Jones to vaccinate the school children in Horry County. "Never has there been such a furore until integration came!" ("Vicissitudes" 43). In 1943 Rebecca Graham Page (b. 1909) began working as a public health nurse. At one point she conducted a survey in Green Sea and Floyds and found that 60 percent of children in some schools had hookworms. "You could tell those who had them just by looking at them. They had pale, hollow eyes" (Zinman). People went barefoot, there were inadequate sewage facilities, and many surface wells had no curbings to prevent groundwater from entering. She reports that there was a lot of venereal disease, including congenital syphilis in newborns–and that her clinic in the back of a drugstore was evicted (Int: 10, 17-19).

Her clients had plenty to eat, and "it might have been a sorry shelter, but they had it." As with vaccinations, however, folks resisted. "People were not ready to accept a person coming in telling them: 'Build ya a toilet,' 'Do this,' 'Screen the house….'" They would say "We've lived all our life like this. We're getting' along all right like this, so let us alone."

> "If you went into the home to visit—we had a lot of crippled children then, club feet, hare lip, and other deformities—you had to wear [kid] gloves when you went into the home to talk to that parent…. If the hen was sittin' over there on the bed layin' a egg, you didn't frighten that hen off the bed." (Int: 5-6)

Not only pride but fear had to be reckoned with by advocates of public health. They couldn't get an African American to return (alive) from the sanatorium as a model for the treatment of tuberculosis because blacks waited too long to be tested (Int. McIver 1991: 10-11).

"I carried the 'Colored' bucket"

"Black colonists," as Rodd Gragg points out, "were among the first settlers in Horry County. They came as slaves, working in the rice fields on Horry's southern fringe or in the naval stores industry around Little River" (32). In the memory of whites, as well as in other records, however, black people tend to serve as the chorus in an opera—abundant, hard-working, and anonymous. A news item records that J. N. Ceiley drowned but "the colored man…saved himself by clinging to the boat" ("Local Matters" 5 May 1871). Usually blacks were in ancillary positions as slaves, fieldhands, fishermen, turpentine-workers, sawyers (who cut wood by hand or by machine), steamboat hands, baby-sitters, cooks, and other servants. Often they got only a first name in the memory-record.

In the census of 1810, Horry District, there were 1,390 slaves, 10 free colored persons, and 2,837 whites, so African Americans made up 32 percent of the 4,349 inhabitants (*Federal Population*). In 1820, according to statistics published in 1826 by Robert Mills, 1,434 slaves and 23 free blacks made up about 29 percent of the 5,025 inhabitants (Lewis, "Little River," 10). John Thomas analyzes the demographics of slavery at the midpoint of the era spanned by this book. In 1850 the 2,075 slaves made up about 27 percent of the 7,646 inhabitants. By contrast, they made up about 89 percent of the population in Georgetown County–18,253 out of 20,4460 ("Slavery").

One reason for the difference was a legacy of the Atlantic:

> "The soil, somewhat sandier than was desirable for the production of such plantation staples as rice, indigo and cotton that were common in Georgetown, turned the local populace toward the establishment of a foodstuff-dominated brand of agrarianism, particularly with sweet potatoes, Indian corn, and peas and beans."

Thomas adds another geographical note: "only about one-fifth of land was low enough to receive the overflowing tides that were so indispensable for a successful rice crop." Hence, an abundance of slaves was unnecessary (22).

Was Horry a bastion of white independent farmers, as often averred? Yes, in contrast to other areas of the state. Thomas points out that about one-half of South Carolina's white population living outside the biggest cities owned slaves, but only one-fourth of Horry's 1000 white households included one or more Negroes. Although statewide 24 percent of slaveowners owned a mere one-to-five slaves, in Horry 56 percent did so. As for owners who held title to only one slave, the statewide figure was 13.6 but the Horry equivalent 23.3. One possible result: seven decades after slavery was abolished, S. F. Horton noted that whites in Loris worked hard in comparison to those in Williamsburg County, who relied more heavily on blacks (Int. 15 May: 8).

Horry did not have the array of large plantations that characterized All Saints Parish, Georgetown District. Their slave life was anatomized by Charles Joyner in *Down by the Riverside: A South Carolina Slave Community*. Yet the area did have its own slave plantations on the coast, inland, and on the Waccamaw, whose lower reaches down to Georgetown could be marked with yellow tape reading "Crime Scene." Christopher C. Boyle lists the following places in Horry:

> "Rose Hill, Ark, Longwood, Crab Tree, Snow Hill, Longwood, Oregon, Bell's Bay, Keyes Field,

Upper Mill, Tip Top (formerly Woodbourne), Oliver, Vaught, Savannah Bluff, Cherry Grove,
Windy Hill, Tampico, and Cedar Creek." ("Interview…Godfrey," 14)

See Fig. 1.13 for a plat of Oregon that shows the two nearby Waccamaw plantations of Longwood and Tip Top at the bottom of the county.

Unlike Georgetown County, however, Horry never developed anything like a riceocracy. One Northern visitor archly observed that the titles "Captain," "Major," or "Colonel," were accorded to any man who owned a Negro: "As my ebony driver expressed it: 'Dey 'm all captins and mates, wid none to row de boat but de darkies'" (Kirke 17).

The prime example of this contrast is F. G. Burroughs himself. In a eulogy in 1897, J. R. Tolar wrote:

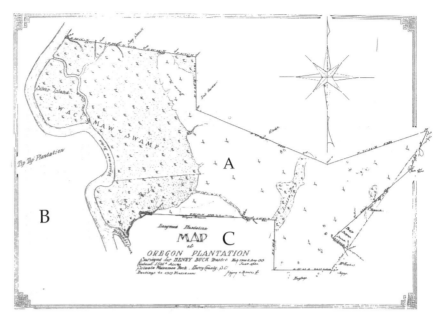

Fig. 1.13. Map of Oregon Plantation with adjoining plantations (1920). A. Oregon. B. Tip Top (Woodbourne). C. Longwood. Waccamaw River at left. ("Map.")

"he never judged a man by his clothes or his money. Prince and pauper were alike his fellow men, and as such entitled to respectful, kindly treatment. Making no undue pretensions himself, he despised shams, pretension and hypocrisy…."

"He was a very unassuming person, very humble, very retiring," according to memories handed down to his great-niece, Evelyn Snider, who was born in 1907, ten years after Burroughs died. "He didn't push himself at all about anything. To look at him, you would not know that he was building an empire."[9]

Despite his egalitarian bent, Burroughs had fought for the Confederacy, an institution based partly on caste. One African American, Ruth Clay "Sabe" Woodbury (b. 1886), hands down memories of her own ancestor:

"My great-grandmamma [Sally Powell] used to tell us—she was the only child that her mother had–and said used to put them on the block and sell them. And said they would save the soap, the grease out of the kitchen like we used to make soap grease. Like they was going to have a sale tomorrow, they would grease them up…and they'd put them on the block to sell them…. And Grandma [Martha Ann Brown, born a slave] said she [the mother of Sally] didn't have but one child and they sold her child. And carried her to Marion. And said she got so disturbed up and mad up about it, she runs away…." (Int: 5-6, 11)

Stitch by stitch, Mother Culture sews people into attitudes. (See Plate 3, "Colored Cafe.") As an extreme example, whites forbade blacks to spend the night above the Dead Line, an area between Chinners Swamp on the north and Brown Swamp on the south, with Jordanville in the middle (Int. W. Davis: 7). The trouble seems to have started around 1907 during the construction of the railroad from Conway. W. Irving Jones (b. 1895) remembers:

"I talked with a man, he was about drunk, at my grandmother's front gate. He was on his way and had his shotgun across his arm and had loaded his shotgun shells with cut nails—just sawed in two." The whites claimed that the Negroes had gone into white folks' pea patches at night. When the whites cussed and hollered at the blacks, telling them to leave, one man "cursed back and told 'em he wasn't going nowhere, so they shot him down and killed him." Fleeing, the Negroes "came back by here the next morning and asked my daddy which way it was to Cool Springs." (Int. 18 Aug: 14-15)

William F. Davis, on the other hand, heard from an old man that Confederate veterans, barefoot, undereducated, and bitter, felt that slaves had caused the war and put up a sign: "No Negroes Allowed in This Area from Sunset Until Sunrise on Pain of Death" (Int: 7). In any case, the railroad stopped at Aynor and never crossed the Little Pee Dee to the outer world.[10]

As water-boy during the construction of the Waccamaw Bridge in the late 1930s, young Ryland Altman (b. 1919) found that some divides could not be spanned: "I carried the 'Colored' bucket and sent it down 30 feet below the river bottom," where the foundation posts had been dug. Thirsty, the white men drank out of the bucket but "told me to never do that again" (Int: 2).

Like the area's insularity, its racial situation during these 222 years is full of complications and contradictions. In the 1920s one man belonged to the Ku Klux Klan yet impregnated a pretty black girl (Reesor, "De Angel," 24). At least one white, a prosperous farmer, went on record in the 1970s to assert that blacks were not human beings, yet he left several appreciative vignettes of former slaves. Different areas of the county, furthermore, had different habits. "Black persons back then was a rarity," declared Marjorie Grainger (b. 1905) from the Loris area: "I don't think I saw but five or six till I was eight-ten years old. If they saw one, they used to pick up stones and sticks and run 'em down the railroad. That was so cruel" (Int. 15 Sept.). Yet in the same area Theatus Garrison used to escape her job hoeing the cotton or tobacco field for a joyride with a white pal, Wilbur, later Dr. Rogers (Int: 7).

Even in poisoned soil, respect and affection could flower. As late as the 1920s, the grandmother of Woodrow Long met weekly with a former slave and talked old times (Int. 13 May: 5-6). A number of people who record their memories on paper or tape recall friendships with those of another race. One tan fellow, Andrew Stanley, even spoke fondly of the white grandfather who had owned his grandmother (Int. 3 Oct: 5), and he looked askance at his less successful and darker neighbors.

Final paradoxes: Henry L. Buck I, the former Yankee and a Union sympathizer, owned by far the most slaves in Horry County–133 in 1850 and 312 in 1860 ("1850 Slave" 11; "1860 Slave" 20). Bill Davis, a child of the Dead Line, was elected chairman of the school board and helped to integrate the public schools slowly but peacefully.

"It was good times in some ways and hard in other ways," declared Claudia Brown, born a century after the county split off from Georgetown District in 1801 (Int. 21 July: 5). Life in Old Horry did have its appealing side: people lived amid bountiful and beautiful nature, under starry heavens (unobscured by ambient light), and close to neighbor, family, church and school, as well as close to the physical processes of getting food and shelter or making a living. "Back those days you would share work," recalled Rilla C. McCrackin (b. 1939). "'Sharecroppers' to me meant you would help one another work. The landowners were the one you had to share the money with" (Int: 4).

Give ear to the declaration of Lunette Davis Floyd (b. 1910). She recalls hog-killings, a communal ceremony when folks roasted potatoes in the hot ashes and ate them along with cracklings made by cooking fat in the wash pot until all the fat was out of the meat: "You young children will never know what you missed!" (14). There was little overindulgence in Old Horry: judging from the record, only one person went on a diet, when a boy got so tired of eating salted mullet and sweet potatoes for breakfast that he skipped a day and went hungry.

The very roughness of the area bred a prickly pride. "They were good people," declared Rebecca G. Page; they paid their debts, had enough food, and had somewhere to stay, "but you didn't tell them what to do." Shifting from nurse to partisan, she added: "You can kind of coax me to it. I'm *full* of Horry" (Int: 7). "I'd rather starve in Horry County," vowed James D. Sanders, "than to be well-off elsewhere" (Int: 2).

The hard side of the county, furthermore, should be seen not only against whatever may be the present day but against life in other regions of the South, country, and world during the era covered by this book. In South Carolina, for example, Georgetown County slaves dulled themselves against the cypress forests they cleared for rice fields; upstate, "lintheads" worked as extensions of weaving machines for all-powerful mill owners.

Many of the recollections in *Swamp* have parallels in other regions of the United States. (One example is *Crackers in the Glade: Life and Times in the Old Everglades*, by Rob Storter.) Despite the many resemblances, in few counties does water seep into daily life in so many ways as Horry: salt or fresh, blue or black, flowing, breaking, steeping, or surging, wet or long-dry and sand-bequeathing.

Notes

[1] Much of the geological theory in this chapter draws on Prof. Douglas Nelson's "Geology of Horry County" or on his private communication with the author. Much theory geological or botanical depends on communication with other professors at Coastal Carolina University: Joseph Pinson, Eric Wright, Paul Gayes, Jim Luken, and Susan Libes.

[2] Jaluco itself was named for the Jackson Lumber Company (Berry, personal communication). It would become the entrance to Carolina Forest development.

[3] Why, in contrast to so much of the East Coast, do no other islands lie off the Grand Strand? Prof. Gayes explains that it composes part of the Cape Fear Arch, terrain shared by North and South Carolina, which rises higher than the coastline adjacent to it on the north and south. This elevated shore makes it hard for ocean waves to cut into the beach, spread out behind it, and start creating an island.

[4] In September 1979, Hurricane David ground away the beach at 29th Ave. S. in Myrtle Beach to reveal the stump of a

cypress tree (a variety that cannot tolerate salt water). Municipal workers cut off the knees with chain saws to protect swimmers (D. Long).

5 *Swamp, Strand, & Steamboat* was written in a bay, or a former one, Carolina or not, that makes up part of Quail Creek subdivision southeast of Conway. One of the small trees out the window is the Southern bayberry, or waxmyrtle. (For names, see Little.) As the source of the name "Myrtle Beach," it has small, wax-covered fruits that used to be made into candles. The leaf of the red bay (*Persea borbonia*) favors the nose when crushed and flavors the soup when dried. The sweetbay (*Magnolia virginiana*) drops a fruit cluster that opens to glossy red M&Ms. "A bay is where the bay flowers grow," declares Elsie Vaught (p.c.). One of them is the sweetbay's fragrant, cup-shaped white petals. Another, which adorns the loblolly-bay (the rare *Gordonia lasianthus*), is a pentagon of white petals that extends from a light-yellow Life Saver. Other species in the yard and throughout the Waterland: blueberry (snack of bears), low gallberry (*Ilex glabra*), and fetterbush (*Lyonia lucida*) with its zig-zag stems. Pond pines bear tight serotinous cones that open after a fire. The titi (pronounced "tah-tah" locally) is a bush-like tree, the Leatherwood or Swamp Cyrilla (*Cyrilla racemiflora*). Its crooked trunk extends a crown over rivers and lakes as well as bays, and in the cold months it has a gender issue: a beard of pine straw along with pendant earrings that resemble tiny grape-clusters.

6 Another example: Lillian Mary Murcek, from Chicago, was "a red-headed Catholic first-generation American of Polish-Austrian descent" who joined the war effort and met James Monroe Hucks, a dashing young Air Force pilot. After they married he said, "You're going home with me." Her daughter adds:

> "Home was a small house on Third Avenue in a town called Conway. Lillian lived there and
> had four children because that was all there was in town. She didn't drive, couldn't get work,
> and was pretty much alienated as a Yankee and a Catholic in foreign territory." (Aceves)

7 Eventually the military took over some 100,000 acres that comprised nine tracts in two counties. The area framed by Highway 90, the Old Ocean Drive Road, the Intracoastal Waterway, and the railroad had "one demolition range, three bombing ranges, a moving machine gun range, and one rifle range" (USAF 8-9).

8 Any victim of typhoid fever, an infection often caused by contaminated water or milk, needed a high-caloric diet to prevent the body from wasting away; yet the treatment was to cut off most food. According to Jesse Byrd James of Galivants Ferry, the grandfather of Timothy Skipper, one patient lay in bed for so long that part of his garment grew into his back. The starvation cure was abandoned after Dr. James Norton recovered from typhoid after being well fed in the Florence hospital (Skipper). Like malaria, this disease was certainly not confined to Horry County or the South: in 1905 Edward E. Burroughs and his mother caught it while visiting the Boston area and spent two or three months recuperating ("In My Time" 23).

9 Evelyn continues with a story. "Papa said that one day the drummer—a traveling salesman—came in, and he had several bolts of cloth spread out on the counter. The clerks were all gathered around looking at the cloth to see what they wanted to buy. [Great] Uncle Frank came in, and he reached over to feel the cloth. He'd been working outside and his hands were grubby and dirty, and the drummer said, 'Get your dirty hands off that cloth!' Well, he got his dirty hands off that cloth and went on out; and all of the clerks were standing there aghast. The drummer knew something was wrong, so he said, 'Who *was* that old man?' They said 'That old man was the owner of the store.' So the drummer packed up his cloth and left, and he never did come back" (Int: 7).

10 Victoria Jones Moore (b. 1876) remembered the story of her grandfather, Henry Jones, the founder of Bethel African Methodist Episcopal Church in Conway. Once near Aynor he was threatened with a beating but released: "Old man, you let this be the fast [sic] and last time you come through here" (Dozier, "Bethel," 7). In 1935, recalls William McTyeire "Mac" Goldfinch (b. 1925), "we were not allowed to send our black gravedigger into that area, so my brother Heyward went and dug the grave" (Int. G. Floyd: 2). Nellie Scott Moore (b. 1939) reported that in the Aynor-Cool Spring sections there were signs on trees as well as ax-prints: "That meant that if you were black…you better get the hell on out because you would get your ears slit or they got beat real bad" (Int: 9).

PLATES

PLATE 2. Dave Carr, World War I, c. 1918. Courtesy Carr family.

PLATE 1. Sweetbay tree prevails over winter.

PLATE 4. Donnie Grant points across river and century to invisible store, 1991. From videotape filmed by David Parker.

PLATE 3. Vestige of store and custom, 916 Third Avenue, Conway, c. 1980. African Americans would enter at the rear of a bakery.

PLATE 5. Freed from its earthly bonds, this raw gum was resurrected at Pot's Bluff by Ron Willman, 2004. Horry County Museum.

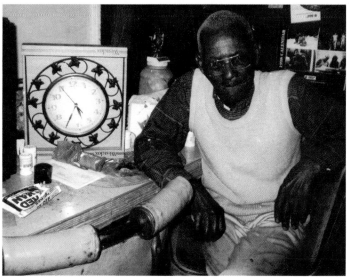

PLATE 7. Robert Bellamy, widower, at his home in the V made by the junction of Highways 90 and 17, 2001.

PLATE 6. Andrew Stanley shows off his old backup tractor, Nixonville, 1991. Photo by Bill Edmonds.

PLATE 8. Janie Johnson tidies up the grounds in Bayboro, 1991. Photo by Bill Edmonds.

PLATE 9. "Miss Flossie" Morris seems to guard the cauldron used by her ancestors in what she would call the War Between the States. Bucksville, 1991. Photo by Bill Edmonds.

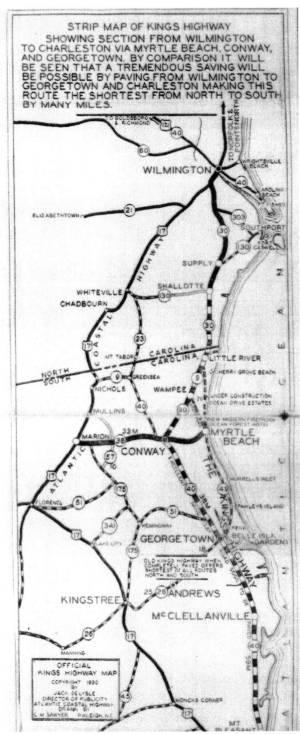

PLATE 12. Henry Small in his 90s, independent farmer, community leader, fast walker, still redoubtable. Burgess Community, 1991. Photo by Bill Edmonds.

PLATE 13. Young Marion Moore and shadow. Courtesy Carolyn Moore.

PLATE 10. Strip Map of Kings Highway, 10 x 4, 1930 ("Official"). Courtesy S.C. Tobacco Museum. North-south axis runs between Georgetown and the point where the S.C.-N.C. border runs off left side. Alternating bars indicate a sand-clay road. Note Highway 40 south of Conway, later 701: "Excellent sand clay road soon to be paved." The work was carried out c. 1931 under the supervision of Winston Granberry Joyner (C. Joyner, p.c.).

PLATE 11. "Reflections from the East." Ocean Drive, S.C., 1930s. Photo by Bayard Wootten. North Carolina Collection, University of North Carolina Library at Chapel Hill.

PLATE 17. A Sunday stroll, Ocean Drive. Photo by Dr. Jerry Hoffer. Courtesy Susan Hoffer McMillan.

PLATE 14. Rusted undercarriage of 1930s log-loader/diving board is inspected by David C. Welsford at Bear Bluff, 2004.

PLATE 15. Author of *Berry's Blue Book* reads upstairs in his once-threatened library, Crescent Beach, 2004.

PLATE 18. In 1991 Virginia B. Marshall stands above the Waccamaw where the vessels of her father and grandfather used to shuttle between Conway and Grahamville. Photo by Bill Edmonds.

PLATE 16. "The Morning After." 31st Ave. N., Myrtle Beach. Photo by Jack Thompson.

CHAPTER 2
THE ROAD

"To illustrate how isolated Horry County really was: in 1954 I came from Statesboro, Georgia, First Baptist Church. We had a moving van, and we couldn't get into this area except on one bridge and one road that would hold the van. I don't know how people got here previously; they certainly did. But we were coming from the south. Highway 378 had an old wooden bridge that they judged unsafe for the van; 701 south to Georgetown had an old wooden bridge that was also judged unsafe. So they had to follow 17 up to Myrtle Beach and come across the old 501 [before the bypass was constructed], and the old road to the bridge—the one bridge into town at the foot of Main Street, which was a concrete structure, to get our moving van in here."
Rev. S. George Lovell, Jr. (b. 1918), Int: 1.

Fig. 2.1. Rev. S. George Lovell, Jr., in 1954. Courtesy Heritage Room, First Baptist Church of Conway.

How to get to the Waterland? How to get around in it? The challenge of transportation underlies all aspects of life in Horry. This chapter and the next explore locomotion that was contingent on water or its vestige, sand.

In 1874 the *Horry News* argued that several cases of fever in Conway could be "traced directly to the want of proper drainage of the streets." The editor urged the County Commission to let the citizens "do their road duty on the streets, instead of being ordered to work the roads four and five miles off" ("Local Matters" 20 June). The primitive status of the infrastructure is itemized in a Grand Jury report of 1893:

> "We present the public road from Socastee Bridge to the Georgetown line in bad condition, and in some places almost impassable. We present the Galivants Ferry Bridge as in bad and unsafe condition. We present the road from Conway to Glass Hill as in bad condition…. We present the

footway over Brown Swamp on the Pee Dee road as down. Foot people cannot pass without wading more or less." ("Final")

Things weren't much better in unofficial reports. When Rick McIver (b. 1912) arrived in Conway, "There wasn't a ditch in Horry County that I could find that would drain anything" (R. Anderson 4). "The water would come up so high," declared Nellie Scott Moore (b. 1939), "'til they had to lay logs in the road for you to go 'cross. It wuttin' but clay highway" (Int: 3).

Others have left vivid memories of travel on the Waterland–by road, bridge, ferry, or tracks-and-ties.

"If there were here no sinners, I would not go along these roads"

Horry County had no paved roads until the 1930s.

The original highway to Conway from Galivants Ferry was a sand-clay road begun in 1919 (Talbert 152). It ran through Cool Spring and Homewood, a segment later named Highway 501 and then 319. As a boy, Barney Dawsey (b. 1912) watched the construction of this road: "They built it with mules and, I believe, mostly blacks were loading the scoop"—i.e., shoveling dirt into the roadside scoop, which would dump it onto the roadbed (Int: 8-9). In Conway it zig-zagged through the downtown, as you can see from Fig. 2.2 (ignoring the numbers). It shared Main St. with the railroad (till '28), then made a left at Third Ave., then a right at Kingston St., then a left across Kingston Lake, sharing a bridge with Highway 905. Then it ran upstream (off the map), made a right to cross the Waccamaw on a bridge and trestle (Fig. 2.3), and continued along the railroad tracks toward Red Hill.

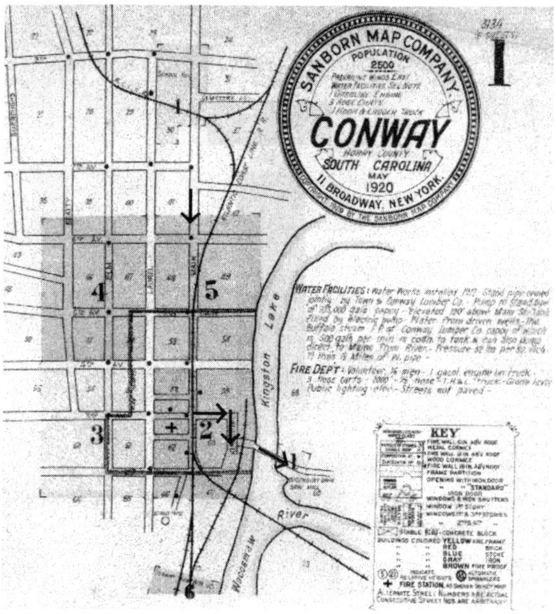

The first road from Conway to Myrtle Beach went via Socastee. Opened in 1914, it was not finished until 1921, when it joined the road that had been improved by Myrtle Beach Farms. Paving did not begin until 1927 (Talbert 153, 181). As seen in Figure 2.4, this Conway-to-beach route took the western edge of the Jaluco Barrier, skirting Impassible Bay as far as Socastee. "It was a cow trail," according to James D. Sanders (b. 1925), "a single rut. One of the skills of driving the Model T was to be able to hear the other car and blow the horn first. He got off the road and you went by." At Gravelly Gully, "when it rained, they turned the Model T around and backed it up that slick hill" (Int: 3-4). (See Fig. 2.5.) At Socastee it turned east on what would become Highway 707 toward what would become the Air Force Base, crossing the unapologetically dubbed Niggerfield Swamp and finally reaching the center of Myrtle Beach on Broadway Street.

In 1937 a new 1500-foot bridge spanned the Waccamaw from Conway with a gentle curve, its lofty arches reminiscent of a cathedral and substantial enough to hold the Lovells' van. For an aerial view, see Fig. 2.6. Also see the view from atop it in Fig. 2.11. The new bridge raised the highway from its humble position next to the railroad tracks to a causeway that stretched to Red Hill; "not a few cars went into the Waccamaw River swamps after crashing off that virtually–unshoul-

Fig. 2.2. Map of downtown Conway, 1920. Numbers unrelated to route of 501. Horry County Museum.

dered road on busy Sunday afternoons" (Ausband, "Roads").

Not until 1948 was the direct route from Aynor to Conway to Myrtle Beach finished. No longer did travelers like Fred W. Hucks (b. 1883) have to ford swamps:

> "Going from Conway to Aynor on what's now 501, you'd ford Crabtree Swamp, Brown Swamp at Brown Swamp Church, Spring Swamp. Come on, next stream is Chinesee; then you're at Aynor, at the end of the world where they ran the railroad up there and stopped it!" (Epps, "Mr. Hucks," 18)

Fig. 2.3. Trestle of the pre-1937 Highway 501 through Waccamaw Swamp, 2003.

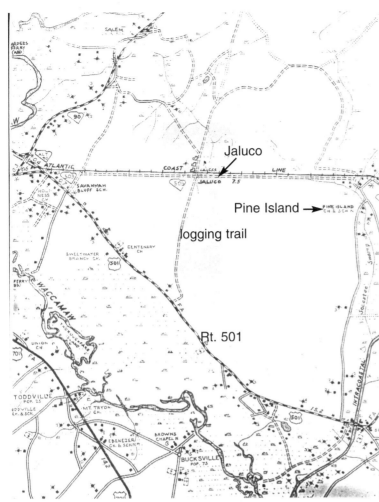

Jaluco

Pine Island →

logging trail

Rt. 501

Fig. 2.4. In this 1939 map Highway 501, later 544, runs south from Conway (located off the top left corner). ("General.")

Southeast from Conway to Myrtle Beach, the impassible was finally breached rather than circumvented. Robert Winfield, a highway engineer (who with his wife gave Rev. and Mrs. Lovell their first roof in Conway) remembers hearing about construction problems on 501:

"They would knock off at night sometimes and come back to find that the bulldozer was down to the top of the tracks on it. They would work for a week to try to get it out. Then they were going through one of those bays and had a bulldozer. I didn't actually go out and see it, but I was told that they came back one day and the Caterpillar you couldn't even see. It had sunk completely out of sight and they just left it there. They just had to dig out that quicksand, pump it out and then haul in new sand. As they pumped it out it just kept going down, so they eventually just covered it up and left it in there." (Int: 4)

The 501 bypass around Conway was completed in 1956, and the highway became four lanes in 1959. Until 1963, however, traffic reverted to two lanes at the Waterway so as to share a drawbridge with the railroad (Ausband, "Roads").

Highway 707 from Socastee to Murrells Inlet? "To go that route was pure sand all the way," remembers James D. Sanders (b. 1925); "The common trick was to let some air out of the tires" for greater traction (Int: 5).

Roads near rivers could disappear, as Highway 905 must have done shortly after World War II when floods reached a cemetery on the Glass Hill Farm. "A trial was going on in Conway," remembers Garland Murrell (b. 1906):

"Two boys had allegedly killed a Little River citizen for a small sum of money. The coffin of the murder victim came up out of the ground…. Law officers are reported to have brought great terror to the prisoners by telling them what had happened." (6)

Road maintenance was often a private responsibility: "Back then," remembered Neal McCracken (b. 1898), "the only way you could fill a hole was to take your wagon and get a load of dirt" (Int. Aug. 22: 23). Ironically, it was the ocean that helped to surface many roads, because it had deposited strata of coquina 1-3 million years earlier. According to Carl Bishop Bessent (b. 1891), "There were many sand and oyster roads through the county" ("Early" 8). For a lump of coquina, see Fig. 2.7.

Even when not flooding, a river could stop a road. A trip to Georgetown via Yauhanna meant one ferry at the Pee Dee and another at the Black. In a drought, however, a ferry might be unnecessary upriver, so that at Red Bluff on the Waccamaw one family "used to sometimes drive across with a mule and buggy when the river was low" (Effie Joyner, b. 1875, Int: 17).

Although primitive, some of the early roads could go where later ones could not. "[They] seemed to follow a snake's path," writes Esther Nance Gray (b. 1916), "with their many turnings and deep ruts, but navigable in good weather. Remember, the Inland Waterway did not cut us off 'til the late 30s" (13). "I have children older than that Waterway," declared Andrew Stanley (b. 1904). In Nixonville, "had a little dirt road, little old boggy road.

"Sometime they waded in water that deep through there; and then branches over the road—you'd stoop your head down…jam to the beach down here where you call Ocean Drive. They called it Windy Hill." (Int. 1991: 27, 16)

The condition of the roads helps to explain the appeal of water as a form of transportation. What do visitors and locals recall about two centuries of roads, or trails, in day or night, in extremes

Fig. 2.5. Sandy precursor of Highway 544 in the early 1920s. "Conway, S.C."

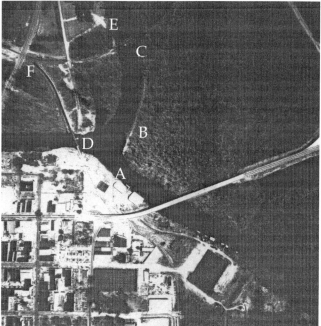

Fig. 2.6. 1937 bridge, undated. Courtesy Sanford D. Cox, Jr., family. Kingston Lake enters at left; lower segment of river flows south. A. Pre-1928 railroad crossing point. B. Pre-1928 railroad bed along the Waccamaw. C. Post-1928 railroad trestle across the Waccamaw. D. Site of former highway 501 bridge across mouth of Kingston Lake. E. Pre-1937 access to bridge over the Waccamaw. F. Later route of highway 905.

of terrain and weather?[1]

Rev. Francis Asbury (b. 1745). *A missionary from England, Asbury was a bishop of the Methodist Episcopal Church. He made four trips to the area between 1795 and 1801, after which at least 14 small Methodist churches came into existence (Benjamin 29). He promoted the growth of the circuit rider system, and his journal entry of February 8, 1791, describes his own circuitous route from North Carolina through what would become Horry District:*
"We came a long, dreary way, missed our road, and at last reached brother S–'s; a distance of twenty-five miles, which our wandering made thirty miles." (I: 666)

In 1795, on his way to Kingston, he tried entering at Longs:
"Cross where you will between the States, and it is a miserable pass for one hundred miles west. I was much led out on Rev. xxi.6-8.[2] This country abounds with bays, swamps, and drains; if there were here no sinners, I would not go along these roads." (II: 69)

S.C. Morris (b. 1836). *Departing from what is now Kingsburg, S.C., Morris traveled to Horry County by "buggy train," a two-horse carriage with buggy hitched on behind:*
"I had to cross the Great Pee Dee at Godfrey's Ferry, and also Richardson's Ferry on the Little Pee Dee on flat boats or ferries, and no roads such as we know them in between. The trail through the swamps was for the most part covered with water, and an unseen cypress knee caught on the step of the carriage, causing the doubletree [crossbar for harnesses] to break, and the horses walked away leaving me and my family and a crate of chickens stranded as if on an ark, miles from any other living soul" ("Tale" 10. See Fig. 2.8.)

Elizabeth Collins. *It was daunting to get back and forth from Hagley Plantation, on the lower Waccamaw, and "the last place God made":*
"Towards the end of January 1862, Mrs. W[eston] made up her mind to visit Conwayboro', a country town (if such a place can be called a town), where she had been informed was a cottage that would be likely to suit her. At an early hour of a very fine day, Prince [a slave] drove us to Conwayboro', a distance of 40 miles, through rough country, full of stumps of trees, and the roads of very deep sand."

A return trip the next year was more taxing on people and animals:
Half of the drive was so rough that the two horses began to give out—in large part because the driver did not know to force the lazier horse, Fidget, to work. So by the time the party reached "a parish called Soccastee, where there was a very awkward bridge to cross, James had to lead the two horses" for several miles. Finally the women decided to walk as far as they could. "This was a hard task, for at this time we encountered some of the deepest sand, as well as two hours of hot sun." Although fresh horses and a carriage arrived to rescue them, the hard-working animal, Miss Nightingale, died a few days later. (*IRQ* 11.2: 14-15)

Rev. William W. Malet. *Another English visitor to the Westons, Malet undertook a journey from Conwayborough to Pawleys Island in 1862 with more success. He appreciates the hospitality, the bounty, the flora, the skill of Prince, and the symbiosis of horse and insect:*
"I left in the buggy and pair at 5 a.m.; at twenty-six miles rested half an hour, at a farm of a Mr. Macklin, who gave good entertainment for man and horse, and would take no payment. In spite of the blockade [by the Union Navy]

Fig. 2.7. This concentration of pectins (scallops) and oysters is cemented with aragonite and calcite, probably with some clay/silt in the matrix. Paul Gayes. Photo by Bill Edmonds.

Fig. 2.8. Cypress "knees," actually modified roots. Photo by Paul Olsen.

these farmers have abundance of good things. Here you are in a 'foreign land,' and meet with a regular old English reception and hearty welcome: corn bread—milk—butter—honey—cider—wine—all homemade; orchards filled with peach-trees and apples—the fruit not yet ripe.

"The road was rough: often when a tree had fallen across it, a detour had to be made some yards through the forest. The woods were beautiful in all variety of foliage: oaks, cypress, cedar, pine, magnolias, azaleas, etc.… 'Prince' never touched the horses once with the whip—only spoke to them; the voice is much used in the management of horses in the South. Though the sun was hot, and flies were numerous, yet the horses went along unmolested, being protected from flies by the 'horse guards,' which are immense black and yellow hornets; two or three of them keep continually hovering around each horse, devouring the flies and scaring them away; they are also constant attendants on cattle, to their great relief and comfort." Because of the sandy terrain, the "'hoofs that iron never shod,' uncontracted, spurn the earth." (*IRQ* 14.3: 30)

Cordie Page (b. 1884): *Darkness might conspire with water:*
"We were coming from Marion one dark night…; my brother riding ahead on horseback had to pull off his coat so we could see the way by his white shirt. After a while my brother said, 'The horse has stopped.' Father said, 'Pull him to the right.' Come to find out, we'd come to a deep slough [a muddy and swampy area, pronounced *sloo*], with an open place up in the trees and had headed right into the river!" (Epps, "Mr. Cordie," 5)

A.J. Baker (b. 1884). *In this narrative ballad (excerpted), the author and his buddy go on a camping trip with a pet horse:*

> We took the road to southward
> Through Autumn's tinted grove
> Where poets paint the dreamland
> And lovers want to rove.
>
> It's [the Waccamaw's] banks we found much
>   overflowed
> The road a darkened aisle
> Then lovely Maude we calmly wooed
> In fear of waters wild.
>
> To Maude again we gave the rein
> A signal for to go.
> She heaved a groan and started on
> Then plunged the overflow.
>
> In such disguise the lone road way
> Meandered o'er the plain;
> We lost ourselves and seeking road
> Drove in the river main.
>
> Down all except Cad Rise and I
> Beneath the river's main
> Then swam on Cad and struggled I
> All tangled in the rein.
>
> Maude could but fight her fearless foe
> Till in a soundless motion
> The river bore its tale of woe
> Towards the mighty ocean.

When I had my refuge gained
From the waters black as night
A man who kept the ferry came,
Came in much affright.

But not 'til Maude was hushed and still,
Hushed all her neighs and groans;
She had but fled to join the dead
To haunt me when alone. ("Fate")

Neal McCracken (b. 1898). *A mule could figuratively drown in sweat while pulling a wagon from Cool Spring to Aynor:*
"[Now] it wouldn't be nigh as heavy as it was back then in these here sandy roads and part of the time uphill. It would just take me about a half a day after hitching up the mules to get back to Aynor with a load. I would do better if I had the two-horse wagon but it was still bad. Most of the time I would only bring about four sacks [of fertilizer], or 800 pounds back. On the one-horse wagon the mule would sweat so bad, and weren't none of it hard [surfaced] then. It was a sight in hell for a mule to pull through." (Int. Aug. 15: 8-9)

Edward E. Burroughs (b. 1900). *In Myrtle Beach around the dawn of the twentieth century, children had to pick sand spurs out of their feet after walking to the store:*
"A board road was built over the high sand dunes on Ninth Avenue to Ocean Boulevard and north along Ocean Boulevard for four or five blocks. Only one car could come down that road at a time." (25)

David Carr (b. 1887). *From the Burgess-Freewoods area, Carr was interviewed in 1991 as part of a televised oral history series sponsored by Rev. Dr. Carl Compton of Myrtle Beach. The centenarian remembers that a trip to Georgetown required an overnight stay:*
To get ice or lightbread [made from wheat flour rather than corn meal] you had to go by ox and cart [pronounced something like *kyaht*]. You'd stay in someone's house or on the deck in the place with the train and the boats. "They had a room that you could buy your ticket to go on the train and we would sleep in there." (Int: 4)

John P. Cartrette (b. 1898). *This longtime resident of Conway lists a few specifics about overland travel:*
"Taking a long axe in the wagon to break the ice in Poplar Swamp so that the mule would not slip on it and break a leg.

"Taking a robe (lap) in the buggy or wagon to wrap our feet in cold weather, and occasionally placing a hot brick or a lighted lantern under the robe for warmth.

"On a trip to Conway after riding until we were nearly frozen, to get out and walk or run on the frozen ground to thaw out.

"The road washed out in White Oak Swamp so that the mule would have to swim.

"At Crabtree Swamp (a crabapple tree grew on the southeast side of the road at the swamp) the road was washed out into a hole. During the freshet [i.e., a flood] a box would be placed on the wagon or buggy seat. One day I was sitting on a box of Brown Mule Chewing Tobacco atop the wagon seat. Coming from town the wagon got into a deep rut in the swamp and the water came up and wet me, covering the box I was sitting on." ("Good" 24)

Also daunting was a trip by automobile in 1924 from Myrtle Beach to Conway via the Socastee road:

"After we left the beach sand, the road became soupy and in ruts. The wheels were in about four to six inches of soup (sand and water), the car axles shaved off the dirt smooth. At places when the car was about ready to gasp its last, the farmer with his team in the distance would start to meet us confident of a fee, but I would get out and push until the car could pick up speed on some firmer ground."

On the way home to Myrtle Beach they tried the Wampee route to the Sand Hill road; Cartrette broke off bushes and limbs to fill ruts, then a tire fell off when it hit a bridge, so they rode along the beach on the rim. ("Good" 10-11)

Once on the way back from Conway, where he had bought medicine for his father, he had to carry his bicycle across Poplar Swamp on footlogs. But when he arrived on dry ground, the handlebar hit the medicine in his pocket, breaking and spilling it. "I had to return the nine miles to town and get the prescription refilled." ("Good" 24)

Charles M. Todd. *Todd's fictionalized memoir draws a vivid portrait of the Brown Swamp area in an unspecified era:*
One young man rode ten miles for the doctor and told him to ride horseback [rather than drive a buggy] because of the swollen streams and frozen ground. Then, "up the road towards Conway, they heard the big pacing feet of old Dan, Dr. Goolsby's [a pseudonym] big black fast horse, rapidly hitting the frozen ground in clanking tones." (13, 31)

Rebecca Graham Page (b. 1909). *Working as a public health nurse after 1943, Mrs. Page (pictured in the Foreword) often got caught in a washed-out bridge, in sand, or in a mud-hole:*
At first she would pay farmers 50 cents to pull her car out with a mule. "But I got so I took me a short-handled shovel along with me. Put it in the trunk of the car. And one place where I went down here to Freemont somewhere, I run over a well—-no cover on it." (Int: 13-14)

William J. Rowe (b. 1886). *Postal service, like medical, had its challenges. As a boy, Rowe often carried the mail home from the post office located in a store run by Burroughs & Collins at Grahamville, four miles away:*
"Almost the entire road in that day before automobiles was composed of deep, white sand. The sand got very hot in the summer and the bare feet of the boy were severely burned. During the winter, the wind had a clear sweep and the dampness made it penetrating and cold." ("Memories" 7)

Susie Lambert Lewis (b. 1898). *In about 1918 during an awful cold spell:*
Joe Jones, the mail carrier for Route 2, drove across the frozen Dawsey Swamp with his Model T. "But the fifth day it broke in." (Int: 15)

Annie Lee Singleton Bailey (b. 1909). *As a child Annie Lee accompanied her father on his postal route:*
Mother would wrap a glass churn, wrap towels around it, and put it on the floor of our Model T, and when we got home, the butter was churned. There were no paved roads anywhere. Highway 9 was "nothing but a sand bed. If you were going to meet a car, you'd have to stop a long time before you got there to get out of the way." In the Hemmingway section, "when I'd blow my horn, the colored people would know to come push me out of the hole" [*laughter*]. (Int: 9,6)

Marion Moore (b. 1931). *Education, too, had to contend with locomotion. Moore took the ferry across Bull Creek from Sandy Island to Bucksport, then a bus to Conway High School, returning home at 5 p.m.:*
"If the roads would get wet and clay hills and the bus slide—we'd be late for school and it'd bog down." The driver would tell the students to get out and push, and not hold the bus. "Now in the afternoon, we was going home, we'd push the bus out. But if you was going to school, if it couldn't get out on its own, it didn't get out" [*laughter*]. (Int: 3-4)

Marjorie Grainger (b. 1905). *Miss Grainger, the daughter of a Civil War veteran, regarded ice as a game:*
"Walking to school with black stockings with holes, worn-out shoes, the ice would spew up out of the ground by a ditch—like icicles. It was fun to kick 'em with our toes." (Int: 3).

Georgia Smalls Lance (b. 1926). *Snow, sleet or rain, young Georgia walked two miles to the St. James Rosenwald School in the Freewoods-Burgess community. Built in 1928 or '29, it was one of fifteen in the county and about 5,000 established for black children in the South with the help of a Northern philanthropist. (See J. Wilson, "Legacy.")*
"When we got to school some days, the teacher was very lenient with us because your feet was soakin', saturated by crossin' the logs and whatever, you'd sometime fall off 'em. You'd take your shoes and socks off, some of them not pleasant odors. 'Course you had to dry your shoes before you'd go back home that afternoon, dry your socks" (Int. Peterkin: 41)

Thomas Clyde Vaught (b. approx. 1907). *One night the horse was ailing, so seven-year-old Thomas and his father walked home from Conway:*
When they crossed the bridge over Kingston Lake, the snowy road "stretched out before us like a long piece of white ribbon." "The trees and bushes grew right up to the road, which was just wide enough for two wagons to pass. The moon and stars were our light. We hadn't gone far before a bough broke under its weight of ice and snow and came crashing down. I walked closer to Papa." Then "a shivering owl let out his woeful cry," and "I was about as close to Papa as I could get, so we walked along in silence, keeping time with the crunching."

It was probably at one dark, swampy stretch that "something tore loose with a blood-curdling scream as if in defiance of our right to tread on his domain. I reached up and took Papa by the hand." At Glass Hill, a coon dog "gave us assurance of his presence with a howl that almost jarred the ground." Every now and then "a dead branch would turn loose and come crashing down, with the ice splattering and breaking other branches, and sometimes it was so close it sounded as if the whole world was caving in." After ducking into a store, they rounded a curve and "could see, through the trees, the lights of the kerosene lamps of home. Mama fed us, warmed us, and put us to bed, and tucked the cover around my head." (29)

Ironically, the pulverized feldspar and quartz of the beach could provide the most reliable thoroughfare. C. Burgin Berry explains that the shore was an official link of the old Kings Highway, a coastal road that "entered the beach near what is now Singleton's Swash…and followed it for some fifteen miles before turning inland." Because of the great Singleton Swash Swamp, travelers through the Province of South Carolina found it easier to cross the swash at low tide ("Withers" 27-28). "The average time we'd try to catch the tide down and go to strand," recalled Andrew Stanley (Int. 1991: 28).

Anonymous, *New Voyage to Georgia. In June, 1734, the writer made his second foray into this same province from Georgia:*
After spending the night north of Winyah Bay, the party left at about 5 a.m., "and about six came on the long bay, the tide just serving for us to get over the swashes. We had twenty-five miles farther to ride on the bay, or sea-shore, and five miles after before we came within sight of a house, so that we were obliged to ride gently for fear of our horses." After fifteen miles, his horse gave out so he took the horse of one of the Negroes, whom he left behind to care for his own. Three more horses gave out before the party reached Little River. (54)

John Bartram (b. 1739). *Also making his way from Georgetown through what would become Horry County was a botanist from Philadelphia who traveled alone through the Southeast before his famous son William. Here is an excerpt from his* Diary of a Journey through the Carolinas, Georgia, and Florida:
"July 19 [1765]. thermo. 81. cleared up in the morning. travailed along the bay, the banks of which is A red soil, which I suppose reacheth into the sea under the fluctuateing sand, insomuch that all the adjacent shells is tinged with A deep orange color. butt the object that engaged my attention most was A solid rock of concreet shels & gravel whose summit just appeared even with the fluctuating sand, but to what depth it decended I cant say. It was so soft as with A sharp pointed knife to cut A little hole into it…." (28) [3] (See Fig. 2.7)

George Washington (b. 1732). *Rolling from the opposite direction was the "Charriott" of the new President, who was touring the Southern states in 1792. He crossed from North to South Carolina on Wednesday, April 27, dined in a private house, then spent the night two miles above Long Bay.*

On Thursday their host "piloted us across the Swash (which at high water is impossible, & at times, by the shifting of the Sands is dangerous) on the long Beach of the Ocean; and it being at a proper time of the tide we passed along it with ease and celerity to the place of quitting it, which is estimated 16 miles,–five miles farther we got dinner & fed our horses at a Mr. Pauley's a private house…." (177-78)

T.A. Conrad (b. 1802). *Four decades later, in 1834, Conrad traveled through the South looking for fossils. He carried a head full of classical allusions as well as a box to hold marine specimens from "the shell-paved beach."*
At Smithfield, N.C., he took a stump-dodging "ricketty jig" of a stagecoach down the coast to a house near the Atlantic. For twelve miles south, "The stage road lies upon the sand of the sea-shore where the ruts are daily obliterated." The next morning he decided to walk. "The day was warm and an easterly wind brought in a mist from the ocean, as drenching as a shower of rain. With the first signs of a road which led off from it, I proceeded through the forest, hardly expecting that so obscure a path should lead to a habitation of a man; but a cabin at length was found where from one of its pallid inmates I procured a vague direction to the nearest inn, which I was never destined to find. Indeed, it would require the clue of Ariadne to direct one through the labyrinths of this sterile uniformity of scene. The pedestrian who traverses the low sandy region of the seaboard meets with few objects of interest sufficient to reward his toil.

"If, when tired of wandering through the deep sand, he strikes into the woods, he will find the brown slippery pine leaves an indifferent exchange for the highway. This most uninteresting country, however, enjoys a winter climate as lovely as a northern October, when the air is unvexed by storms. The pine forest is here and there varied in the low, moist, richer portions of soil, by a growth of oak, hickory, and a variety of less conspicuous trees, nearly every one of which wears a beard of Spanish moss which a Turk might envy, and on almost every limb, stripped of its panoply of leaves, the mistle-toe, as if in pity, hangs its emerald and perennial mantle. The swamps resound with the singular cry of the ivory-billed woodpecker [very large, presumed extinct], and the pileated woodpeckers, with their crimson crests flashing like meteors, are seen chasing each other in frolic pastime around the grey trunk of the dismantled tree…. (19)

Carl Bessent (b. 1891). *Another man veered off the sandy highway but with less profit. Referring to himself in the third person, Besssent recalls heading for a picnic at Windy Hill:*

"He dressed and hitched the blind horse to the buggy, and drove along the Strand by Ocean Drive, S.C. He went to sleep driving. When he awakened, the horse was standing in the breakers." ("About" 6)

"They really make me appreciate a bridge": Ferries

Before and even after the rivers were spanned, Horry County was dotted with what might be called shuttling bridges. In 1954 all the points that the Lovells' furniture could or could not cross had once been ferries. First, where Highway 378 crossed into Horry from Marion County at the former Potato Bed Ferry. Next, where Highway 701 crossed into Horry from Georgetown County at Yauhanna, a bluff on the Pee Dee. (From a trading post here in 1716, one trader returned to Charleston accompanied by "several Indian oarsmen and a load of 549 deer skins"–Michie 9.) Then where Highway 17 crossed into Horry County from Georgetown, over the confluence of the Pee Dee, Black, and Waccamaw Rivers, a ferry had operated until just nineteen years earlier when the Lafayette Bridge opened.

Ferries operated across the Waccamaw until the 1920s. Dr. J. A. Norton lists those between the North Carolina line and Georgetown:

"Wortham's, almost opposite Little River;
Bellamy Landing, some ten miles lower down;
Star Bluff, off of Wampee;
at Bear Bluff at one time;
Reaves Ferry, Nixonville;
Hardee Ferry, Savannah Bluff;
a local ferry; Cox's ferry;
Peach Tree Ferry...." ("Ferries" 7. See Fig. 2.9)

According to Dr. Norton, there were several types of ferry: (A) poled across in a flat-bottomed scow [a large boat with a flat bottom used to carry freight], (B) pulled by a notched club along a wire rope (see Fig. 2.10), or (C) pushed across the current while attached to a pulley ("Ferries" 8). Any wires lay slack across the bottom of the river until needed.

Fig. 2.9. Flat at Enterprise Landing on the Waccamaw, 1920s. Note ferryman with pole. Horry County Museum.

Born approximately 1887, Donnie Grant stood on the bank of the Waccamaw where he had worked for "Ol' Man Bill Reaves" (1853-1923):

"I had a cable across the river with a flat, and I'd pull the cable. [*He holds his cane parallel to the ground and threads it hand over dark hand*]. Pull the flat across. And the boat had a paddle. [*Shifting his cane to the side, he pushes it backward as if through water.*] No charge. Anybody come and holler they wanted across, whoever was there, they would put them across. Some would come over here to buy fertilize [sic]. Some would come to buy grocery." (Int: 23-24)

See Plate 4 for a photograph made from the videotape filmed by David Parker.

Sometimes with the help of Grant's flat, a mule, and "an old road cart about wide as this chair," Andrew Stanley (b. 1904) carried the mail from the Wampee Post Office to the one in Conway: "I know him well. He put me across the river when I was driving that mail a million a million a million days. He's fifteen years older than me" (Int. April 1991: 3).

Soon after 1874 the ferry even enabled one congregation to build a place of worship. According to the oldest members of Socastee United Methodist Church, interviewed in the early 1960s, the best timber was donated, cut, hauled to Peachtree Ferry, floated across the Waccamaw to the Bucksville sawmill, and sent back as boards (S. Cooper 15). But water itself could put ferries out of commission: "Heavy freshet," announced the *Horry News*, "in the Pee Dee River, Long ferry, at Bull Creek, and Yauhana. Gallivant's ferry is Impassible for horses and vehicles" ("Local Matters" 17 Feb. 1874).

Fig. 2.10. Ferryman's club, 25" long. Horry County Museum. Photo by Paul Olsen.

John Bartram (b. 1739). *The diary-keeping botanist recounts his approach to Horry in 1765, river by river, coin by coin*:

"July 18. then set out over much savana ground & some piney dry sandy soil to monks ferry on black river, 6 pence; then over pede [Pee Dee], 6 pence; then Wocama, 1 shilling, half A mile broad; then very poor sandy soil & some savanas." (28)

Rev. William Malet. *Not so routine was Malet's return to Conway from Georgetown District a century later. First, because of the Civil War the ferryman's place had been taken by a black female. Then, when the raft reached the western bank:*
"Our dusky propellor held on her pole at the stern, and I seized the iron ring at the prow; [the slave] 'Prince' gave a pull, and out sprung the steeds—but alas! back went the boat, in spite of my pull and her push. Nobly the horses struggled up the slippery bank, their hind feet in and out of the water: the bank was steep, the water deep; in a moment the boat had slipped away, and the carriage was in the river, and poor 'Prince' in a very uncomfortable position.

"I kicked and thumped the near horse, and urged them with my voice, telling 'Prince' to let go the reins; and just as the horses made a last desperate effort to escape being dragged back into the stream with the floating buggy, both splinter bars broke, and away they sprang with the pole and reins. I rushed to the near fore-wheel, which was just disappearing, and by unexpected strength held it up to the edge of the bank. The moment the horse broke loose, 'Prince' scrambled over the splash-board, sprung up to the bank, and held the other wheel. The poor Negro woman stood aghast; the horses began eating grass."

Luckily a few overseers from plantations were headed to Conwayborough for conscript day (i.e., to perform public labor), and they helped pull the carriage to terra firma. The splinter bars were then patched, and the party went off "with no more damage than my valise, with all its contents, my white surplice, my books and journal, stained with the dark-brown waters of the Wakamah." (*IRQ* 14.3: 31-32)

James A. Norton, M.D. (b. 1876). *"I can remember well the time when these ferries were all in more or less active use":*
"And the hallooing of the ferryman up, especially at night, when it was dark and perhaps cold and rainy, and the ferryman curled up snugly in his bed on the other side of the river, and it seemed to me that the ferryman was usually on the other side of the river on a cold, wet, and mean night, was quite an adventure in and of itself.

"There was only one consolation, and that was when you did reach the ferry, the worst and darkest part of your trip was over, for always the ferryman's house was on the opposite side of the swamp, usually situated on a bluff, and the dark and sometimes deep swamp would then be behind you, and only the steep bluff to cross on the other side."[4]

The ferry itself could bring respite:
On hot or even cold days, crossing on the ferry was a special moment, "breaking the monotony of a long drive with its consequent cramping and leg-weariness of possibly an all-day's drive in a small buggy." Livestock enjoyed "a space of breathing and rest as the flat took its slow way from one side of the river to the other."

Female members of the family often substituted for the males. "And that was one outstanding trait of the women of this county anyway—indoors or outdoors, they were at all times not only willing, but did take their place shoulder to shoulder with their men folks in any kind of work." ("Ferries," 7, 8-9)

Eunice Watts Hardee (b. 1910). *Star Bluff extended from the Waccamaw River through Longs Community, across the woods, and to the beach at Chestnut's Cross Roads. Even the twelve-year-old daughter of Duke and Bertha Watts worked at the Little House on the Ferry:*
At all times someone had to be on call, literally, for that loud "Hello!" The charge for each passenger in a rowboat was 10 cents; 25 cents for families with horse and buggy, wagon, or car. Eunice used small blocks of wood called "billets" to pull the ferry across, one car at a time. Once she ran to the river to see what had happened: "My daddy pulled the man out of the back of the car and lifted the car out of the river with a windlass" [a drum wound with rope and turned with a crank]. When the water was high, the ferry was unloosed from the cable and poled by hand across the wider distance. Eunice saw an accident with a wagon: "Daddy quickly unhitched the mules and one swam to safety. He rescued one man hollering and praying but the other man drowned." (W. Thomas, "Watts")

Mark Bellamy (b. 1891). *Interviewed by C.B. Berry, Bellamy remembers an incident involving a dozen or more mules at Wortham's Ferry. Quotation marks indicate Berry's original paraphrase:*
"John Vereen and Will Stone went into the horse-and-mule business and bought a carload of mules—unloading them from the railroad in Loris." The mules followed a horse to the ferry, where the men managed to get them aboard--but about half of them bolted off the ferry into the river. "Most continued swimming across to shore but one was carried far downstream in a fairly swift current and had to be pulled from the river." (Berry, "River")

James "Son Rabbit" Bellamy (b. 1893). *At Wortham's Ferry a horse caused the demise of humans:*
"Henrietta Bessant, she was coming home for Christmas—her and her baby daughter. Somebody ran mule or ox or horse and the horse got scared and jumped. The women got drowned. I remember that good." (Int: 5)

Pratt Gasque (b. 1908). *A trip to Murrells Inlet from Marion, via Conway, required that a farmer abandon his team:*
A plowshare hung from a tree, and we would beat it with a piece of iron. The farmer across the river, Rufus Graham, who was usually plowing, would unhitch his mules and put them in the barn. Then he would amble down to the flat. "After checking his cables and nodding a greeting to us," he pulled the ferry to the other side. He used wooden mauls [heavy, long-handled hammers] about the size of a baseball bat, with grooves in the large end that he placed on the cable. When he reached them, he secured the ferry to a tree with a thick cable to keep the Model T from pushing the flat away when it drove off. (4)

E.R. McIver, Jr. (b. 1912). *Born in Florence County, Rick co-founded McIver-Shaw Lumber Company in Conway after surviving campaigns in Africa during World War II. He has many memories of ferries, "not all of them good":*
"Usually when I got to the landing, the ferry was on the other side. In winter, the cable used to pull the ferry across was cold, wet and rough on your hands, unless you were fortunate enough to find a stick with a slot cut in it to pull the cable with, but that was usually lost.

"The land approaching the ferry was sloping, wet, and muddy and slick. If you got on the ferry without slipping into the water or getting your vehicle stuck, you could figure luck was with you. When it rained it took a long time bailing out the ferry. It always seemed to me that over a thousand gallons had to be splashed out or bailed out. If you ever made the mistake of overloading it, it would sit flat on the bottom and there was no way to move it. You had to unload and make several trips.

"Accidents were very common. I remember my father cranking his car up when we hit the far bank and starting off with a mighty roar before we could secure the ferry. It kicked the ferry halfway across the stream and the car did not move forward one inch, but plunged into the water with only the radiator cap showing. In high water when the cable was under water, problems really came up. One time during high water we attempted to cross by paddling the ferry. The wind and current caught us and we ended up under trees and on logs....

"One thing I can say about ferries, they really make me appreciate a bridge." ("Water" 4-5)

Theatus Graham Garrison (b. approx. 1920). *As a child in Loris, she and her family would take an overnight trip to the beach to celebrate the completed harvest. They traveled in a wagon with a top made of brownish, unbleached muslin:*
A boy stood on one side of the ferry and a girl on the other. "They would drive the horse right up to the river and put the horse on the flat and then my father would [unhook the wagon] just in case if the horse got scared or anything. If she jumped, she could go over and wouldn't carry the wagon. So we were sitting in the wagon, the little ones." "I was always scared because I thought the horses might jump off and carry the wagon, too. [Often] I stayed here with Miss Maggie, my schoolteacher."

Whoever was first, black or white, boarded the ferry. "[Sometimes] it would be two—a white and a black on there because they were in line and they would let them cross like that." (Int: 19-20)

Jesse Mills (b. 1893). *A ferryman once connected two young people in marriage:*
Old man Singleton's uncle was guarding Maude Macklen, age 15, and everywhere she went, "he's right with her." As the couple made their way toward the river, "her walking in one cart and me at the other," they arrived at Peachtree Landing ahead of the chaperone. He had to wait for the next ferry and caught up only as they were emerging from the Georgetown courthouse, married. Mrs. Mills lived until 1977. (Int: 7-8. See also Pollard 37.)

"All of the bridges was wood"

The Little River bridge appeared on a map dated 1808 (Berry, "The Little"). At least from that time, a ferry operated across Kingston Lake near the point where it entered the Waccamaw (Murrell 5), but not until 1874 were the piles for a bridge driven into the mud ("Local News" 28 April). Thereafter travelers on wheels, hooves, or feet could move with less tediousness between Conway and the area later served by Highway 905 (called Pireway Road for a town just over the border in North Carolina). A new steel bridge was constructed in 1916, visible in the top corner of Fig. 2.11.

Often, according to Rick McIver, the main challenge wasn't bridging a river or branch, it was *getting* there, because the preliminary swamps were so wide. The first bridges through the Little Pee Dee and its swamps were built in 1902 or '03, according to Winnie Holliday Coles, b. 1892 (10-11). From upstate, Evangeline Wideman Page Collier was escorted in this style to her first teaching job in 1919 or 1920: "Mr. Kemp Cooke, trustee of the Sandy Plains School, met me at the train in Marion and brought me through the Little Pee Dee Swamp. The road was a winding swampy trail over rickety wooden bridges" (3). When a turnbridge was finally constructed across the Waccamaw, it was kept in the open position until about the time of World War I for lack of money to construct the approaches ("HCHS" 6). Finished in 1912, it remained a steel sculpture until funding was located (see Talbert 98-101). "Mac" Goldfinch, as a child in Conway (b. 1925), could hear people driving to the beach on that bridge: "Clack-aclack-a-clack-a-clack-a. All night long" (Int. G. Floyd: 19-20).

Not until 1937 was the concrete-and-steel, van-bearing structure erected over the Waccamaw at Conway. From this bridge the photo of the Conway waterfront, Fig. 2.11, was probably taken. Downstream from the earlier one, the new bridge replaced the circuitous route over lake, rails, and trestle, and indeed its funding came mainly from the railroad-crossing elimination program sponsored by the federal government ("Bridge Goal" 12). Albert Carr (b. 1906) stayed at a work-camp during the week and helped to construct the bridge (along with three others, as well as the Waterway they all crossed). Sixty-five years later he explained the steps of its construction, from coffer dam to cement finishing. "I have been down on the bottom" (Int: 19).

Until after World War II, there were only three concrete bridges, according to Robert Winfield (b. 1918):

The work on Highway 378 was replacing a bunch of old wooden bridges and in some places no bridge at all. When it flooded, the swamp was flooded and you couldn't go through that place. They built a fill through the swamp from over near Britton's Neck back to just before you get to the Pee Dee Road coming into Conway. The fill was left because the war came along and stopped the construction, but the bridges were all completed. The project just set there until after the war. Then the Highway Department came in and finished the road work, paved the roads, and 378 was about the third road that was paved in Horry County at that time. (Int: 2)

Fig. 2.11. Junction of lake, river, rails, and roads, the economic center of the county for decades. Note the steeple of Kingston Presbyterian Church. Horry County Museum.[5]

Until the new Highway 501 was finished, vehicles could cross the Inland Waterway only in North Myrtle Beach and Socastee. Before the Waterway was dug and spanned by a turnbridge at Socastee, the "very awkward bridge" of Elizabeth Collins rose above Socastee Creek, which flowed into the Waccamaw, and above the entire swamp. (See Fig. 2.12 for the 1936 Waterway bridge.)

Paul Sarvis (b. 1888). *This structure was awkward indeed for one particular animal, as two brothers learned:*
An old fellow, Shed Stalvey, had an ox he'd drive from his place; when it got loose it would come back down for the nice grass. After a freshet, "Directly Reuben says, 'Paul, let's go see where that old ox went.' Can't find him. But he'd swum the river--and he was on the old bridge but the boards had floated up. And in stepping he got [caught] down in there." They managed to get him pried up with some old boards and pushed him into the water so he could swim out. "He come to this side in a hurry." (24)

Barney Dawsey (b. 1912). *Over the Little Pee Dee at Galivants Ferry:*
"it was a wooden bridge in about center way down in the river swamp. They had a wide section in it where you could pass. So the closest one to it, if he saw somebody else coming in front of him, he'd pull over and wait on that place." As you'd cross, "the boards would go bam-a-lam-bam." (Int: 24)

Virginia B. Marshall (b. 1914). *"The year I went off to prep school, my brother took me to the train station in Marion":*
"He was the last car to go through Little Pee Dee Swamp at Galivants Ferry, because the water was coming up through the boards of the bridge. And the people were about six weeks without getting in and out." (Int: 11)

Annie Lee S. Bailey (b. 1911). *As a child in Loris, this future mail-carrier accompanied her dad on his route:*
"Father would put me out sometimes before we would go across the bridge, if we had a real heavy rain. Because they just laid the planks across the bridges, the road, the ditches; and he'd have me to walk across to see if all the planks were there...."
There used to be just a plank lying across Buck Creek; "Once I pulled up my dress and he had me to walk across that bridge to see if all those planks were in before he got in [the water], because that was a pretty deep ditch at that time." (Int: 6-7)

Marion Moore (b. 1931). *"All your branches and your swamps had wooden bridges across them":*
"There were timbers and your bridges was narrow. One vehicle crossed them at the time. The roads [bottom planks] went crossways and then you had drive-strips parallel with the road that you drove on across the bridge—what they called 'double deck' under where the vehicles went because all of the bridges was wood." (Int: 12)

Fig. 2.12. Future bridge gets a purchase on former swamp. Horry County Museum.

Robert Winfield (b. 1918). *In a wooden clock, J.O. Cartrette inscribed a list of sixty events that occurred between 1940 and 1968. One was the burning of the Yauhanna Bridge on April 11, 1941, the details of which are provided by Winfield:*
"There was a long wooden bridge from one side of the swamp to the other. It caught fire and burned out several spans on the Conway side. It was built out of creosote timber pile and burned like grass once it got started. They hauled dirt in and put a fill in that burned-out space rather than building a wooden bridge back."

"There was a lot of rain that fell and rivers and everything flooded. The road had not been completed on 378 yet, so the swamp filled with water and you couldn't get out that way. You couldn't cross 701 because the bridge was burned out. So to get to Georgetown or Charleston you had to go to Myrtle Beach and go to Georgetown or either go to Florence and go around by Hemingway and back down to Charleston." (Int. 9-10).

"Smoke and soot poured in": The Railroad

Before the train found Horry, citizens had to find the train. For example, in 1861, as a new Confederate soldier, William Burgess (b. approx. 1840) left Socastee and took a steamer to a camping place up the Black River from Georgetown. "Next morning we left Brown Landing and reached to Kingstree, where we took the first train I ever saw..." (4). Travelers going to or from Columbia had to take the Atlantic Coast Line between Georgetown and Lanes, a junction on the South Carolina Railroad. Daniel Jordan Carrison, a fifteen-year-old in 1894, recounts an experience that various Horryites would have shared:

> "There on a siding waited our train to take us to Georgetown, its little locomotive resplendent in shining brass trimmings, a set of deer antlers on its headlight and its great bell-like smokestack belching clouds of black smoke from the fat pine put into the firebox by the Negro fireman." (21)

The Wilmington-Columbia line first grazed the northwest corner of the county in 1854. But not until 1887–eight years after the first transcontinental railroad got its final spike in Utah–did Horry become a terminus when the *Shoo-Fly* pulled in from Chadbourn, N.C.

The last segment of the roadbed had been hard to establish when it reached the Conway Barrier. "Located upon a sand knoll two miles long by one wide," wrote the *Horry Herald*, the town was "elevated considerably above the surrounding country, [so] no route can be chosen but there will be considerable grading to do to reduce the road to anything like a level" ("Local Items" 17 Nov. 1887). A week later the hands were working in the area of Crabtree Swamp (which would later soak young Cartrette's tobacco box). There they threw up an embankment on the south side of the swamp; "It was wet and muddy and consequently slow progress was making" ("Local Items" 24 Nov.). But finally steel and wire met river. To mark the occasion B.G. Collins sent a telegram: "The whistle of the locomotive in the Main Street of Conway, the completion of the Wilmington, Chadbourn and Conway Railroad and the Western Union Telegraph united us with the outside world for the first time" (*Horry Herald* 15 Dec.; qtd. in McMillan, "A Brief...Railroads").

What brought steam to Horry County was water. According to Catherine Lewis, the Chadbourn brothers had been shipping timber from Wilmington, but as they sawed farther and farther away, they looked toward Conway to transport the wood: "That riverport gave access to the world beyond" ("Chadbourn"). Until 1928, when the roadbed was exiled to the edge of town and a new bridge constructed upstream, log-carriers as well as scheduled freights and passenger trains ran down Main Street. (See Fig. 2.13.) According to Kelly Paul Joyner, passengers descended at either Platt's Pharmacy or at the Jerry Cox Company ("Priceless" 9).

The Burroughs & Collins Company built the Conway & Seashore Railroad to Pine Island and then to New Town (Myrtle Beach). The train departed from the eastern side of the Waccamaw, so passengers and freight had to be floated between barrier islands, as recorded in Fig. 2.14. A drawbridge for the railroad was not completed until 1904 (McMillan, "A Brief...Railroads"). Its

Fig. 2.13. Pedestrian shares street and world with locomotive. Horry County Museum.

successor, a turnbridge open, can be seen to the left and right of the tugboat in Fig. 2.11, its inland section extending from between warehouses and the other folding back. (The "drawbridge" was probably this turnbridge.)

The railroad's former route down Main Street can be seen on the map in Fig. 2.2. After 1928 the old bridge was used for a spur that served Conway Lumber Yard downstream as well as for the Quattlebaum Light & Ice Company (J. Goldfinch); locomotives pulled in from across the river. See Figs. 2.15, 2.16, and 2.17 for traces of the old route.

The engine that chugged over the new steel-and-wood road to the beach had formerly carried logs over a tram-road in N.C. Equipped with broad-rimmed wheels for use on either iron or wooden rails, the *Black Maria* itself had been hauled by ox to the rail line at Whiteville, N.C. "The first engine to be used on the completed road was bought in New York when the old steam-driven elevated trains were being replaced by electricity" (Godfrey, "Some," 18-19; McMillan 19. See Fig. 2.19.)

Later the Conway, Coast & Western began its thwarted extension inland from Conway toward the Little Pee Dee and the outer world. Captain Phillip H. Sasser (b. 1867) served as conductor between Aynor and Myrtle Beach. On one excursion he "stuck his head in the door of the coach and shouted, 'She's headed for the ocean and we can't stop her!'" (Mrs. Altman 11). Ruby S. Jones (who reported on vaccinations in Chap. 1) described her father's train:

> The engine was an old wood-burner that had to stop about every ten miles to get wood and water. Great stacks of wood were placed by the railroad and a great water tank stood nearby. "There were no window screens, so it was wise to wear dark clothes. The smoke and soot poured in through the windows. The [later practice of] coal-burning increased this necessity." Sometimes the train hauled logs, and sometimes it was a "potato train" from Myrtle Beach Farms to another train going to Chadbourn and Northern markets. ("My Father" 14)

Fig. 2.14. Ferry to train. Horry County Museum.

About ten years after the entrance of the *Shoo Fly*, passengers became separated by race. The *Horry Herald* reported the debate over the Jim Crow Car Bill, one provision of which states that railroads

> "shall furnish separate apartments in first and second-class coaches or separate first and second class coaches for the accommodation of white and colored passengers provided equal accommo-

Fig. 2.15. Andrea Wells and Stella on the eastern pillar of turnbridge, 2003. Photo by Paul Olsen.

dations shall be supplied to all persons...." ("General")

On the route from Conway to Myrtle Beach, there was a reversal of racial decorum noticed by Geraldine Bryan Burroughs (b. 1911):

> When the engine came to Myrtle Beach, the cars for baggage and colored people enjoyed the privileged first position. When it headed back out, however, it first pulled the cars to a siding, then reversed its own direction on a turntable, then returned to pull the white people's car in front. (Int. F.G. and G. Burroughs: 22-23)

Theatus Graham Garrison (b. approx. 1920) remembers the little train that came through Loris near the other end of the line:

> "It had three cars–the baggage, the car for the colored people to ride in, the car for the white people." Children would have fun going down to the station: "The white folk would be on one side and the colored people would be on the other." (8)

Fig. 2.16. Trees between ties, once the Conway & Seashore Railroad, 2003.

Fig. 2.17. Wireless communication. Photo by Paul Olsen.

For a photo of an African-American crew member, see Fig. 2.18.

Like the tricycle pedaled by Dr. Burroughs, there were unofficial trains. One was "Oscar's railroad bicycle," recalled by William J. Rowe (b. 1886):

> During the summer when Rowe was working at Burroughs & Collins' store in Myrtle Beach, someone became sick and a friend asked him to go with him to get Dr. Burroughs in Conway. It was at the end of a long, hard day, and Rowe had to be back at work by five the next morning. They each pedaled and reached Conway about midnight, slogging through the Waccamaw, which "had overflowed the railroad track for the width of the swamp and was about one foot deep." On the return trip Rowe fell behind, having grown so weary he "could hardly push one pedal down to where the other pedal could be reached." At sunrise he was severely scolded but not fired. ("Memories" 12)

For these two centuries of recorded memory, overland travel in Horry offered many challenges and a few pleasures to those who negotiated its patchwork of former islands and intervening lowlands:

Sand–firm, deep and white, dry, soupy, burning, cold, or quick. The bay, the slough, the swash, the swamp rising over the box to the boy. The lurking knee, the missing plank. Stumps in the road, or logs, or fallen trees, or sand spurs, or head-stooping branches. Heavy orchards, the sterile uniformity of the pine forest, the richly varied foliage. A slotted stick nowhere to be found, a floating break in the monotony. Smoke, soot, segregation, and stars twinkling through the umbrella. Clay hills, slippery banks, brown slippery pine needles. Darkness, ice, the hot sun, a hot brick, a cold, wet and mean night, a mist from the ocean. A sweat-drenched mule, stinky wet socks. Roads that merged with the river main, rails that ended at the bank, a bridge that was rickety or on fire. The clank of hooves on frozen ground, the crash of boughs laden with ice and snow, the terrified neighing of Maude, a blood-curdling scream, the cry of an ivory-bill, the holler at the riverside, the bang of a saw, clack-aclack, bam-a-lam-bam!

Fig. 2.18. Guard on payroll train? Horry County Museum.

Fig. 2.19. Conway & Seashore Railroad, its Forney engine, formerly used on the elevated tracks of New York City. Horry County Museum.

Notes

[1] Memories are often presented in *Swamp* as a mixture of quotation, paraphrase, and summary. Even in a block of type that indicates a recollection, direct quotations appear only within quotation marks.

[2] In these verses God promises an inheritance to him who overcomes, and consigns the fearful, unfaithful, and sinful to hell.

[3] Probably Hurl Rocks, just southwest of downtown Myrtle Beach. These deposits, according to Prof. Gayes, are called beachrock. They date from the last time sea level was at or near present levels (80,000 to 100,000 years ago). Examined closely they look exactly like the material beneath the breaking waves: coarse sand and robust shell fragments that have organized into large ripples, cemented together by calcium carbonate.

[4] After Maude joined Miss Nightingale in horse heaven, Baker and his friend were carried to a refuge: "The ferryman in small canoe/Bore us across the deep/And placed us in his humble home,/To bathe our cares in sleep" ("The Fate").

[5] Foreground: one of the Jerry Cox Co. buildings, which sold tickets for both ferry and train. Extending from it is the riverboat dock for passengers and freight, and tied to the dock is the Burroughs family boat. Just past the fixed section of bridge stands a warehouse for riverboats. Last building upstream: Burroughs Lumber Company with smokestack. The two stacks in background mark the power company. The steel bridge over Kingston Lake carries Hwy 905 (earlier 501, too). James Goldfinch.

CHAPTER 3
THE BOAT

"When freight had to be transported by boat, there were certain landings along the Waccamaw where families and storekeepers would meet the steamers. People sometimes walked for miles to purchase supplies and even the children helped carry the sacks of provisions home. At times folks got so hungry that they would stop and make a fire to parch corn. When the corn was cooked, the ashes would be blown off and the corn eaten."
Lewis Asbury Dozier (b. 1876) as reported by his children (Dozier, "Mount Calvary," 9).

Fig. 3.1. The *F.G. Burroughs* docks at Conway behind an empty log-barge while the tugboat *Bicford* churns upstream. Note the absent bridge downstream, to be constructed in 1937. Horry County Museum.

Before fossil fuels such as coal, kerosene, gasoline, and diesel, boats in the Waterland were powered by arm, wood, wind, current, and moon.

In September 1989, the remains of a Native American canoe were excavated at Ocean Lakes Campground by the archeologist Hugo. (See Fig. 3.2.) According to Stewart Pabst, Director of the Horry County Museum, pre-Europeans living along the coastal plain of South Carolina exhibited a semi-nomadic lifestyle, moving seasonally from one food resource to the next throughout the year.

As the moon pulled at one side of the earth, seawater spilled over the edges of the shrunken other side, floating vessels on the tide, lifting them above sandbars or oyster beds. Pirates, smugglers, and fishermen could make use of this 4-6 foot swell, as could privateers during colonial days (McIver, "Water," 14). As the tide ran out, vessels on the Waccamaw slipped toward Georgetown with the current, for example log rafts, solitary or chained together, which floated downstream, vessel and cargo identical. As the tide ran upstream, vessels got a boost inland.

According to an old joke, Mississippi has two cities, New Orleans and Memphis; likewise Horry has two ocean ports, Georgetown and Wilmington. But Little River offers a modest connection. In 1826 Robert Mills reported that it

Fig. 3.2. Paddles long disappeared with paddler. Horry County Museum.

"admits vessels drawing 6 or 7 feet of water up into the harbor, 4 miles from its mouth. There is a little difficulty at the entrance, but the harbor is perfectly safe from the effects of storms." (Qtd. in Lewis, "Little River," 10)

To help complete the nation's Intracoastal Waterway in the 1930s, this short river was channeled and extended through swamps. These marked the flat that partially separate the Myrtle and Jaluco Barriers.

Memories of boats in Horry County tend to involve one of the few rivers in the world that both originate and end in a coastal plain (Shuping). It starts as a trickle at spring-fed Lake Waccamaw in North Carolina, then twists roughly parallel to the Atlantic for approximately 112 miles, swelling on the way as it drains eight watersheds and 626 stream miles. Its gradual slope averages half a foot per mile (*Flood* 2).

During periods of high water, shipping on the Waccamaw could go upstream as far as Reeves Ferry in North Carolina (far past Reaves Ferry in South Carolina); in low water it might cease at Conway. During 1954, according to records at the Longs station on S.C. Highway 9, the maximum daily flow ranged 2520 cubic feet per second to a mere 2 cubic feet. In the next year the maximum flow quadrupled (USGS).[1] For an aerial map of the junction of the Waccamaw and Highway 9, just below North Carolina, see Fig. 3.3. The river, undammed, rarely constricted by retaining walls, passes an occasional "bluff"—i.e., land elevated enough to hold dwellings.

A blackwater river, the Waccamaw runs dark not from stolen topsoil like the Missouri, or from upstate rocks eroded into silt and clay like the Yadkin-Pee Dee (Thom 4), but from decomposing organic matter in swamps. This infusion turns white swimmers a luminous amber until they disappear a foot below the surface. In the winter, low, dark, misty clouds can turn its surface to the matte-iron of despair.

The Waccamaw flows southwest in every direction. Its flat and swampy flood plain (the area that has been or can be covered by water) averages two miles in width in the Conway area (*Flood* 2). The river immerses cypress trunks with their wooden stalagmites, and it partly inundates trees that have been felled in identical alignment by a hurricane. In the cold months, a boater can gaze through hardwood branches and their nests of mistletoe to behold the sun setting in the east.

Above Conway, current meets tide, which at its ebb exposes a black substratum of roots and soil. Below town the river veers directly south, where it continues to thrash silently amid its own backwaters and the arabesques of former courses. An unwary

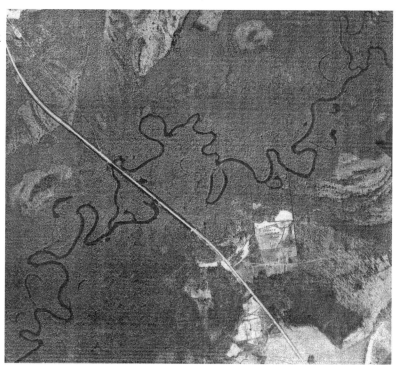

Fig. 3.3. Like a moth evading a bird, the Waccamaw zig-zags past Highway 9. Note sand outcroppings on former barrier islands. Courtesy family of Sanford D. Cox, Jr.

boater can take the wrong turn, make a circle, and come upon the same marker recently passed. The Waccamaw joins the Intracoastal Waterway (formerly Socastee Creek) just above Bucksport, near Enterprise Landing at the edge of Big Swamp. That confluence then runs between former rice plantations at the tip of the county, joins Bull Creek, then flows toward Winyah Bay in Georgetown County.[2]

Paddles, oars, or poles drove vessels up or down the Waccamaw as sweat dripped into the water. Steamboats, like early locomotives, burned wood to transform water to vapor. Even living trees were enlisted as hoists to wind boats upstream. Flossie Morris (b. 1894) remembered how yawls made of dugout logs operated: "They put a man on shore;

and they fastened to a tree or something and had a winch pull them up some" (Int: 11). Henry Small (b. 1897) also remembers such a boat: "It ties to the river [to anything stationary]. Drifted close to shore enough to tie up until tide done to tell 'em ready to go" (Int: 16).

Barges transferred goods to and from large vessels that could only progress so far up the Waccamaw. Until 1875, when that river was dredged, schooners (sailing vessels with two or more masts) could venture up only so far. At Pot Bluff (also spelled Pot's or Pott's), six miles below Conway at Toddville, they transferred their goods to lighters or wagons. For the "down trip," the empty vessels might use ice blocks insulated with sawdust for ballast (Godfrey," Some," 9). The *Horry News* occasionally marked the arrival of these boats:

> "Schr [schooner] Ridgewood—W.M. Johnson, from New York, arrived at Pot Bluff on the 10th, to Burroughs & Collins, with Mdz [merchandise]...." ("Local Matters," 17 Feb. 1894)

In 2004 divers at Pot Bluff discovered a barrel-shaped, amber mass of raw turpentine gum that had preserved itself (instead of ships) for over a century. A whiff of its pinene cleared the author's sinuses. See Plate 5.

Even someone born as late as 1933 can remember, although "barely," when vessels still docked at Kingston Lake, a major tributary of the Waccamaw. "They came from as far as Norfolk, Wilmington, all the way down the coast–Georgetown, Charleston–bringing in supplies," said Doug Smith.

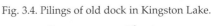

Fig. 3.4. Pilings of old dock in Kingston Lake.

"Fertilizer, food, hardware, all kinds of freight that they'd unload here at Jerry Cox. Had a dock here—the old pilings still out there, some of 'em [see Fig. 3.4]. They'd unload the boats, and the farmers and the people who lived in this area would come here and buy what they needed for their households and their farms. Drive a mule 'n' buggy down here and pick up their stuff. The mules used to paw a big hole there [*gestures*] around the hitching posts" (Int: 2). See Fig. 3.5 for a souvenir.

To keep the rivers navigable upstream, a snag boat operated. In 1879 Captain Thomas W. Daggett contracted with the U.S. government to remove obstructions in the Waccamaw and other rivers. A former steamboat captain, sawmill operator,

Fig. 3.5. Hitching post in wall next to Kingston Presbyterian Church, Conway, 2003.

and Confederate soldier, he had been raised in Massachusetts ("Died"). According to the ancient ferryman Donnie Grant (b. 1887), a "gov-ment boat" used to park in old Grahamville (the future Wild Horse community off Highway 90), and then run up and down the river. "They'd come up from Conway into Red Bluff and stay here for weeks and months cleaning out the river and cutting the snags" (Int: 13). In the next century, two other federal boats–World War II landing craft—were converted into a tug and a pile driver by Thomas W. Rich, Sr. (Int. Rich. See Fig. 3.6.)

This chapter weaves together scraps of memory that deal with navigation on the Waccamaw, other rivers, and other kinds of water.

Fig. 3.6. From war to wood. Courtesy Col. Thomas Rich, Jr.

"Row across the river"

Before plywood was available, explains James D. Sanders, boats were stored in water to keep them from shrinking and leaking (Int: 12). Gary Mincey (b. 1907), a former wildlife officer from the Wannamaker Community, analyzes the "lost art" of boatmaking:

"They'd take these logs, nice cypress. Back then they had ideal trees for that. And they'd split the log about the length they wanted the boat, and they'd shape the outside of the boat. They'd begin to hew out, but for fear they'd hew too deep in the wood—it'd go through—they made a few auger holes [bored them with a special tool], and they could keep checking the depth." They'd take cypress, make pegs, drive them into the auger holes, and smooth them off. "Sometimes if you didn't check on it real close, you'd never know they had been put in there."

It would take two or three people, or a wagon, to get a new boat to the pond. Lawton Huggins had one made of juniper when Mincey first started to work. The lumber on the bottom of that boat went crossways rather than longways from bow to stern. "He threw it out there in the sun for two or three days, or a week or two, and there'd be cracks in it all around. Then if you wanted to use the boat, you had to throw it in the pond overnight; and it would swell up. If you made that boat with dry lumber and put it together good and tight, it was going to swell and buckle up." (Int: 3-4)

Fig. 3.7. In the early twentieth century this group of beachgoers made a painting-like composition with their large wooden boat. Horry County Museum.

A rowboat or canoe was a fishing vessel, car, taxi, truck, schoolbus, or pleasure boat. (See Figs. 3.7 and 3.8.)

As a boy William L. Rowe (b. 1886) worked on a farm several miles upriver from Conway where strawberries were picked, sorted, packed with sawdust and blocks of ice, and crated. "I rowed the boat down to Conway, picked the [crates] out, and saw that they got in the boxcar," properly labeled and sent to Northern markets ("Memories" 9).

The family of Julia Smalls (b. 1890) used to paddle across the Waccamaw from the Freewoods: "There was a general store in Bucksport; we got there by boat. There we could buy groceries and cloth" (Dozier, "Interview…Smalls," 31). Another African American, Katie Bellamy Randall (b. approx. 1900), was raised on the Neck, a narrow peninsula between Cherry Grove Marsh and Little River (see Fig. 10.3). People would cross the river, go to the store and trade, and row back. "Prop your leg up so you won't fall. I'd take a boat by myself—one of the chillun—row across." Once while gathering oysters her boat hit a staub (stake) and knocked her into the drink. "The tide was high and it was comin' the way we was going." [*Laughing at the question "Who saved you?":*] "I saved *myself!*" (Int.) .

Fig. 3.8. Boys in canoe. "Conway, S.C."

Mitchelle Collins (b. 1886) remembers getting around in a flood: "We would go down the steps [of the Beaty-Spivey house on Kingston Lake] and I had an old colored man meet me there" who would row her out to Red Hill" (Int: 23). Elting Holliday (b. 1919) preserves the rare glimpse of a Native American in connection with the "Bingham freshet," a flood in the 1920s during a notorious murder-trial: "We had to go by boat to Conway from Glass Hill," one mile up the Pireway Road. The boat, which carried milk for delivery from the Hollidays' dairy farm, was paddled by "Uncle" Boss Bullard (W. Thomas, "Elting"). During the freshet of 1945, Mr. J.C. Bennett, Sr., started working at the Williams Box Mill across the bridge from Conway. "My dad said, 'I'll take you over to the mill'; they had some paddle boats out there and we paddled all down the highway, past the commissary and to the office of the mill" (Bennett, Int. 2003: 3. See Fig. 3.9.)

What adventures occurred while paddling or rowing across two centuries?

Anonymous. *New Voyage to Georgia,* publ. 1735. *For their second reconnaissance mission from Georgetown, the party traveled beside Long Bay (see p. 26), but for their*

Fig. 3.9. Flood of 1929. The Heritage Room, First Baptist Church, Conway.

first, they had ventured up the "Waccumaw." They departed in a large canoe, February 7, 1734, spending their third night on the west bank somewhere below the bluff "on which Kingstown [later Conwayborough] is to be established." The largesse that promised to enrich them threatened to swallow them:
"[W]e encamped there, and found a great deal of good oak and hickory, and the pine land very valuable, and a great deal of good cypress swamp, which is counted the best for rice."

While a few surveyed the land, others took the boat upriver to look for more, "leaving only one bottle of punch, and a biscuit a piece, promising to be back again in the afternoon; but in short, they never came near us that night, nor the next day, in which time we had like to have been starved."

The stranded men began to construct a raft—"a barque, as the Indians call it"—to reach the other side, when their companions returned. One of the men "had straggled out in the wood by himself a shooting" and had been found only with great difficulty. The rescuers also brought back the guns, however, so the party was able to kill some birds to live on. (45-46)

Rev. William W. Malet. *In 1862, one of the Georgetown refugees offered Malet a ride back to Hagley Plantation aboard a "four-oar"–on the very river that had stained his papers:*
The boat left Conwayborough soon after 4 a.m. in the middle of July, after the Negro captain, a jolly fellow, blew a loud blast on his conch shell to call his men together. "The Wakamaw is a very winding river. There was no wind for sailing: the sun was extremely hot, and there being no awning to protect us, its effects were felt severely, but the Negroes rowed merrily, every now and then singing their boat songs." Because the tide was "for some way dead against us," the party did not land until 9 p.m. (35)[3]

Nathaniel H. Bishop (b. 1837). *At dusk on January 18, 1875, Bishop crossed into South Carolina on his journey from Quebec. His canoe was made of paper molded to a wooden frame and waterproofed:*
"When darkness settled on the swamps, a heavy mist rose from the waters and enveloped the forests in its folds. With not a trace of land above water I groped about, running into what appeared to be openings in the submerged land, only to find my canoe tangled in thickets." Giving up, he prepared to climb a giant tree and tie his body onto its forks to spend the night. (233)

Moses Floyd Sarvis (b. 1836). *By contrast, two boys found themselves on land without a trace of boat:*
Moses' father arranged for him and his brother to board with a man on the east side of the Waccamaw at Gravelly Gully so they could go to a school at Socastee Bridge. The boys, however, "not caring to stay away from home, got up before day, walked to Bucksville, paddled down the river to Peachtree, and walked to school. The entire trip was about six and a half or seven miles. "If we could find them, each of us would paddle a boat and tow one, so that we would be sure to have a boat on the afternoon. One afternoon we came to Peachtree and all of our boats were gone. We were preparing to swim the river, but Mrs. DeLettre loaned us a boat. Thereafter, we carried as many as we could find."[4]

Agnes Mishoe Gause (b. 1919). *Ms. Gause remembers a small boat filled with African Americans, among them her father, born in 1898 below Bucksport in the Tip Top section–earlier Woodbourne Plantation, where his own father had been sold:*
"Back in 1929 and the early 'thirties, work was hard to find. Boston, his brother John, and his friends Charlie Johnson, Keeler Sumpter, Fred Frazier, and Bob Pino would get up at three o'clock in the morning and 'whoop!' for each other. Then they would walk down to Bucksport, take a boat, paddle up to the Inland Waterway bridge in Socastee, and work on that bridge from sunup until sundown." (Int: 4; "History" 4)

Florence Epps (b. 1907). *At night in the 1930s, "boats from Wilmington would anchor offshore and smaller boats would row out to meet them and bring in the bootleg booze."*
One morning a boy "asked my mother permission for me to walk on the Strand with him so he could look for his watch he had lost on a sand dune the night before. We walked hand in hand till we reached a spot where he began furiously to dig. He soon unearthed a quart jar of moonshine whiskey which he slipped under his coat as we trudged back home." ("Bootleg")

"Three flat gone round wid all the vittles"

Flat-bottomed boats were used to carry freight. "Flatboats on the river," noted Edward E. Burroughs (b. 1900), "were being pulled by Negroes who often weren't very careful about using lights on them at night. One time a steamboat almost ran one down..." (30).

Tugs maneuvered rafts of logs, then later barges of them. Sometimes they pushed the barge, sometimes pulled

40

it--either driving alongside or in front, contingent partly on the width and navigability of the river (Int. Rich). In 1899 the *Horry Herald* noted that "Capt. S.W. Fulton of the tug *Pender* of Georgetown…came up here Monday evening after a raft which he towed out the following morning" (Nolley, "Matters," 15 June). "Daddy had a little gasoline tugboat known as the *Pathfinder*," reported F.G. Burroughs (b. 1908), "which would help maneuver logs into position" at the Burroughs Sawmill on Kingston Lake (Int. 1991: 5).

Ellen Godfrey (b. 1837). *Once a slave at Longwood Plantation in Horry County (see Fig. 1.13), Godfrey was interviewed in 1936 and 1937 by Genevieve W. Chandler. She remembered that during the Civil War, the Joshua Ward household moved to relative safety on three flatboats. Normally used for work in the rice fields, the vessels now carried "two hundred head o' people and all they things" (Chandler, "Mom Ellen," 159). After hiding out, the slaves began a five-day expedition back to Horry County. The parentheses in Chandler's transcriptions are always hers:*
"Git to Bucksport, people gin to whoop and holler! Three flat gone round wid all the vittles. (And with the very young and very old.) Easier coming home. Current helped. (Going up against the current, only poles and cant hooks—tedious going.)[5] Git 'Tip Top' (Plantation) all right. Come home den! Git to double trunk (rice-field trunk) [i.e., sluice gate] at 'Tip Top.' Whoop! Come bring flat. Mother Molly dead on flat! Bury she right to Longwood grave-yard." (Chandler, "Aunt Ellen," 154, 157-58)

G.W. Watts (a boy in 1864). *The few stores in Conway "were supplied with goods brought up from Georgetown":*
"The flats were propelled by paddles and poles, with time a change to oars made of oak or longleaf pine. There was no good way of protecting the goods such as cloth or notions on the trips up the river so that very often the stocks for the stores were damaged goods to start with." (11)

W. Irving Jones, Sr. (b. 1895). *Fertilizer came to Galivants Ferry from Wilmington via Georgetown, where it was picked up by the crew that worked for Joseph William Holliday (1827-1924):*
They pulled a flat upstream with long poles—"stick 'em in the river bank; you know it was a long process with tons of that stuff. The fertilizer that they sold was Big O. That was 8-2-1. That was for everything, corn, potatoes." (Int. Aug. 18: 2)

Carrie Doyle (b. 1901). *Mrs. Doyle remembers such a vessel derelict at the Ferry:*
"After they parked it there it just sat in the water and rotted away. It was just a long flat thing with logs around the edges. Every Christmas the people around there would order whiskey and it would come in on that flat." (Int. 8 Sept: 14)

Walter A. "Sonny" Stilley III (b. 1930). *One tugboat hand was Joe Horry (b. 1893), who lived in an apartment behind the Stilley house at 702 Elm St. in Conway and served as a "black daddy" to young Sonny.*
In the early 1900s Joe met Sonny's grandfather, Walter Stilley I (b. 1875), who traveled through North and South Carolina selling saws to lumber companies. On one of his trips, the cabin boy who brought him coffee in one of the staterooms on the *Comanche* was Joe Horry. They got along well, and later when my grandfather came back to Conway and helped build the old Veneer Manufacturing Company around 1914, Joe came to work on the company tugboat, which was captained by Joe McMillan. It pulled log rafts off of the Pee Dee and other rivers into Conway. (Int: 1-2)

J.C. Bennett (b. 1928). *"About fifty yards over here is the river," explained Bennett at the ruins of the Veneer Manufacturing plant (a.k.a. Williams Box Mill):*
The tugs—like the big *Samson*—would bring in the barges and dock up and secure them beside the Waccamaw. Each barge had a tall boom pole that would hook the logs off. "It rotated along the base and had cables. They would hook cant hooks into the end of those logs and raise them. They'd swing them around and load them. The employees would then cut them into [lengths], 54-inch 'blocks.'" (Int. 2003: 3, 6. See Fig. 3.10.)

Fig. 3.10. View from pilot house. Courtesy Col. Thomas Rich, Jr.

Henry Bonnette (b. 1909). *After 1936, barges would ply the Inland Waterway, but not until two construction-dredges finally met each other after plowing between Little River and Socastee Creek:*
"They sent me out to help the drill. Me and another fellow was puttin' inch-and-a-half sticks of dynamite [*motions with hands*]. We'd put four, five, and sometimes six ten-inch lengths of dynamite together. Later I worked on the dragline. We had to do a lot of levelin' out and pushin' around."

"Big steamships—they were three of 'em"

Early oceangoing ships were vulnerable to pirates. (For an example see Chandler, "Uncle Sabe Rutledge," 63.) They were also prey to storms. In 1830 or '32, on Cherry Grove beach, there was "nothing but sand, shells, and pieces of wrecked vessels" (Berry, "Great," 24). The schooner *Cassie F. Bronson* was wrecked on the Little River beach in 1906. It was 193 feet long, had a 40-foot beam, had an 18-foot depth of hold, and registered 1,124 tons gross and 952 net (Berry, "Schooner," 6). "'Member the shipwreck," declared Sabe Rutledge, who also remembered when part of Surfside Beach was a farm: "Two men and lady come to the Ark [Plantation]. Stormy time. Massa take them to town. Old anchor there now" (Chandler, "Uncle Sabe Rutledge," 60).

Julius "Joe" White (1910-1997), who came to Myrtle Beach from Georgetown in 1939, told Jack Thompson that a lot of African Americans in town were descendants of crew members who survived shipwrecks in the 1890s (Int. Thompson: 7). However accurate this idea may be, proof of one shipwreck occasionally emerges from the sand at 43rd Ave. N.: the hull of the *Freeda A. Wyley*, a 507-ton, three-masted barkentine. "There is a wrecking crew still at work upon the Steamer…which came up on the Singletons Swash beach some time ago," reported the editor of the *Herald* in 1893.

"The lumber with which she was laden is in tolerable good condition; but her stern is badly burned and much damage done in other parts by fire" (E. Norton, 28 Sept. 1893). See also B. Floyd, *Tales*, 73; and J. Thompson, *Reflections*, leaf 17. Another example is handed down by Andrew Stanley (b. 1904): "Piled-up old ship went to wreck in the ocean," he remembered. "And they'd build 'em a casket—the first one I'd seen was built out of that lumber" (Int. April: 33). When Harriette S. Stogner (b. 1921) was small, a boat ran aground, and it was finders-keepers: "I think practically every woman in Conway got a fur coat. [*Laughter.*] Mother got a Hudson seal" (Int. G. Floyd: 65).

Ships also carried rocks. At the ruins of the Upper Mill in Bucksville, the bank of the Waccamaw is reinforced by "smooth 'Belgian blocks'" that came as ballast, i.e., heavy material carried in the hold of a ship to make it more stable. These were "unloaded from trade ships when lumber was taken aboard as cargo" (Chandler, "Pre-World War II," 35). James R. Holbert, Jr. (b. 1917) remembers that between Bucksport and Eddy Lake "you could see these imports all along the river, especially at low tide" (Int. G. Floyd: 5). See Fig. 3.11.

Schooners gave wooden-way to steamships by World War I.

Fig. 3.11. Ballast rocks, Bucksville. Courtesy Capt. Henry L. Buck IV. Photo by Paul Olsen.

Waccamaw. *Writing in 1868, a newspaper correspondent described a village "situated on Little River, a tidewater river, properly an arm of the sea, two miles from its mouth":*

"Vessels of one hundred and fifty tons burden can come up to the village, and so make regular trips between this place and Northern cities, as well as to the West Indies. A large Schooner, commanded by Capt. Davis, was taking on cargo for New York during our visit." (Qtd. in Lewis, "Little River," 12)

Fig. 3.12. Ship and steamboat, Georgetown Harbor. Horry County Museum.

Lucille B. Godfrey (b. 1891). *Before the* Shoo-Fly *connected Conway to the junction at Chadbourn, reaching the main line might require a three-steam trip:*

"Aunt Effie graduated from Greensboro College in 1887. It is difficult to grasp the fact that the first year she went to Greensboro, she had to go by boat to Georgetown, then by ocean steamer to Charleston where she caught the train to Wilmington." ("Some" 15)

Paul Sarvis (b. 1888). *Also traveling by ocean was fruit: Sarvis's father used to ship a hundred or more barrels of pears from Socastee to agents in New York.* "They put 'em on the boat right there at Peachtree Landing, then they go on down to Georgetown and then on those big steamships…. They were three of 'em." (Nichols 27. See Fig. 3.12.)

42

Eatofel Vereen Thompson Arehart (b. 1913). *Even clams sailed from Little River:*
"We had a ship called the *Menhaden*. It went to Wilmington every week and came back with whatever there was to carry. This was the only way to get produce out, particularly clams. There was a clam industry, and on down the river there was a fish plant where they made fertilizer. (Int: 11)

"All I need is wood and water"

Hoyt McMillan, author of "A Brief History of Water Transportation in Horry County, S.C.," writes that the first known steamboat to ply the Waccamaw was the *Francis Marion*, which picked up Confederate soldiers in Conway, 1862 (5-7). The earliest extant schedule of the first boat to make regular runs was printed in the *Horry News*, 1875; the vessel *Bull River* was based in Georgetown (Bedford 103).

In the early 1880s, Burroughs & Collins bought the *Juniper* to inaugurate the Waccamaw Line of Steamers. The *Driver* was then built from this pioneer at the Kingston Lake shipyards. William J. Rowe (b. 1886) recalled that Burroughs & Collins used flats until they bought the *Juniper*, which was "pretty sorry":

"Capt. Williams said he could tell when he got in the Pee Dee River because the water in the hull commenced to turn yellow" [*laughter*]. He added that if he were to let us get on a mud bank until the tide sank down, that would jam up the mud in the cracks and re-caulk her. (Int: 12)

Fig. 3.13. *Mitchelle C.*, "the largest and finest steamboat to operate on the Waccamaw River"—HCHS 6.

More boats followed: the *Altamont*, a tugboat; the two *Maggies*, named after the daughter of Captain Williams; and the *Ruth*, named after the daughter of F.G. and Addie. The *F.G. Burroughs*, completed in 1898, a year after its namesake died, could carry 130 passengers and 150 tons of freight. The last vessel in the fleet was the *Mitchelle C.*, named after the daughter of Mr. Collins (Fig. 3.13). All were sold in 1919.

The Waccamaw boats were sidewheelers, which had two large wheels, one on each side; as they revolved, boards (like seats on a Ferris wheel) scooped into the water to propel the vessel. The sidewheelers, as Franklin G. Burroughs (b. 1908) explained, "were highly maneuverable vessels." Each wheel could be operated independently, even to the extent of driving one forward and the other backward, so they could easily negotiate the turns of the river ("Steamboat" 7). By contrast the Pee Dee boats were sternwheelers, which had one wheel behind the vessel, a type nicknamed "wheelbarrow boats." The *Ruth*, as a smaller boat in the fleet, was iron of hull and light of draft (Epps, "Have you heard," 18); it worked the upper Waccamaw, the Pee Dee, and the Little Pee Dee. According to Lucille B. Godfrey, "They had to rebuild [the steamboats] every few years: the wooden hulls didn't last long" (Int. Rowe: 11).

Other steamboats were headquartered in Georgetown: the *Sessoms*, the *George Elliott*, and the *Lucy V.*, named after the daughter of John Vereen of Murrells Inlet (F. Morris Int: 9-10). There was also a boat that thrashed up the Pee Dee River as far as Mars Bluff: the *Planter* used to carry Flossie Morris's mother (maybe from Port Harrelson across from Yauhanna), who would ride it to the terminus then catch the train to visit her family in Chester (Int: 12). The last boat to make regular runs between Conway and Georgetown was the *Comanche*, which quit in the 1920s.

According to an advertisement in 1894, "the Steamer will leave her wharf at Conway every Monday and Wednesday morning for Georgetown at 4 o'clock, touching all intermediate points. And will leave her wharf at Georgetown every Tuesday and Friday morning for Conway at 4 o'clock…" ("Waccamaw Line"). Since the boats left before daylight, some passengers spent the night in staterooms (Quattlebaum, "Early Conway," 26). "You went to bed," recalled Lucille B. Godfrey, "and lay listening for awhile to the moving about on the lower deck, the soft sounds from the engines, and finally you waked up before good light to find yourself underway" ("Laws" 12). Henry Small (b. 1897) remembers that the boat from Longwood to Georgetown cost 50 cents, and from Enterprise, 60 cents (Int: 15).

The *Horry Herald* kept track of such comings and goings: "The freight on the river keeps the boats busy. The *Maggie* went to Georgetown on Christmas day. The *Ruth* went up the river as did the *Driver*" ("Local News" 28 Dec. 1893). "Capt. Zack Dusenbury has gone up the Santee river with the steamer Driver. Capt. F.A. Burroughs took charge of the Str. Maggie making the Georgetown trip this week" ("Local News" 8 Nov. 1894). "There was quite an exodus of our young people Monday on the early morning steamer to Georgetown and the evening train taking a goodly number away who had been at home for the holidays" ("Matters Local" 5 Jan. 1899). And a sad homecoming for two people:

"Miss Ruth Burroughs and her brother, Mr. Arthur Burroughs, were summoned home a few days ago on account of the extreme illness of their sister, Mrs. H.L. Buck, Jr. They were met at Georgetown last Saturday night by special steamer.... ("Matters Local," 14 Sept. 1899)

Edith Ella Burroughs Buck died from complications of childbirth.

Besides passengers with their workaday and emotional baggage, there were products: naval stores in barrels, cotton in bales, lumber and wooden shingles from the mill in Bucksport. See Fig. 3.14 for a partial list of items carried on decks in 1885. "The amount of freight handled by the Waccamaw Line is increasing," noted an item in the *Horry Herald*, 1893; "Cotton is beginning to come in and rosin, turpentine, and spirits are being more freely shipped" ("Local News" 23 Sept.). Vessels brought in manufactured or processed goods: lumber, fertilizer, molasses, coffee, rice, medicine, empty barrels, hasps (metal fasteners), millstones, even bricks from England for the county jail. Ice in 300-pound blocks was also taken from Conway to Bucksport for ice cream suppers (Int. Staley: 20-21). Notice the bales of cotton in Fig. 3.12.

Interviewed in 1959 by C.B. Berry, Thomas Walter Livingston, or "Mr. Tom" (b. 1875), recalled when there were almost as many businesses at Red Bluff as at Conway until the railroad was built. He and his partner sold turpentine and rosin for shipment elsewhere:

> Steamboats came up the Waccamaw with express [goods]. You could order a gallon of liquor or any other merchandise and have it sent directly to Red Bluff. The *Ruth* made weekly trips, but when the river was too low they poled in with shallower-draft boats. (Berry, "Rambling," 16)

The steamboat, according to Austin Todd (b. 1901), abetted a major economic change in the area above Conway and below Red Bluff:

> "In the early 1900s when I first remember it, turpentine was going out and people were turning to farming. Farmers would buy fertilizer and supplies at Conway and would have it sent to Board Landing by the steamer *Ruth*." Later the *F.G. Burroughs* was used. (7)

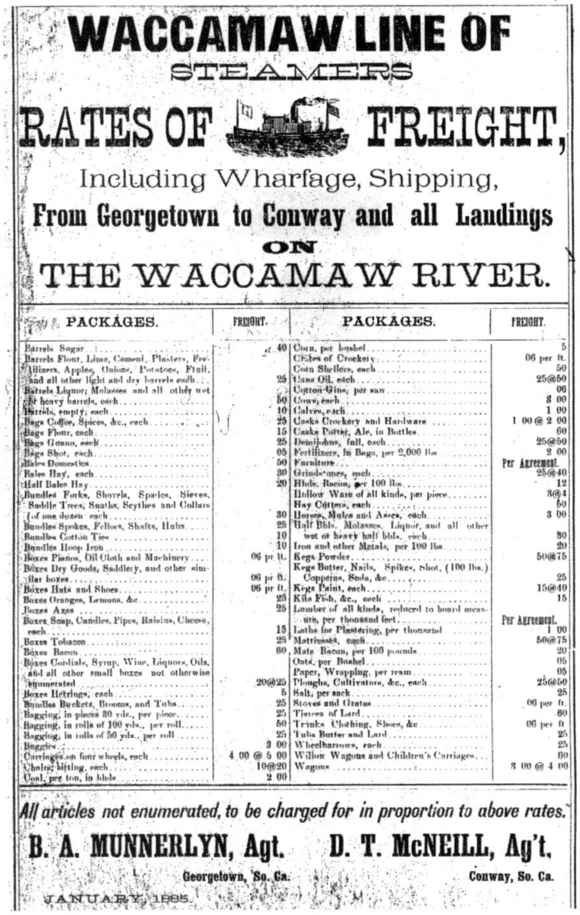

WACCAMAW LINE OF STEAMERS

RATES OF FREIGHT,

Including Wharfage, Shipping,

From Georgetown to Conway and all Landings ON THE WACCAMAW RIVER.

PACKAGES.	FREIGHT.	PACKAGES.	FREIGHT.
Barrels Sugar	40	Corn, per bushel	5
Barrels Flour, Lime, Cement, Plasters, Fertilizers, Apples, Onions, Potatoes, Fruit, and all other light and dry barrels each	25	Crates of Crockery	06 per ft.
Barrels Liquor, Molasses and all other wet or heavy barrels, each	50	Corn Shellers, each	50
Barrels, empty, each	10	Cans Oil, each	25@50
Bags Coffee, Spices, &c., each	25	Cotton Gins, per saw	06
Bags Flour, each	15	Cows, each	8 00
Bags Guano, each	25	Calves, each	1 00
Bags Shot, each	05	Casks Crockery and Hardware	1 00 @ 2 00
Bales Domestics	50	Casks Porter, Ale, in Bottles	60
Bales Hay, each	30	Demijohns, full, each	25@50
Half Bales Hay	20	Fertilizers, in Bags, per 2,000 lbs	2 00
Bundles Forks, Shovels, Spades, Sieves, Saddle Trees, Snaths, Scythes and Collars (of one dozen each	30	Furniture	Per Agreement.
Bundles Spokes, Felloes, Shafts, Hubs	25	Grindstones, each	25@40
Bundles Cotton Ties	10	Hhds. Bacon, per 100 lbs	12
Bundles Hoop Iron	10	Hollow Ware of all kinds, per piece	3@4
Boxes Pianos, Oil Cloth and Machinery	06 pr ft.	Hay Cutters, each	50
Boxes Dry Goods, Saddlery, and other similar boxes	06 pr ft.	Horses, Mules and Asses, each	3 00
Boxes Hats and Shoes	06 pr ft.	Half Bbls. Molasses, Liquor, and all other wet or heavy half bbls. each	30
Boxes Oranges, Lemons, &c	25	Iron and other Metals, per 100 lbs	20
Boxes Axes	25	Kegs Powder	50@75
Boxes Soap, Candles, Pipes, Raisins, Cheese, each	15	Kegs Butter, Nails, Spikes, Shot, (100 lbs.) Copperas, Soda, &c	25
Boxes Tobacco	25	Kegs Paint, each	15@40
Boxes Bacon	60	Kits Fish, &c., each	15
Boxes Cordials, Syrup, Wine, Liquors, Oils, and all other small boxes not otherwise enumerated	20@25	Lumber of all kinds, reduced to board measure, per thousand feet	Per Agreement.
Boxes Herrings, each	5	Laths for Plastering, per thousand	1 00
Bundles Buckets, Brooms, and Tubs	25	Mattresses, each	50@75
Bagging, in pieces 30 yds., per piece	25	Mats Bacon, per 100 pounds	20
Bagging, in rolls of 100 yds., per roll	50	Oats, per Bushel	05
Bagging, in rolls of 50 yds., per roll	25	Paper, Wrapping, per ream	05
Buggies	3 00	Ploughs, Cultivators, &c., each	25@50
Carriages on four wheels, each	4 00 @ 5 00	Salt, per sack	25
Chains, lifting, each	10@20	Stoves and Grates	06 per ft.
Coal, per ton, in hhds	2 00	Tierces of Lard	60
		Trunks Clothing, Shoes, &c	06 per ft
		Tubs Butter and Lard	25
		Wheelbarrows, each	25
		Willow Wagons and Children's Carriages	00
		Wagons	3 00 @ 4 00

All articles not enumerated, to be charged for in proportion to above rates.

B. A. MUNNERLYN, Agt. Georgetown, So. Ca.

D. T. McNEILL, Ag't. Conway, So. Ca.

JANUARY, 1885.

Fig. 3.14. Waccamaw Mart. Courtesy the Trestle Restaurant.

The grandmother of Andrew Stanley (b. 1904) would "sham sheeps" [shear them], sell the wool, "load it in a cart, carry it to Little River, and put 'ton a boat and ship it to Wilmington" (4). "When the rum boats came in from Wilmington," wrote Rebecca Clark Snyder (b. 1899), "you would hear groups of sailors, high on rum," singing as loudly as Long John Silver (25). The written word also traveled by water. Gertrude McDowell (b. 1901), raised in the Burgess Community, said that the mail floated from Conway to Georgetown:

> "There was a mail carrier that met the boat at Longwood Landing, exchanged the bags, and came to our post office. I can remember how the children would listen for that boat to blow." (39. See also Johnson, Int. Peterkin: 43)

"We'd listen for that whistle to blow," recalled Flossie Morris in 1991; "I certainly missed the boats when they took them off" (Int: 12).

Franklin G. Burroughs (b. 1908). *In about 1914 Franklin (son of Arthur) rode from Conway down to Hagley Landing on the boat named for his grandfather. As articulate as he is observant, he describes the boat's layout, schedule, ports of call, cargo, and meals:* The white passengers traveled on the upper deck; its "island" comprised the pilot house, the captain's quarters, a galley (kitchen), the dining saloon, and a few staterooms. Behind this structure was open deck, railed and covered with a canvas awning, and alongside it was a promenade, somewhat constricted by the sidewheels.

"The lower deck was given over to freight, fuel, and the engine room, and perhaps to some passengers of the 'economy class' (in today's parlance). In those days accommodations were most certainly 'separate' but a far cry from 'equal.'" "Cotton and naval stores or turpentine were the important downstream items, while fertilizer and manufactured products were brought up from the port of Georgetown."

Other than a regular departure time from Conway or Georgetown, scheduling was erratic. One variable was the flood stage of the river. Another was loading or unloading: "Cotton would be taken aboard at one stop, shingles or naval stores at another," and wood had to be taken on at various "yards."

Because indoor plumbing was a rarity at the time, the toilet had special appeal. It was located inside the sidewheel housing, so that "below the opening one could see the massive paddlewheel churning away and providing a constant flushing system" ("Steamboat" 5-6).

Fig. 3.15. Decks of the *F.G. Burroughs*. Horry County Museum.

M., V.I. *(writing in 1905). The utilitarian steamboat could also provide "the most romantic trip which can be taken in South Carolina," according to a Baptist preacher traveling around the state:*
"I am in the midst of the trip as I write this, a guest of that splendid man, Captain R.G. Dusenberry [sic], on the boat *F.G. Burroughs* [see Fig. 3.15]. I am sitting quietly behind the right wheel house, my feet aloft on its expansive rotundity, the sun beaming down genially, the wind cheated of its teasing tugs at hair and hat and paper by my position, the exhaust from the engines a nerve-quieting soporific, keeping time to the drowsy lullaby of the great paddlewheels as they contend with the water." (16)

Jessie Dusenbury *(b. 1889). Her father, Zack Dusenbury (1848-1910), was captain of several Burroughs & Collins boats:*
"I remember I was kind of frightened when I had to pass by the long arms of the engine that were going up and down. Papa said they were saying 'Going to Georgetown, going to Georgetown, all I need is wood and water,' but I was always glad to get to the upper deck." (20)

Edith Proctor Woodbury *(b. 1900). Mrs. Woodbury remembers hearing Dr. H.H. Burroughs tell this story to her father:*
As a lad Homer decided to go to Florida to seek his fortune. Things didn't work out, and he had to walk all the way back to Georgetown. There he sought Captain Zack Dusenbury. The master of the *F.G. Burroughs* took him aboard and served him a meal, his first in a while. "Soon he was in the Captain's bed for a long snooze." After reaching Conway he vowed never to leave home again. (8)

Paul Quattlebaum *(b. 1886). In a nostalgic speech given in 1954, Quattlebaum remembers something like a cruise ship:*
"The Negro deckhands sang as they worked. The odor that came up from the galley of ham frying and coffee boiling was enough to give anyone an appetite…. The captain was jovial and always had a good yarn to tell. The deck crew were happy." (26)

Carew Rice *(b. approx. 1900). A steamboat could also be a moving van:*
"I remember our moving day, when we rode down the river to Georgetown on the old sidewheel steamer *Burroughs*—it was bitterly cold and when a deck hand drew up a bucket of water from the river and splashed a little on the deck, immediately it turned to ice!" He adds that at one of the landings, someone gave Captain Dusenbury "a giant head of collard" (20).

William J. Rowe *(b. 1886). Having boated strawberries down the Waccamaw and pedaled a railroad bicycle through its overflow, Willie eventually took its current away from his friends and beloved grandfather toward the College of Charleston:*
Frank A. Burroughs wrote him a pass that included a lower berth on the *F.G. Burroughs*. "Finally the hour had come on that lovely September day to board my steamship. As I sailed down dear old Waccamaw, I did not know that I was leaving Conway and Horry County forever." ("Memories" 13)

Lucille B. Godfrey *(b. 1891). One trip confirmed a permanent separation:*
"A rather shabby old gentleman got on at one of the lower landings. He sat down by Mama, and they got to talking. He was a Confederate veteran and when he found that she was Addie Cooper [Burroughs], he told her that he was with her brother, Tom, when he was killed. All those years the family only knew that he was missing. It was at night after the

Battle of Cedar Creek [fought in the Shenandoah Valley of Virginia, 1864], and their group was around a campfire cooking supper. A sniper's bullet struck Tom, and his friends buried him there. Mama told me that her brother Tom was the only one in the family who had brown eyes." ("Some" 16)

Bertha Paul Staley (b. 1907). *Although a pharmacist could send medicine by steamboat to young Bertha (K. Joyner, "Priceless, 9), she had to visit the dentist in person, traveling from Bucksport to Georgetown:*
"Oh, that was heavenly! Mama always fixed a picnic lunch; and of course, it had a big deck out and those heavenly rockin' chairs—reed rockin' chairs…. And we were amazed at the blacks that would meet the boat at these little stops like Longwood and Hagley; they'd talk Geechee" [a blend of English and African tongues]. (Int: 23)

Roberta Ward Rust (b. 1909). *Roberta, who worked for 42 years as teacher and principal in the Savannah Bluff and Tilley Swamp areas, also worked in her parents' general merchandise store at Wampee:*
"Sometimes they'd bring as small amount as three eggs and we would crate them and send them to Wilmington on the boat." The store would order goods from Wilmington: nails, plow points, plow lines ("I could fix a plowline for you in no time flat"), sugar, flour, rice, dried apples, cloth, hot cologne, hardware, groceries. "The best old brown sugar you ever tasted in your life came in barrels. And the first wastebasket I had at school was a tub that lard came in."

When the boat arrived at Little River, "someone would hear the whistle at the sand ridge. One of the colored men that we called 'Uncle' Joe Green would ring a bell, a big farm bell. The colored people would then take the wagons to Little River to pick up the goods" (Int: 7-8, 11). See Fig. 3.16.

Lucille B. Godfrey (b. 1891). *Riverboats were vulnerable to fire, the same element that destroyed houses, mills, businesses, schools and even a bridge; one night the* Maggie *burned, as did the* Lucy V. *at Bucksville. Water itself was a threat, and the* Sessoms *went under near Hagley. (See F. Morris Int: 10.)*
The *Mitchelle C.*, heavily loaded with fertilizer for delivery up the Little Pee Dee, lay at the wharf. The backwash of the *F.G. Burroughs* caused her to sink, with the help of a slow leak. Don Burroughs bought a pump that had been used in the rice fields, but the

Fig. 3.16. Boat at Little River. "Conway, S.C."

first time they put the line down in the hull it was too near the bow. "When we saw the boat beginning to stand almost straight up, we were terrified." With the pump placed closer to the center, the steamboat righted itself. ("Some" 17)

Fig. 3.17. *Comanche*. Horry County Museum.

Franklin G. Burroughs (b. 1908). *The sidewheelers were finally replaced by the* Comanche, *a propeller-driven craft that burned coal and had much sleeker lines than the older boats. (This vessel is pictured in the Foreword and in Fig. 3.17.)* "In contrast to the boisterous thrashing of the *Burroughs*, this steamer seemed a ghost ship as it moved along." As Franklin was angling on the Waccamaw, it would suddenly appear around a bend, leaving little time to brace for its wake.

Burroughs notes that the captains reflected the personalities of the two vessels:
"Captain Thompson of the *Burroughs* was a hearty man of operatic-basso build and volume, sporting a walrus moustache and capable of making his orders heard all over the ship; Captain Sarvis of the *Comanche* was clean-shaven, slight of build, and generally soft-spoken, although he could assert himself if need be." ("Steamboat" 7)

Stanley Coleman (b. 1915). *The son of Preston M. Coleman, overseer of the Holliday farm, Stanley reports that the* Ruth *met an ironic end for a such a workhorse:*
"They would haul fertilizer from Georgetown up Little Pee Dee. And every now and then, after they stopped using it, the thing would get loose and float down the river [*laughter*]. And it was Daddy's job to go get the darn boat. He took a stump-puller and two or three mules and would go down there, put a cable around that thing and then wrap it—had the mules go 'round and 'round till they could pull it on up…. And when they got it back up the last time, they pulled it out on dry land and that made a good card place up there" [*laughter*]. (Int. 13 Oct: 21)

"Cook all the way back": Boats and Jobs

Fig. 3.18. Shipyard in future parking lot of Kingston Presbyterian Church, Conway. Horry County Museum.

Over decades, shipbuilding created employment in Bucksville and Conway. (See Fig. 3.18.) Operating the boats, too, meant jobs.

Sarah Burroughs Sherwood (b. 1884) remembers "Frenchy, the cook on the boat, who came from the Isle of Madagascar" (Kearns 89). In one case, working must have been easier than commuting: Ben Horry (b. 1850 or '51) walked from Murrells Inlet to Conway every Monday to work on the *F.G. Burroughs*, then returned every Saturday (Chandler, "Uncle Ben Horry," 306).

Regularly-scheduled runs depended on waiters and cooks, as recalled by Franklin G. Burroughs (b. 1908):

> "Meals were served in the dining saloon, and in keeping with rail and ship travel of that era, were of excellent quality and abundance…. A white-coated waiter, or steward, was at hand to care for the needs (or wants) of the diners. The Captain presided at the communal dinner table." Breakfast on the *Comanche* was "a huge platter of bacon and an endless supply of the largest-ever-seen pancakes, brought hot to the galley to be smothered in local cane syrup…." ("Steamboat" 5, 7)

Franklin's Aunt Lucille (b. 1891) writes that other workers cared for the appetite of the vessel itself:

> "There were certain landings where cord wood was stacked for firing the boilers—the Negroes would form a line, a sort of bucket brigade, and pass it quickly to the deck. Often there were women as well as men, and they would sing, and cut steps, and shout back and forth to the crew." (Godfrey, "Some," 16)

Sammy Brown, the uncle of Ruth Clay "Sabe" Woodbury (b. 1886), was an engineer on several riverboats (Int: 9). Her mother, Sara, got work on leisure-runs to Georgetown:

> "Every excursion my mama used to run a table. She'd cook all that good stuff and—say we going tomorrow, she'd cook all day today. And used to come crackers in little boxes and she'd fry that box full of fish, then fry another one. Then she'd put the stove on the boat and have the grease fried hot. The people didn't have a whole lot of stuff—they'd buy them. Give 10 or 15 cent piece, 25 cent piece. And she'd be sold out all that food, going to Georgetown. Got down there, she'd have to buy more and cook all the way back on excursions." (Int. Latimer: 10)[6]

How did Joe Horry get that job on a steamboat that led to one on a tug? "Sonny" Stilley (b. 1930) retells the story of the hiring:

> "The cabin boy for the *Comanche* quit, got sick, or something happened to him, and Captain Thompson told the black members of his crew that he needed a new cabin boy." They suggested that the captain talk to the widow Horry, who was having trouble raising her son of about eleven years old. When they put ashore at Brookgreen Landing to pick up wood, the captain negotiated with her for several hours. The two agreed that he would pay her ten cents a week for Joe's services, on several conditions: that he have a good place to sleep and good food, and

that the captain teach him how to 'figger.' Joe slept in the captain's cabin and ate at the officers' mess, and every night they had lessons from the Bible and the almanac.

When the second engineer on the *Comanche* quit, got sick, or something, Captain McMillan, the chief engineer, suggested they try Joe. Horry later declared that he was the proudest man in the world—a teenager at this point: "I was the only nigger on the river that had a berth, clean sheets every week, ate at the captain's mess, and was paid three dollars a week" (Int: 2). "Joe also told me that there were twenty-some African Americans in the crew—firemen, roustabouts, and deck hands. 'Joe, where did the other black crew members sleep?' He said, 'Wherever they fell'" (Int: 5).

Horry also talked about another African American (last name unknown) who stood about seven feet tall and worked as a human depth-finder for the *Comanche*:

> They went up the Waccamaw River to North Carolina every spring, usually on high water, to deliver fertilizer to many landings. "Ben would be put overboard with a rope around him, and he was a pretty good swimmer. Joe said he dog-paddled real well, and he would get out in front of the boat, which would go at very slow speed in shallow areas. As Ben and Joe and Captain McMillan said, 'When his tits were out of the water, he turned around and waved his arms.' That meant the boat had to back down and Ben would wade around and find the deepest point and they would try to get over.
>
> "Joe said he'd seen Ben in the water in the late winter or early spring when there was ice on the edge of the river, and they would pull Ben in periodically, take him down in the boiler room, stretch him out on a blanket in front of the boilers, very hot, rub him down with towels, give him a good slug of corn liquor, and put him back overboard. I said 'Joe, didn't he get sick a lot?' He said 'Ben never even had a cold.' I thought that was a remarkable story to show how hard times were." (Int: 5. See also McIver, "Water," 11.)

"First time in a boat that had a motor"

The familiar buzz of the outboard, the throb of the inboard on a luxury vessel—these were unheard until toward the end of the timespan explored by this book.

Carl B. Bessent (b. 1891). *In 1906 Bessent, tired of rowing his family from the Battery to Little River, vowed to buy a powerboat. He took the steamer to Wilmington, bought one for $150, tied it to a two-masted schooner, turned it loose—and couldn't start it. But success followed, both mechanical and financial:*
"I would tow boats to the oyster beds near the mouth of the river charging fifty cents each way. Often I would tow twenty rowboats. Also I collected oysters; sometimes one hundred bushels a day. Oysters were bought at the factory for ten cents a bushel" [about 35 liters]. ("Early" 8)

George W. Floyd (b. 1918). *Floyd remembers a Sunday afternoon spent with Edward and Arthur Norton, known as Hoagie and Wack (the sons of Dr. J.A. Norton, who listed the Waccamaw ferries in Chapter 2):*
"The first time that I'd ever been in a boat that had a motor would have been in 1936 or '37." The fellows put in somewhere on the Waccamaw, went to the Inland Waterway and back. "I didn't have on a thing in the world but just a bathing suit, and I was burned the worst I've ever been in my life." (Int. G. Floyd: 36)[7]

Geraldine B. Burroughs (b. 1911). *In 1936 Geraldine opened the Inland Waterway—which had been dug, dredged, and dynamited from Maine and Florida—with a pair of scissors:*
"I had on a white sharkskin suit. I know that the ceremony was in the middle of the day and at that time, why, you wore gloves and hat and patent shoes. I had on a white Panama hat with a lavender band and a lavender blouse. I do remember that because I had to go to Columbia to buy it. And Colonel Holmes B. Springs was the person that asked me to cut the ribbon." There at Socastee the dignitaries, including the governor, watched from a little stand. "I got in—well, I guess you'd call it a yacht," and cut the ribbon right on the water. (Int. 1993: 2)

Frances Jessamine Buck Richardson (b. 1879). *Later that year the* Horry Herald *noted that the Waterway was "dug about fifty years too late" because it now competed with trucks ("Local and Personal"). It primarily became a seasonal migration route for people who did not have to ask how much that boat costs.*
"It was channeled through here, and when yachts began to come, one came down like the *Queen Mary*, the biggest thing we'd ever seen." A young woman got off, said she would like to tie up for the night, and invited us to come aboard to meet the owner, a retired Presbyterian minister. "Well," said my husband Don, "he sure didn't get this boat preaching!" (Epps, "Precious," 35)

As roads improved, water meant less as transportation—or as a barrier to it—and more as recreation. The canoe held nature-lovers rather than traders or surveyors, while the rowboat joined the rotting wagon in the yard. Boats were no longer made of juniper or cypress, but of the same synthetic material as the all-weather giraffe atop the volcano. The wooden paddlewheel gave way to the rimmed wheel of the train, and then to the rubber tire under the automobile, RV, pickup, tractor trailer, and log truck. The wind propelled weekend sailboats rather than schooners. The ebb and flow of the tide began to have significance mainly to those who walked a narrower or wider beach.

Two decades after the closing year of this book, the author heard a profound rumble on the Waccamaw, recognized it as a diesel engine, and beheld what looked like a ship full of logs passing upstream. On the superstructure of the tugboat behind it, the nameplate read *Samson II.* The last tug on the river, operated by Stilley Mill, it eventually followed the *Samson I* around the bend to oblivion. It also followed sacks of Big O, cypress pegs, boat-poles, the aroma of corn parching or of fried fish mixed with engine fumes, and Ben overboard. No longer heard were the blast of the conch shell, the songs of rowing men, the steamboat whistle, undiluted Geechee, the whoop of slaves returning home or of bridge-builders being roused, the drowsy lullaby of the great paddlewheels, the clang of the annunciating farm bell, or rum-scented jingles.

Notes

[1] The drought was so extreme that salt water began to work its way into the Sampit River in Georgetown (Grelen).

[2] For insights into the political dimension of the Waccamaw and Little River, see Bedford on the "river establishment," *passim.* For an artistic and reflective trip downstream, see Franklin Burroughs (b. 1942), *The River Home: A Return to the Carolina Low Country,* originally published as *Horry and the Waccamaw.*

[3] For an account of such a boat on the lower Waccamaw, see Carrison 21.

[4] Young Sarvis would become a soldier in the Tenth South Carolina Volunteers and live for a century. His daughter was Flossie S. Morris, who would die at the age of 103. One of his brothers would fight at the Battle of the Crater and another would lose his life in the Battle of Atlanta. (F. Morris, "Early," 19; Int: 3.)

[5] Peaveys, hinged hooks used by loggers.

[6] This valuable interview with the half-sisters was conducted by Catherine Lewis and Etrulia Dozier in 1970. Twenty-five years later it was transcribed from reel-to-reel audiotape by the interviewers and the author.

[7] In 1943 the Norton twins, pilot and co-pilot on a bombing run over the Netherlands, perished when their B-29 went down in the North Sea. Lewis, *Horry County,* 134-35.

CHAPTER 4
THE GUM

"More than a hundred years ago my great-grandfathers, Dusenbury & Sarvis, owned the main part of present day Myrtle Beach when they were in the timber and naval stores business. In 1881 they sold 3,654 acres to Burroughs & Collins for $1,000. They considered the land on the ocean of little value because trees wouldn't grow near the water."
Mary Emily Platt Jackson (b. 1921), "Recollections," 5.

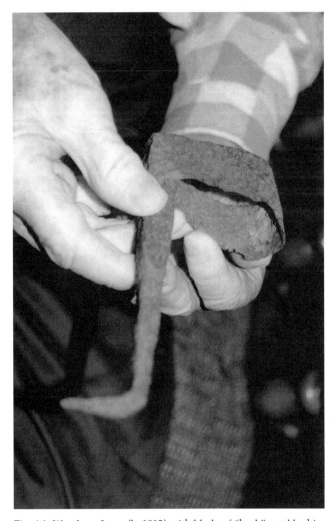

Fig. 4.1. Woodrow Long (b. 1913) with blade of "hack" used by his father to score the bark of pines (2003). Hook anchors in handle.

Trees thrived in the sandy dirt or spongy lowlands of Horry. The insides of the longleaf pine floated downstream in barrels, while softwood and hardwood, as timber, traveled by raft, barge, rail, or truck.

Often the trees themselves aided locomotion.

Alive, the longleaf exuded an oleoresin (oil-resin) that was distilled into protective agents for wooden sailing vessels—hull, deck and rigging—against water, weather, shipworms, and marine growths (Butler 13). The dead pine's rotted-away bark and sapwood left this pungent substance in trunks, branches, and roots to be baked in a kiln and drained out as tar. Sailors would climb the rigging and smear it on the ropes. Indeed, a "tar," or sailor, got his name from tarpaulin, a waterproof covering. According to Lawrence S. Early, "A three-deck ship of the line in 1844 carried six barrels of tar on a one-year voyage, nine barrels on a two-year voyage, and twelve barrels on a three-year voyage" ("From Cowpens" 4).

Tar itself was often boiled or burned down to pitch, used to waterproof the ship's wood and to help stop the

50

seams after planking was caulked with oakum (treated hemp or jute fiber). The tree's wood became masts and spars, the poles that supported rigging. (Kingstree in Williamsburg County was named for specimens chosen to serve as masts for ships of the Royal British Navy–B. Floyd, "Trees.") Longtime-rooted trees also aided movement when pines and hardwoods became the hulls of vessels that were constructed inside and outside of Horry County. Lumber even became railroad ties. Both the turpentine and logging industries, furthermore, caused the movement of people by attracting immigration to the county and emigration from it.[1]

The longleaf, also called yellow pine, reigned. (See Fig. 4.2.) All along the Atlantic Coastal Plain, it thrived in terrain that was too sandy to cultivate (Earley, "From Cowpens"). When T.A. Conrad hiked down the coast in search of fossils, this was probably the tree whose "brown slippery leaves" (fallen needles) made little improvement over the deep sand of the beach, and whose monotony was occasionally broken by hardwoods (19).

François André Micheaux, who visited American forests in the early 1800s, wrote admiringly about the *Pinus australis*. Southward down the East Coast it appears near Norfolk, where the pine barrens begin, and it "seems to be especially assigned to dry, sandy soils," the term "swamp pine" being inaccurate. (By contrast the loblolly pine was named for a mud puddle, its frequent site—Little 298.) The longleaf is found in the lower part of the Carolinas, Georgia, and Florida, in a swathe more than six hundred miles long and one hundred miles

Fig. 4.2. Virgin longleaf pine forest. Gamble, *Naval Stores*, leaf 1.

wide. The tree stands sixty or seventy feet high (80 to 100 according to Little 291). Its needles are about a foot long, "of a beautiful, brilliant green, united to the number of three in the same sheath." "The cones," adds Micheaux, "are very large, being seven or eight inches long, four inches thick, when open, and are armed with small retorted spines" (9). (See Fig. 4.3.)

The longleaf, Frankenberg points out, is the only tree in the region whose seedlings can survive one ecological constant: fire. (See Fig. 4.4.) In fact longleaf savannas (open grasslands) cannot be sustained without fire, whether sparked by lightning or by Indians flushing out deer. According to Earley, less than 3 percent remains (p.c.).

Like the *Giving Tree* in the book of that title (Silverstein), the longleaf yielded itself up completely.

Along with the white pine it was a source of "excellent good Plank for Building" as well as for

Fig. 4.3. Cones of longleaf and shortleaf pines. Photo by Bill Edmonds.

"Masts, Yards and several other Necessaries," according to Dr. John Brickel, who wrote in the 1730s, around the time the surveyors first reported on the swamp-lined Waccamaw (Averit 27). The deadwood on both the tree and the ground, self-embalmed, was chopped into "fat lighter," "fat-wood," or "lighter'd" (lighterwood), used to kindle fires. The roots, too, were burned for tar ("Tar") and its needles mixed with sand to help cover the kiln.

Needles of young longleaf were cut by the Negroes for brooms, according to Micheaux. And the seeds? "Sometimes [they] are very abundant and are voraciously eaten by wild turkeys, squirrels and the swine that live almost wholly in the woods." Only the violet flowers, which "shed great quantities of yellow pollen" in the springtime (9), escaped second use. But in the late 1800s even its aroma would be sought as a curative by invalids, especially those with tuberculosis, who flocked to Southern Pines and Pinehurst in North Carolina and other places in the South (Earley, "From Cowpens").

Before the advent of Bright Leaf tobacco at the end of the nineteenth century, a tree was the closest thing to an ATM. Whether a pine or a hardwood, it was a plant that nobody had ever seeded, hoed, fertilized, poisoned, cured, or prayed over.

Fig. 4.4. Young longleaf, six feet high and slow-growing. Lewis Ocean Bay Heritage Preserve, 2003.

"And a pair of rope lines"

With its manifold uses, a tree epitomizes the way Old Horry resisted specialization as to plants, skills, roles, activities, and objects. Things tended to be homemade, re-used, used for more than one purpose, or done without.

Work was often communal recreation: steamboat-loading, house-raising, hog-butchering, sugarcane-grinding, tobacco-curing, lumber-sawing, fish-seining.

The ocean meant frolic, air-conditioning, and nourishment (along with the salt to preserve it). A seashell provided live food, an eating utensil, and a souvenir. The beach was a road, as was the river, while a boat was a bridge. A train carried passengers, mail, and freight, as did a stagecoach and steamboat, whose deck was a bed. Sand was a pleasure for beachgoers, a hazard for vehicles and boats, a nuisance and blessing for tobacco farmers. Land grew food and the family tree. The back yard was a bank. A lake was not only a swimming venue but an industrial center complete with turpentine still, sawmill, grist mill, and cotton gin. Swimming was bathing. The same basin and passed-around cloth served to wash a rural family and the schoolmarm who boarded with them (Epps, "Mildred Bedsol," 27).

Things were money. A fraction of a harvest paid the rent for the land or bought the provisions needed to grow the crop. In one negotiation a first-rate mule was worth two plain mules, one bull yearling, a pair of shoes, and a pair of rope lines (Int. W. Davis: 37). Overalls were swimsuits or pajamas. A shirt was a lantern. A flour sack held seeds, which came from the garden itself. A croker fertilizer-sack, folded several times and punched with holes at the ends, served as a back-band to keep the traces from dangling next to one farmer's draft animal (Int. J.M. Vaught, Jr.: 25). Four hempen fertilizer bags, stitched together, formed a sheet onto which newly-picked cotton was dumped or under which large piles of cured tobacco were protected. "Later in the 1940s and '50s, bags were made of coarsely woven cotton and used for clothing and linens (quite durable), as well as for holding chicken feed" (D. Long, personal communication).

A bare foot served as a shoe, a shoe served as a wallet, and a pair of high heels carried the teacher across two miles of sand. A baby plate became a soap dish. A baked corncob helped to press clothing: "They could open a little damper and swing the iron back and forth to get a breeze on the cobs that would almost turn the bottom red-hot" (Int. J.M. Vaught, Jr.: 24). Patent medicine was liquor. A saw or plowshare became the ferryman's doorbell, an old buggy-spring the blade of a drawing-knife. A catalogue was recycled in the privy, a calendar was turned into stationery (each sheet the back of a month), and newspaper was glued to inside walls as insulation. A school lunchroom provided a frame for a house, which was then supported by brick salvaged from abandoned houses and chimneys and lit by the fixtures of the demolished auditorium (Int. J. & E. Vaught: 1).

A store was a place to buy staples, a corset, a casket, a farm animal, and an implement; a bank that lent on credit and kept money in a safe; a gathering place for companionship and news; a pharmacy; and a post office before rural free delivery (Int. W. Davis: 4).

A church was a place for worship, a community center, and a burial yard; a school was also a community center and an outpost of Christianity. A courthouse was a center of entertainment. A home could serve as a shed, a barn, a textile manufactory, a funeral parlor, a boarding house, a free hotel and restaurant; a room might be a trade-off for groceries. For one sixteen-year-old teacher (who wore the high heels), a wire strung between two nails was a closet, a skillet of water placed on coals or by the fireplace was a bedroom heater, a jigsaw puzzle was a shirt-box card with a picture drawn on it, beans and corn brought from home were counting aids, and bushes were toilets—girls to the right, boys to the left (Epps, "Mildred Bedsol").

A turpentine wagon became a car, moving van or bed. Every autumn one tobacco truck became a school bus when it was backed into the shed under a stored body, the wedges or jacks were knocked out, and BOOM! (Int. J. M. Vaught, Jr.: 18).

A child was a laborer, a grandparent often a parent. Someone with latent abilities in realms social, political, artistic, scientific, technical, commercial, mathematic, academic, or communicative was a farmer. A farmer was also a midwife, a logger, a turpentiner, a millworker, a waterway-builder, a minister, a mail courier, a teacher in "singing school," or someone who also did "public work" for wages. A preacher was a farmer or a businessman (like B.G. Collins, the partner of F.G. Burroughs), while a teacher was a role model and tax-saving fund-raiser. A mailman was a taxi driver and an emergency phone-caller. A prisoner was a road-worker. Captain Sasser conducted a train, pulled teeth, and sewed wounds.

A pet was a work animal, a cow ran wild with the pigs or mowed the lawn, and a goat pulled a cart or even a plow (Int. Hemmingway: 5-6). A person was a work animal or machine. Slaves were property along with colts and feather beds, and a farm was a recycling center. Workman's compensation? "If they got hurt, they were outta work" (Int. J.M. Vaught, Jr.: 29).

And a tree?

A big cypress anchored one end of the ferry-cable; any stout trunk worked as a stanchion for pulling a boat against the current or keeping a raft from slipping back with the tide; a tall rig-tree with a block and tackle dragged logs out of the woods. A limb was a framework for hoisting a pig for slaughter, for unloading logs, for hanging a murderer, or for playing tag: if you were holding on to a limb of one of the small oaks, "you were not poison" (Epps, "Mildred," 27). A log was a dugout boat; a church-bench if hewn on one side; a footbridge; a "pole" framework of a house, barn, church, or hut; a support for earthworks around a tar-kiln; a home for a new swarm of bees; a burned-out mortar for a rice-grinding pestle. A tree supplied fuel for a stove, a locomotive or other steam engine, a moonshine still, a hog-scalding fire, or a tobacco-curing barn. It even yielded up smoke to preserve meat.

"Long sweetgum poles—maybe sassafras"—helped make up the trace chains for one farmer's ox; a long pole that stuck out from a tree with a weight on the end and a hollow log beneath a fulcrum made a chewing-tobacco press; and where the dirt road crossed the tracks, poles laid about two inches apart at right angles to the rails made a cattle guard (Int. J.M. Vaught, Jr.: 27).

A stick was a coupling between rafts, a support for a clay chimney, part of a roof for an outdoor church, a hook for drying corn-shucks, a primitive tobacco-transplanter, a percussion instrument, a doodlebug-teaser, and a means of punishment–as after two students lobbed a potato at Flossie Morris (Int. G. Floyd: 33). A stick was also a means of teaching someone the ABCs in the dirt (Int. D. Carr: 1-2). A squared-off stick with a hinge helped to time the engine of a grits mill: "To retard the spark or increase it, [Babe Bratcher] would just move that stick around a little bit in relationship to that big wheel" (Int. J. & E. Vaught: 3). "A piece of wood about from here to here and this long" was like a thumb on a merchant's scale: "It was nailed in the bottom of a half-bushel measure, stayed there. And when you bought a half bushel of meal, well, you didn't get no meal out where that there block was" (Int. W. Jones, Aug. 18: 22).

Twigs were shaken onto the winter field from an apron-sack to serve as fertilizer (Int. Hemmingway: 3). Lighter'd furnished a resinous piece of kindling, a mosquito repellent, and the black smoke that churned from a locomotive. Sawdust became a road, a packing material for ice, or a mountain for a tobogganer sliding down on a sheet of bark.

"The Gum" presents rare memories of the naval stores industry, while the next chapter will take up the other main commercial use of trees: logging. For an overview of both industries in Horry County, see C. Joyner, "The Far Side of the Forest." This chapter benefits from corrections made by Lawrence S. Earley, author of a forthcoming book, *Looking for Longleaf: The Fall and Rise of an American Forest* (Univ. of North Carolina Press).

How did a tool called a "hack" make its way to the Waterland? In colonial days, Britain had encouraged suppliers of naval materials, especially in North Carolina, in order to avoid dependence on sources in Norway and the Baltic. A royal petition in 1704 noted that few such supplies had been brought from colonial plantations, "tho in those parts there is great plenty of timber for building of ships and also to produce pitch, tarr and rosen, and a soil capable to afford hempe" (Gamble, "Early History," 19). Naval stores were already being produced before the village of Kingston was settled: the unnamed canoeists of 1734, paddling for two February days above Georgetown, reached a bluff over the Waccamaw, found two half barrels of pitch and, "being very cold, set fire to them" (*New Voyage* 45). (In common usage, "pitch" could mean either the raw gum or its doubly-distilled offspring; "turpentine" could mean either the gum or the thin oil now sold in a can; and "sap" meant the raw gum, although the oleoresin comes not from sapwood but from heartwood.) In 2004, divers in the Waccamaw salvaged the gum shown in Plate 5.

According to A. Goff Bedford these products, "necessary for the world's navies and commercial fleets," were the most important crop for a hundred years after the collapse of the indigo market in Horry County (21). In later years not only ships but factories ran on the pine-tree products: "Indeed, turpentine derivatives were to manufacturing of that day what petroleum is to the present," notes Catherine Lewis about the sticky treasure:

> "Few manufactured goods did not depend on it at some point in their production. It was an ingredient in medicines, disinfectants, soaps, waterproof cements, explosives, waxes, printing inks, paints and varnishes…. Horry District became one of the chief producers of this essential commodity." ("Little River" 10-11. See also "Principal Uses.")

Each issue of the Conway newspaper had advertisements for commission merchants who dealt in naval stores from their base in New York City. In 1874 the *Horry News* reported that during the previous year the three ports of Pot Bluff, Bull Creek, and Little River had shipped more than 80,000 barrels of naval stores:

spirits of turpentine:	13,854
rosin	: 64,631
crude turpentine	: 500
tar	: 1,047

All these tapped substances shared the deck with goods that had been raised, grown, or caught: peanuts, cotton, cowhides, furs, beeswax, sweet potatoes, salt mullets, oysters, chickens, eggs, cattle, and turkeys ("Local Matters" 17 Feb.). See also "Shipments…from Little River…1873."[2]

After the Civil War, as iron drove wood from the ocean, the importance of tar and pitch declined while the demand for rosins and spirits of turpentine increased with industrial expansion (Gamble, "Charleston's Story," 36).

"The debit side of the ledger"

All manner of people extracted treasure from Pinewood Mine. "It was customary," writes Lucille B. Godfrey (b. 1891),

> for the turpentine operators, of which there were many in the county, to hire large groups of slaves to work the woods. My grandfather [Anthony Burroughs] had been hired either by the operators or the slave owners to bring a number here. Those from North Carolina were trained in the work. The Negroes below us were more familiar with rice culture. This group [of turpentine workers] probably came in near Little River." ("Some" 10)

Her mother's sister, Ellen Cooper Johnson (b. 1844), witnessed such groups: "I have seen as many as a hundred slaves brought back by these businessmen. These hands were hired from the large slave-owners for the year, and they must be fed and clothed" (Kearns 73).

One ex-slave, Willis Williams, born approximately 1845 and interviewed in Conway in the 1930s, remembered that "Mass" John A. Williams of North Carolina owned four hundred slaves:

> "He was a man *had* the colored people. He didn't work all on his own plantation. He'd hire out his people to work turpentine.--Put 'em out for so much a year. He'd give 'em blanket, suit, coat, pants. First of the year come, Boss would collect wages for all he hire out."

Willis himself "was a grown man pulling boxes" (tapping pines) when the earthquake of 1886 hit (Chandler, "Ex-Slave…Williams," 211).

William Oliver was one of the 18 slaves on Daniel W. Oliver's plantation just north of Bucksport (Boyle, "Interview…Oliver," 14). He reported decades later: "When I married, was working turpentine. Rent timber and cut boxes" (Chandler, "Recollections," 219). Any farmer could work his own trees or lease acreage to others. Anthony Burroughs's son F.G. arrived in Horry County in 1857 and ended up owning thousands of acres of timber, which supplied his turpentine distilleries.

A.J. Baker (b. 1884) grew up in the Baker's Chapel section. A farmer and surveyor (and commemorator of the horse Maude), he recalls that during the 1800s and the first decade of the 1900s, the turpentine industry was one of the chief occupations of the male laboring class in Horry County:

> "I had every opportunity to observe just what was going on in and around that small farm surrounded by almost primeval forest where workers of the industry were constantly seen during the summer season. Nearly all of the farms were small and provided only provisions consumed at home. Hence the turpentine industry to bring in a little cash." (Int: 1)

He defines the economic hierarchy:

> "As in the system today of tenant farming, the landowner would share-crop his timber land to producers as tenants. I think the method varied in different communities. The small owner would be his own producer, while the large land owner would perhaps have several tenants and producers in common. The tenant usually was allotted a certain number of boxes or pines as a crop…. ("Turpentine" 14)

In turpentine jargon, a crop was about 200 acres of pine timber that produced about 10,500 cups or boxes of gum. This amount, when dipped the first year, would yield 50 barrels of spirits and 160 barrels of rosin (Pridgen 104). Baker notes that the workers themselves might be tapped dry because any profits had to reimburse the company store:

> "When I worked in the commissary as a boy with my uncle [in the Brown's Bay section north of Conway] they usually had taken up their part of the turpentine in provisions before it ever went to market. They were always on the debit side of the ledger, of course." (Int: 4)

Most of these laborers have gone "jam out of remembrance" in the words of the unnamed old man of Chapter 1. But he does leave a sketch of his grandmother Isba (who married her cousin):

> "She went and hunkled right down (97 years old). Was wore out. I've known her to dip turpentine like that all day and send after the old Granny woman [the midwife] that night. 'Fore she knocked off [died] she had ten head of chillun. (Chandler, "Old Man," 3)

He also recalls another character whose dwelling resembled the earthen banks made for storing sweet potatoes:

> "Old man Dave make him a hovel like a 'tater hill. Straw inside. When he wanted to fiddle he'd climb on the ridge pole. House had all burned down. Burnt his furniture all up but he saved his fiddle. He worked turpentine." (Chandler, "Old Man," 4)

Dorethea Long (b. 1927) remembers her tall grandfather, William Dempsey Lewis: a "chipper," or ax-wielder, he leased someone's land for its turpentine around 1900-1910 and was known as the strongest man in the community located two miles from Allsbrook toward Gurley. Her husband Woodrow (b. 1913) heard that workers would play tricks on each other. One man put a pine burr (cone) under the tail of an ox that was pulling a cart, and "the camp was torn up" [*laughter*]. Woodrow recounted the well-known story of a turpentine worker in the early 1900s who had such a long walk from Lewisville to Poplar that he cut a switch, whipped himself along the way, and exclaimed "Now you've gotta *move on*" [*laughter*].

Each year a tree would produce less gum. With large operators leasing vast areas, the turpentine industry depleted the forests of the Carolinas then moved on to Georgia and other Southern states. Eventually the forests whose beauty, variety, and abundance had so allured the explorers in 1734 began to float like them upon the rivers, and the longleaf was nearly barreled and rafted into oblivion. Ironically, as A. Goff Bedford points out, turpentining slowed the development of the county because it:

> "discouraged the clearing of the land for agricultural purposes and the development of permanent communities. All a man needed…was a handful of odd tools and some thirty or more trees which, scarred once a week, would produce about a quart of sap each before the scar healed" and the farmer would gash it in another place." (21-22)

A Turpentine Calendar

How would laborers translate resin from bark and rings to staves and hoops? Here is a brief summary of the annual process as recalled by those who took part in or observed it.

• Cut a "box" and score the bark

Like the raw material of maple syrup, the "sap" of the pine had to be brought to the surface. In winter, when the tree was dormant and the resin down, the laborer took a heavy axe and chopped out a "box"–a cavity in the trunk–to collect the semi-fluid gum. (See Fig. 4.5.) One "chipper" was Woodrow Long's father, William Mack (b. 1881), who was born the same year that Dusenbury & Sarvis sold its land for 27 cents an acre. "He could chip out a box that was so precise in size that the oval paddle of wood could scoop the collected gum clean out."

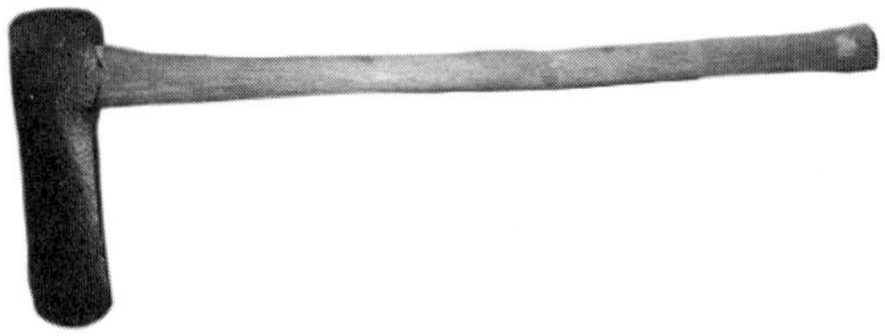

Then, wielding a "hack," a long, wood-handled tool with a sharp metal beak, the worker made a vertical cut within easy reach through the bark and sapwood. (See Fig. 4.1.) He made another stroke on the left of it, then on the right, to form a V (W. Long, p.c.). According to Pridgen, each "streak" was about two-thirds of an inch wide and a little deeper. The worker added a new gash to the face every week for about thirty-four weeks (102).

Fig. 4.5. Boxing axe, 34" long. Horry County Museum. Photo by Paul Olsen.

The oleoresin produced during the first year, called "virgin dip," was lighter than in subsequent years, when the turpentine and rosin became progressively darker and less valuable. To make a profit, operators abandoned forests after a few years and moved on (Earley, "From Cowpens"). See Fig. 4.6 for a living memento of those days. Many years later, Sam Cox, Jr., observed that a few V-scarred trunks ended up as part of a dock on the Waccamaw: "They had cut them and then turned them upside down…and driven the small end into the ground, and there the cat-face was, just as pretty…" (Int: 13). (See Fig. 4.7.)

Fig. 4.7. Trunk with streak-whiskers. Horry County Museum. Photo by Paul Olsen.

Fig. 4.6. Tree scarred by turpentine cuts. Maple Section, 2003.

Rev. William W. Malet. *In 1862, Malet visited a farm near Conwayborough owned by E.F. Graham, who had been discharged from the army because of ill health:* "He has pines in his woods, which he 'hacks' for turpentine. The 'hack' is a steel instrument shaped like a 'drawing-knife.' The bark is hacked in a V shape up to ten or twelve feet [i.e., from the bottom of the tree]. "After four weeks' hacking, about one inch a week, turpentine begins to run down into the cavity or 'box' cut in the tree, the root of which holds from one to two quarts. One thousand of these boxes full will fill four barrels, 230 lbs. weight each, in four weeks. The price at New York before the war was four dollars a barrel. One man can tend 1200 boxes." (23)

• "Dip" the gum

Right after the bark was scored, the resin began to ooze. A few weeks afterward workers began "dipping" (gathering) it with a paddle or a "dip iron." Gathering went on all summer. (See Fig. 4.8 and Fig. 4.9.) One improvement in the process that was increasingly used in the twentieth century was the external, artificial box (Earley, p.c.). "The last turpentine work I saw," remembers Woodrow Long, "they had metal pans hanging, but that wasn't the vogue earlier" (Int: June 2000). Dorethea Long notes that in some areas a tin cup was attached to the tree (p.c.).

W. Irving Jones (b. 1895). *Then they took a dipper, scooped out the raw gum, and poured it in a bucket that hung at the bottom of the cut:*

"Rake it off and get the dipper clean." After pouring the load into a barrel, they would leave the bucket cocked with a brace to continue draining the gum [into the barrel] and start filling another bucket (Int. Aug. 11: 7).

• Haul the gum to the still

After axes, hacks, and paddles came wheels and hooves. The job of Dorethea Long's father (b. 1902) "was to take the cart with his ox 'Blue' through 'Anderson Woods,' between Bayboro and Gurley, and pick up the turpentine" (Int: June 2000. See Figs. 4.10 and 4.11.)

Fig. 4.9. Dipping somewhere in North Carolina, South Carolina, or Georgia. Pridgen 103.

Silas "Dock" Beverly (b. 1881). *The distillery required water not only to boil the resin but to transport the resulting spirits and rosin downstream:*

Fig. 4.8. Paddle, 49". Horry County Museum. Photo by P. Olsen.

"The gum was hauled to the still located at Toddville [on the Waccamaw], owned by the Burroughs & Collins Company. For there it was graded. Good turpentine sold for about $3 a barrel. Rosin and spirits were made from the turpentine." (25)

A.J. Baker (b. 1884). *The barrels of crude gum were "hauled to market by mule wagons":*

There were no trucks then, "and if there had been, the roads were inadequate for their use." Generally the big merchants owned the stills. At the market the product was bought "at a certain price per gauge weight of 280 lbs. or 320 lbs., whichever was in force." (14)

Susie L. Lewis (b. 1898). *In Galivants Ferry, before trucks:*

"There were just certain hands that drove the two-horse wagons to Marion and to Conway…. They had 4-plat lashes [i.e., braided with four strands] and you could hear them popping their lashes every evening coming in and hollering" [yodeling].

Fig. 4.10. Mr. Hallie P. Martin, 1983.

Fig. 4.11. House where Martin lived with his grandfather, R.M. Prince, in Gurley. Photo c. 1915. Courtesy Dorethea Long.

J.C. "Don" Ayers (b. 1893). *The last person Ayers ever saw hauling a cartload of turpentine was Newton Blanton, a Civil War veteran from North Carolina:*

Called a "trip cart" by some, it had two wheels and a bed or body about four by five feet. To prevent the barrels from rolling off, it had one vacant space in front of the axle and one behind that were designed to fit barrels lying down. Directly above the axle there was a floored space. "This little cart provided a wonderful conveyance for a small family. They sat on the crossboards hanging their feet and legs through the front opening." (14-15)

Andrew Stanley (b. 1904). *Barrels were carried to the Gully in Nixonville to be soaked like a juniper boat:*
"I see a old gentleman named Collins Moore had four mules to a wagon, and they'd dip that turpentine. And he'd sit there, continues like he's going to put it in close to the pond. When he got the barrel filled, he'd put the lid on it and rolled it in that pond to keep the barrel from leaking–the water swelled up the staves to make the barrel tighten. Then he'd put 'im up two skid poles to the wagon and to the ground, and roll that barrel of turpentine up those two poles, and load it his self." (Int. April 1991: 23)

•Dump the resin into the boiler

From his paper canoe in 1875, Nathaniel H. Bishop noted the "turpentine distillers on the little bluffs that jut into the fastnesses of the great swamps of the crooked Waccamaw River" (vii). These operations may also have announced themselves to the nose, for according to much later testimony about stills in Georgia, the odor was strong enough to wake up a car passenger at midnight (Int. Jones, undated fragment: 48). In 1874 the *Horry News* reported that the run of new virgin turpentine had been retarded by dry, cold winds: "At the distilleries up the river and in the country it is also coming in very backwardly" ("Local Matters" 14 April).

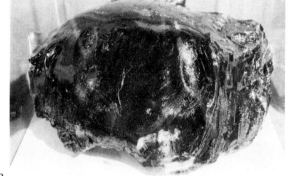

In Conway, Braxton Brown, the father of Lillie B. Latimer (b. 1882), ran a still for "Old lady Mary Beaty": "Used to carry my father dinner and breakfast many a morning" (Int.: 5). Carrie D. Doyle, born the same year that Mrs. Beaty died (1901), and the same year the Conway & Seashore reached New Town, used to salvage material from a former still in Galivants Ferry: "I've been there many a time to dig rosin to make soap. People would dig pretty, clear hunks" (Int. 31 Oct.: 15-16). See Fig. 4.12. Such operations hung on through the early part of the

Fig. 4.12. Rosin nugget, 15" x 15". Horry County Museum. Photo by Paul Olsen.

twentieth century. Almost ninety years after James Clyde Williamson was born in 1906, he vividly remembered the rolls of black smoke coming from the still owned by the Stone Brothers in Little River (Berry, "James").

Edmund Kirke (b. 1822). *In* Among the Pines: or, South in Secession-Time, *this Northerner recounts a trip to South Carolina between its secession in late 1860 and the beginning of the Civil War in April, 1861. Here he outlines the distilling process:*

> "The crude turpentine is 'dumped' into the boiler through an opening in the top…; water is then poured upon it, the aperture made tight by screwing down the cover and packing it with clay, a fire built underneath, and when the heat reaches several hundred degrees Fahrenheit, the process of manufacture begins. The volatile and more valuable part of the turpentine, by the action of the heat, rises as vapor, then condensing flows off through a pipe in the top of the still, and comes out spirits of turpentine, while the heavier portion finds vent at a lower aperture, and comes out rosin" [see also Int. Baker]. Rosin produced by the newly boxed tree, valuable because of its clear color, is used for fine soap and "Rosin the bow"—i.e., for the strings of a musical instrument.

He and the secessionist "Colonel" rode on horseback to an unrefined refinery:

> "About four hundred yards from the farmer's house, and on the bank of a little run [creek], which there was quite wide and deep, stood a turpentine distillery; and around it were scattered a large number of rosin and turpentine barrels, some filled and some empty. A short distance higher up, and far enough from the 'still' to be safe in the event of a fire, was a long, low, wooden shed, covered with rough, unjointed boards, placed upright, and unbattened [without strips of wood nailed atop the seams]. This was the 'spirit-house,' used for the storage of the spirits of turpentine when barreled for market and awaiting shipment.

"Two 'prime' Negro men, dressed in the usual costume, were 'tending the still'; and a Negro woman, as stout and strong as the men, and clad in a short, loose, linsey gown [i.e., linsey-woolsey, a rough wool], from beneath which peeped out a pair of coarse leggins, was adjusting a long wooden trough, which conveyed the liquid rosin from the 'still' to a deep excavation in the earth, at a short distance. In the pit was a quantity of rosin sufficient fill a thousand barrels" (29-30).
For a smoking distillery, see Fig. 4.13.

Ellen Cooper Johnson (b. 1844). *The sister of Adeline Cooper Burroughs, Margaret Ellen wrote her memoirs shortly before dying*

Fig. 4.13. Burroughs & Collins turpentine still in Conway. Horry County Museum.

in 1925. This excerpt comes from a long, dramatic, even cinematic account of raids by Confederate deserters (or survivors) in the last months of the Civil War:

"It was a beautiful, calm, moonlit night, but how helpless and lonely we felt! The two old faithful servants [who had not fled to the Yankees] had gone to visit their families who lived some distance from Cool Springs. About eight o-clock we saw that a fire had been started on the turpentine still-yard. What could we do? Over one thousand barrels of turpentine and resin were on this yard, and it was burning!

"My sister told me and the colored girl to run and call old man Bart and his daughter, or they would be burned to death. We ran, shouting 'Fire, fire!', but no answer. When we got to the yard, we saw them in the shed which stood a few feet from the road. Old man Bart was throwing out new spirit barrels which had been packed there the first year of the war…. We knew that this fire had been set to draw us away from the house." (13)

Susie L. Lewis (b. 1898). *In Galivants Ferry there was "a great big old tub as big as this room and a big old pot runs all the way around it:*
"They put that lighter somewhere another down in the furnace, and it goes up, sweats out that tar, and the turpentine comes down through there and drops down into another little container down there, and they burn the rosin out of it. I've seen cakes of it…. They had to pave the sidewalks when we moved to Cool Spring. Our wood and such got kinda scarce around there and the colored people and the white ones, too, got to burning it in their fireplaces, and all the black smut and smoke--just as bad as coal." (Int: 11)

Mitchelle Collins (b. 1886). *For children a distillery appealed to the feet, eyes, and jaws:*
Everybody had walks made of rosin blocks. "In the summertime they'd get hot and the children would walk on them, all that sticky stuff would get on their feet." Children would go over to a neighborhood still and watch them make turpentine. They'd let us go get the top hard layer from a barrel: "You'd chew that crusty part" (Int: 3).

• Transport barrels to a ship

As the next phase of routine gum-distillation, the barrels had to be transported to the Atlantic. In Little River, freighters that had discharged their merchandise into a large warehouse "would load up with barrels of tar and turpentine, cotton, corn, and other farm produce for shipment to Wilmington, N.C., Charleston, and other ports" (Berry, "Little River"). On March 4, 1903, the Georgetown *Times* recorded the arrival of the *F.G. Burroughs*, "from Waccamaw, with 196 bbls of rosin, 75 bales of cotton, 12 bbls of tar," and a forlorn "2 bbls of spirits" ("Marine").

Edmund Kirke (b. 1822). *This Northern sojourner explains how naval stores were transported from the backwoods to the big city:*
"In the creek, and filling nearly one-half of the channel in front of the spirit-shed, was a raft of pine timber, on which were laden some two hundred barrels of rosin. On such rude conveyances the turpentine-maker sent his produce to Conwayboro'. There the timber-raft was sold to my wayside friend, Captain B–[Buck], and its freight shipped on board vessel for New York." (30)

Nathaniel H. Bishop (b. 1837). *From his 58-pound canoe, Bishop glimpsed already-rafted products of the upstream distilleries when he passed through Conwayborough:*
As Negroes roared with laughter at his outlandish double-ended paddle, he "shot past the landing place where cotton and naval stores were piled, waiting to be lightered nine miles to Pot Bluff," a dock "reached by vessels from New York drawing twelve feet of water." He was beginning to feel the influence of the tides. (237)

Donald McNeil Burroughs (b. 1877). *One transshipment downstream from Conway involved a lucky error for F.G. Burroughs:*
After the Civil War Don's father returned to Conway and went into the turpentine business. "To do so, he borrowed a stake and collected enough naval stores to make a shipment North. Schooners came up to Pott's Bluff at that time to pick up the turpentine and resin. Papa's shipment was rafted here, put aboard a ship, and the Captain handed over the bill-of-lading and prepared to sail. Before Papa could look over the bill, the schooner got underway. "Papa realized that the bill-of-lading was short several barrels. He mounted his horse, raced to Georgetown, arrived there with the ship, and demanded settlement." An argument ensued that was arbitrated by a Mr. Hazzard, who impressed F. G. so much that he

insured his shipment with the man. "A very fortunate thing this was, too, because the unlucky ship was lost at sea...." (Kearns 66-67)

Carrie D. Doyle (b. 1901). *Naval stores also traveled down the Little Pee Dee to Georgetown:*
"They had a big old flat they used. They would put in barrels and then [poled] it down the river.... I would hear [Will Marlowe's] wife talking—he would be gone about a week sometimes. They would all gather down there whenever the flat came back."[3] (Int. 31 Oct: 17)

• Salvage residue from the "face"

In 1909 J.W. Ogilvie wrote that before the railway there were only three frame houses between North Carolina and Conway, mostly "crude log cabins with mud chimneys generally backing the road as if they were gruesome sentinels placed there to challenge the entrance of improvement and progress." His sardonic quip about the residents: "Seemingly their ambition lay in scraping a pine tree" (19).

A.J. Baker (b. 1884). *Not all of the resin of the tree would reach the box below, so part of it would lodge on the face:*
"Here it would harden flake-white, lose much of its liquid appearance, and become a sort of dry turpentine." A substantial amount accumulated as the successive gashes exuded resin. "During the fall and winter, this turpentine was scraped from the face of the tree, gathered in suitable boxes, packed in barrels, and was ready for market. This was known as scraped turpentine [called "scrape"] and gave the workers something to do during the off season" ("Turpentine" 13). See Fig. 4.14. for the unambitious tool.

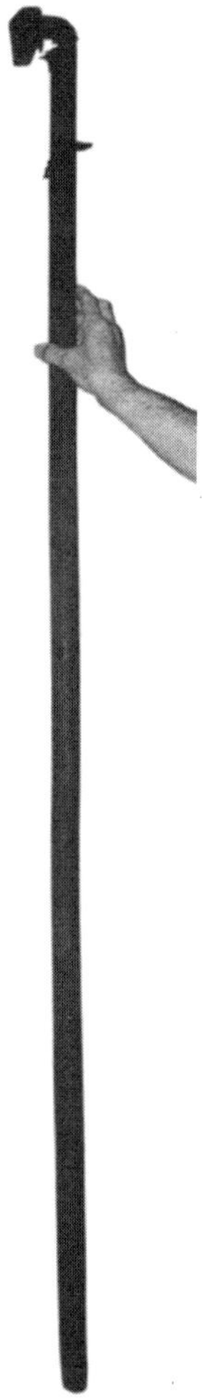

Making Tar and Pitch

Tar could be made by the controlled burning of deadwood under a mound of wood and dirt. Cad Holmes (Int. Peterkin: 37) remembers seeing former tar kilns in the woods around Burgess Community. "Right in the back of my house there's some charcoal—*from* the tar kiln. I can get a handful of it anytime." (Such relics from the Maple Section appear in Fig. 4.15.) In her earliest memory, Nellie H. Johnson (b. 1918) carried dinner to her grandfather as he made tar near Holmestown Road:

He'd cut lightwood from the pine trees and bury it—"Dirt on top" [*illustrating with hands*]. Then he'd "make a drain, a little ditch.... And he would dip the tar out and strain it. With a screen right there" [*pointing to a window screen*]. (Int. Peterkin: 36-37)

A report from 1771 explains that managing a kiln required great expertise: if it burns too quickly, it wastes tar; "if there is not air enough let in, it will blow (as they call it) and often hurts the workmen" (Catesby; qtd. in Berry, "Horry County's," 14).[4]

Fig. 4.15. Charcoal of yesteryear next to David Long's boot, 2003.

Fig. 4.14. Scraper with handle, 71". Horry County Museum. Photo by Paul Olsen.

C.B. Berry (b. 1919). *Almost two centuries later, in 1968, this surveyor-historian described a recent surveying expedition at Ocean Drive Beach where a golf course was being laid out:*

"We noted a large hole in the ground some thousand feet from the nearest road. The hole was obviously very old, having moss growing about in it. While trying to determine whether this was caused by sand haulers, a wartime bomb from a plane, or perhaps the uprooting of a huge tree, we noted a circular area adjoining the hole that was nearly two feet higher than the level of the adjoining land and speculated that this had once been a tar kiln." The proof: "Upon digging into the area we found masses of large pieces of charcoal...." "Further digging revealed the clay floor and a circular imprint where once had been the wooden tar pipe that led to the hole. This kiln was thirty feet in diameter.... We have personally observed other old kiln sites at Little River and in other parts of Horry County." ("Horry County's" 14. See also Berry, "Tar Business.")

Proximity to the ocean helped to finish off the turpentine industry. "[It] was almost ruined by the hurricane in 1893, which felled most of the trees being used. After this the trees were burned in tar-kilns to get tar for sale, and some of the land was cleared for farming" (Ayers 15).

Wood tar itself could be reduced by about a third. "Pitch it within and without with pitch," God ordered the ark-builder of Genesis. This material is made "either by boiling tar in iron kettles set in furnaces or by burning it in round clay holes made in the earth" (Nairn, qtd. in Berry, "Horry County's," 13). Dorethea Long remembers that some kind of vat stood in the Bayboro area, which Earley suggests was a "pitch kettle" used to boil down tar into the more concentrated pitch (personal communication).

Destructive Distillation

One man's experience gave an ironic edge to the term "destructive distillation"—the treatment of resin-rich deadwood under heat and pressure to release the oils and acids. To conduct this process the Walker Chemical Works of New Jersey built a plant just upstream from Conway. By a contract dated 1910, Burroughs & Collins agreed to sell the company "all of the lightwood, dead long leaf pine timber" suitable "for cross ties and manufacturing and distillation purposes" ("State").

Working there was Arthur Burroughs, who earlier in this book hosted the excursion train, tucked in one sister aboard the steamship, and visited another on her deathbed. His wife, Frances Coles Burroughs (b. 1882) writes that he

> "was terribly burned in an explosion at Mr. Magrath's chemical plant in August of 1912. They
> were afraid to move him, and sent the *Ruth* down the river to bring him home. They placed him
> on a sheet on the bow and brought him to Snow Hill [on Kingston Lake]. He died a few hours
> after reaching home." (21)

An African American, name unrecorded, died in the same accident (Godfrey, "Some," 14).

After the dissolution of the company in 1914, L.D. Magrath (1885-1962), from New York City, stayed in Conway to become mayor and "in many respects a symbol of the town itself" (Wachtman). His father-in-law, George Officer, who was from Canada, and whose sawmill had burned down at Eddy Lake, taught Frances how to do bookkeeping. She worked for Stilley Plywood, a business that as one person declared "put food on the table for many a family." Her son, Franklin G., grew up in straitened circumstances to become what Catherine Lewis called the premier lawyer of Horry County. Although he had vivid memories of steamboat captains, he had only a single dim one of his father.

At Pitch Landing, just below Conway, the declining sun brightens the already-light-green cypress trees on the opposite bank and, beyond them, the white puffs of cloud. The reflection, a wet mosaic of Army green and silver-blue, with a hint of purple, manages to avoid sliding downstream.

At the nearer bank, where the Waccamaw becomes shallow and tan, a fellow backs his pickup down the ramp and unwinds his speedboat into the river, where his companion starts the motor. Perhaps a descendant of Granny Todd, she wears no bonnet but instead a two-piece swimsuit. A pontoon boat hoves into view with sluggish determination and eight waving hands, then a speedboat tows a crescent of spray.

This evening the river seems to be reserved for white people. Who would think that black and white laborers once came to the place in mule wagons to unload massive containers onto flats or steamboats? As the boaters get an occasional whiff of the two-stroke engine, they can little imagine the heady scent of pine oils that must have surrounded laborers as they hacked, dipped, distilled, and hauled the summer away.

Gone with the rowboat and the ubiquitous longleaf are the "boxing ax, the hack, the puller, the dipper, the scraper, the bucket, the scrape box, and the barrel" (Baker, "Turpentine," 14). Gone is the air-splitting pop of the four-plat lash. As with the tools, gone are the old phrases: "crop" of trees, "pull a box," "scrape a pine," "following the turpentine." Good riddance to the wrong side of the ledger. As time passed, cash was scraped less from the bark and more from the timber. For around the end of the nineteenth century—also the era when Bright Leaf tobacco began to sprout—the log began to replace the barrel as the main form of extraction.

Notes

[1] Uprooting oneself to seek the longleaf was called "following the turpentine." Men with tarred heels walked from N.C. and ended up as farmers in northern Horry County (Ayers 14). The father of W. Clyde Clardy (b. approx. 1892) moved the family to the Wampee area to work in turpentine:

> "Malaria killed a lot of people, and many of them were put in a zinc casket that had a chain on it,
> then buried on their property. They planned to have the casket lifted out and returned to their
> former home in North Carolina to be permanently buried there, but none were ever moved."(29)

Migrant laborers, black and white, worked as employees of big-time operators who leased vast acreage and eventually moved on. As Cad Holmes understands it, "They would farm boys out to go to work for a company, which might be out of state." Sometime before 1880 his ancestor, London Holmes (an African American), departed at the age of fifteen and came back five years later with some money, probably from turpentine work (Int. Peterkin: 21).

Susie Lewis (b. 1898) remembers "the Georgia Turpentine Rush or something like that" in the early 'teens (Int: 13). William Mack Long joined a turpentine gang from the Maple Section and followed the trade to the same state, where he married a local woman. (This was the patriarch who disconcerted little Willie Ruth Hucks by putting a worm in his cheek and letting it roll around.) According to Bedford, turpentine connects many names in Tift County, Georgia, with those in Horry (114). Alabama and Florida also attracted workers as the longleaf played out. Social life could be bleak for the laborer and boss, as described by Pridgen (104).

[2] The *Horry Herald* featured a regular Market Report on naval stores:

> "Rosin, 87 1/2 per bbl. for strained, good strained 92.
> Tar, 1.15 per bbl. of 280 lbs.
> Crude Turpentine, $1.00 for hard and $1.50 for Yellow Dip and $1.70 Virgin." ("Market" 1894)

[3] Originally Punch Bowl Landing (on the Little Pee Dee below Potato Bed Ferry) may have been called Punch Pole.

[4] For an analysis of the firing process written by one of the Carolina Indian Commissioners, see page 13 of this same article.

CHAPTER 5
THE LOG

*"Wasn't nothing but one store and a boardwalk for walking and no street—
the street was so sandy. And when they cleaned up them big farm on Myrtle
Beach there—[Burroughs and] Collins Lumber Company come over here and
bought the timber and I snaked the log [i.e., dragged them with a chain], and
they pay me extra to pull the tops kind of up together so they could burn it.
That whole farm, I did."*
David Carr (b. 1887), Int: 12.

Fig. 5.1. Dave Carr. Courtesy Nellie Holmes Johnson.

Logging has been a trade at least since the Babylonian hero Gilgamesh journeyed to "the country where cedar is felled" (*Epic* 70). During the era covered by this book, Polish gentiles in Europe worked in the lumber industry in the winter, as recalled by Abraham Livshein (b. 1903):

> "They would put the trunks on sleighs, and pull them by horses out of the woods to the nearest river that was not frozen, tie them together, and float them to Germany." (Coan 157-8)

Lumbering defined the word "strenuous" in the experience of Donnie Grant (Plate 4):

> "Like see that swamp there, cut a road through there. Sometime I'd come into a tree—great, great big old, big old tree. And I'd take it down: I'd get on my knees and I'd take my ax…and sometimes it would take me a day. And then I'd climb the trees. I'd hang my rig up the tree and I'd cut the tops out. Go up a tree and have a belt, stick my ax down there, and I'd go walking up that tree [with spiked boots]. I'd know which way it was going to fall to keep it from falling on me." (Int: 7)

Fig. 5.2. Crosscutting. Horry County Museum.

Not until the middle 1880s did the crosscut saw come into general use (Cain 144). Fig. 5.2 shows four hands on one saw. Young Woodrow Long (b. 1913) and his brother both took a side of the crosscut but "the two of us were no match for our dad" (Int. May 8: 5). "This tool doubled the output of loggers: where a pair of strong men could chop up to twenty five logs in a day, they could saw more than fifty (Earley, "From Cowpens," 9, based on Cain 145 and Napier 128). Nevertheless, this work was done by calories rather than combustion. When Fritz O. Sutter of Clallam County, Washington (b. 1899), was asked to name the most amazing invention of his ninety years, he thought for a while and replied: "The gas-powered chain saw":

> "I just couldn't believe that a huge Douglas fir could be cut down in 15 minutes—something that would take two men and a 'misery whip' dang near a whole day of hard work!" (Int. Oakes)

The chain saw came into use only near the end of the time explored by *Swamp.*

Although naval stores were still being loaded onto the *F.G. Burroughs* when young Franklin rode it in 1914, the industry was doomed like the steamboat that hauled its barrels. As turpentine waned, logging waxed. "In the present scarcity of money," wrote the editor of the *Horry News* in 1874, "owing in a great measure to the low price of turpentine, this cash demand and rise in the timber market will be a Godsend" ("Local Matters" 25 July 1874).

After 1895 the South led the country in log production. The region's peak years were 1907-10, after which primacy shifted to the West ("Lumber"). In Horry County and nearby areas, logging started to flourish about 175 years after the unknown explorers had admired the trees along the February "Waccumaw." Before the end of the 1800s, Burroughs & Collins, realizing that turpentine was on the way out, and needing a more efficient mode of transport than ox- or mule-cart (see Fig. 5.3), began surveying for a railroad to remove timber and lumber from its vast holdings east of the Waccamaw. Then in 1900 the *Black Maria*

Fig. 5.3. Muleteers, caisson, and former trees. Horry County Museum.

chugged alongside that river and across the sand with Arthur Burroughs as the conductor (Fetters 6).

Cutting trees offered both full-time and part-time work. "Logging paid the taxes," declared Woodrow Long, and supplied fathers with Christmas money (Int 8 May: 6; Int. June). Even as a boy of six, he was "big enough to carry the kerosene can that sprayed the saw to keep the turpentine [resin] off it so it could go through the log" (Int. May 8: 5). In the early twentieth century a dozen lumber operations sawed through the county at one time or another. Rilla C. McCrackin (b. 1941) walked to Rehobeth School "through a wet swamp on old hollow cypress logs left by loggers many years before" (Int: 2).

Willie Rowe (who took the steamboat to college) remembered one of the best pool players in Conway, Mr. Howell, who "measured almost all logs and timber which were floated down the Waccamaw River for sale" ("Memories" 9). In high school, Oscar Bellamy (b. 1897) worked as a tally man for Hammer Lumber Company. When the logs floated down Little River, someone guided them into a trough where a bracket caught and pulled them up to the mill by a continuous chain mechanism. When the wood emerged from the saw as lumber, Bellamy kept count of it (W. Thomas, "Little River").

Conway Lumber Company, the town's major industry, operated from 1902 until 1944 at the end of Laurel Street on a flood-prone bend of the Waccamaw. (See Fig. 5.4. Railroad spurs to this plant appear at the bottom of Fig. 2.2.) The commissary was located on the northeast corner of Main St. and Third Ave. At its height, Conway Lumber was the second largest mill on the Atlantic coast and

Fig. 5.4. Conway Lumber Company around 1920. "Conway."

employed up to 400 men to cut timber and saw lumber (Fetters 8; see Fig. 5.5). The plant had two or three signs, according to James D. Sanders, announcing that it cut 100,000 board-feet a day (Int: 11); this figure was the equivalent of nineteen miles, about the distance from Conway to Aynor. See Fig. 5.6.

The grandfather of J. Marion Vaught, Jr. (b. 1923) was a millwright who helped frame up lumber mills. "He and my uncle would get off from Conway Lumber and Burroughs Lumber Company (or W.H. Winborne) and go to Bucksport for a cool drink," non-alcoholic during Prohibition. John M. Vaught, Sr., "cruised timber" (i.e., bought it) for various lumber companies that didn't use ash or maple. He shipped the ash, which was unusually tough, to Louisville Slugger in Kentucky, for bats, and to Santee River Hardwood Company in St.

Figure 5.5. Hands at Conway Lumber Company. Horry County Museum.

When in need of LUMBER
SEE THE LARGE STOCK AT

The "BIG MILL" At Conway

DAILY CAPACITY 100,000 FEET

Grades, Working and Courteous Attention Guaranteed to Everyone.
CONWAY LUMBER COMPANY

Fig. 5.6. Advertisement for Conway Lumber Company, *Horry Herald*, 1937.

Stephens for wagon tongues and spokes (Int. J.M. Vaught, Jr.: 6-8, 17).

The industry seems to have been vital to black men, and vice versa. For example, the Lexington Lumber Company of Conway listed the names of 500 people on its payroll between 1944 and 1950; ten had the notation "white" (Lexington). Will Crawford, a little black man with a high-pitched voice, used to haul his logs to Reaves Ferry and put them in the river; then he would ride the ferry with his ox cart while his oxen swam: "Hey you fellows, *come on, come on*!" (Int. J.M. Vaught, Jr.: 9-10). An abundant supply of labor did little to ameliorate harsh working conditions. An extreme case, reports W.I. Jones, Sr., was one man who worked a lot of Negroes in his logging business; "He said 'You could kill a nigger and hire one and kill a horse and buy another one.' He was rough" (Int. Aug. 11: 36).

As with the turpentine industry, exporting logs meant importing and exporting people: "The logging business brought many newcomers to the area from Sweden and Finland, including the Andersens, Becks, Lehtos, and Lynns" (Ham 6).

What kinds of trees were chopped or sawed? The pine has soft wood and a straight grain, which makes it easy to turn into building materials, shingles, or furniture (B. Floyd, 9 January 2003). Emphasizing the longleaf, Larry Earley writes in "From Cowpens to Fairways":

> "Heart pine lumber [taken from the center] was rot-resistant and had a beautiful finish. Heart pine planks made sturdy and durable floors for mills and factories as well as homes, and they took a fine polish…. Giant squared dimensional timbers from heart pine logs were desirable all over the world for use as foundation supports, uprights, and roof timbers, and also in the construction of mills, warehouses, bridges, trestles, and pilings—anyplace where great strength and durability were demanded." (8)

The well-burning oak, fuel of steamboats, also provided crossties for trains, whether or not saturated with creosote (McIver, p.c.). The sweetgum (*Liquidambar styraciflua*) is pretty and smooth; although it warps as a board, it is used for plywood veneer or cut turned as furniture (Berry, p.c.). See Fig. 5.7.

The water tupelo, or tupelo gum, grows up to 100 feet in swamps of the Southern coastal plain and has soft, light wood. The red maple (*Acer rubrum*) expresses its signature color by bud, stem or leaf almost year-round. The trunk of the river birch seems made of scraps of paper bags torn by an artist and loosely glued (Fig. 5.8). Wet soil feeds the massive trunk of the sycamore (*Platanus occidentalis*, Fig. 5.9), while from the trunk of the black tupelo or blackgum (*Nyssa sylvatica*), branches stick out unimaginatively at right angles (Fig. 5.10).

Fig. 5.7. Sweetgums reach toward winter sky.

Prized by lumbermen around the world for its durability, the bald cypress (*Taxodium distichum*) thrives in flooded swamps and along stream banks, as illustrated in Fig. 5.11. Its needles and most of its twigs drop off in winter, and in deep water, root-growths protrude into the air to form "knees" (Patrides 22).[1]

As Dorothy O. Magrath recalls, the lumber sawed and planed at Eddy Lake "was so nearly flawless that a cut of the tree would be sent as a guarantee that the boards were really cypress" (Snider, "Story," 13). "What we have today we call a yellow cypress," explained W.A. "Sonny" Stilley: "There is almost none of the old black cypress or the red heart cypress, and that required tidewater. Cypress can grow on high land as long as it has enough moisture. But it likes a swamp" (Int: 8).

In 1990 Woodrow Long (b. 1913) mused upon Crabtree Swamp near its junction with Kingston Lake in Conway:

> "These trees here, I guess, were in the bottom of this wet place; and nobody was able to cut them with the equipment they had at that time—with a log cart and a mule team and all. They're too old now for anything but to look at as history. The largest one that I ever remember down here was almost twice as big as this one. All the boys would get in there and make out like they were in an Indian teepee." (Int. March: 9.)

Fig. 5.8. River birch, *Betala nigra*, and muscadine vine.

Twelve years later, despite his own fragility, Woodrow hiked to this same living monument, a reunion preserved in Fig. 5.12. (Afterward the author, a friend and former neighbor, discovered weeds sticking out of his car, which had bounded through Mr. Long's pasture.)

This same nourishing wet element, when high, allowed loggers to extricate logs from the woods. One mill operator (reported a descendant) had to ask his creditors for an extension because there had been no freshet that year.

Early logging—however valuable the products and the jobs—fell on the wrong side of the environmental ledger. Like the turpentine industry, with its destructive boxing and cupping, it had no concern for sustained yield, for replanting, for waiting, for selecting. Clearcutting, moreover, left nothing but ugly and flammable debris. The sapless pines may have resembled the unhealthy schoolchildren as described by Zach McGhee: "There was a lifeless, stupid air about everything and everybody."

Fig. 5.10. Black tupelo. Photo by Reggie Davis.

Fig. 5.9. Sycamore with trumpet creeper and poison ivy.

For an overview of the logging industry, with photographs, see Tom Fetters, "Loggers of Conway and The Independent Republic," *IRQ* 20:1: 4-18.[2]

"'Til you had you a whole big raft for me"

At least one mill transported log-rafts by salt water. When the Winyah Lumber Company first enlisted the *Black Maria* (bought from Conway Lumber Company) to haul logs from a camp at Enterprise crossroads to Garden City Beach, workers lashed them together and towed them over the waves to the mill at Georgetown (Fetters 15). Although rails might be enlisted, a river, swamp, or stream typically furnished at least a segment of the passage. "There was no such thing as a dual-wheel truck around here" in the early 1930s, explains J. M. Vaught, Jr. "The trucks couldn't take more than about three or four logs because the roads were so bad. They normally got to the place they would put a two-wheel trailer on the back with a couple of poles" (Int. March 17: 14).

This advertisement from 1898 specifies the who, what, where, and how of one rafting deal:

To Loggers of hreato [heart] Pine.
I am now buying
Short Leaf Pine Logs
delivered at Bucksville, S.C.

All Logs to be 16 feet, 1 inch: 14 feet, 1 inch, and 12 feet, 1 inch "between pin holes." 80 per cent. to be 16 feet, 1 inch long, balance may be 14 feet and 12 feet....
All Logs must be well Rafted and Pinned at both ends.

Jacob Savage,
Georgetown, S.C.
("To Loggers")

Fig. 5.11. Cut stump of cypress.

How to transport cypress wood? This species, which "favors tidewater and gets thin and scraggly the farther it gets away," will not float when newly cut. Woodrow's father would "dead" the tree—that is, chop a ring around the bottom of the trunk—then wait a season until it was dry and float it down in a freshet (Int. June). During the 1960s Woodrow discovered a cypress log in the creek during road construction, had it hauled out, and fashioned it into a mantel and picnic furniture (Int. June).

Before barges did the job exclusively, rafts were used to transport logs saw-ward. One problem among others: if any logs stayed in the water too long they would sink (Int. Rich). For more on the construction and operation of rafts, see McMillan 46-47. Here are memories of rafting hoisted from the drink of yesteryear.[3]

Fig. 5.12. "One of the greatest Christians" (Ward) next to one of the oldest trees.

Flossie S. Morris (b. 1894). *Miss Flossie remembers when river traffic was active at Bucksville, where the Atlantic Coast Lumber Company operated between 1902-04, and*

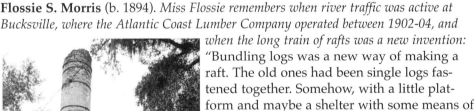

when the long train of rafts was a new invention: "Bundling logs was a new way of making a raft. The old ones had been single logs fastened together. Somehow, with a little platform and maybe a shelter with some means of having a fire for the raft man to cook his meals and a 'raft man' frying pan to fry meat"—to supplement his coffee.

Fig. 5.13. A lone chimney serves as a monument to the Upper Mill, 2003. Courtesy Capt. Henry L. Buck IV. Photo by Paul Olsen.

"My father said that when the old mill was running at Bucksville (Fig. 5.13), he could have walked all the way across the old dock on hewn logs [cut with an axe].... They were hewn to a square." "I don't know how many bundles were fastened together on the river for the tugboat *Robert E. Lee* to pull to Georgetown. At that time rafts and barges were pulled, not pushed." ("Atlantic" 14)

W. Irving Jones, Sr. (b. 1895). *When Conway Lumber Company was operating, tugboats on the Waccamaw would handle a concatenation a half mile long:*
"They were all chained together; they had to have one man on each raft of logs with that pole for when they were going around the curves and crooked places to guide away from the banks and [keep from] getting hung up." (Int. Aug. 18: 4. See Fig. 5.14.)

Oscar Bellamy (b. 1897). *Interviewed by Wyness Thomas in 1988, Bellamy recalled logging*

Fig. 5.14. Chain to connect rafts. Horry County Museum. Photo by Paul Olsen.

done for the Hammer Lumber Company, which operated a mill on the bluff at Little River until the 1920s:
His father, William, made use of oxen to haul logs out of the swamp because their divided hooves allowed them to walk in mucky soil. These animals dragged logs to firm ground to be loaded on carts, chained together, and hauled to the river. There they were rafted together with 100 feet of chain and a "dog"—a piece of metal with a hole in it fastened to each log. (Thomas, "Little River")

Andrew Stanley (b. 1904). *In 1991 "Andr'" was interviewed by C.B. Berry next to the tobacco barn he had constructed out of cypress poles daubed with clay. (See Plate 6.) He was resourceful of stick and grammar:*
"They hauled 'em [the logs]. They cut 'em so long and they rolled 'em in the river, one—down to the edge—and they bored a hole in it. Then they had a long pole. They bored a hole in hit. Then they took a peg—where you cut off the same stump you cut the tree off of, you could use that. And trimmed it good and drove it through the hole into that log. Then you would roll another'n in the river. You'd bore the hole through the binder and drive you a peg through that into the log [*illustrates with stick*]. You bored a hole in the log, too. Then you shoved it further out. Then you bored you another hole, and bored a hole through the log, and drove your peg in that. And you've shove it further out, and to the thing 'til you had you a whole big raft for me out of that tree." Then you would beach that

Fig. 5.15. Pike, 66", with near end broken off. Shove with the point, grab with the hook. Horry County Museum. Photo by Paul Olsen.

raft, made up of fifteen or twenty logs, so the tide wouldn't carry it off; using a like technique you would bind a new one to it, and so forth, until you had five, six, maybe eight rafts in a train. "They'd take an old long pole, get behind 'em, and shove 'em [*punches with stick*], and mind 'em off the banks of the river" and float them down to Conway Lumber Company. (Int. April: 43-4. See Fig. 5.15.)

J. Harry Lee (b. 1908). *Chuckling, Mr. Lee remembered cutting logs and hauling them to the river around 1930:*
"Called them log landings—anyplace we could get 'side the river, that we could clean out a big enough place to roll the logs in the water. We would haul 'em till we get enough in there to get the road full and roll 'em in and raft 'em up...." Although the Stilley Company had big lighters (barges) to haul logs down to the sawmill and plywood mill, rafts were still used. "I have drifted all along the river like that. You didn't have much time to sit. Just when the tide rise, you would go back [upstream]; you had to tie up when it starts rising tide and let it loose when it starts falling."
One, two, or three people would stay aboard the raft with food and water. If you had some dry wood you could build a fire on a few small pieces of tin. "If it rained, you'd just get wet; have an old coat or something." (Int: 8-9)

Chester Jenerette (b. approx. 1909). *At eighteen, he and his brother guided 200 logs down the Waccamaw River to Conway from Pireway, N.C., a journey of one week. Their raft had a steering mechanism, perhaps like the one in Fig. 3.1 (seen as a reflection at the near end), a notched framework for a long rudder (Hill). Although traveling by daylight, they could begin to exploit the moon at Grahamville:*
An oar secured to the front binder allowed his brother to steer, but the raft could not go backwards, only float with the current or falling tide. If caught against the bank or a tree, it was difficult to dislodge. Sometimes people slept on a raft in tents made out of sheets that might be rendered semi-waterproof by powdering them with flour. Rafters cooked over a fire built on a mound of dirt. (W. Thomas, "Pireway")

Anonymous. *A "veteran Waccamaw lumberman" was interviewed in an undated newspaper article reprinted in the* IRQ. *The man, drifting a "batteau" of about 300 logs, was forced to tie up because of a snowstorm:*
"He built a roaring fire on the bank and prepared his supper. Then he built a brush shelter with a bed of pine straw and Spanish moss." There he slept warmly through the storm. "He awoke the next morning, he said, in an igloo. His raft, covered with two feet of snow, was beautifully contrasted by the black water in the Waccamaw River. Carrying tons of snow he resumed his voyage, and two days later arrived in Conway, where no snow had fallen. A crowd lined the banks to admire his long, white procession." On another lonely trip he was navigating by moonlight when a storm came up. "It was dark as ink, save when intermittent flashes of lightning silhouetted the horizon and mirrored it in the deep, dark water. Thunder rocked his raft and echoed among the coves. "The torrential downpour made it impossible to steer the raft and one of the logs rammed a small tree with overhanging limbs. The impact dislodged a giant water moccasin from

the limb of the tree and he fell onto the raft. Then the lightning flashed and the lumberman saw the snake squirming about his feet. He stood motionless for a moment, a cold sweat gushing from his forehead, then plunged blindly into the water and swam to the bank." From there "he caught glimpses of his raft as it rammed the bank, jack-knifed, and finally cracked up. Disassembled by the impact, the logs floated wildly down the river." (Stevens, "Tales," 6)

Woodrow Long (b. 1913). *More routine are the details remembered by Mr. Long, who retired as a mail carrier to work his small farm and big garden:*
The width of a raft depended on the depth of the water. "You might start with two logs up in Maple and add logs as you went downstream." The tide came up to Smith Lake, which drains into Kingston Lake and then the Waccamaw, making the rest of the trip more predictable. "Hauling logs was a real chore. Roads were rough and muddy, and the logs were heavy, and the teams had been worked on farms all year, so any way they could get them there without just dead-pulling them with mules, they did it. "So they would pull them to the nearest creek that had water, and they'd roll them in and raft them. Some of us fell in the river sometimes when we were going down. And at one time there was ice on the water, but we got out all right." To frame the raft they'd put beams across the front and back. Then they'd put a coupling between rafts until they had a train perhaps two or three hundred yards long. His father—the ace chipper—"could make the little square coupling. It would have to fit the hole, and the auger was one size, so the little pin had to have just enough resistance to hold but be easy enough to drive. He could do that off-hand with an ax without any problem at all." Dogwood was the best wood for a coupling because it flexed. (Int. May: 3-5; June)

Evelyn Snider (b. 1907). *In her youth Kingston Lake was the industrial center of Conway. Although the turpentine still had departed for Georgia, there was a cotton gin (which separated seeds and hulls from the fibers), the Burroughs sawmill, and a grist mill (which ground bulk quantities of corn or grain):*
"Logs used to be floated from up the lake. Many a time they would be poled past our house. One day Papa [Charles H. Snider] went down and put me on a boat; he and I rowed to the raft and he asked the men if I could ride. So I did and he followed me on down in the boat. At the bridge, I got in and came on back home." (Int: 2)

Florence Epps (b. 1907). *The first editor of the* IRQ *shares her own memory of rafts:*
"My generation as well as ones older recall the thrilling sight of logs lashed together, rafted down the Waccamaw to be cut into lumber. The farmer who owned the logs would pole them down at ebb tide, sometimes tying up at night or for other reasons. Such a waving as would accompany the approach of these logs, and oh, joy unbounded to find a raft tied to a cypress or willow trunk! Then we children would walk on the logs and sway with the rhythm of the river." ("Have," *IRQ* 1.2: 18)

Marion Moore (b. 1931). *Moore's grandfather, George Cornelius McCormick (b. 1878), floated timber in rafts or in isolation:*
"Back then, you would go in the woods and notch timber and deaden it and then let it die and then cut it. When spring freshets come, you could float it out and down the river to the mills. My grandfather rafted timber and carried it to the Eddy Lake Sawmill, and then it closed. When Bucksport come along, they pulled logs with the boats there and [with the] railroad. You'll find sunken logs now occasionally in some of the creeks that's got timber logs still drove in them that broke loose from the raft and messed around and finally got wet and sunk." (Int: 24)

J. Marion Vaught, Jr. (b. 1923). *They called Ucie Dusenbury a "deadheader":*
His little gasoline boat had an inboard motor, two pontoons about twenty feet apart, and a rack between them. He would go up and down the river with a pike pole 18 or 20 feet long, pry loose a log (which weighed little more than the water), and pull it up "to where he could hook his tongs in it or wrap a rope cable around it. He would wrap the windlass and move them over to the side. He'd balance the logs till they filled up his boat. Then he would go down the river to Conway Lumber Company, or if he had hardwood he might go by Stilley's or Veneer Manufacturing Co. He pulled it right on in to the log pond." (Int. J.M. Vaught, Jr.: 6-7)

"Without one wheel in the water!"

In one case, a logging locomotive had to be hoisted out of the river: see Fig. 5.16. For railroads temporary and permanent began to supplement rafts, then to supplant them.

When loggers had reached trees located too far from the swamp to float back, small trains, called trams, carried the logs on temporary wooden rails to the river, mill, or main line. (Notice the railroad track in the foreground of Fig. 1.1.) Conway Lumber Company even owned "a track-laying machine, a steam shovel to build up an embankment, and a dedicated train of sand cars for continuous track building into new sections of the swamp" (Fetters 14).

Myrtle Beach itself was at first a logging town. The ubiquitous *Black Maria*, which had originally chugged along tramroads in North Carolina, started hauling timber back to the Waccamaw in 1901. The father of Mrs. W.H. McNeill ran a locomotive in Myrtle Beach: "a log train from that big swamp where they haul out their big cypress logs and all out to the beach where the mill was. They first had a shingle mill and then they got lumber" (Int. McNeill: 5).

Dave Carr (nephew of Sabe Rutledge, the former slave) worked for logging companies as a barber, cook, and railroad master ("mahstuh"). Later he drew on this expertise in France: "They'd blow up the railroad and I'd take rail on the train ties and a saw and a drill so they could cut the railroad and could bore a hole through it, put bolts in it and cool it down" (Int: 10). "He always did schemy work," declared his brother Albert—i.e., brainwork, notably as a foreman for Conway Lumber Company (Int: 9).

Fig. 5.16. Derailment, place and date unknown. Horry County Museum.

Willie Page (b. 1910) left Aynor to work on the logging railroad owned by Camp Manufacturing in Marion County, an outfit that moved around, cutting through Santee Swamp toward Charleston: "I drove them spike many a days until I was tired. It was a 10-pound hammer" (Int: 17). One such line ran "between Ketchuptown and Lake Swamp" (Fig. 5.17). Ruth Ham writes that abundant timber in that area was hauled to the main line, which cut the corner of Horry, and on to the giant Schoolfield Lumber Mill in Mullins (6).

Ghosts of such lines criss-cross Horry farmland, new-growth forests, malls, back yards, and golf courses. For a map, see Fetters 4; for a photograph, see Fig. 5.18.

Eugenia Buck Cutts (b. 1912). *Eugenia's aunt, Jessamine Buck, married D.V. Richardson, "the first man in Horry County to abandon rafting of logs down the river":* "He put in the first railway into the hitherto inaccessible swamp area, greatly enlarging production, but this was viewed with distrust by his associates. My father [H.L. Buck III, b. 1872] and Uncle Frank [A.] Burroughs, after an overnight visit there, returned to Conway saying, 'I don't know what this man Richardson has got, but he's sure fixing to lose it all with railroad logging!' And 'Uncle Sip,' an old inhabitant of that area, upon viewing the railroad engine, which had been shipped to Conway by barge, scratched his head and said, 'I don't see how it'll run without one wheel in the water!'" ("Industry" 33)

Fig. 5.17. Ketchuptown crossroads, 2003.

Albert Carr (b. 1906). *How did they build a railway through the swamp? Carr, the bridge-builder of Chapter 2, now almost a hundred years old, almost blind, explained the process while tracing his finger on the back of the interviewer's hand:* "You would lay it across the side on a hill and get to low land. Then you would build something like a truss [a rigid framework of beams]. You would lay logs across and across, up and down the swamp. Then you would come back down and cut some big heavy poles. You would stand them together and pin them down on them logs. Then you would go on and lay your train back up with your crosstie….

5.18. Tramway in Eddy Lake. Courtesy George N. Magrath, Sr.

"There would be a man on this side who said 'O.K., put a rail!' and you pulled the rail by him on that side. You had a man on this side who said, 'All right, pull a rail,' and he would pull that and jam it together. Then they nailed it down with a spike [*illustrates with a poke of the finger*]. They would build like that until they get across…. Some places it would be a little hilly and they would take the bulldozers and push it down." (Int. 18-19).

J. Marion Vaught, Jr. (b. 1923). *A logging company ran a track from Jones Big Swamp to the Waccamaw:* One Plymouth locomotive used an internal power unit. "Had a chain drive on it that drove the wheels. The railroad was not completely aligned, and as a result, the flanges on the wheels—from the engine and the cars—would rub the rails, and you could hear it squealin' and a-squawkin' for a long ways. You could hear it from the time it started way down in the swamp till it came clean outside and got all the way to Bear Bluff on a calm day." (Int. J. & E. Vaught: 2)[4]

Thomas W. Rich, Jr. (b. 1934). *Rich, Sr., born in 1910, logged from North Carolina to the Santee River. His son remembers his father as determined to bag the elusive hardwood. A skidder was a tree, pole, or other vertical device to which cables were attached that, rewound, dragged cut logs to a loader (Fig. 5.19):*

There was no way to get a skidder back there in the swamp where the cypress, gum and tupelo flourished. It would have gotten tangled up among the trunks and cypress knees.

So working mainly with blacks from Bucksport, he built tracks up on tree stumps as part of the roadbed. They put a "rehaul" skidder on a flatcar and backed it in. The loggers put down their cross-cuts and hooked the tongs into the log; the skidder pulled them back to the steam locomotive (later converted to diesel). Another skidder had a boom that loaded them onto two or three cars. The locomotive pulled them out to high ground, where they were loaded onto trucks. Or the train pulled them to the riverbank, where they were loaded onto barges. (Int. Rich.) See Fig. 5.20.

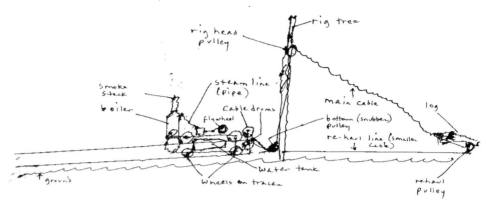

Fig. 5.19. Sketch by J. M. Vaught, Jr. Main cable pulls log as rehaul cable (below) winds out.

Fig. 5.20. Locomotive pulls three log cars of hardwoods from Waccamaw Swamp, Loggers: Thomas W. Rich and George Pino. Courtesy Col. Thomas W. Rich, Jr.

Donnie Grant (b. 1887). *Donnie worked for Trexler Lumber Company, an outfit that "built tram roads to Grier Swamp on the south, to Maple Swamp and the Baker land on the west, and to Pireway, N.C., on the east." The foreman came to build the railroad tracks in 1907 and later supervised the workers and bought timber (Rowe, "Memories," 14; Epps, "Captain," with photograph):*

"There was a foreman by the name of George Byrd. He kind of liked me, and he'd take me on to an old lever car he had. He'd run up and down the railroad. He said, 'Donnie, you set right here, and put your foots over here; you won't get hurt.' And I'd sit up there and I'd ride all day with him, and me and him would talk." (Int: 4)

The tram locomotives "looked like a little tumble-along comin' through the woods. They were small and there was some on 'em were a pretty good size. They had them named as No. 2 and No. 1, and No. 3, and No. 4, like that. They all was a smaller size. And the one they called No. 2, that was the one that took the logs to the main line—I mean to the mill. And these others, they'd pull them out of the swamp out to the main line. And then they'd couple up and she'd take them on into the mill." (6)

James R. Holbert, Sr. (b. 1890). *As a new graduate of Burroughs High School, he worked for Gardner & Lacey Lumber Company on the Waccamaw River:*

"I worked on the locomotive as flagman and engineer. We would haul the logs from the woods to the river where they were pulled off the flat cars and dumped in by a big tackle [pulley] hung in a high tree. In the river the logs were tied together into a raft then pulled to Georgetown by a tug. We would drive the locomotive into Conway to pick up supplies from Burroughs & Collins. Our line joined the main line at Red Hill." (19)

Andrew Stanley (b. 1904). *"Had a railroad run from Conway right out there" (Holbert's line):*

"I can show you the old print [roadbed] of it now—from here and the Little River Neck." The train hauled longleaf pine—"got a big burr" [cone]. [For view of raised bed along Highway 90, see video footage at end of Int. April.]

Franklin G. Burroughs (b. 1908). *As a child Burroughs lived on Main Street in Conway, near a V in the tracks:*

"The Conway Lumber Company ran a log dummy and log cars out the Atlantic Coast Line Railway toward Aynor; they were logging over in the Little Pee Dee River Swamp. And I can remember cars coming in there with logs that were as high as a man. The diameter was high as a man's head." (Int: 16)

Flossie S. Morris (b. 1894). *She describes the "donkey engine" [a small locomotive] that brought logs to the Bucksport Mill:*
"It didn't look like a donkey to me…. It came puffing back to the river where the logs were bundled by a horse that circled around." ("Atlantic" 14)

Agnes M. Gause (b. 1919). *Retired from AVX in Myrtle Beach, Ms. Gause remembers the way loggers were transported from Bucksport:*
"They used to go on an old train you call a 'locomotor' and go way back in the swamp. And you could hear it coming way back in the swamp. It would come in just like a train on the track." (Int: 9)

"Beside the railroad—a long string of 'em"

Large, permanent mills existed in town, but if they operated out in the country the logger, like the turpentiner, might be cut off from civilization. Quarters for both the mill and the remote camp, furthermore, were segregated by race.

Fig. 5.21. Logging camp near Port Harrelson or perhaps in Nixonville, S.C., probably in the 1940s. Courtesy Col. T.W. Rich.

When the Trexler Lumber Company set up a camp above the Dead Line, some people tried to frighten the Negroes away, but Foreman George Byrd put a stop to it (J.P. Cartrette, "Allen," 42). See Figures 5.21 and 5.22.

Before fireproof shingles, wooden ones were hand-made at sawmills. To do so the worker used a froe. The type illustrated in Fig. 5.23 had a handle with a heavy blade jutting perpendicular to it. The worker positioned the blade near the edge of a log, and whapped the top of it with a heavy mallet to cleave off a thin slab.

"Ground sawmills" would move from place to place, according to Thurman Anderson (b. 1909). (See Fig. 5.24.) They were set up about seven miles apart, "close enough for most everybody to take their logs to when they needed some lumber" (Int: 2). One of these outfits was run by Ed Andersen's grandfather Oscar (son of the Ole who had helped construct the *F.G. Burroughs*). Oscar had come to Horry after the Georgetown mill burned, circa 1910. Laborers moved from tract to tract around Horry, Georgetown, Charleston, and Berkeley Counties, sending most of the wood to Dargan Lumber Company in Conway and commuting home on weekends. Ed worked every summer from the time he was nine years old, in 1945, until 1953: "I learned to drive a lumber truck at 12 years old, and Uncle Dave Carr taught me to drive a mule." Anderson believes that the small sawmill operators disappeared in the early 1950s due to competition with large companies for woodlands—a situation aggravated by the cutting of small trees for pulpwood, used to make paper products (Donald E. Andersen).

W.H. McNeill (b. 1885). *McNeill began working for Burroughs & Collins shortly before World War I. For a time he had a job at the commissary, when there was a giant swamp near Myrtle Beach:*
"They started out making cypress shingles and decided there was too much waste; [so] they pulled

Fig. 5.22. Moving from stump to stand. Horry County Museum.

up a mill and sold the biggest cypress, I know it was, in the world. Tremendous big logs…. They tell me them people that live in the North doesn't believe it was lumber…"[*laughter*]. (Int: 7) Burroughs & Collins "worked a big bunch at that sawmill. Mostly colored people. There were three or four white families on the beach." One day the bookkeeper left to go seining for fish in the swash. Soon after he left, the mill-whistle blew and a crowd of blacks came in. Everyone wanted a token—"big round pasteboard things with dollars and half-dollars printed on them—called them 'checks.'

Well, I commenced looking in drawers and I found one, pulled it open, and I give every one of them a check to Leroy Allen. I'd ask him his name, if he worked that day—'Yes,' I'd give him a check" (11. See Fig. 5.25)

Donnie Grant (b. 1887). *Grant handled a saw many decades before a cane. He "went from one job to another" as he became a skilled logger. For his first job, he would arise at 4 a.m. on Monday, cross the Waccamaw on the ferry he had once operated, walk to Hickory Grove, and cross the swamp to Allen. On Saturday night he would return home by the same route:*
After his days of riding around with Mr. Byrd, he joined the team crew and received a pair of mules. "The boss man told me, he said, 'Now I want to learn you how to be a driver. We're not looking for you to pull logs like the rest of these all; but you just take these mules and pit up and down the road, and when you can pull a log, pull a log.' "I took them mules, and I saw that I was man enough to holler at them. And I put them to work, and I'd bring in just as many logs as the rest of them would. They'd make a lotta 'miration ["myration"] at me, and I drove wagon until I learned to do that good. Then they took me and put me to a skidder to top load [train] cars. A skidder was a machine that had a big, high tree—and the blocks all up there, a line, and they'd pull logs out of the swamp. And I top-loaded them logs on the cars until I learned to handle the loader. Then they put me up on the machine, and I loaded the logs. And I done that for awhile until

Fig. 5.23. Froe. S.C. Tobacco Museum. Photo by Paul Olsen.

I got a little bit higher. "Then they put me to the levers…. Like this is the skidder sitting right here [*points to interviewers' photograph*]. Here is a drum [i.e. that rewinds the cables]. And right here, that's sort of what you give it the gas with. The one right here is what you press down on to pull your log by." (Int: 3-5; 7)

Paul Sarvis (b. 1888). *In what he calls "them-time," Sarvis, last seen rescuing an ox from Socastee Bridge, handled the commissary for lumber companies. Because he moved around so much, he and his wife remained engaged for five years:*
"Well, after we got married I was still in the log woods and just be with her on weekends where I board there in Andrews [a lumber boom-town in Georgetown County]. And sometimes she

Fig. 5.24. Ground sawmill. Horry County Museum.

could go out there and spend a week with me…where she could board with some people that lived right at the camp. The camps [i.e., cabins furnished by the Atlantic Coast Lumber Company]…wasn't much bigger than this room…. Like you see little children build little dirt houses with their foot…. And they built so that when they moved from one place to the other they could put it on a log car…. The average camp was about, well, just room enough for two. One man have a bed in that end and one in this end. And they had a stove in the middle." The last time he worked in the woods, Conway Lumber Company had what it called a "house," which was a good place to live. "I just got forty dollars [a month], but I had to pay all my expense out of that. Left me about ten or fifteen dollars." (Nichols 20-21)

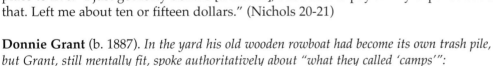

Fig. 5.25. Merchandise coupons, company store. Horry County Museum.

Donnie Grant (b. 1887). *In the yard his old wooden rowboat had become its own trash pile, but Grant, still mentally fit, spoke authoritatively about "what they called 'camps'":*
"Beside the railroad—a long string of 'em. Sometimes there would be two or three stay in a camp; and we'd have what you called old bunk beds in those days." "We'd have our fireplace outside, and we'd sit on out there and cook our food; and then we'd go inside and eat, fix our bucket, and set it up for the next morning. We'd go to work sometimes 6 o'clock, sometimes 6:30. Worked till 12 and knock off; and then we'd go back, and we would work till 6. We didn't stop for a rainy day unless it got too bad…. We'd always have us a [dry] pair overalls, a pair of pants and a shirt, or something in there. When we'd go on back in wet, we'd pull off our wet clothes and put them on and dry our clothes, then, for the next day." "We had to buy our own food. And of course we could take a dollar 'long then and buy what you could buy here now with fifty dollars. You could take 10 cents, buy a piece of meat that long. Take a dime and you'd buy a quart of rice. The grits—you had no limit to them." (Int: 9)

Albert Carr (b. 1906). *"If it rained and you knocked off, you ain't got no work.*

"Somebody else didn't want to work, hire another man. You had a little raincoat, but it ain't doing much good. It would come a rain sometimes and you can't work with a coat on." Heat was provided by a "trash-burner," which expelled smoke through a pipe in the wall. "You would wake up in the morning and make a fire out the door." (Int. 18)

Alice Little Whitson (b. approx. 1900). *The Eddy Lake Cypress Lumber Company was set up around 1890-91. Logs were hauled to the mill by tugboat from up the Pee Dee River, or floated down from logging camps; then they were sawn into lumber for ocean-going schooners to the North. Mrs. Whitson's father, John W. Little, was a partner in the venture with George Officer (who later taught bookkeeping to Frances C. Burroughs):*
"As a child of five, I thought Eddy Lake was a paradise. Endless sandhills to play in, huge live oaks to climb, a mysterious river to explore, a variety of unusual pets, the world was ours. The schooners that came from Baltimore to load lumber were always exciting. We became friendly with the captains—they brought gifts to the children and let us have the run of the ship. Both our house and the Officers' was full of visitors." (10)

James Clyde Williamson (b. 1906). *Almost ninety years old, Williamson said that his father had approached Capt. Jim Ellis of the Hammer Lumber Company and asked for a job:*
He became the foreman of six or eight men with crosscut saws who were paid one cent per tree, and he also became a saw filer. The Williamson family lived in logging camps and moved about from time to time. James recalled small boats named *Kitty Hawk* and *Togo*, as well as commercial craft such as *Prince* and *Atlantic City*, which unloaded freight at a long wharf extending into the woods. (Berry, "James")

Leola Hicks Burroughs (b. approx. 1912). *Interviewed by Wyness Thomas in 1993, Burroughs spoke with Gullah-influenced vocabulary, grammar, and intonation. As a girl she had two choices in life, the saw or the froe:*
Leola, her father, and her grandfather crossed the Pee Dee River on a ferry, then walked on unpaved roads from the Pee Dee Section of Georgetown County to Myrtle Beach. Depending on when their jobs were completed, they left for home on Friday or Saturday. Grandfather carried a lantern so they could find their way along wagon paths. Working like a man, she sawed logs and carried shingles. ("Interview" 16)

Agnes M. Gause. (b. 1919). *While logging in Nixonville, her father had to cobble up his own hut:*
"Boston said he took some old logs, then dug holes and set them upright. He nailed some tin around the frame and over the top. Taking a big drum, he cut a door in it for a heater. He cooked on it and slept in that little house for a couple of days during the week while working. The big boss made him overseer to make sure that the others worked. On Thursday night they would set traps for 'coon, then come home on Friday and sell the hides." "When working for the Richardson Lumber Mill in Bucksport, he was stacking lumber for 90 cents a *day*. When that part of the company went down, they made cypress shingles to cover houses. They dug stumps for 10 cents each and a bag of hog cracklings if you were a good worker." ("History" 4)

Mary Sannie Gause *Interviewed by Etrulia P. Dozier in 1975, she remembers the shingle mill before it burned in 1918:*
"Men graded the shingles, bunched them into bunches, and they were shipped to their destination on the boat *Louisa*. My husband Wheeler worked at the mill." (Cutts, "Formation," 15)

J. Marion Vaught, Jr. (b. 1923). *In the 1930s Vaught's grandfather allowed one company to establish a camp between Jones Big Swamp and the Waccamaw, where he ran the commissary:*
The track split off for a service track. Whites lived on one side of Thomas Road—there were four camps about the size of a boxcar—while blacks lived across the cattle guard by the blacksmith's shop. "Sometimes they stretched wires between four trees—had a tarpaulin with weights in hot times. Lean to's. Old boxes with peep-holes, handmade with vertical boards and laps." "That is where he got rid of all his sweet potatoes and cracklins." (Int. J.M. Vaught, Jr.: 15.)

"Stay all week and then go home on the weekend. Some didn't care about going home—nobody there because they were single. One of them was Howard Hughes. He was from Union section in Georgetown County and married a girl from the community. He had what we called a Geechee brogue. If somebody asked him which log should come next, he'd say [*imitating with enjoyment*], 'Doesn't make any difference—all them chillum gotta go.'" (Int. J. & E. Vaught: 29]

"I wore out a couple pairs of brogan shoes": Making Plywood

Plywood, introduced into the United States in 1865, is a "manufactured board composed of an odd number of thin sheets of wood glued together under pressure with grains of the successive layers at right angles" (*Columbia*). Its production became an important industry in the Conway area. One mill, founded in 1932 by Walter I and II, was Stilley Plywood, which paid the hands weekly in silver dollars (B. Stilley). An earlier plant just downstream on the Waccamaw was Veneer Manufacturing Company, which in the days before cardboard made the sides, tops, and bottoms for plywood boxes. (For more technical and historical details, see Int. J.M. Vaught, Jr.: 8-9).

In 2003, more than fifty years after working there, J.C. Bennett (b. 1928) explored the brick pillars that once raised the floor above the low ground, and the iron rods and concrete vats that now protruded from vines. He explained how wooden cylinders became boards composed of thin layers.

• Shave the bark

"One person's job was to take an ax or something and get all the bark off because the bark and dirt on the 'blocks' or logs themselves had a tendency to dull the lathe blades which cut the veneer."

• Steam the log

Each log had to be submerged in hot water. "That was real dangerous because the water would splash and sometimes burn people–not bad, but for safety reasons they built vats on top of the ground." (See Figure 5.26.) Little rails pushed them back into the vat where live steam was turned on them to soften them up for cutting. Heavy canvas covered the vats.

• Peel the log

"They would cut it at different thicknesses. I guess a 32nd or a 16th or an 8th of an inch. Really few times would they cut as much as a quarter because the thicker it was, the less pliable it was." They would

Fig. 5.26. "Who'd have ever thought that that would be history?"

hold the log up on a chain and then the automation would put chucks [clamps] in each end of the lathe, or "peeler," and bring those chucks together. "Then when they released the chain, the log would start rotating and wood would come off like unto a toilet tissue roll. "The guys would get the veneer that was coming off and run it back on the 'table,' they called it. Two or three guys would run back and take it about 60 feet and drop it. When they got it breaking off at the lathe, another guy would get a piece and he would run down there and it was your turn again. I wore out a couple pairs of brogan shoes [i.e., heavy, ankle-high] one summer doing that job."

• Glue the sheets

"Upstairs, over at the glue pot, they had hundred-pound bags of soybean meal and a big old vat. You would put these chemicals in the soybeans and mix the glue. They had a little lever which they pulled out, and a roller. They put glue all over the roller and when they put a piece of veneer through it—which was the trough vat, the centerpiece—they would get it saturated with glue. Then you would have a back and a face. Then you would have another back, a cross-band, and a face. You would keep building it up and building it up."

• Press the sheets

"Then you would put it under great pressure. They would put big steel buckles over the top of it and twist those buckles overnight for 24 hours. Then it would be dry enough to tear down.

• Clip the sheets

"You take the veneer that was just dried to a clipper. You had a little treadle [a pedal or lever operated by the foot] and you would mash a little button and it would cut the veneer square. It was dangerous. Right after the clipper, they would have those pieces cut into different pieces of veneer based on the orders they had taken. They would build so many pieces—say, 2 feet by 4 feet of veneer and then rag it on each edge. Then you would put it through a power saw and then through the rip saw [coarse-toothed]. You would square it up to the sizes which you wanted.

"You'd see that stump go up in the air": Building the Waterway

Another form of logging deepened creeks, cleared swamps, and dug through higher land.

Donnie Grant (b. 1887). *"Well, I should remember because I done a lot of work on there":*
When they first started, Donnie got a job working with an old man they called "Dynamite King." "He'd get out there in

that water up to here, and I'd tote dynamite to him; and he'd tell me which way to go, you know, to get out of the danger spot. He'd put that dynamite down on it. They had him a long rod; and he'd crouch down on under a stump, so he'd say, 'Alrighty, buddies,' he'd say, 'Come back this way now.' And I'd be floated in that water back there a ways. He had a little wire…and he'd touch them wires together like that, and you'd see that stump go up in the air!" Not afraid of the water, Donnie worked with the King until they got some skidders to pull the stumps and logs. "Then I hooked tongs in the woods. I hooked the one skidder and Keeler Sumter [Sumpter?] hooked to the other one, and we cleaned that whole—right over here—all the way up." (Int: 20. Keeler was one of the laborers who paddled to the Waterway Bridge.)

Andrew Stanley (b. 1904). *"Mr. John" Vaught, Sr., would come from Nixonville to hire laborers:*
"I holped clear the right-of-way." "We was cutting the tops off 'em and piled 'em up, burning 'em"; others dynamited the stumps and roots out. (Int. April: 27-28)

"When will we be going back?"

Loggers, sawyers, and their families could feel the sharp metal teeth of disease, isolation, and accident.

Born in 1885, Mrs. Dorothy O. Magrath was interviewed by Miss Evelyn Snider about life in the Eddy Lake Cypress Lumber Company. The very water that nourished the prized trees bred the mosquito:

> "Whenever a member died, a coffin was hand made, fashioned from the first cypress boards. Then the women lovingly padded and lined it with the softest and loveliest of materials. Most often these were for infants and small children because infant mortality was high, especially during the summer when malaria took its grim toll." ("Story" 13) "Getting anywhere from Eddy Lake was a challenge. In order to escape from the scourge of malaria, every June the family moved to their summer home at Murrells Inlet…." Her father "would arrange a date with Burroughs & Collins for the family and all their belongings (including cows and chickens) to get on the boat at Bucksport," then disembark at Wachesaw for the trip overland by oxcart. (11)

Alice Little Whitson (b. approx. 1900) reports that her father lost a hand in the planing mill at Eddy Lake, and her mother made another kind of sacrifice:

> It seemed a paradise for a child, "Yet over it all hung an air of tragedy, for by 1903, the dread malaria had already claimed the lives of three members of our family…. My mother was frightened, and wanted desperately to get back up North, where we children got the impression that people lived forever. The early days must have been very hard for her, coming as she did from the heart of New York City, which she loved." The sawmill adventure, originally intended to be temporary, dragged on. "By this time my mother had given up asking the old question 'When will we be going back?' Secretly, I don't think my father ever wanted to. It was my mother who, in her own words, was 'poised for flight.' She regarded the whole episode as so temporary that she resented spending money for 'good' furniture or in any way indicating that we were putting down our roots to stay." (10)

Arthur Burroughs started a mill across Kingston Lake from Snow Hill, homestead of the Burroughs family. His sister Lucille tells this story:

> "He had put on a new pair of leather gloves and when he attempted to show one of the [mill] hands something about a saw, his glove got caught and his arm badly mangled. He almost died of shock. He used to tell me that he would rather I tie his neckties and shoes because Aunt Effie cried every time—not that I didn't feel like it." ("Some" 13-14)

Boston Mishoe, working for a logging outfit in Nixonville, rode a more dangerous form of transport than a loco-motor, as his daughter recalls:

> The company "had log trucks without metal bodies, and riders sat back-to-back on coupling poles. Two men had fallen off and gotten killed, so riders were very scared after that. Boston would ride the truck to a place in the swamp where they would continue by paddling boat. Ice would sometimes cause trucks to skid on the road." (Gause, "History," 4)

She remembers a vivid detail about winter logging:

> "When my father was working [near Bucksport], now he had to wear hip boots. And when it was cold, I've known him to come home and—it was so cold, the old overall pants they'd wear them with the bosom on 'em, straps—it was frozen. And when he'd pull them off, they stood on the floor just like that"[*illustrates*]. (Int: 19)[5]

Between seed and lumber came water.

The swamp nourished the wood and then suspended it as logs–hardwood and pine, sometimes with cat-faces inscribed by turpentine workers. The swamp challenged the logger with his mules, oxen, wagon, tongs, and chain, and it safeguarded at least one giant cedar as a teepee. But the skidder, loader, and tram eventually probed so deep into the Waterland that the only unlogged forest in the vicinity rose underwater about fifteen miles off Murrells Inlet at the prehistoric mouth of the Pee Dee River (Gayes).

The hoof-marks of oxen have faded into the muck, but the "print" of the tramroad still exists as a tree-overgrown elevation or depression, as a narrow sandy road, or as the name on a street sign. Gone are the metal dog, the donkey engine, and the drop-in moccasin. Nobody hears the locomotor, the all-day back-and-forth of the two-man saw, the dynamited stump, the squealin' and a-squawkin' wheels, the rain falling on the logger's tin roof or on the rafter's floured sheet. Poles no longer connect rafts or mind 'em off the bank. Gone are the auger and peg, the lever car, the payment token, the spikes for wooden rails, the 'coon trap of the logger, the froe, engine Number 4, drums to rewind a cable or shelter a fire. Mr. Rich no longer devoutly carries the saws out of the woods on Friday to sharpen them on Saturday.

In 1954 the Lovells' van crossed into Conway just downstream from where the *Black Maria*, half a century earlier, had dumped log-loads into the current. Just downstream from that bridge, ten years earlier, the Conway Lumber Company had ceased operating. Upon that river, as logs or board-feet, had floated a great portion of Horry County and not a little of coastal North Carolina.

Even as the industry reached its peak around the first decade of the twentieth century, a new source of cash was ascendant. Unlike the tree, its value resided in the leaves; it had no sap yet was sticky; and it took only a year to grow but had to be planted twice.

Notes

[1] In 1701, John Lawson made a horseshoe-shaped journey through the Carolinas and, although he skirted the future Horry County, he saw the kind of bald cypress that must have lent majesty to the Waterland: "These Trees are the largest for Height and Thickness, that we have in this Part of the World; some of them holding thirty-six Foot in Circumference" (103). To envision the size of this trunk, imagine sixteen loggers taking a nap on the stump with their heads in the center and their thirty-two boots pointing outwards.

[2] Did turpentiners beat the loggers to environmental pillage? A government report in the *Horry Herald* (1893) claims that tests on "bled and unbled" longleaf show that "the resinous contents of the heart wood are in no wise affected by the bleeding; the oleoresins of the heart wood being non-fluid, the whole turpentine flow is confined to the sap wood" ("Tapping"). An editorial in the same issue offers a rebuttal:

> "One, two or three years working of pines may not affect the strength or durability of the timber, but several years working will so impair and deteriorate the timber, even the heart, as to render it very inferior to the timber from untapped trees...." The tapped trees "look sickly and lifeless" while the untapped are "green, vigorous, and healthy" ("The Long Leaf").

According to the Secretary of Agriculture in 1921,

> "The method of exploitation commonly followed during the last hundred years is crude, wasteful, destructive, and sadly shortsighted.... The trees are exhausted in from four to six years and turned over to the sawmill man showing a loss due to turpentining of from 20 to 50 per cent. (Meredith 90)

Earley affirms that although turpentining killed trees (and incurred the hatred of loggers), it did not damage the strength of the lumber. He refers to a USAD document by Gerry, 1935 (p.c.).

[3] Originally the Waterland was more raft-worthy. An example is Lake Swamp, on the edge of Pleasant View community. According to Ruby Williamson, when settlers first arrived, "cedar, cypress, pine, white oak, red oak, ash, poplar, holly, and many other varieties of timber grew there, with tupelo gum and sweet gum and cherry nearby." A fairly navigable stream ran through the swamp, and down it floated rafts of logs through the Gerrald Lakes (probably a vestigial course of the Little Pee Dee), and from there to Galivants Ferry and other points. "Through the years, however, because of hunters and people cutting wood and throwing logs across the stream, it has been stopped up" (12).

In many other parts of Horry, human activity has altered the old drainage patterns. Roads and highways divided swamps as they did neighborhoods. The Intracoastal Waterway served as a 43-mile-long ditch, while the Simpson Creek flood control project converted bottomland to acreage. Woodrow Long points out that farms themselves make a double change in hydrology: "There wasn't so much cultivated land, so the water stayed in place. Farmland tended to fill in the streams because of soil-runoff; and the ditches cut to take water off fast added to its velocity and took more soil to the swamp" (Int. June).

[4] The Plymouth Locomotive Co., named for a town in Ohio, built industrial diesel-powered locomotives for light-industry service (Copeland).

[5] Earlier working as a raftsman, J. Harry Lee (b. 1908) became a foreman at the finishing department of Stilley's Mill in Conway:

> "I was running a sander, and it got to messing up. It wasn't running smooth. I got to examining it, to try to see what was the matter. I shut the thing off and run my hand under there to see if I could feel what was making it cut bad, and I hit the end—well, knocked my finger off [*holds up left hand with top of middle finger missing*]. And I worked there till the mill burned down." (Int: 7)

CHAPTER 6
THE WEED

"That man didn't farm that place good and it was sandy to grow a crop in. Nothing came up good. Walter went with me over there and he said, 'This is nice land—this land will grow some tobacco. You get that man to furnish you with good fertilizer.'"
Neal McCracken (b. 1898), Int. Aug. 26: 14.

Fig. 6.1. Boy with tobacco drag. Horry County Museum.

Nicotiana tabacum has a close relationship with long-disappeared water, for "Tobacco likes sandy soil" (C. Munnerlyn).

Over thousands and millions of years, the ocean helped to weather rocks transported by rivers from the Piedmont and the Blue Ridge Mountains (the easternmost range of the Appalachians). When waves withdrew, they left upland particles mixed with mineral remains of sea life that had sunk to earth. As time passed, organic matter joined this mix to produce a sandy loam. (See Fig. 6.2.) Such soil offers a home to 'bacca plants, which do not require much nitrogen, a nutrient that can be managed with fertilizer (Gooden).

According to Taylor, farmers trying to get the best yield and quality for flue-cured tobacco (i.e., dried by pipes filled with heated air) "would strive to grow a big plant that became nitrogen deficient near maturity, a process that required sandy, coastal soil" (16). Eldred E. Prince, Jr., notes that early tobacco farmers valued sandy acreage because it imparts a lighter color to the leaf. As the years passed, they were able to exploit richer soil by using different varieties of tobacco. He also points out that sandy fields do not become sodden after heavy rains (p.c.). In any case, this same loose, gritty material that John Bartram judged "very poor sandy soil" in 1765, that engulfed wheels and hooves, provided a surfside highway, impeded construction of the railroad, hung up steamboats on a bend, and anchored the longleaf, welcomed the weed.

H.L. Buck reported that his father, Henry L. Buck II, experimenting with tobacco in the latter part of the 1800s, put it "in a sorry piece of land where I used to hunt rabbits" (C. Thompson 20). The father of J.C. "Don" Ayers came to Mt. Olive Community from Robeson County, N.C., in 1882, whereupon he bought some of the vast holdings of the Minceys and began farming. In 1898 he planted tobacco and happily sold it in Mullins for an average of about 8 cents a pound. "I remember his saying, 'As long as I can make $50 per acre, I guess I'll continue to plant it'" (Ayers 15). Around 1911 George Holliday of Galivants Ferry said, "Look at that big old cotton patch–made more money on that little six

Fig. 6.2. Sandy field along Pee Dee Highway at the western edge of the Horry Barrier.

acres of tobacco than we did all that" (Int. S. Lewis: 6).

In 1899 an advertisement for the Horry Warehouse in Conway touted "the weed" as a substitute for an all-cotton crop and bragged: "Our water transportation gives us an advantage over any other point in the Tobacco belt" ("Horry Warehouse"). But as Prince notes, tobacco ended up being shipped mainly by rail from Conway to North Carolina and Virginia (p.c.).

How did broadleaf succeed longleaf? Tobacco had meant the type called Burley, which was dark, strong, grown in Northern latitudes, and air-cured (hung out to dry on the stalk). It was smoked in pipes or cigars, inhaled as snuff, or chewed—for example the Brown Mule brand that furnished a seat for little Cartrette. Lucille Godfrey reports that one woman, glad that a promising helper had stopped chewing tobacco, was "a little dashed when the girl told her that she did not mind quitting…because she liked dipping snuff a lot better" ("Some" 16).

Then in 1880 a patent was awarded for the manufacture of cigarettes by machine. In *Long Green: The Rise and Fall of Tobacco in South Carolina*, Eldred E. Prince, Jr., explains that the popularity of this inhalant increased the demand for a mild variety. The dried-yellow leaf was invented accidentally by a farmhand who, having fallen asleep in the curing barn, tried to compensate by piling logs on the fire. Cultivation of Bright Leaf then expanded beyond the "Old Belt" of North Carolina and Virginia into new areas. "One of these was the eastern corner of South Carolina—the Pee Dee region"—usually defined as those counties touched by either of the Pee Dee Rivers (Big or Little): Horry, Georgetown, Williamsburg, Marion, Dillon, Florence, Darlington, and Marlboro (*Long Green*, xv, xx, 47).

In 1887, the same year a bill was entered that would have outlawed cigarettes in South Carolina ("General"), tobacco seeds were advertised in the *Horry Herald* (21 Jan.: 3). The Horry Warehouse (J.E. Coles, Manager) also advertised "The Money Crop." This newspaper began to print advice and encouragement on the subject of tobacco-growing–how to prepare plant beds, sow seeds, top plants, and build pole-barns cheaply, even by enlisting animals:

> "Just have your hogs to work up the clay to daub the barn with by mixing a little corn with your clay, they will mix it to perfection, and will not charge you one cent but his regular feed." (Watson)

Marlboro, Chesterfield, Raleigh, Winston, Salem—each of these places in the Carolinas gave its name to a cigarette. Horry could have joined them. "Say 'O-Ree,'" each pack could have urged while an attractive person blew a smoke ring around the "O." However imaginary, this brand had definite economic benefits, cultural effects, and agricultural requirements. Here are memories of people familiar with 'bacca through the 1950s, a decade that Prince calls the "golden age of the golden leaf" (*Long Green* 179).

"We did have a nice piano"

An editorial in the *Horry Herald*, Nov. 9, 1899, cited the average per capita income in Horry County as $2.50. In the poorest area it was 50 cents, and in the most affluent, $5-6 (*Lewis*, "History," 32). The county was used to bartering, buying on credit, and paying by chits that were converted to merchandise in the company store (Fig. 6.3). The editor, observing that the tobacco industry put money directly into the hands of the producer rather than the creditor, supplied dollar amounts to define this new prosperity (Nolley, "Horry"). Although a landowning farmer typically went into debt, he at least received cash for his 'bacca rather than a token, so even after buying on credit in town he could shift to the money side of the ledger. The influx of cash can be sensed from D.B. Watson's testimony: "A sewing machine agent told me the other day he had collected four times as much money this season as he has ever done before. I asked him how. His reply was, they are planting tobacco" (Watson).[1]

Fig.s 6.3. Coupon for merchandise. Horry County Museum.

Figuratively speaking, the tiny seeds jingled in overall pockets. "With the monetary gain, the farmers were able to make improvements in their homes, educate their children in schools and colleges" (Pinner 15). Ancillary businesses also gained: "The great amount of Tobacco Flues being hauled out from Conway to the country," noted the editor in 1899, "is a new feature in the life of our town" ("Matters" 29 July). Two weeks earlier he had insisted on the *Herald's* cut: "There will be a number of people here at the tobacco sales the latter part of this month and we shall expect subscribers who are owing the paper to call and settle" (Nolley 13 July). The benefits of this new crop were spread unevenly from person to person, and, moreover, profits fluctuated from year to year. As with naval stores, overproduction plagued the industry; growers found it easier to spell *oligopsony* than to combine forces.[2] Yet tobacco, whether planted full- or part-time, whether bringing in 23 cents a pound or 9, became the principal source of money for everyone from the minister to the strip-dancer.

William F. Davis (b. 1914). *One of Horry County's first tobacco growers was George Holliday (1875-1941). Davis began working for the Hollidays' Pee Dee Farms in 1935, first at the Jordanville store and then at Galivants Ferry:*
"You see no plantations in this county. The terrain is such, with all the branches and swamps, there just wasn't room. And that's the way tobacco came in as big as it did. A fellah could take his family—of course the families were large—and could make more off of five acres of tobacco than he can make over fifty acres of cotton." At one time the Holliday tobacco interests, "scattered over a wide area from Loris to Conway to Toddville," supported between 1200 and 1500 people. (Int: 8, 10)

Hester Summers Medlen (b. 1911). *Schools also benefited, according to Mrs. Medlen (who taught for decades), because there were no funds for extra things until the tobacco was sold:*
"You could put on the box suppers in the fall when the farmers had made money on tobacco. They were very generous with us because we did have a nice piano. We seated the auditorium down at Inland School" and bought equipment at Maple and Horry Schools. (Int: 10)

Mildred P. Brown (b. 1915). *Farmers could also pay off merchants. Brown's father, E.W. Prince Sr., was owner of a store in Gurley:*
"Credit was the way the families made it from January until September. Many times the tenants never paid out of debt from one year until the next. I can remember seeing some of the tenants, after about the third tobacco sale, come home with a new linoleum rug for the front room, a bolt of white homespun for underwear and bed linen, and maybe a new piece of clothing for the children. Just after tobacco season a big car from up North would come by packed with bedspreads and other household goods to sell. Everybody stopped work and went to the porch where the peddler could spread his goods out for viewing. He always sold at least one bedspread. (6,8)

John C. Spivey (b. 1871). *In 1947, Spivey (the uncle of Ann Ludlam Winfield) worked with stewardship revivals for the Waccamaw Association, Baptist. His group visited a church of about 200 members and a budget of $600:*
"This was in the fall of the year after the farmers had sold tobacco but had not sold their cotton." Although the stewardship group recommended a raise in the budget to $1500, "one old brother"resisted the sum as too great an increment. Spivey replied that the Bible called for a pledge based on income, not on custom. He had gotten field measurements from a government worker and put them on a blackboard. From 132 acres the farmers had received $66,000, so a tithe would be $6600. "You can't promise the Lord for next year," he asked, "one-fourth as much as you owe him on this year?" They voted in the proposed budget and paid for it. "This church now has a parsonage with a pastor…." (22-13)

Theatus G. Garrison (b. approx. 1920). *In the Loris area,*
"Every time my father would sell tobacco, he would always bring us home a piece of candy. Little balls of mint candy, and that was a treat. In later years he got a Ford. He was making a little [tobacco] money and he was the first man to have a car—the first colored family around here." (Int: 11)

Agnes M. Gause (b. 1919). *In Bucksport her father, Boston Mishoe (also a logger and bridge-builder) let the children have scrap tobacco:*
"Not for candy money! It was to buy your books…. And we had to buy material to make clothes. And all the yellow tobacco, he gave it to us; and we'd have to buy a bolt of homespun, a bolt of ginghams. And that was to make your dresses and your slips to school." (Int: 16)

Jerry Ausband (b. 1937). *"Saturday was the only day to shop if you lived on a tobacco farm":*
"This was the day for second-best dressing, saving the best stuff for Sunday church. This was the day when everyone came to town to look at and touch the clothing for school that fall, but couldn't buy until the crops came in or the credit slips from the farm owner were distributed to be paid back from tobacco earnings." ("Nostalgic")

Marion Moore (b. 1931). *About the time the buyers paid for the crop,*
"Everybody would go to the circus and all the teenagers went to the hoochie-coochie…"[*laughter*]. (Int: 22)

"She'd always have prayer"

In Horry County the weed grew in every square foot of life. For numerous accounts and photographs of tobacco as a family venture, see the Loris *Sentinel*, Tobacco Edition, 27 July 1988.

Drying-sticks doubled as legs for a chopping block (O'Tuel) or, daubed with clay, made chimneys (Doyle Int. 31 Oct: 4). At Collins Creek Baptist Church people waved fans that advertised tobacco warehouses as well as other businesses (McDowell 38). At White Oak School No. 2, boys made their baseballs out of tobacco twine (D. Long 9). As children, Ben, Ella, and Mary Emma Reaves (b. 1921) would mount their mules and pony from a tobacco barn bench, used by people tying 'bacca leaves (W. Thomas, "Reaves"). (See Fig. 6.4.)

Tobacco work reinforced social cohesion. In this respect it contrasted with the turpentine and lumber industries, which pretty much relied on adult males who, furthermore, were often separated from family life at the mill or in the woods like soldiers waging a campaign. Although much labor was done by tenants, sharecroppers, and hired hands, both white and black, the locus of tobacco farming was the family: children, parents, and grandparents.

As a child of five or six, Claudia A. Brown (b. 1901) stood on a box and handed leaves to her mother for five cents a day:

> She said, "You won't like it long because that smell of that strong tobacco will make you sick." But it didn't, even in the heat. "Hit'd near about knock you down, it was so strong. Specially if you put poison on it."
> But when it was curing in the barn, it smelled good a mile away. "When it came outta there, it'd be just as pretty yalla as gold." (Int. 21 July: 2)

Fig. 6.4. Tobacco bench, S.C. Tobacco Museum. Photo by Paul Olsen.

"I can remember cooking dinner for tobacco hands when I was nine years old," writes Lunette D. Floyd (b. 1910), "and had to stand on a gunshell box to reach the pots." She also remembers the social life fostered by 'bacca–growing in the area of Jordanville-High Point. "When someone needed a new tobacco barn, they would have a 'barn-raising' and invite all the neighbors. They'd put the barn up in one day. The wives came along to help cook, so that was one of our social get-togethers" (20).

In the Cane Branch Section of Allsbrook, Merlene Rheuark (b. 1934) worked on her daddy's farm:

> "We used to think it was fun to crop the top leaves. Usually, though, when the men were cropping, the women would be stringing it or doing something else in the barn. We [females] used to go from the fields early so that we could fix a big dinner. We would make fried chicken, beans, rice, mashed potatoes—a lot of Southern food. Everyone who worked with you would come eat. But it was the only time you could ever get out of working in the field." (Hanson)

Unlike the passenger train, the tobacco field was not segregated; many blacks worked for and with whites. "We'd gone down there to get some tobacco help," remembered W. Irving Jones, Sr. (b. 1895), and a colored fella said to his grandmother, a former slave:

> "'Momma, I'm gone.' She said 'Well, son, got everything with you?' He said 'Yes, Mammy,' and he went on a little ways. She called him back again, said 'You sure that you got everything with you?' He said 'Yes, I do, I got it all.' Said 'Well, let me ask you this: have you got your manners with you?' He said 'Yes,' and she told us that day that would take you further than money would." (Int. Aug. 18: 12)

On Holliday land around Galivants Ferry, as reported by Carrie D. Doyle (b. 1901), "They didn't go get the tobacco gatherers then like they do now for everybody around:

> "the thicket was full of little houses and somebody lived in every one of them, and each one would swap work…. Mr. [Preston] Coleman would go around and see he had one to gather one day and 'nother to gather another day." They all worked together and got along well, although the blacks knew their place. (Int. 8 Sept: 12)

Jones' son Irving (b. 1930) explains that farmers in the Cool Spring section later brought in help from areas that did not grow tobacco—i.e., from cotton country, where the black population was high: Orangeburg, Santee, Lamar, Florence, and Marion. Farmers in Horry County paid more for help than any others: "It was a sort of vacation, a big family of blacks. They would sing, stamp their feet, clap their hands, and sounded good to me as a little boy" (p.c.). Raised in the Galivants Ferry area, Rilla McCrackin (b. 1941) was the daughter of sharecroppers Walt and Pincey Cook.

Her memory is less sanguine about the hired African Americans:

> "Some landowners had small buildings that the black people stayed in. No running water or bathrooms. Some had a small wood stove to cook on. Hand-wash their clothes and hang them on a fence or limbs of trees. They did not go into white people's houses; I think people were afraid of them because of their color and few had any education. They didn't have very much to say. They worked hard for what they got. Some would have to hitchhike back to their home if they failed to work or couldn't handle the heat. Some were middle-aged women with their children that were old enough to work in tobacco." (Int.)

Carrie Beach Smith (b. 1934), a sixteen-year-old from the North Santee Community of Georgetown County, was recruited by her sister to live on a white couple's small farm:

> "They had a nice place to stay but it was a lot of work. Had to do a little of everything—crop tobacco, string tobacco, clean the worm off tobacco. It was hot and it was scary, because if the worm sting you, it hurt and would make a wale [welt]." After two weeks as the only young person there, she took the bus home.

Things went smoother for Lewis P. Gould (b. 1913). "We used to go over [to Cool Spring] about 6:30 or 7:00 and you'd have to eat something. And she'd always have prayer—I don't care what time you got in the tobacco field, you'd have to have prayer" (Int: 15). [Mrs. W. P. Johnson] or her husband would thank the Lord for his blessings or would ask Him to take care of us during the day (p.c.).[3]

A 'Bacca Calendar

From seeding to sawing, the whole process meant hard labor. Here are directions for a year of tobacco-growing before mechanization, sophisticated chemicals, and bulk barns (which eliminated the need for stringing and hanging the leaves to cure them). The memories of John P. Cartrette (b. 1898) are taken from "The Good Old Days," written in 1974 (22-23). Those of Mrs. McCrackin (b. 1941) come from an interview conducted by her daughter (the transcription then expanded by Rilla), as well as from personal communication with the author. Her memory is as sharp as her eye for details, technical, sensory, and social. (For an analysis of the rice-growing process, which was vital to Georgetown County during slavery, see Joyner, *Down*, 45-50.)

•Grow seedlings in a bed

It was an annual reforestation with seeds that resembled precious spices.

Foy Stevenson (b. 1909). *The family, headed by James Edwin Stevenson, a Confederate veteran, lived near Zoan (ZOH-ann) Church:*
"One day [my sister] Charlotte noticed that the tobacco plants growing so lushly next to the house were in sad need of suckering. Not only that, but they had been so neglected that tall shoots of lavender blossoms had been allowed to grow from them." The three sisters zealously broke off the suckers and flowering tops, "sure their industry would win Papa's approbation." Then he returned from a business trip and sat in his customary chair on the porch: "Who in thunderation suckered that tobacco?" We had destroyed the seed for next year's beds. (10)

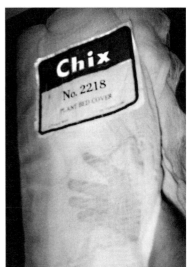

John P. Cartrette. *The hot curing-barn started with cold weather:*
"In December a new piece of ground was spaded up for the tobacco bed. Then in January seed was scattered and raked in the soil. Canvas [a gauzy material] was stretched over this to keep the bed and plants from freezing. Later, weeds had to be pulled out by hand." (See Fig. 6.5.)

Sam T. McCrackin (b. 1936). *From the Methodist Rehobeth Section, S.T. explains that tobacco beds had to be sterilized:*
"We'd take a bush ax and go out in the field and chop corn stalks at the ground in such a way that caused them to fall together in the middle, easy to gather. Cotton stalks were pulled by hand, roots and stalks together, then carried to the beds and stacked on the tobacco beds to burn."

Rilla C. McCrackin. *In Galivants Ferry, "The beds were tilled and made ready to sow in mid-January.*

Fig. 6.5 Tobacco cloth, S.C. Tobacco Museum. Photo by Paul Olsen.

"Then when a few days passed, the beds would be sown and the canvases stretched over the beds, then pegged down with green reeds that were about 10-12 inches long, spaced about 1 yard apart. The beds ranged in width and length a few inches either way but came out 8 feet wide and 100 feet long. When the plants started growing, the weeds also grew. Then the weeds had to be carefully plucked from the beds. Sometimes you would make three or four trips and days to pick the beds (with help, of course). This was a very back-breaking job. You would squat, sit, bend, get on your knees, and any way you could to relieve the back pain. The plants sometimes would be found to have a disease called 'blue mold,' which would cause the leaves to wilt and turn yellow. This disease was doctored with a fungicide called Fermate. It helped to save the rest of the plants. There were lots of problems in growing tobacco crops."

•Transplant them in rows

Replant seedlings where ancient sea oats may have rooted in dunes. Keep the rows straight and the same length with tall measuring sticks (Fig. 6.6.). A boy holds one of them vertical while a mule runs a line from it down the field to another boy; then they turn the sticks horizontal to equalize the space between rows with a notch.

Fig. 6.6. Row-lining stick held by S.T. McCrackin.

John P. Cartrette. *"In the middle of April or the first of May, when the plants in the seedbed were large enough,* "they were pulled up by hand. Holes were made with a stick in the tobacco rows; plants were dropped in by hand; water was poured by a dipper; and soil was mashed against the plant by hand."

Susie L. Lewis (b. 1898). *The mercantile stores began to sell "these little hand transplanters that you set tobacco with":* Her husband bought one and "it was pretty good: you didn't have to hurt your back. Used to, one would go along and drop the plants and one would go along and set that one. You had to pet tobacco to make a dollar out of it." (Int: 16)

Rilla C. McCrackin. *"You had to pull the plants from the 'baccer beds :* "Everybody's back hurt. You would be tired and cold in the dew of the morning. Your fingers ached, your back ached, and your knees were wet and cold. You were glad when the sun warmed things up in the morning." "Women were carrying pasteboard boxes with holes in each end tied with string and put around their necks that came down to their waist" [Fig. 6.7]. The plants was put in a box and then put in a [hand-]setter by the ladies [Figs. 6.8 and 6.9]. They had to face the men and walk back'rds to drop the plants in the setter. The men carried hand-setters—with a place for water. It had a handle, and under the handle was a place where the water went—a trough. When I was a little girl I had to tote buckets of water down to the field, where it was taken from a barrel and carried to put in setters."

•Plow and fertilize the land

Unlike turpentiners and loggers, tobacco farmers made their cuts with the plowshare. Francis Gardner (b. 1925) began turning up the dirt of the Freewoods in eleven-year-old bare feet: "We had one pair of shoes, and those were for Sunday. I remember getting up early in the morning, 6 a.m. or 7 a.m., and plowing tobacco in the cold dew" (J. Wilson, "Preserving," 3-C). Once the ground was harrowed, the farmers applied nourishment.

Claudia A. Brown (b. 1901). *Fertilizer could be home-made:* In winter, the mules would make a furrow with a plow, then farmers would put stalks in it. Then the mules would plow a furrow on each side to cover it [i.e., to let it rot]. As a child she used to pull fodder off corn stocks and would have to reach up. Or they would rake up pine straw, make a pile as big as a house. Take an old car [cart], two-wheeled, to the woods. They'd hoe where the pine straw lay—that syrupy dirt that was under the [half-rotten] straw; they put this on top of the dry pine straw. All through the winter they'd put water on it that was used to wash clothes. "I've had a sack tied

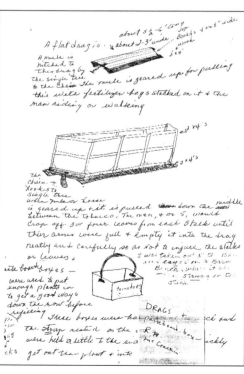

Fig. 6.7. Sketches by Rilla McCrackin. Bottom: Pasteboard box.

around me—threw compost on the tobacco rows." (Int. 21 July: 4)

Agnes M. Gause (b. 1919). *Potassium was also scarce in Bucksport:*
"If they'd plant tobacco they didn't make anything on it because they didn't have the fertilizer to put to it. They used to put ashes and stuff like that to it—gardens and whatever." (Int: 20)

Fig. 6.8. The McCrackins' old hand-setter.

•Top and sucker the plant

The tobacco stalk rises to a flower, a sweet-scented, pink or whitish thief. Snap it off, along with the side-shoots, to redirect growth to the leaves.

Sally Hemmingway (b. 1918). *"Tobacco grows up about so high [gestures],*
"and when you top it off, you see, comes shuckers in it. And it would get so hot, but you still had to get every single one off. And they were so sticky. (Int: 13)

•Pluck, spray, or fumigate

Tobacco is subject to any number of predators, including the larva of a species of sphinx moth, usually green, with horn-like processes at its hind end.

Foy Stevenson (b. 1909). *"Farmers did not use pesticides on tobacco in those days:*
"Even though the children were squeamish about touching the horned, juicy worms, they sometimes engaged in the activity as a pastime rather than a duty." Her father paid a nickel for each can of worms. The children "picked off the big fat worms and dropped them into the can with great caution. The worms were soft and squashy, and they did not want to mash them" but "to retain their full, natural size and rotundity" to fill up the container. (11)

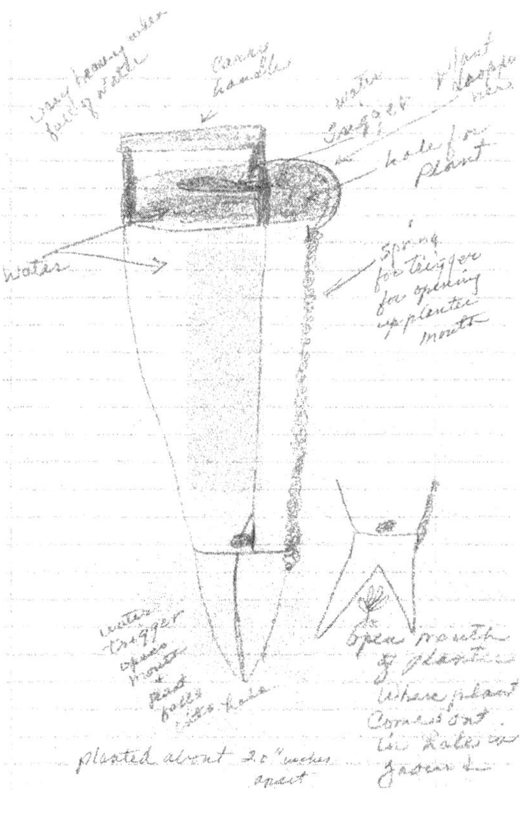

John P. Cartrette. *"When the worms began to eat the leaves,*
"they were plucked off by hand and stepped on to kill them. Sometimes arsenic of lead was dusted on the plants to help kill the worms. When suckers (or other small leaves) came at the base of each leaf, they were pinched out."

R. Cathcart Smith, M.D. (b. 1914). *Powder was applied—*
Either a poison called Paris Green or a form of arsenic lead. They walked down the rows and shook it onto the plant from a can or an old pair of ladies' hose. "Sometimes you'd be in the hot field sweating, and you'd inadvertently wipe your hand across your mouth—it was bitter."

Rilla C. McCrackin. *At "poisoning time," maybe in the early spring,*
the mule pulled a barrel with a sprayer down the rows on a drag. "We had to go down rows and put poison in the bud of plants with our hands to kill the bud worms when it was a foot or two high." (See Fig. 6.10.)

Fig. 6.9. Sketch of hand-setter with instructions, Rilla McCrackin.

•Crop the plants

According to one native, if the leaf rattles, it has the proper body–"but if it don't do dat, it ain't a good grade o' 'baccer." See Figures 6.1 and 6.11.

The top leaves, or "tips" (also called "wrappers") are the smaller, greener leaves. The highest-quality tips were made into cigars or blended with plug (chewing) tobacco. Ordinary tips and middle stalk leaves were called "cutters" because they were shredded for cigarette manufacture. As the main source of the crop's value, they were also called "mortgage lifters." Lower leaves were called "trash" or "lugs"; they were typically used as filler in low-price products, or exported to the Orient to make cheap cigarettes or even filler for opium (McDaniel, E. Prince, p.c.).

Fig. 6.10. Poison sprayer. Courtesy the McCrackins.

Fig. 6.11. Farmers amid profit. Horry County Museum.

Remove the leaves one at a time from the bottom as they mature. First harvest the rain-beaten "sand lugs." Tuck leaves under your arm and carry them to the drag (Fig. 6.1). Be careful: leaves are fragile and can bruise. The sand clings to fingers covered with gum from the bottom of leaves.

The earliest methods of carrying a leaf-pile? According to J.C. Roberts (b. 1892), "We'd tie it off, then two men toted it off in a sack sheet attached to poles. Then you finally got to rolling it out with wheelbarrows. Finally made drags and drag it with mules" (Int: 11). The mule would pull a drag (which had runners instead of wheels) between rows, and gatherers would carry leaves to it from multiple rows to the left or right. As Nellie Scott Moore (b. 1939) recalls, "The one man driving the drag, they would always tell him 'Hawk!' when to stop" (Int: 4). Eventually a drag or tractor rolled down a "fifth middle"—an empty row with four rows on each side.

R. Cathcart Smith remembers that croppers earned more out in the hot sun than stringers in the shade, while Roberta Rust (b. 1909) recalls that in and around Wampee it was black people who worked in the cotton gin and in the tobacco field (Int. 30).

Rilla C. McCrackin. *"Come time to take the tobacco out to the flue-cured barns,* "we had a 'bacco drag and lined it with fertilizer sacks that had been washed and sewn together by hand and placed on the inside and sewn in to hold it in place. It lasted all season through. A flat drag is 5-6 feet long and about 2-3 feet wide. The top boards are 4 or 5 inches wide; the frame is 2 x 4 wood. The chain is hitched to the singletree [crossbar of the harness] on the mule. The mule is geared up for pulling this with fertilizer bags stacked on it and the man riding or walking." (See Fig. 6.7.)

"The summers were suffocating. There was no ice water—barn or field—just a gallon jug taken to the field. The menfolk cropping tobacco would drink from the branch in the woods if the water was running and clear. Daddy said it was all right to drink unless you saw a dead varmint close by" (Int: 7).

Manning Elliott (b. 1914). *For years he and his wife Frostie Johnson Elliott farmed with the Hollidays at Moore's Mill in Galivants Ferry. "You would just get your help, go in the field:*
"You had a black boy coming behind you in a drag." He pulls it with a mule while croppers empty tobacco leaves onto it from under their arms or in their hands. You holler at the mule to stop there in the field and put your tobacco on. "And if the drag can't hold [any more leaves], at the end of the road, well, there is another drag coming in behind you." The drag boy takes the cropped leaves to the barn.

"You would pull the leaves off the stalk and there they would be": "I've seen people that would take a snake by the tail and pop his head off. I had some colored people—this guy took a rattlesnake and put him under his arm and I told him he was gonna get bit. Used to you would hear about spiders stinging ya while cropping" but not anymore because of pesticides. "Used to be them little old black spiders running all over the tobacco."

"If me and you and somebody were to get out there and crop tobacco and you would get so hot, I would 'monkey' you and you would 'monkey' me. We would put you under the shade where you won't be able to crop. Maybe you go off that night to see your girl and don't get home till late, then have to get up and tend the barn and then get in the field and crop that tobacco all day long—maybe you had left home without any supper—you would come back in and the 'monkey' would get you that day. 'Cause you couldn't stand to crop, 'cause you got so hot and weak you can't work…. They called it 'monkeying': you just dropped out."[4] (Int. 2-4)

Robert Bellamy (b. 1917). *A fisherman, construction worker, and church singer, Bellamy also cropped tobacco every day except Sunday five miles out of Loris:*
"Us mens would crop tobacco and the womens cleaned it. You would get two to six head of us cropping; you could fill up two bags." We would stay in a large house, and on weekends we'd come home to Little River Neck; "the old folks would be on the wagons and we'd be walking." In another place, "every time we touch a tobacco leaf, we see a pilot [copperhead] run. That's the snakiest place I have been in [*laughing*]. I've seen white fellows kiss snakes. Course it was cold and that snake couldn't bite 'em. They'd kiss 'em on the neck like that, but I ain't going to kiss them" [*laughing*]. (Int: 13-15. See Plate 7.)

Janie B. Johnson (b. 1906). *Both serene and doughty, Mrs. Johnson earned her practical nursing degree from S.C. State College in Orangeburg during the Depression. "I've been in this spot since 1930," declared this former midwife:*

"You couldn't scatter the tobacco. My husband was careful how to broke it off of the stalks, careful how to handle it when they got it to the barn. Friday of last week, I said [to a hired hand], 'You all don't work like we did. If you was as observant and take care as my husband did in his lifetime, you'd be worth thousands of dollars. Where you's not worth a nickel!'" (Int: 14. See Plate 8.)

Theatus G. Garrison (b. approx. 1920). *Between 1890 and 1960, the ten-year censuses recorded an average decline of 35 percent among South Carolina blacks between the ages of 20 and 34 ("S.C.'s Blacks"). In the 1930s, Miss Graham rode the train up to New York, where she became a nurse and caterer:*
"I would always come home in August, 'cause that was tobacco season down here. I would help my father for a month and then I'd go back. When I would leave, they always would gather around the little train down at the station to see me off." (Int: 9)

Merlene C. Rheuark (b. 1934): *"When I was at least ten years old,*
"we used to have to get up around 4 o'clock. We had to bring the tobacco to the house on our arms until we got the barn empty so we could fill it up again that day. It was a thrill to find a watermelon in the drag of tobacco."

• Tie the leaves onto sticks

Nobody wants to puff on hairy green leaves. Tobacco must be cured, unlike cotton, which could be picked and immediately baled. So before the advent of metal bulk-barns, which allowed heavy piles of tobacco leaves to be put on racks and heated in a sealed, easily-regulated space, people had to tie leaves onto sticks to assure a good surface-to-volume ratio. Roberta Rust, interviewed in 1991, declared: "I even have a ball [of tobacco thread] in yonder I saved. I think I might string some later" [*laughter*] (Int: 30). Stringers were shaded by an overhanging roof on each side of the barn (Fig. 6.12).

Fig. 6.12. Winding leaves of weed. Horry County Museum.

"Tobacco sticks were 4 feet, 6 inches long," remembers J. Marion Vaught, Jr. "A split stick worked much better in the barn than a sawed one, which might have cross-grain in it and break easily. But a split stick runs with the grain, and they would hold up better in a barn when the heat got on 'em or the weight was on 'em" (Int. March 17: 22). "I was so proud when I strung my first stick of tobacco," reports Catherine Lewis (Int. A. Jones: 21), "I thought I had graduated." She also remembers "how heavy a stick of green tobacco is…" ("Cordie Page" 35).

Rilla C. McCrackin. *"Someone was always available to take [the cropped 'bacca] out of the drag and place it on the tobacco bench with stems toward handers and stringers.*
"The handers picked it up three or four leaves at the time, keeping stems level to be strung by the stringer. Just anyone wasn't chosen to string tobacco. It had to be done a certain way—neatly and tight so as not to fall out of the thread wrapped around it because the tobacco was being heated, and gradually the stems would shrink and could fall out of the wrapped strings." "Children could hand tobacco and women strung it on the stick by wrapping thread around the bat, then gripping it and sliding it up tight to the stick. The next bat would be wrapped with the string the same way and thrown over the stick, and this continued to the end of the stick. The twine would be bound to the end of the stick with about five inches left to hang on the tier poles."

Agnes Nichols Roberts (b. 1898). *A longtime teacher from Cool Spring, she handled more than chalk:*
"Some of [the people stringing] went under the stick and some over it; I turned mine over…. Unload it, and the man sits up there, a boy, and pitchforks it. You better not drop or step on it." (Int: 21)

Claudia A. Brown (b. 1901). *"I use to work for Mr. Mansey Gause up here, and Paul Gause and Charlie Gause:*
"Went up there one Monday morning to put in tobacco and he didn't have but one stringer. Paul says, 'Mrs. Brown, what we going to do?' I says, 'Well, you bring the tobacco out the field and I'll string it fer ya.' We put in two barns of tobacco that day and I strung every leaf of it." (Int. 24 June: 2)

Willie Page (b. 1910). *Page taught two white boys, Aubrey and Jimmy Winburn, how to cure tobacco when their father was working in the Charleston shipyards around the time of World War II:*
"I made [the sticks] myself: cut down a pine tree and cut it to links, saw the links out about as thick as these and bust it up. Then get on down there to where you cut it up, kind of like you making shingles." (Int: 15)

Ethlyn Davis Missroon (b. 1913). *As a girl she lived with her grandparents, Mr. and Mrs. Joseph Tindal, at Pawley Swamp in the southwestern corner of Horry:*
At weed-curing time, after a day's work, "my grandfather would line up his adult workers and place a crisp green dollar into the hand of each…." His grandchildren, however, would find only "a bright silver coin, a dime or sometimes a quarter, resting in our grimy paws at knock time." (25)

Agnes M. Gause (b. 1919). *"My husband decided he'd plant his sister's little acre-half acre in the back":*
"I said 'Well, you won't have to get anybody to hand it to the person who's going to put it on the stick. I'll hand it to them.' I guess I stayed out there about an hour, and I saw one of these old, big green worms that's on the tobacco leaf." She threw the leaf around "like that" and kept walking away from that barn. "I haven't been back under once since." (Int: 16)

•Cure the leaves in the barn.

"Got to have a certain amount of heat to turn dark on you, to be pretty," affirms Willy Page (Int: 21).

According to Reginald McDaniel of the S.C. Tobacco Museum, the curing barn was typically square in order to promote uniform heating, and it measured either 16′x 16′ or 20′x 20′, although some barns were built "according to the whims of the individual farmer." Connected to the furnace was a network of pipes that were about the same diameter as dinner plates. "It was necessary to have a fine mesh fence-wire placed over the metal flues to catch any falling leaves, lest they hit the red-hot flues and send the barn up in flames" (Berry, "Area"). The process required about a week of stoking before it reached the optimum temperature of 170 degrees. "We used to have a Brown & Williamson thermometer in our barn," said McDaniel, "that designated 190 degrees as 'scorching.'" In her parents' general store, Roberta Ward Rust sold many such thermometers (Int: 30).[5]

The process?

Gradually push a log across a roller made from another log into a clay or brick furnace heated by wood (later by kerosene). The log is 8, 10, 12 inches in diameter and 16 feet long. "Sometimes if you had a big tree we'd split the wood–make four or five pieces out of it, try to cut it about 5 foot long (D. Smith, b. 1933). Have two cords on hand to fire each barn—a cord being a stack 4 feet wide, 4 feet high, and 8 feet long. J.P Cartrette remembers "lying on a hard bench and waking up every hour or so and replenishing the fire."

Fig. 6.13. Mr. McCrackin climbs tier-poles in barn next to Methodist Rehobeth Church, 2003.

In the barn, hang the heavy sticks of green 'bacca on poles "made from young pine trees with their bark skinned off." The sticks were placed on the tier poles in a staggered position so the heat could circulate better (Int. McCrackin: 7). The poles ran between the front and back of the barn, four feet apart, and rose high to the roof in parallel ranks, maybe seven or eight levels high. "Most times," explained J.M. Vaught, Jr., "we'd gather tobacco on the same day. Put it in the barn at the same time and divide it with a piece of twine that hung down" (Int. March 17: 25).

A worker or two would have to straddle the poles far above and scramble around like a circus performer (Fig. 6.13). Rilla recalls that sweat and water dripped down to the dirt floor.

Despite all these demands, a farmer might give up one day of work. "My daddy was a very religious man," remembered Barney Dawsey (b. 1912), "and wouldn't burn [cure] a barn of tobacco on Sunday. If we put it in on Saturday, there wasn't no fire till Monday" (Int: 12).

John Fowler (b. 1881). *Interviewed shortly before his death in 1978, Mr. Fowler remembered his vigil at the wood-burning furnace:*
"You would have to stay right near it. My daddy planted four acres and I was the one in the family that would come in the farm day and night and watch—some of the others would sucker the tobacco and keep things going that way.
"I told my mother to fix me something to eat and said 'When I get through watching, I don't want nobody to bother me till I get in that room and get a nap,''cause I would sit there day and night punching wood. Took about two nights and three days of solid burning." (Int: 5-6. See p.1.)

Mrs. G.W. Collier. *Recalling Aynor life in the 1920s, she speculates that the tobacco barn gave rise to something that was both an occasion and a dish:*
"Chicken bogs [a pilau of rice and meat] originated in the tobacco barns when the farmers had to sit up all night to fire the hardwood furnace. Becoming bored, the young men planned parties. They would secure an iron pot and snitch their neighbors' chickens! Often the owner of the chickens would be a guest, enjoy the bog to the fullest, not knowing that he was eating his own bird! For 'twas always a great secret where the chickens came from. You can imagine the sly looks, quips, nods, and becks that ensued. A bog afforded much merriment and finally the host let the fellow know that he had

furnished the chicken." (4)

T. Arthur Pinner. *Pinner grew up in the Evergreen Community. Writing about the 1930s, he recalls, "Farmers formed labor pools to harvest and cure their tobacco":*
"It was a situation of 'I help you today, you help me tomorrow.' The method of curing tobacco usually meant firing a barn furnace with wood and keeping a 24-hour vigil on the curing product. The process usually took four days and four nights to complete. During the nights, there were fish fries, chicken stews, and candy cookings. Many youthful romances developed."

Manning Elliott (b. 1914). *"You would get ya a piece of wood or two and start your fire," a step that began a period of about three months:*
"You run that furnace just about to death and cram it down full to get your heat up…. When it come night you would be sitting there. You might drop off to sleep, your fire may go out and your wood fall out the furnace. You would just have to start it back. "I would sit up and then maybe you would sit up part of the night and maybe some of the rest part of the night. You have to push that fire all night long and then all day long, and then maybe you would have to gather tobacco the next day and get up at four o'clock in the morning and run to the barn. You are going from eight o'clock in the morning till maybe after ten o'clock that night." (Int: 1)

Rilla C. McCrackin. *Curing was a joint effort of family and friends:*
Watching the furnace, Daddy would "run up on the tobacco." That means elevating the heat slowly to the temperature that best sets a golden color, not too green or brown, and that retains strength in the leaf. If the leaf was too dried out it would be called "trash," a cheaper grade. "The tobacco also has a better aroma when cured well" (Int: 6, 4). "We slept outside under the roof of the barn's shelter and on top of the tobacco bench. My daddy and mama made us a bed by folding a homemade quilt for each of us on the bench. The mosquitoes whined all night; to keep them out, Daddy would take an old tobacco canvas to hang up around us.

"On the weekends there were git-togethers. People grew peanuts and would have peanut-poppins. They would also have chicken bog and invite people over to work in the tobacco. The men would saw wood to fuel the barn's furnaces and for cook stoves and fireplaces. They would be in the yard, the children playing, them having their mandolins, guitars. There was harmonicas sometimes. Some would have a fiddle. Sometimes they would be a dancin' and some drinkin' 'stumphole' [moonshine] and homemade grape wine. The little kids playing chase and hide-'n'-go-seek. They didn't have to have a flashlight back then; their eyes adjusted to the light—moon and stars."

Doug Smith (b. 1933). *The heat of the barn might serve both curing and canning:*
"Me 'n' my grandmother would peel tomatoes like 40 or 50 quarts at the time, sometime put 'em in half a gallon jars, and set 'em in the barn by the tobacco flues and cook 'em. About 11 o'clock at night we'd have to go in there 'n tote them hot tomato jars out of the tobacco barn and tighten the lid on 'em 'n' seal 'em so it would keep."

• "Order the tobacco up" and remove it

"You needed one day to put the leaves in," as J.C. Bennett remembers it, "seven to cure them, and you had to cool the barn down first" (Int: 15). "After the tobacco was cured," recalls Rilla McCrackin, "the barn doors would be left open all night for the night air to soften the tobacco. The leaves would become more pliable and soft (easy to work with)—not break or shatter. Sometimes the nights would be very dry and the next morning the tobacco would shatter; you had to be very careful with it." Wink Prince notes that the dried leaves would absorb a little moisture from the humid atmosphere and, once pliable, the tobacco was "in order" (p.c.). "The cured tobacco," Rilla told her daughter Amanda, "was taken out of the barn as early as possible before the sun came up:

> "Men climbed up on the tierpoles and handed the tobacco down to the man below him. The lantern was used to break the dark inside the barn and outside. The men always came out washed down in sweat. The tobacco was packed into the drag lengthwise. After reaching the top of the drag, the sticks of tobacco were turned crosswise and laid from the front to the back of the drag as high as could be reached."

• Grade the leaves

In "taking off tobacco," the dried leaves were unstrung and then separated into three qualities: first, second, and trash (R. McCrackin). As with rosin, the lightest color is best. "We'd sit down there on the floor and grade it," recalls Andrew Stanley (Int: April 1991). Rocks and shell fragments stuck to the 'bacca: "Making all those different grades and all that sand, oh, I hated that," declared Agnes M. Gause (Int: 16).

• Pile the dried leaves

Having kept the leaves apart on the curing stick, now store them in bulk form. "Gather a handful, with level stems. Folding a leaf, carefully wrap it around the top part of the others and you would push the stem through the leaves to hold [the bundle] in place. Then later it would all be placed in sticks again and packed down in a neat pile to take later to the warehouse" (R. McCrackin).

Sometimes the dried leaves were stored on the premises: "We had nowheres else to keep the tobacco," recalls Merlene C. Rheuark (b. 1934). "We slept on the floor or on top of the tobacco while it was in the house." After the sale "we had to wash down the whole house and put the bed back up." Young Rilla Cook had a similar experience. "At that time we had no packing house on the farm Daddy sharecropped:

> "Our beds were moved out on the front porch usually first of July and the tobacco was piled up to the ceiling on both sides of the bedroom. A piece of cloth was put over the window so the sun wouldn't bleach the color from the tobacco. Our quilts were thrown over it to keep the moisture in the tobacco."

S.F. Horton (b. 1911). *"Tobacco was selling cheap in 1933":*
The Agriculture Department decided to close all warehouses in the tobacco-growing states and to set up allotments for each farmer. For several weeks, farmers had to continue to gather tobacco, but most of them did not have pack houses. People would crop their green tobacco and cure it, and just take a bedroom and take down the beds and pile up the tobacco. "One tenant asked his landlord, 'Captain, when are they going to open up these warehouses and let us get rid of some of this tobacco?' Said 'We've already had to take down all of our beds–I done slept on the floor so much my hips is done riz twice'" [*laughter*]. (Int.1:3; p.c.)

•Transport leaves to auction

> "A can of bait, a fishing pole
> A basket of tobacco to 'American' sold
> A place to swim at the old soak hole
> Somehow remind me of Daddy." (Majar)

Farmers could haul their cured leaf to be sold in warehouses (Fig. 6.14). "We had three or four grades of tobacco," notes Merlene C. Rheuark, and "we were all extremely happy when the last loads were taken to town and sold."

Cordie Page (b. 1884) explains that after the cooperative was established, the half-dozen warehouses in Aynor disappeared, so many farmers went to Mullins instead: "I remember at my house on the Pee Dee Road hearing the wagons all through the night" (Epps, "Mr. Cordie, 6). James Bellamy (b. 1893) "sold some in Loris, some in Tabor, some to Whiteville…. Carried some to Fairmont" (Int: 7). Andrew Stanley (b. 1904) recalls his mode of transportation: "You drove a pair of mules up there, or ox and cart, and backed up there, and load it, and carried it to Conway" (Int. April 1991: 22).

Fig. 6.14. Tobacco auction. Horry County Museum.

Farm-to-market transportation was a challenge before trucks and pavement. Penny G. Floyd (b. 1896) lived on the Pee Dee Road between Jordanville and Galivants Ferry: "We grew anywhere from two to five and six acres. But we didn't have any good way to get to the markets" (6).

At the warehouse, buyers from several large companies walked beside lines of tobacco-piles and responded to the auctioneer's indecipherable syllables with indiscernible gestures. Lewis P. Gould (b. 1913), a longtime employee of Loris Drug Store, recalls those days: "Sale started—biggest day of the year. Drugstore would always carry out drinks to the tobacco buyers and people out there on the floor" (Int: 15). A journalist who grew up in Conway, Jerry Ausband recalls that young fellows with baskets "yelled out 'Boiled peanuts for sale.'" For a recollection of market-time in the same town, see Franklin Burroughs (b. 1942), "Returning," 30-31.

W. Irving Jones, Sr. (b. 1895). *In Aynor, Jones was employed as a ticket-marker; he followed the sale and recorded the buyer, price-per-pound, and grade wanted on each ticket:*
Outside there was a pump and a horse trough. "They give every man that went in there to sell tobacco a tin cup with a handle to it [to take home]. In the bottom, it would have the name of the farm. In mine it had 'E.O. Branford,' who was

one of the first tobacconists in Mullins. Later on they got those cups that were kind flexible" (Int. 11 Aug: 3). "I got to where I could grade the tobacco and put the class on it 'cause I done so much of it. Some of them said, 'Well, if you're working for three warehouses you are making money'; I said, 'Well, look, I got $9 a day for that—each one give me $3.'" (Int. 1977: 18)[6]

Willie Page (b. 1910). *While J.L. Winburn (b.1915) was working in Charleston,*
"I would take tobacco to the place and sell it and have the man to the bank to split the check, put his part in the bank and give me my part…. When he come back, he was surprised at how much money he had. I gave him all them slips. I had all the bills where I sold tobacco." (Int: 21)

Sally Hemmingway (b. 1918). *One farmer, however, was an ethical sand-lug:*
Sally and her husband got up early and, before breakfast, walked from Cedar Branch to a farm on Highway 9, where they sharecropped for a white man all summer. They "stricked [stripped] that tobacco, got it all cut and tied up…." "We worked all day long, then we'd have to walk it all the way back. He sold that tobacco under some other name. His daddy's name, some his brother's name, and we didn't get a dime out of it. I said 'Look, you got it, and I can't get it. Can't get it by law….' That's OK as long as he's on this earth. But when he dies, that same thing is going to be hanging over his head, and he'll have to pay for it then." (Int: 15)

J.C. Bennett (b. 1928). *Another farmer was quite straightforward. He was interviewed in 1946 or '47 by Jack Hawley, when tobacco in the warehouse was bringing about 30 or 40 cents a pound:*
"I can see the farmer now, wearing those bib overalls. He saw the microphone and didn't know what it was. Hawley said, 'How is the tobacco going?' And he said, 'Not worth a durn.' Hawley says, 'Well, Mr. Smith' (or whatever), 'if you would get a dollar a pound for your tobacco today, what would you do?' He said, 'Well, sir, I would — in my frock.'" (Int: 16)

•Cut the stalks

What had lifted the flowers, suckers, spiders, and broad leaves sunward now impeded the next year's crop.

Merlene C. Rheuark (b. 1934): *"We would have to cut the stalks that was left in the fields with a hoe:*
"My brothers and sisters didn't want to work, so I would make a game out of it. I would half all the rows up and whoever finished their rows first would be the winner. That's the way I tricked them into working. (But there was no prize.) We would put the stalks in piles and burn them at night."

•Cut firewood

Wood was stacked—as it had been to heat the boiler of the turpentine still, steamboat or locomotive—to fuel next year's curing. "We'd have a pile of wood 6 or 8 feet high and a long pile of it to run one barn a year" (Barney Dawsey, Int: 11). As when vessels rode the tide in or out, lunar power was exploited, because more wood could be chopped under a full moon.

The mule would eventually go the way of the crosscut saw, and the tenant farmer would become an isolated case:

> **"WANTED**
> Tenant farmer with team.—Keyes Field Plantation located at Toddville 6 miles from Conway on Waccamaw River. Irrigated farm with tractor. Tenant may have at least 6 acres of tobacco. See H.B. Hardwick, Toddville." ("Want Ads" 1954)

With more automation, fewer people would load a drag, monkey out, or string 'bacca under the granny-skirted porch, and Emma Page would have to demonstrate the rhythms of tobacco-tying with ersatz materials–white string, broomstick, and newspapers. Growing the 'bacca weed would become less of a communal experience, even an initiation into the Waterland. Fewer people would vow "Never again!"

Who could have guessed that the flower-topped fountain, so carefully defended by arsenic of lead, was itself the poison? Tobacco acreage would plummet over the final quarter of the century. Unlike turpentine, however, the crop would remain vital economically. On the family level, the Hardwicks might have a 10,000 pound quota that they once worked but now cash-rented to someone else. On the community level, tobacco profits would help to keep alive businesses, churches, and even towns.

Not a few prosperous tobacco farmers invested in tourism: George J. Holliday once owned what would become Surfside Beach and was a principal in several development ventures (see Jackson, "Memories," 6), as was D.A. Spivey, who owned a tobacco warehouse. So the combustion of cigarettes helped to drive the engine of the Grand Strand.

Notes

[1] "When they sharecropped, that was next door to slavery," declared J.C. Bennett (b. 1928). Describing what could have been many a person in Horry, he said his granddaddy in Turbeville (Florence County) "was fortunate that he had a couple of milk cows, chickens, and hogs":

> "Of course, he had to give the landowner so much of the corn and if he planted two or three acres of wheat, he got enough to get him two or three barrels of wheat out of it. We lived good eating-wise and getting clothes on your back, but at the end of the year you didn't have a thing. You started with nothing and at the end of the year you had nothing. You couldn't get ahead."
> (Int: 15)

Despite the relative prosperity brought by tobacco, sharecropping and tenant-farming persisted. James R. Holbert, Jr. (b. 1917) remembers a diary entry made by George Holliday after learning that Jim Jerdon's mule had died:

> "'I told him to get a new mule and to charge it to his account at the store' [wrote Holliday]. That was a good gesture because Mr. Holliday being the landlord, if the tenant didn't have a mule, he couldn't work the crop…. Then when the man would sell the tobacco, they'd split 50-50…. And he would deduct the cost of the mule from the tenant's share, so he got paid back, but he also had a crop." (Int. G. Floyd: 68)

[2] The term means "a market with few buyers and many sellers"; see *Long Green* 83. This award-winning book analyzes other determinants of tobacco prices, whether up or down: exploitation, addiction, weather, wartime, Hollywood, new female smokers, and governmental efforts to control crops and support prices. Professor Prince also has an unpublished compilation of memories having to do with tobacco-growing.

[3] Even in one sinister context, there was the weed. Just over the North Carolina border from Loris, W. Horace Carter edited the Tabor City *Tribune* and earned a Pulitzer Prize for his crusade against the revived Klan. He remembers a rainy November night in 1950 when, between Mullins and Loris on Highway 917, at least ten thousand men and women flocked through a soft, sandy field. Along its borders stood a few tobacco stalks that had eluded the mule-drawn harrows:

> "The truck that would be the stage carried a twenty-foot-tall cross made from pine poles. It was wrapped from top to bottom with fertilizer sacks…. A Klansman quickly dug a hole near the parked truck, and after dousing the wrappings with kerosene, he and others stood the cross in its hole…." At the order of the Grand Dragon, "A bright, smoky flame raced to the top of the cross as the burning kerosene and sack material cast an eerie glow across the field. Like a regiment of soldiers, both men and women started walking slowly around the cross. Six rode white horses. The well-known hymn, 'Amazing Grace'… rolled across the field. The spectators were quiet."

If these details weren't surrealistic enough, the speakers played several Negro spirituals and light classical music (*Virus* 48-49, p.c.).

[4] Elliott elaborates on the custom. "I've said it many a time this year at them colored boys. 'All right, boys, don't let him monkey y'all.' That hauler jumps tobacco from one row to another, and he looked over and said, 'Hey, did you see that?' to one of them colored boys. He said, 'Hey, what did you see?' Hal said, 'I saw a monkey—did you see him?' He said, 'No, I didn't see him.' But when one dragged behind and they don't stay together, they say, 'Well, the monkey's about got him.'" "Yes, they get tobacco-sick, you know. We had a hand the other day cropping tobacco and he got sick on tobacco. He dropped out—monkeyed out." J. Marion Vaught, Jr., remembers that Heck Vereen, the father of Link (a.k.a. Donnie Grant), would declare, "You can't monkey pewter!" "I's the Pewter Man. You just can't melt pewter down" (Int. March 17: 10).

[5] During World War II, "old Bud Fore" wanted to build tobacco-curing furnaces, but without fuel for his truck he had to carry his tools over his shoulder in a sack, with little help from a once-broken leg. W. Irving Jones, Sr. (b. 1895) tells this story:

> "'Mr. Irving, I come to see if you could help this old nigger.' And I said, 'Well, Bud, what is it?' He said, 'I wanted to get down to the ration board and get me some gasoline so I can go build these furnaces. They won't give me a bit. They gave me a card for my family, and that's all.' So I

went to the board and told 'em what was what; they said, 'Well, we'll give you a B card for him to have for that purpose.'" (Int. Aug. 18: 13)

⁶ Were merchants sometimes cheated, or "beat"? Jones describes a trick that may have been used to circumvent the quotas introduced in 1933:

"Two fellas back there used to pick all the better tobaccos, carry 'em to Tom and sell 'em on the floor, and then they would take the other tobacco and carry it and sell it in their name. But the good tobacco they sold differently and of course that wasn't right. A lot of that stuff has gone over the dam and a lot is being transacted today. (Aug. 18: 23).

"A 'pin-hooker,'" reports Dr. R.C. Smith, "was a speculator:

"Although he worked for himself rather than a tobacco company, he was allowed to buy tobacco by the warehouse people. If he thought the price was too low, he would buy somebody's tobacco, dress it up—take out the dead leaves—and put it on the market later in hopes of getting a better price. Or he would buy [a pile or two] from a needy farmer before the market began; he'd ride out into the country or the farmer would bring in his crop." (See also Prince, *Long Green*, 81.)

CHAPTER 7
THE BEACH

Cad Holmes (b. 1945): *"You couldn't mingle in the water then, anyway."*
Georgia S. Lance (b. 1926): [shakes head] *"Oh, no, no, no, no, no."*
Nellie H. Johnson (b. 1918): *"You could wade the water far as your knee*
[moves hand to shin] *or your ankle. That's all."*
Cad Holmes: *"But you couldn't be on the beach in the summertime."*
(Int. Peterkin: 44)

Fig. 7.1. Old times on the Recent Barrier. Horry County Museum.

As his chariot rolled over the shell fragments and petrified sharks' teeth of Long Bay, President Washington, a slave owner, could little imagine that people from all thirteen former colonies would frolic along the shore–and that Negroes would be among them, splashing in the very waves that had borne their ancestors from Africa.

The future resort would subsume plantations. The Ark, for example, owned by John M. Tillman. In 1860, according to the U.S. Census, the farm comprised 250 acres of improved (developed) land and 3,000 unimproved. It produced upland rice, sweet potatoes, and 2,000 bushels of Indian corn, and included 63 slaves (Boyle, "Interview…Rutledge," 11). The house was located near the future Willow and 3rd Ave. S., Surfside Beach (Jackson, "Memorials," 6).

In the late 1930s, Genevieve W. Chandler interviewed Sabe Rutledge, who reminisced about his childhood at the place (see Fig. 7.2):

"Boil salt? Pump! Pump! Pump it! Had a tank. Run from hill to sea. Had a platform similar to wharf…. Go out there on platform. Force pump. My grandmother boil salt way after Freedom. We tote water. Tote in pidgin and keeler [a small tub]—make out of cedar and cypress…. My grandmother had two pots going. Boil all day and all night. Biling [sic]. Boil till he ticken (thicken). Cedar paddles stir with." ("Uncle Sabe Rutledge" 59. See also Rhyne 46-47.)

Dave Carr (Fig. 5.1), the son of Rutledge's sister, was also born at the Old Ark. "But now it's named Surfside and my foreparents were slaves…" (Int: 1). Its plantation house remained standing until well into the twentieth century.

During Sabe's childhood, the Atlantic helped supply the sodium chloride needed to preserve fish and other meat. "You must remember that all of the salt that we had during the Civil War had to be boiled out of sea water," wrote Ellen Cooper Johnson (15). The rogue soldiers who burned the family's naval stores in Cool Spring stole not only meat but salt. During the war Woodrow Long's grandfather, allowed to go home and die from a fever, hitched a ride on a wagon going from Arkansas to—of all places—Cherry Grove Beach, for the Yankees had taken Vicksburg and cut off access to the salt mines in Louisiana (Int. March 1990: 4).

In Plate 9, Flossie Morris stands by the salt-making kettle used by her uncle, Louis Floyd Sarvis, and her aunt's husband, James Dusenbury (Int: 17). Another such vat was taken from its brick foundation by Noah Scarborough Hardwick (b. 1870) and used for fifty years in the Adrian Community to wash clothes, make syrup, scald hogs, make lye soap, and bathe people (Hopkins 26-27).[1]

Fig. 7.2. Sabe Rutledge, identified by Genevieve Chandler Peterkin. The site was identified by Nellie H. Johnson as his home on the Sand Ridge (off the later Glenns Bay Road). Photo by Bayard Wootten. North Carolina Collection, University of North Carolina at Chapel Hill.

Myrtle Beach Memories, a lighthearted video-postcard (SCETV, 2003), passes over the historical constraints on African Americans. "If you saw a black man up and down here," declared one motel owner in Crescent Beach, "he worked for a white man" (p.c. July 2000). Jack Thompson reports that if black people crossed Kings Highway in the '30s, '40s, and '50s, they had to be going to or from a job. They were not allowed on the shore. "But the blacks," he points out, "were actually responsible for building much of Myrtle Beach:

> "The wonderful old white guys took a lot of credit for building piers, hotels, roads, and most of the infrastructure. Actually that hard blood, sweat, and tears was done by black people. The meals that were cooked and served that Myrtle Beach became noted for were done by sweet black cooks. A lot of the recipes that are famous today were created by the black folks that worked in these kitchens." (Int: 6-7)

As a young woman Genevieve Chandler Peterkin (b. 1928) and her relatives drove to the deserted Garden City Beach a year after the causeway was built. A Mr. Stroud arrived in a pickup full of boys—white and black, probably his children and field-hands, all of whom had helped to crop tobacco. The kids scrambled over the dunes and waded in the surf, whereupon another white man arrived with his wife and children: "He actually picked up small rocks [*illustrating*] from the beach, throwin' 'em at the children tellin' them to get back to the truck 'n off the beach" (Int. Peterkin: 44-45).

Ironically, some of the coastal property had been owned by African Americans. "The Singleton Swash tract was bought from a Negro, Frank Keel" (Godfrey, "Excerpts," 9). Andrew Stanley's sheep-raising grandmother in Nixonville "I guess she had—oh, 5000 acres":

> "She [her property] went all the way to the ocean, where the swash across the road down there to Windy Hill, the bridge across the road—that was belonged to two brothers live right across there. They come there from the ocean to right 'cross that branch there—you can see to it just to look out the woods 'way down,…from there to the ocean. Highwater mark. Now they doesn't own nary a foot of it." (Int. 3 Oct. 1993: 6)

Robert Bellamy (b. 1917) performs a title search:

> "I know Cherry Grove, in Ocean Drive, used to belong to colored people on the right all the way through there and the colored people left and went North, like they did in Wilmington, and the white folks took all the land." (Int: 4)

His adoptive sister, Katie Bellamy Randall (b. approx. 1900), remembered that Sam and Mary Bellamy had 32 acres that ran clear to the creek on Little River Neck: in debt, they couldn't pay money for their mules and fertilizer, but [*her century-old eyes widening*] "they had *land.*"[2]

Despite their property and labor, African Americans had but one small area where they were welcome to swim. Testimony comes from Leroy Upperman, M.D. (b. 1913), who was interviewed in Wilmington while consulting a map drawn in 1946 by "A.J. Baker, surveyor." Dr. Upperman once belonged to a consortium that purchased the Atlantic Beach tract in the 1940s. He said that whites wanted people to work for them either as domestics or entertainers, but the big bands and others couldn't stay in the white areas. So George Tyson, a black man, wanted to develop a beach that would serve the needs of black people, including school teachers:

> "Atlantic Beach was the only one—except for the small one of Sea Breeze, which is about fifteen miles from Wilmington—that blacks had available to them. Compared to nothing, this was very promising." (Int: 2).

Many families visiting Myrtle Beach, as Stanley D. Coleman recalled, would take their cooks along. "Sometimes their boyfriends would come get them and take them up to Atlantic Beach, then bring them back when it was over that night" (Int. 21 Oct: 12-13).

Although white people might have difficulties reaching the surf, nobody could turn them away. Indeed, even before the beginning of the twentieth century, when Burroughs & Collins established New Town, whites from Horry County or further inland would go to Pawleys Island to escape from the malarial swamps, or go elsewhere up and down the future Grand Strand. They would also go for a holiday: "Cherry Grove and Windy Hill Beaches were resorts long before Myrtle Beach came into existence. Indians, too, from North Carolina, used to go to the beach at Cherry Grove "and bring their tents" (Int. W. Jones, Sr., 1977: 51).

At the beginning of the 1900s, when loggers were turning the woods horizontal, and a "crop" was beginning to mean a field of sticky leaves rather than a stand of resinous pines, tourism made its naked footprint on the strand when the Conway & Seashore train came to a halt at the Myrtle Beach depot.

Travel the Strand of Time

This itinerary follows the entourage of President Washington. Remember that for the first third of the 21st century, Highway 17 between Wilmington and Charleston snubbed the beach in favor of Marion and Florence (*Official*), and Kings Highway, despite its august name, was still a clay-sand road on a 1930 map (Plate 10).

• "Only one house you could rent": Little River and North Myrtle Beach

In Little River, as Louise Stone (b. 1911) testifies, a person could walk down a sandy road to the waterfront, where nothing much was built, although the Bryans constructed a hotel in the late 1920s for people coming to fish (Int: 4). When the relatives of Annie Lee S. Bailey's father came to visit from Georgia, a trip to the beach was a must for them via Wortham's Ferry: "They only had one house you could rent. And it was right up on the strand" (Int: 7).

Anonymous. *In 1892, one tourist describes a group that visited from Williamsburg and Marion Counties:*
"The party was composed principally of young pleasure-seeking individuals—young ladies and gentlemen possessed of great talents for music who were bent on having a Golly time, and spared no means in entertaining those around them. With their string band, accompanying vocal music, old Ocean's roar was lulled into oblivion…." ("Little River Beach")

Eatofel V.T. Arehart (b. 1913). *Into oblivion went some of the terrain itself, according to this former schoolteacher:*
"I remember being very upset because a man had filled in what had been a natural drainage basin, a lake. Filled it in and sold it as a beach lot. Well, all the water that came backed up all around people's houses and they began complaining about it. The beach looks nothing like it looked. When I was small they would fish on Waties Island (Fig. 10.3). They'd take the mules and the boats and seines and spend the fall fishing." Sometimes the children were allowed to spend a day or two. "But it seemed to me it must have reached to the sky—the biggest sand dune; we couldn't wait to go up and just roll down. Well, there's no sand dune there now."

"It was not until 1925 that a group of people from Florence came and sold lots at Cherry Grove. I guess Miss Belle Edge probably built the first pavilion there…. It had a porch all the way around it and it had a little snack bar. That was pretty modern to have a bath house to be able to go to the beach and have a place to change your clothes…" (Int: 15-17).

Theatus G. Garrison (b. approx. 1920). *Before emigrating to New York, she would go camping with her family:*
People used to treat themselves at the end of the harvest by spending the night at the beach. "We had a big wagon and it had a top. It would mostly be made out of unbleached muslin,…brownish. They'd be working on that thing a month or more before we went to the beach." There "we'd go in the woods and hunt hickory nuts" to put in our bags. I'd be scared of the river because I thought the horses might jump off and carry the wagon, too. A lot of times I stayed [home in Loris] with Miss Maggie, my school teacher." (Int: 19-20)

Catherine H. Lewis (b. 1928). *Long before 1968, when North Myrtle Beach was formed from Cherry Grove, Ocean Drive Beach, Crescent Beach, and Windy Hill Beach, Catherine donned one of the wool swimsuits that ladies could rent at Ocean Drive:*
"The water would drain out of them so that they would feel dry to the touch, but they were still so cold. But it didn't bother anybody apparently that everybody else in the world had worn the same suit." (Int. Arehart: 17)

96

Fig. 7.3. Post card of Atlantic Beach scene. Courtesy Susan H. McMillan.

Andrew Stanley (b. 1904). *Even farm animals might enjoy a vacation:*
"Sometimes a sheep would go to the ocean—to Windy Hill, to Cherry Grove—and let out the flies in the summertime and lay down and then to stay for a few days. [Grandmother'd] get uneasy about 'em, she'd hitch up the old oxens and get a little bit of feed and go to hunt her sheeps, and drive those oxens down there until she found 'em. Then she'd talk to 'em and give 'em a little feed, get in the street and follow her back."

James Stevens (b. 1920). *A native of Loris, this powerful state senator was once a boy:*
"I can remember the dirt road from here to Ocean Drive and Cherry Grove, [which] had five cottages," one of them owned by a relative, as well as a dilapidated salt mill. Mr. [Nicholas] Nixon had a store with a dancehall over it. On a dirt road at Ocean Drive there was a bath house, one side for women and one for men. On top was a full barrel: "The sun warmed the water so it was nice to take a shower in it." Mr. Dan Hardwick used to load them up in his car and take them to the beach on Sunday afternoon. "He had room for about nine of us—we were all small—and I well remember one time that we drew lots and I was the one left out. I looked so disappointed, undoubtedly, that he said, 'Well, we've always got room for one more.'" (Int: 2-3)

Leroy Upperman, M.D. (b. 1913). *People would drive down early from Wilmington and spend the day (Fig. 7.3):*
"If you were young enough, you'd go to the various places of entertainment" where you could eat seafood, drink beer or, if you knew someone, get booze. "Sometimes the streets were so crowded that it would take you maybe a half hour to drive" from the ocean highway four blocks to the ocean front. Anyone spending the night had the choice of rooming houses, the Gordon Hotel, or private homes. (Int: 2-4. See also Dozier, "Dr. Peter C. Kelly.")

Genevieve W. Chandler (b. 1890). *Traveling to Windy Hill from Marion, the family pitched tents near the home of an Irishman, the red-haired and freckled Mr. Patrick:*
"He would say 'Wife, pass the fry,' meaning pass the ham…. The only family I remember was the King family, rich in chickens, hogs, and children. We had a white-coated cook cooking in a Dutch oven [a heavy metal pot or a metal device equipped with shelves and placed before the fire]. We ate Mr. King's cabbage, a big Irish cobbler, potatoes, and butts meat. The hogs would try to get our dinner; we'd run out in the rain to run them off." ("Going" 3)

• "Almost like quicksand": Singleton Swash

Mitchelle Collins (b. 1886). *Near the swash at the northern tip of Myrtle Beach, the daughter of Benjamin Grier Collins enjoyed a fringe benefit:*
"That was the only beach we knew then because Burroughs & Collins owned this little cottage for the employees. They let them go down there in the summer. We stayed about one week, I guess. That's the first time I saw the ocean, of course; I was about five or six years old." (Int: 21)

Donald M. Burroughs (b. 1887). *The family "would leave Conway by steamboat and go up to Papa's branch store:*
"Here the huge turpentine wagons were waiting to take us to the shore. As children, Old Green Wilkins was our favorite wagon driver, for he would keep us entertained with wonderful tales. We would ride for a while, jump off, and walk along the sandy roads, picking blackberries until we were tired, run to catch the wagon again, hop on, and ride. It was a full-day trip.

"If the tide was right when we came to Singleton Swash…, we could wade across. It was very exciting when the tide was high and the mules would have to swim." Across the swash rose a large dune that supported a one-room house where the women would sleep on pallets while the men would sleep on the wagons or in any other shelter. "Once the boys rolled one of the wagons filled with sleeping men, including the preacher, down into the swash." (Kearns 100-02).

Lucille B. Godfrey (b. 1891). *Donald's sister records more details about the trip to a place that, as President Washington noted, "at times, by the shifting of the Sands is dangerous":*
Most of the supplies having been loaded on the boat the night before, the *Driver* left Conway around sunrise and went to Grahamville, a center for the naval stores industry. There it was unloaded, mattresses and camping equipment were put in turpentine wagons…. The children played games, hopped rides, picked huckleberries, and ate raw peanuts and

peppermint sticks. "Mama rode in a buggy and I can still hear the sand creaking as the wheels turned. Once the teams got in a stretch of soft sand in crossing the swash, almost like quicksand." They arrived at low tide so as to ford the creek from the side. Food was prepared over open fires and on crude platforms with a heavy layer of sand. This saved much stooping. "Bathing suits were old clothes for the men, the myrtle and scrub oaks affording all the privacy needed. The women and children, of course, had their own 'baths': I remember they had stylish suits made of bed ticking [woven fabric used to cover a mattress or pillow], high at the neck, long sleeves, and gathered at the ankles. They wore big straw hats tied close under the chin—sometimes bonnets." ("Some" 22)

J. Harry Lee (b. 1908). *As a boy, Lee and his family would head toward the Atlantic from Sterritt Swamp:*
We would take a road across one branch and across another; some branches would have water, some wouldn't. "There was a ridge between the branches, right long ways in there right on to Singleton Swash. It would take us about a day going and a day to come. We'd tie the mules up there and the flies would eat 'em up" [*chuckling*]. We camped there in the open air—"just built us a fire under the trees. At that time there weren't nobody down there. There was one old house out there over the hill. There was a big hill back between [us and] the water." (Int: 10-11)

Annette E. Reesor (b. 1909). *For summer residents of Myrtle Beach, it was worth an eight-mile walk in the broiling sun to go crabbing:*
Their destination was the summer cabin of Mr. D.T. McNeill, shipping agent for the Waccamaw Line (see Fig. 3.14). "Every August his five Bell grandchildren and their parents escaped the heat of their Wampee farm to its cool comfort." Before making coffee from the spring-water in back, the adults would laughingly pluck out the "wiggle-tails" (mosquito larvae). "Our catch on one particular outing was especially bountiful. Bushel baskets were filled with angry, spitting, squirming blue crabs. 'Aunt' Mary Jane had the huge iron pot boiling, and as she dumped the live crabs into it, some of them were so uncooperative as to crawl out and scurry around the kitchen floor. Their sharp, open claws were a menace to the children's bare toes." ("De Angel" 24)

• "'Clams, crab' hawked from tubs": Myrtle Beach

Myrtle Beach was more a shoreline than a town. "There was one vast sand dune starting below Withers Swash and reaching to Singleton Swash…. The dune line stood about to Ninth Avenue and Kings Highway" (Edward E. Burroughs 22). As Lucille B. Godfrey remembers the place, it "was white, with big sand hills behind—the myrtle, scrub oaks, growing just beyond." Even as late as World War II, "There were 20-foot sand dunes," remembers Mickey Spillane. Beholding a long, white strand from the cockpit of a P-52, he told the crew chief to invent a problem with the plane, landed at the airbase, stayed for a few days fishing and crabbing, and ended up living in Murrells Inlet (Armor 24).

Fig. 7.4. Seaside Inn. Horry County Museum.

Burroughs & Collins constructed the railroad primarily to get access to timber, when the late F.G. bought tracts large and small from owners who had leased the rights to turpentine operators (Godfrey, "Some," 18-19). Before summer houses were built, Lucille and her family and others "spent one or two summers in small company houses that were built for the 'force'"–i.e., loggers (Godfrey, "Excerpts," 7). "Parties who have been on the beach of late at the site of the new town," reported the *Horry Herald* in 1899, "give a gratifying description of the location and say that it is barely one hundred yards from Front Street to the water's edge" ("Matters" 22 June).

In 1901 the Seaside Inn was constructed (Fig. 7.4). People had to walk there from the depot on boards laid over sand. "Big bones of a whale that rested in front of the hotel provided sport for the children as they stepped in and out of his jaw and jumped over his backbone" (Epps, "Have," 14). Like recreation, public health was barebones. "Most people in the area had shallow wells," according to Edward Burroughs (b. 1900), and were afraid to drink the water because of typhoid fever. So when you ordered groceries from the store, you ordered one or two demijohns of deep-well water" (25-26).

Burroughs & Collins made some modest efforts to develop the land for more than timber as well as the vegetables grown to feed the hands. Some buyers came from Conway and west to Florence and Columbia: "Front lots sold for $25 if you agreed to build" (Godrey, "Excerpts," 8). Boarding houses sprang up in the mid-20s.

In about 1927, when Kings Highway was straightened, new streets were laid out, new businesses were opened, and "North Carolinians poured down" (Epps, "Editorial," 3). Sam Cox, Jr., recalls that the manager of Myrtle Beach

Farms, James Bryan, would use a cow chain to measure lots. "If somebody wanted to buy a front row lot, he would measure off 2 links of it, 60 feet, or 3 links, or 4—it would have to be increments of 30 feet (Int: 10). Around 1930, Bryan "said if you'll build a house on it costing $5,000, he'd give you the lot" (E. Benton 9).

In 1920, a large concession stand-plus-bath house was built. The first summer vacation house, according to J.P. Cartrette, stood at the northwest corner of Ninth Avenue North and Chester Street:

> "It was later called the Sand Hill House because during the winter the wind would blow over the dunes stretching a thousand feet or more to the ocean, piling it up about a foot deep on the wide porches surrounding the house. In the spring Mr. Bryan would send men to shovel off the sand, then the women to sweep and scrub." ("Good" 22)

Lumber and vegetables became less valuable than the land that gave them root. In 1926, the Woodsides from Greenville bought out 65,000 acres from Burroughs & Collins, a tract bordered on the north end by Singleton Swash. The land was repossessed in 1933, but not before the Woodsides had built Pine Lakes Golf Club as well as a million-dollar hotel—both harbingers of times to come. It was also in the 1920s that the Greek community began to arrive, most of them in the restaurant business; besides the draw of north-south traffic along Highway 17, there was the climate, because "Many of the immigrants could not bear the bitter cold winters of the North." (Spirakis 6. See also Dino Thompson, *Greek Boy*, a memoir of growing up in the bosom of Myrtle Beach.)

For photographs, see J. Thompson, *Reflections* and *Memories*. For photos and vintage postcards, see S. H. McMillan, *Myrtle Beach and the Grand Strand* as well as *Myrtle Beach and Conway*. For stories, see B. Floyd, *Tales*.

Fig. 7.5. Ruth Burroughs, b. 1875. Courtesy Mrs. Adeline Merrill.

Lucille B. Godfrey (b. 1891). *"The night when they voted on a name for the new resort"*– "The guests and many of those working there met in the old pavilion. A great many names were written on paper slips and handed in. The only other that I recall was 'Edgewater….' Because of the lovely [wax] myrtle which grew there in great abundance, Mama's suggestion was 'Myrtle Beach' and this seemed to meet with general approval and received the most votes" ("Some" 19). At the Seaside Inn music was furnished by local black musicians–fiddlers. Her late father had supervised a Negro driver named Wade: "the hotel guests found out that he could play the piano and they would not let him stop—threatened him—he was exhausted by early day light." "One hot day, an old Negro couple drove up in a wagon from Murrells Inlet. They had caught and boiled a wash tub of shrimp the night before. The shrimp were nicely covered with myrtle leaves for protection from the sun, but Ilo [Iola Buck Burroughs] and Frank warned us all of the danger of eating them. It was a major tragedy for them and a minor one for the house-keepers. There was no refrigeration except the blocks of ice sent packed in sawdust in freight cars." ("Some" 21)

Sarah B. Sherwood (b. 1884). *This was an era before lifeguards literal or figurative. On July 29, 1902, Effie, Frank, the late Edith Ella, Arthur, Sarah, Donald, and Lucille (see Fig. 7.5) went down to the breakers with a party of young people:*
"As Ruth started into the water, she handed her engagement ring to her friend, Elma Cole. Ruth could swim, as we all could, but a huge wave separated her from her friends and she was swept out to sea. People searched the strand all afternoon and through the night with torches. She was found very early the next morning by Charlie Barron of Columbia, about eight miles up the beach. She was unmarked, and lay as if sleeping, with a strand of coral seaweed twined in her hair." (Kearns 126-27. See also Godfrey, "Some," 20.)

"And that's a seat"—The Train to the Beach

Daylight, unapologetic after revealing the ringless, lifeless young woman, continued to reappear. It shined upon the fishermen as they rowed out to sea on their daily run, upon the street-peddlers, and upon the little steamboat *Ruth* as it chugged up and down the rivers on its mundane business.

The second-hand locomotive also shuttled back and forth. During the summer it remained in Myrtle Beach until morning so that commuters could spend the night (R. Jones, "Myrtle," 12). Around suppertime husbands and fathers returned from Conway to enjoy the scenery and the cool air that blew off the surf (Reesor, "Sand," 8). Captain Sasser "would back his train up on Main Street [in Conway] at 6 p.m.," remembered John C. Spivey (b. 1871), "to pick up the businessmen for the beach. If Dock Spivey, who was then the owner of Red Hill, was aboard, Captain Sasser would holler out, 'Doodle Hill' as he arrived at Red Hill." The arrival of the train "was the only thing the women and children had to look forward to," and they all helped carry luggage over the dune. At six-thirty the next morning, Sasser would blow the whistle. "That meant 'Get ready and come on.' At seven o'clock he would begin checking to see if we were all on board. If he found one missing he would blow the mad whistle…" (30).

Carl B. Bessent (b. 1891), who once awoke to find his blind horse standing in the waves, drove another buggy to Conway from Little River and then rode the train to Myrtle Beach. "There was a hotel, a pavilion, a store, and a few cottages. A generator provided electric lights. I remember that night because Jack Johnson was fighting a man named O'Brien. Everyone was interested because a black and white man were fighting. We stayed up until midnight when we received the results by telegram" ("Early" 8).[3] Born the first day of the twentieth century (1901), Claudia A. Brown used to travel the rails near her house in Homewood. "Some people carried a big ol' frying pan to fry fish, and a pot for rice. Most carried sweet potatoes. Everybody was laughing and enjoying themselves. They sat in a regular passenger car with windows, and the train crossed the Waccamaw on a trestle" (Int. 21 July: 1).

"Moving to the beach was a task," according to Edward E. Burroughs (b. 1900), the son of F.A. and Iola Buck Burroughs. The railroad placed a boxcar in front of their house on Main St., whereupon the vacationers loaded the furniture in one end, and in the other, the cow and calf (the only milk supply), plus the horse and wagon. In later years the family did ride in a passenger car, but on the first trip that he remembers, they crossed the river at Conway on a flat to reach the newly extended railroad (25-26).

There were also special excursion trips. In 1904 Cordie Page (b. 1884) took one of these to Myrtle Beach from Aynor: "I rode on a flatcar that had been hauling dirt. They put some blocks down there, and some plank boards, and that's a seat" (C. Lewis, "Cordie Page," 32). One Sunday, J.O. Cartrette (b. 1892), along with several other boys from Homewood, took his first excursion and, after wandering around for hours with nothing to do, decided to take a dip—with no thought of renting a bathing suit, which would cost half as much as their railroad fare. "We removed our clothes, left them on the sand, and waded in. Had a good swim and no rush." When they came out, "The hot sun soon dried us and what salt stuck to our bodies was only a pleasant memory that we had been in the ocean" (20).[4]

Marguerite W. Altman (b. 1907) remembers that her husband's family rode the train from Aynor when there were only two rental cottages at Myrtle Beach. "For swimsuits the boys used overalls with bibs. After swimming, Purdy started shaking. Everybody thought the mighty ocean had scared him but good. He was about to freeze and no one had thought to bring him an extra shirt or jacket" (11).

See J. Thompson, *Reflections*, leaf 23; and S. H. McMillan, *Myrtle Beach and Conway*, 13.

John C. Spivey (b. 1871). *Before volcanic giraffes and elephants, many wild animals frequented Myrtle Beach. Spivey's brother-in-law Charles H. Snider called his summer home "Turtle's Nest":*
Soon after the name was displayed, a turtle was caught in front of the place. Mr. Will Bryan identified it as one that had lost a foot in a trap at Little River a few years before. "He said he kept the turtle long enough to teach it to read and then let it go back to the ocean." This explained why it had come out in front of that particular house. (7)

Lucille B. Godfrey (b. 1891). *"Myrtle Beach Sanitary Department was handled pretty efficiently by 'Uncle' Billy Rainbow":*
"He had a cart and mule and several helpers. He made the rounds early in the morning and soon his barrels were full with feed for his pigs…. 'Uncle' Billy was ably assisted by an old sow and her brood. She began her day soon after sunrise, coming up from Spivey Beach, snorting, squealing, and upsetting containers" outside the various cottages. "Early one morning we heard a great commotion in the kitchen—the old sow had walked up the back steps, torn through the mosquito netting screen door into the kitchen, and ripped open a sack of flour" ("Some" 19, 21). Before a statewide law required fences, cattle roamed everywhere. "When there was a land breeze, great droves came down to the strand and stood right at the water's edge, patiently waiting for the wind to shift."

Mr. Bryan, overseer of Myrtle Beach Farms, hired Jule Cooper to buy fish "and scour the country for fresh eggs, chickens, and vegetables." If the weather prevented the Negro fishermen from going out along the coast, he would order her to kill another goat. "Finally Jule said, 'Mr. Bryan, I have already fed those people so much goat that they are walking around on banisters.'" ("Excerpts" 7, 21)

Florence Epps (b. 1907). *Miss Epps inventories the fauna:*
"oil cloth on the tables, mosquito netting at the windows, fans made of newspaper strips attached to a rod which brushed the flies away at mealtime, alligators under the porches on warm summer day, and razorback hogs roaming wild through the woods…" ("Welcome"). "Just as the narrator reached the chilling climax [of a ghost story], a monstrous grunting beast loomed over the crest of the dune! Brave dog Skeezix hastened to the rescue with ferocious barks that turned terror-by-night into swine!" ("Sand" 9)

Annette E. Reesor (b. 1909). *Every day was a celebration for Florence's sister, "Dickie":*
News and reading material arrived on the evening train. One lady saved all of her magazines for the year to read all the installments of a story at once. Children rode the waves, swam beyond the breakers in mild weather, paddled in shallow water and rough, and "laughed at novices who screamed and clung to each other in fright" (see Fig. 7.6). They collected

shells as well as Indian arrowheads and pottery. On rainy days they played games and did crafts. "Evenings were glorious starlit wonders. All the children and dogs in the neighborhood gathered on the sand dune between our house and the Barretts' to gaze at the stars and tell ghost stories. We swapped information about constellations that were so clear we could almost touch them."

Fig. 7.6. Group in surf, Myrtle Beach, c. 1920. Horry County Museum.

The first Pavilion, 1908-25 (see Fig. 7.7) was connected to the hotel by a boardwalk. Having so many sides that it appeared round, it was electrified by a Delco generator system. "For music there was a squeaky Victrola [a phonograph wound with a crank] with a small morning-glory speaker, and about a dozen records. Sometimes there was a marvelous string band of Negro musicians. Then one summer here was a live orchestra of college boys!" As young people danced, older people rocked and children played on the surrounding porch, "which was frequently covered with encroaching sand dunes." Then it was back home along the boardwalk. The first to open the door did so with exceeding care "lest a sudden gust of wind blow the flame in the kerosene lamp high enough to smoke the chimney black. Then to bed with the hushed murmur of the surf for a lullaby…" ("Sand" 8-10). George, who helped her father at the drug store in Conway, also did odd jobs around the summer cottage. A week before school resumed in the fall, "As he nailed down the shutters, his hammer had the sound of doom in it." ("De Angel" 22)

Fig. 7.7 First of several Pavilions, c. 1920. Horry County Museum.

Eugenia Buck Cutts (b. 1912). *Eugenia remembers jumping and dancing at the Pavilion:*

"My best experience there was climbing up on the roof because the sand dunes were so high we could jump off the roof into them—and look at the stars." "I went to the opening of the Ocean Forest Hotel [in 1930] and I was taken by my first cousin, Henry Burroughs [the brother of Edward]. We went in a party…. My biggest treat was dancing with Collins Spivey." (Int: 16)

E.R. McIver, Jr. (b. 1912). *The same boy who watched his father's car kick the ferry and sink into the river had another misadventure:*

"They had house parties, fine dances at the Pavilion. We camped in 1924 or '25 on the beach—*eaten up* by mosquitoes, I swear. Went down in an old car 'n' that thing got stuck in the sand. We left it down there—had to hitchhike home. I went back after the war—and that thing was still there stuck in the sand" [*laughter*]. (Int. Wells. See Fig. 7.8.)

Fig. 7.8. Follow that chariot! Horry County Museum.

E. Horry Benton (b. 1913). *Benton's dad lent some farm animals to help build the Ocean Forest Hotel:*

"They was down here working and they needed some mules to pull slip-pans [big pans with side-handles for dumping dirt], grade the streets, and everything like that. There wasn't no trucks. So my daddy, in the wintertime, he had two pairs of mules, so we let them. Of course, the company paid him for the mules and fed and looked after them." "It was a huge undertaking to do by hand and every one of those bricks had to be unloaded off the train, onto a truck, carried up there and unloaded…. "They relied on local people to work and I think everybody around Conway and Loris and the whole county, Georgetown County, too, that wanted to work had a job…. It was hard for them to get here and most of them could come and stay five days and work." Some would camp nearby in tents. (Int: 1, 7. See Fig. 7.9.)

Fig. 7.9. Construction nears Depression: the Ocean Forest Hotel in the late 1920s. Horry County Museum.

Blanche W. Floyd (b. 1920). *In 1930, the finest hotel between New Jersey and Miami dominated the crescent of Long Bay:*

"It could be seen for miles. To some of us, it was a fairy tale magic castle, unbelievably modern: It had elevators (in a world of one-and two-story buildings). Painted white, against the ocean's blue backdrop, it seemed incredibly beautiful." Its décor was fancy and its staff refined. "To people in the tiny fishing and lumbering village of Myrtle Beach, the Ocean Forest Hotel seemed a world apart" (*SN* 17 July 1999. See also *Tales* 93-96. For photographs of its construction, grandeur, and demolition, see J. Thompson, *Reflections*.)

Jack Thompson (b. 1936). *"In the late 40's and early '50s the Ocean Forest was in its glory days"*:
"It had an outdoor amphitheater called the Marine Patio [Fig. 7.10], where people could dance under the stars by the music of big national bands like Tommy Dorsey and Tex Beneke. The hotel was situated exactly halfway between New York and Miami, and most of the bands traveled in buses. They would trade out their stay for three or four days by playing." (Int: 4)

"Groups of kids from a certain area, a college or high school, would rent a big old house and come for a week. They would usually bring a chaperone to keep them all separated so they didn't all sleep together. In the daytime they are scattered out sunbathing, raising Cain, and dancing all night." (Int: 8)

Fig. 7.10. Advertisement for the Marine Patio, Myrtle Beach *News*, 4 June 1954: 1-C. Horry County Museum.

Stanley D. Coleman (b. 1915). *Young and old had different ideas about recreation:*
A lot of elderly folks would walk up the boardwalk to hear the big band at the Pavilion. Young people might play a practical joke: "maybe a black stocking stuffed a little bit and pulled with a fishing line" would make a girl jump over it and scream "Great God, there's a snake!"

They would also have house parties. "One night you could look up and down the strand with that moonlight and I could count nine blankets and the mosquitoes were about to eat us up. This couple came along and I said, 'Let me ask you: have you got any mosquito citronella?' He said, 'No, I hadn't got any. I tell you what. The third blanket down there—the guy has a bottle.'" (Int. 21 Oct: 11-12)

Marie Gilbert (b. 1924). *Marie and her family would travel from Florence to spend the summer, accompanied by two Negro servants. In her book of poems,* Myrtle Beach Back When, *she celebrates this primitive but idyllic experience—its scenery, people, animals, food, sensations. Here is an excerpt from "Morning on the Back Porch":*

"On the ocean side
the sun comes blinding
steaming away night mists.
On the street side the house itself
makes long shadows across the chicken yard,
cool breeze wanders to the tune
of contented cackling, to the tune
of 'clams, crab' hawked from tubs, and
baskets brought to back steps.

"'Corn, butter beans, potatoes
squash, okra and tomatoes'
sings the driver to his mule
pulling the wagon slowly—
slowly enough for Kaleb in his brown bag hat
and Myrtle in her blue uniform dress
to step up to the swinging scales,
purchase from the driver." (7)

Elizabeth Goldfinch Singleton (b. 1924). *Raised in Conway, she recalls housing in the late 1920s-1940 that must have resembled logging cabins:*
"A beach vacation for the majority of us not fortunate enough to own a cottage involved renting one for a week or two and invariably having a cast-off stove, no hot water, a huge table and benches for eating, discarded iron beds, no closet space, and usually a 'pass-through' for food from kitchen to dining area." (5-6. See Fig. 7.11.)

Fig. 7.11. Some vacationers stayed at Myrtle Beach State Park, the forerunner of camping towns. Horry County Museum.

Julia Pryor Macklen (b. 1902). *Julia and her husband, H. Lloyd Macklen, were early grocery store, motel, and restaurant owners:*
Turnips, rutabagas, and cabbage were available locally (Int. 1993: 2). "After my husband would work in the store all day,…often stay there till seven or eight o'clock, he would drive to Wilmington and sleep in his truck until daylight, when farmers had the habit of bringin' produce…. He would also buy a barrel of fresh shrimp and fish, packed in ice." (Int. 1992: 3)

There were only two motor courts (i.e., with separate cottages); the Macklens bought the Travelers Motor Hotel, the second one constructed at the beach. "We could sit down in our living room, which was our office, and see the cars slow down and then go on; we would realize that we had failed to turn the sign from 'No Vacancy' to 'Vacancy.' We could fill up in a matter of hours" (Int. 1993: 5-6). Then the couple bought a motel-restaurant on Kings Highway just north of Chapin Memorial Park. (See Fig. 7.12.) "People who were here for fun would be at the kitchen door when we would open with fish that they just caught" (Int. 1992: 6). "I've known of people bringing a whole 24-pound size flour sack full of shelled, fresh butterbeans" (Int. 1993: 7).

The restaurant operated year-round, its winter guests mainly people going to or from Florida. She used many of her own recipes and Mr. Macklen introduced the broiled seafood platter (Int. 1993: 27). The business always had white waitresses, but since professional caterers did not work, Mr. Macklen started training four colored boys who were dishwashers. "He would approach them and say, 'How would you like to make twice as much money as you are making now?' 'Yes, sir,' they would say. And he would say, 'Furthermore, if you do that as well as I want it, I wouldn't mind doubling it again'" (Int. 1993: 14). In the late 40s her husband worked out an advertisement: a beach scene that featured moving waves and an animated lobster. "Parents many times had to take their children and watch the sign." (Int. 1993: 18)

Bertha P. Staley (b. 1907). *In the 1950s Bertha (who as a girl had taken the steamboat to Georgetown) drove to Myrtle Beach with the United Daughters of the Confederacy:*

Fig. 7.12. Lloyd's Motor Court and Restaurant, 1951. Courtesy Jack Thompson.

"We looked for a place and nobody served lunch! There were no Hardees, and the few guest houses served meals only to their guests. We finally went to this little motel that said they would serve a lunch." (Int: 24-5)

Jack Thompson (b. 1936). *Jack began his photography career in Myrtle Beach after hitchhiking there with two other teenagers from Greenville, South Carolina:*
"The older guys would come back from Myrtle Beach and talk about the girls, the sun, the sand, and the dancing, not to mention the beer and the great times away from home. In 1951 very few people knew where Myrtle Beach was, so we thought we should be there in a couple of hours." With $2.71 among them, the boys caught numerous short rides in the back of trucks with hogs and chickens. The farmers, going ten miles an hour, knew only of Folly Beach, so "Myrtle Beach must be down around Charleston." Sleeping under a church porch in Society Hill, they arrived a day and a half after starting out. An hour later Jack was working at a photography stand owned by Dwight Lamb. (Int: 1)

Other young men from Camp Lejeune in Jacksonville, North Carolina, would visit a place named for them–the Marine Room, located at the site of the future Yachtsman. Also men would come from Myrtle Beach Air Force Base and, on buses, from Fort Jackson in Columbia. "In the '50s, when you mixed all the service people into fun-sun-and-suds time with college and high school kids, you had a volatile mix. Free-for-all-fights occurred down on the beach at nightclubs, between the lifeguards, somebody trying to be king of the beach." "There was a rough and rowdy group of young people out of Conway—we called them the 'farmers….' They were always ready for a fight…. Some of the local boys had a habit of meeting the train and picking a fight with the tourists. They tried to be tougher than the Conway boys…" (Int: 2, 5-6). "Beer in the early '50s—anybody could get it. You just had to look like maybe you were shaving. There were a number of places that you could buy it on Sunday; you just had to be real cool about it, discreet. (Int: 5)

Billie Mae Benton (b. 1927). *On the genteel side, school groups like the Home Economics Club of Conway High School would attend camps:*
"The first day it was cloudy and we didn't think we would burn and we got cooked. The four of us had to sleep cross-way in the bed. It was just a double bed and every one of us was blistered—we hollered all night—someone was touching someone else [*laughter*]. Needless to say, we stayed in that week. We didn't do nothing, 'cause we couldn't stand to have our clothes on." (Int: 7)

O.T. "Tommy" Collins (b. 1942). *"We used to come to the beach from Fort Mill, S.C.":*
"That was our vacation. Lotta times we'd come for just one day. We'd get up at five o'clock in the mornin'–Mama would throw boiled eggs and a ham biscuit in a basket and down the road we'd come. We'd stop around Monroe or McBee or somewhere like that and Daddy'd just pull over to the side of the road. We'd spend all day and Daddy'd turn around 'n drive all the way back home. You're talkin' a five-and-a-half, six-hour drive.

"But then we'd come and spend the night, after my dad worked for Springs [Cotton] Mills—which put up Springmaid Beach for his employees—in 1953-54, somewhere along then. We could stay there for a dollar a night. Per room. You'd have two little concrete beds. With a little inch-and-a-half mattress on 'em [*chuckles*]. You had a bath, you had a little screened-in porch. And there was like three rooms on it with two beds in each one of them and at the end of the hall you had a little shower. If you were lucky enough to be able to afford all three rooms, you had a private shower with your family. But if you didn't, you showered with somebody else's family." (Int. 1-2)

Mark C. Garner (b. 1920). *Garner moved to the area in 1948, co-founded the Myrtle Beach* Sun *(which heated and then absorbed the* News*), and eventually became mayor:*
"I always remember riding down Ocean Boulevard on Labor Day and seeing the men and women who operated the guest houses…; they had their suitcases and trunks packed on the porch waiting for the final guest to check out so they could go back to Greenville, Spartanburg, or Columbia or wherever they were from." (Int: 7. See Fig. 7.13.)

Belle Miller Spivey Hood (b. 1934). *D.A. Spivey's real estate company began buying land on the south end of what is now Myrtle Beach in the 1920s,*
and in the 30s and 40s this stretch was known as Spivey's Beach, which ran for about a mile between 1st and 17th Avenues South. The waterfront fish shack, where the boats of Joe Sarkis had landed, gave way to Spivey's Pavilion: "It was constructed of lumber taken from a tobacco warehouse that was being dismantled in Aynor…. In the 1940s the 'Big Apple' with its large circle of dancers progressed to the 'Little Apple,' then to the 'Jitterbug,' and finally in the '50s to the state dance, the 'Shag.'" Known on the Atlantic coast as the home of the shag, the pavilion began many a romance on its dance floor. ("Spivey's" 9)

Fig. 7.13. Aerial view of Myrtle Beach in 1953, the highest point a church steeple or watertower. Courtesy Jack Thompson.

James D. Sanders (b. 1925). *A number of Conway families had places at Spivey's Beach—"basically four walls and a roof."* Sanders' father, the foreman at the Burroughs & Collins sawmill on Kingston Lake, "carried some slabs from the mill and put them on top of the sand to go on down to the waterfront. It was considered a little foolish to build a house on the waterfront; the higher-price property was back up around where Business 17 is today." (Int: 5)

• "Indian had big camping ground": Surfside Beach

Tourists weren't the first people to walk barefoot on Surfside Beach: "Chillun have not a shoe!" declared Sabe Rutledge (Chandler, "Uncle Sabe…Story," 65). Even whites and blacks were newcomers. According to Rutledge, "Indian had big camping ground on beach near the Ark. After big blow you can find big piece of pot there. I see Indian. Didn't see wild one; see tame one" (59-60). The area later became known as Floral Beach, named after the wife of George J. Holliday, Floramae (b. 1903). (For more recollections of Surfside Beach, see H.T. Willcox.)

David Carr (b. 1887). *Logger, soldier, and railroad master, Dave was also a good Samaritan:*
"I know a boy come down the beach where I was fishing at. A white boy–drinking and messing with women and lost

his pocketbook with $150 in it. Come back next morning, crying. *I* had it. I said, 'What did you loss [sic.]?' 'I lost my pocketbook.' 'How much money was in it?' He told me. 'What's your name?' He told me. I'd say 'Here, this is it.' And he was so glad he was going to give me $10. I said, 'No, you go ahead and be particular and not loss what you got.'" Once another white boy appeared on the beach with no money or shelter, so Dave "let him stay in the fishing camp and feed him, let him fish with me and make a little money." (Int: 14)

Louise Chestnut Squires (b. 1916). *During the 1920s her father was caretaker for Floral Beach:*
"In the winter we moved into the old hotel which was located behind the huge sand dune that ran from up at Lakewood Family Campground down to what is now Garden City Beach. Over the years the dune has been leveled." The hotel, called the Ark, had been a large plantation house. The floor of the lobby had been chopped out by fishermen who, as refugees from the hurricane of 1893, had made a place for the water to escape.

A pavilion stood about two blocks south of the later pier. "The bathhouse was on the bottom or ground floor, and upstairs was a large open-air floor with a grand view all around. An orchestra was hired for the summer months and that is where I learned to do the 'Charleston.' 'Carolina Moon' became a popular new tune. I looked forward to the summer because I could see friends of the summer before and make new ones." "There were no houses or anything but myrtle bushes from Floral Beach to what is now the Point" [the tip of Garden City Beach]. (13-14. For a plat, see Martin 10.)

James Calhoun. *In 1952 a group of men negotiated to buy Floral Beach–800 acres and a dirt road on the ocean side of Highway 17, 900 acres on the other:*
G.W. "Buster" Bryan, Calhoun's lawyer and his partner in a lot of things, went down to the Garden City fishing pier and traded with the owners. Calhoun was lying down at his house, later destroyed by Hurricane Hazel, when Bryan came walking up the steps. He said, "Well, I bought it–$150,000…." The Burroughs family held 337 acres in the north end; the group sold the 900 acres across Highway 17 to Dr. Vivian F. Platt, then bought the Burroughs acreage, with all that oceanfront, for $50,000. Calhoun was elected president of the corporation by Buster Bryan, Collins Spivey, Craig Wall, Sr., Ervin Dargan, and Jamie Nettles. Bryan's wife had been down to Florida and picked out a name: Surfside. "That sounds good to me," Calhoun said. "Just add Beach to it and we will have it." (Jackson et al., "James Calhoun," 10-11)[5]

Lonely in Paradise

Sunbathers, swimmers, waders, surfers, sailors, joggers, fish-catchers, metal hunters, shell-finders, castle-builders, kite-flyers, cone-vendors, volleyball players, Frisbee-throwers—all these beachgoers make it hard to imagine the place as isolated.

In a storm, a cottage could seem as vulnerable as a ship, recalls Annette Reesor:

"'De Angel of de Lawd standing right dere, an' he ain't gwine let nuttin' hahm you chillern.'" Thus Shiney, "her round Indian-Negro face reassuring us with calmness and courage," comforted four white children gathered in "The Shelter," the E.J. Sherwoods' first beach house. The occasion was one of those sudden, terrific thunderstorms that plagued Myrtle Beach during my childhood days. With few buildings to absorb the crack-boom of thunder and lightning that played a lively game of 'miss the house, hit the water,' there was a fearsome aloneness when one came upon us." ("De Angel" 21)

Isolation could also stem from race:

"Our Negro servants came with us year in and year out. They shared our sorrows, anxieties, and joys. It was pleasant to hear them humming during meal-preparation, or singing spirituals somewhere around the place after the supper dishes were done. At first they had as complete freedom of the beach as did their employers, but when 'foreigners' came from such sophisticated places as Sumter, Florence, and Columbia, the Jim Crow Laws limited their activities. "Once Lue confided in me, 'I ain't gwine come down to dis place nex' summer.'" The beach with a stranger in Lue's bedroom was not to be contemplated. "Now I realize the loneliness these good people must have experienced with their leisure-time activities so limited." ("De Angel" 23)

The strand as remembered by Ruby S. Jones (b. 1894) could be as beautiful a place of exile as Mrs. Little's Eddy Lake:

"Great, pure white sand dunes dotted the shores beyond the strand. These were decorated with great clumps of deep green myrtle," and at night sea turtles would come ashore to deposit their eggs. "It gave one a yearning to walk in the brilliant moonlight, but pray whom would you walk with? For with all this, it was a lonely place for young people. We were glad to greet September and get back to Conway—and to us—'Civilization.'" ("Myrtle" 13)

In the 1930s, Mrs. Mary Cornelia Dusenbury Platt declared that "Myrtle Beach was getting too crowded for us," so Mary Emily moved with her parents down Kings Highway:

"There was no one living from Myrtle Beach State Park, three miles north of us, to the few homes at Floral Beach three miles south. For a girl in her teens those were lonesome summers." (Jackson, "Recollections," 4-5)

At first, lodging was what you brought on a wagon, and food what you packed on the cinder-spewing train or caught in the saltwater. Primitive the transportation, the bathhouses, the bathing attire, the measures for health and safety. Mules swam, wiggle-tails darted through spring-water, and seaweed twined in her hair.

Dunes once extended in land-waves a thousand feet to the ocean. With more animals than people around, the strand could evoke loneliness, but life for white folks was enriched by the black aunts and uncles who caught fish, peddled food, cared for children, and furnished music. Pavilions were oases for young and old, and the bones of a whale the first amusement park. Crabbers were broiled, shrimp was warm, and suits were so cold.

Anybody could get beer, a beach lot was a giveaway and the Ocean Forest a vision. As the beach developed, it became less like the Indian camping ground; with better highways the New-York-to-Florida trade increased and "Myrtle" became the white Carolinian's second home. When the Conway-to-beach train carried off passengers for the last time in 1955, the lobster waved goodbye with its neon claw. Although more and more guesthouses and motor courts appeared, suitcases and trunks still stood ready to go home on Labor Day.

Notes

[1] One of the salt works probably manufactured gunpowder (Gragg 44); it was located on Singleton Swash where the Dunes Club would be constructed almost a century later. For the magnitude of this operation, see Berry, "C.B. Berry Speaks," 18.

[2] George "Babe" Bratcher joins the multitude of those too practical to enrich their descendants. "Granddaddy told me he had an opportunity to buy land in that area [Ocean Drive] for $.50 an acre" but did not because it was nothing but useless sand (S. Smith).

[3] In 1908 Jack Johnson, a black man, defeated Tommy Burns for the world heavyweight title (Burns).

[4] In 1960, at the Jerry Cox store in Conway, Lucille B. Godfrey met Bill Cox, who had managed the first bathhouse at Myrtle Beach. "To begin the summer season," he recalled, "they had twelve suits—six for men, six for the ladies." The suits were long:

"I asked if the ladies did not wear corsets and he said, 'Yes, but you weren't supposed to know that—they were hung back to dry.' He said he cut the top out of a tomato can, punched several holes in it, put a piece of haywire for a bail—this was fastened under the water spigot to make a shower." ("Some" 25)

[5] Surfside Beach has been a fishing spot, a farm, a playground, and a war zone. Sabe's mother told him of a skirmish that had taken place down the coast at Magnolia (later Huntington) Beach:

"Ma tell me bout they had the to-do. Blockade at inlet. Had 'em out to drill (the Yankees came to shore to drill). Old man John Tillman lose all he China-a-way (chinaware)! Every bit of his china and paints (panes of glass) out the window [i.e., from the concussion of guns]. Yankee gun boat sojer (soldier) to Magnolia to drill. They [i.e. the Rebels] 'tack 'em…to cut 'em off. When Rebs tack 'em, small boats gone back. She had to brace 'em. Shoot dem shell to brace (gun boat fired to frighten Rebs who were cutting Yankees off from escape). I hear old man Frank Norris…say lot of 'em [i.e., shells] bog…. Bomb shell hit and bury them in the sand. Had to dig out." (Chandler, "Uncle Sabe Rutledge," 60-61)

CHAPTER 8
THE FISH

"They used to keep that [Little Pee Dee] river bank just as slick as glass setting on it fishing. Sometimes when one [person] would go there and see somebody at a certain place, they would have them get away and say that it was their fishing place."
Carrie D. Doyle (b. 1901), Int. 8 Sept: 18.

Fig. 8.1. And we came all the way from Hartsville. Myrtle Beach *News,* 4 June 1954: 7-C. Horry County Museum.[1]

People in Horry have always fed upon whatever stuck to creekbanks in sharp shells, burrowed under wet sand, or wriggled under brine or blackwater.

Native Americans left middens of oyster shells in several places. In Cherry Grove marsh, people harvested oysters, clams, shrimp, crabs, and fish, maybe swapping oysters for meal and flour (Katie B. Randall, b. approx. 1900). Julia Smalls' clamshell became a spoon (Dozier, "Interview," 32). Thomas C. Vaught (b. approx. 1907), reports that one Negro, Cain Dyne, sold shucked, raw oysters from Murrells Inlet. On Saturdays he brought them to Conway in a 50–pound lard stand and served them in lard trays, at least a half a pint for a dime, spicing them with pepper and vinegar (27). Surprisingly, according to J.M. Vaught, Jr. (b. 1923), people inland "wouldn't even eat shrimp," fare that came in later (Int: 10).

The man who had boiled the Atlantic shared this recipe: "Bile conch. Git it out shell. Grind it sausage grinder.

Little onion. Black pepper. Rather eat conch than any kind of nourishment out of salt water" (Chandler, "Uncle Sabe Rutledge," 62). Rutledge described this exotic catch-of-the-day:

> "You ought to been there Monday. Catch a sea monkey. You couldn't argue it from a monkey. Curl he little tail up. Move he little head quick just like a monkey. Brown. Have little old fuzz just like a goslin'-down on him…. Little nubs for feet. Work he little nub. Work it backwards and forwards. Work 'em just like they feet." (Chandler, "Uncle Sabe Rutledge," 62)

People also ate other species that depend on water to eat and reproduce. Alligator tail suited the palate of Rutledge; Henry Small would catch a turtle, cut open the side, "get that meat out of it," and make a stew (Int: 20-21). The brother of Theatus Garrison caught bullfrogs under a bridge and sold them to another fellow (Int: 15). In 1893, mammals swam right onto land, whereupon citizens cut out the blubber and extracted the oil from seventeen whales ("Local" 8 March).

But most of the protein that came from water had fins, gills, and a backbone. There are about 800 species of fish in the area (Moore), any one of which might be diverted by a communal net from the ocean to a barrel, or snagged from salt or fresh water by a variety of techniques.

"All hands to the boat": Ocean seining

One type of fishing had triple importance: dietary, economic, and social.

At times the Atlantic held so many fish in the last half of the nineteenth century that they could be scooped ashore. "I see thing in my time," declared Mundy Holmes, interviewed in Holmestown Community: "I see 'um make some haul and fish pile high as that sand hill there. Didn't been so much a seine" (Chandler, "Ex-Slave Talks," 1). But such a net, long or short, became the tool of choice. "The mullet at high tide would come right up in the suds almost," declared Sanford D. Cox, Jr., "and with one of those hand seines…you could pick them up pretty good" (Int: 23).

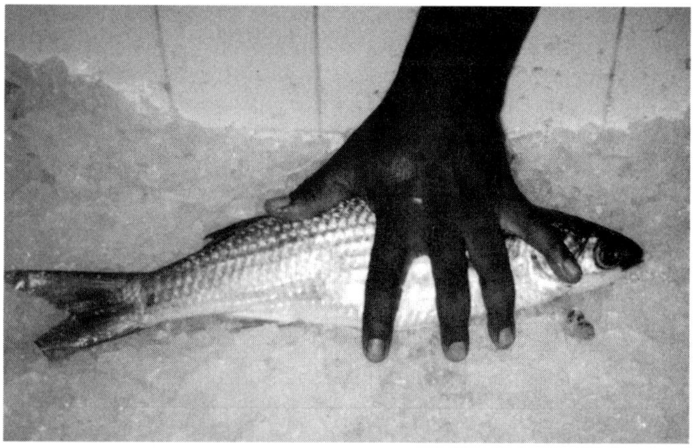

Like tobacco-growing, however, seining was typically communal. When schools of mullet and spot "ran" southward in the autumn (i.e., migrated), people brought long nets and worked together to divert them. (See Fig. 8.2.) These seiners

Fig. 8.2 Today's menu for breakfast, lunch, and dinner features Mugilidae.

were both private and commercial. As a child in Nixonville, Roberta Ward Rust (b. 1909) saw people in covered wagons coming from North Carolina to the beach to fish: "They would shoot guns, letting us know they were coming. Sometimes they even brought a dog; he would bark at us whenever I'd come to the railing fence and look over" (Int: 12-13).

Fig. 8.3. Spot (bottom) and whiting. Berry's Seafood.

Spot: "our most abundant, easiest to catch, and best tasting saltwater panfish," asserts Donald Millus (66). (See Fig. 8.3.) Robert Bellamy (b. 1917) tells about Ocean Drive, where the fishermen accumulated six rows of spot for a businessman from Wilmington:

> "They had the camp full, yard full. They had a few rows of spots piled up that high [*illustrates about three feet*]. And they'd go back from Highway 17 back down to 90. He had long-distance trucks he would bring down to get it." (Int: 7)

Until the coming of the railroad, paved roads, and trucks, however, fish could not be sent to market but instead would be carried back home in wagons. "They are certainly a Godsend to the lower classes, and none the less to the wealthy, for we all like the nice fat September mullet" (L., S.T.). According to Bernard Dawsey (b. 1912) of the Aynor area, some pupils would even carry a lunch of sweet potato and fish (18).

Raised in Homewood, J.P. Cartrette (b. 1898) describes the ritual:

> "September caravans of neighbors would take their mules and wagons, carts and buggies, and drive thirty or forty miles to the ocean and bring back barrels of mullet. We forded the

Waccamaw River at Reaves Ferry on a flat barge poled or drawn by ropes across the stream."
While they camped one night at Windy Hill Beach, rain began to fall: "My father turned the cart
upside down, and we slept under it." ("Good" 21).

As Louise C. Squires (b. 1916) remembers, "People came with wagons, boxes, and barrels to buy fish to salt down. Many campfires were built to fry fresh fish and roast sweet potatoes in hot sand close to the fire. The aroma would tantalize you real fast!" (14). Claudia Brown (who remembered frying pans on the train) unrolled a net across the mouth of a swash with several other people, and when the tide went out, they trapped the fish (Int. 31 Oct: 1). Sam Cox remembers that children might help to pull and men might go skinny dipping (Int: 22, 24). "We didn't do the hand-seine in the daytime," explains J. Harry Lee (b. 1908): "Had to wait till dark"—the fish were too far out in the daytime to get a net around them. "I been down there many a night and I would go in the water and it would be so cold my clothes would freeze on me" (Int: 12-13). Protocol was observed near Dick Pond: "After the white folks took their turn in the fish camp, the black folks came down from Socastee and the Free Woods..." (Jackson, "Memories," 5-6).

Catherine H. Lewis (b. 1928). *Catherine tells a well-known story about an escapade in the late 1920s or early '30s:*
During a house party at Crescent Beach thrown by a group from Loris, several of the men decided to go seining and drinking. To pull out a heavy load of fish, [person 1] got the idea of hitching the ends of the seine to his brand new Plymouth. He got bogged down in the sand; when they struggled unsuccessfully to free it, one of the men went for help. The others worked for a while, then shed their clothes and went to sleep in the warm dunes. In the meantime, the rescuer comes back with help. "Here is the car half-full of water, washed in the tide, their clothes floating about, no sign of them. So he goes home and tells [person 2's] wife, 'Oh, Ruth. He's gone. We've lost him.'

"Well, the next morning the sun rises and wakes our drunken fishermen. No clothes, broad daylight, and some distance from home. So they set out and by chance, they come across a clothes line with some women's bloomers flapping in the breeze.... Attired in those, they go home to greet their families." (Int: 4-5)

What were the steps of communal seining when undertaken with the help of a boat? Here are memories of those who got wet or stayed dry. (See also Berry, *SN* 2 Aug. 1997.)

• Set a lookout
Sabe Rutledge had a "lifeguard tower" [*gestures in air*]. As Genevieve C. Peterkin remembers, "Somebody would be up there as a lookout. A school o' mullet comin', and the ocean would darken, just like a big dark cloud (Int: 35).

Genevieve W. Chandler (b. 1890). *Peterkin's mother interviewed the man himself, "who was sitting on the 'LOOK OUT' at the Floral Beach Fishery":*
He "continued to let his eyes play all over the sea like searchlights, ready to wave the black flag and march down toward the fishery holding it aloft keeping himself in a line with the fish if fish were sighted. Since way before what he called 'the big war' he and his people have eaten mullet and rice for the three fall months." ("Uncle Sabe...Story," 69)

Florence Epps (b. 1907). *As a child Epps looked forward to beholding the stands erected by Joe Sarkis:*
"Made of pine poles and branches," they were "a sign that schools of mullet were on the run. Visitors, I believe, offered to help haul in return for the thrill of following Big Joe's commands, pulling on the seine, and the wonder of the catch." (Hobeika 10)

• Make the "strike"
"The men," wrote Clarke A. Willcox (b. 1896), would feed out the net in a huge half-circle. These nets were deep enough to reach bottom and several hundred yards long" (viii).

L., S.T. *Writing to the* Horry Herald *in 1905, this unknown person describes the process of "making a strike" as a group by using a gill net (set vertically in the water), a haul net, or a cast net:*
"The lookout is up the seine [i.e., toward the fish] all ready for the fray. All eyes are watching the lookout and his is watching the fish. You will hear some one of the crew say 'all hands to the boat.' The lookout is waving. Then the man in charge goes up to see if the school is worth striking and as soon as he decides to strike them, he waves the boat down to the water and follows the fish on until they get within about 300 yards of the boat." After he waves the boat to sea, the order is given, "Bow-oarsman in second bow amidships, strike seine-thrower." The next order: "Give away, boys, altogether." The captain signals to the bow-oarsman, who gives orders: "Throw the staff," "Ease inside," "Heavy outside," "Give away altogether." Then they jump. "Pull, boys, pull!" And again. "By this time the fish are all hemmed and jumping, thousands at a time. I have gone to the staff to turn it when there was danger of being killed by a large fish hitting

me on the head and I have been sore for several days by being bit by a roe fish [egg-laden]."

J.P. Cartrette (b. 1898). *Once about 100 people in families drove from Homewood to Conway and met the train:*
"The men reached down in their pockets and brought out enough silver dollars" to pay for a special trip back to Myrtle Beach. Upon arrival, they saw fishermen about a mile up the strand: "We joined them as they were unable to pull in the net due to the great number of fish, and they offered to let us share equally with them in the catch. We were only able to hold the net until a team of mules were brought to hold it until the tide went down." ("Good" 22)

Robert Bellamy (b. 1917). *After dodging copperheads in the tobacco, Bellamy had to fight high waves when his group worked on Hog Island:*
"If there come back a big tide, then you got to take that boat and bring the fish back to the hill [dune]." One time the breakers got so high "we had to go back and get the boss man–he is on top of the fish-house." (Int: 5-6)

•Haul in the catch

Mary Sarkis Hobeika (b. approx. 1904) explains that her father, Joe, came from Lebanon and originally peddled goods house-to-house in a covered wagon. Then he began a seine-fishing business near Withers Swash, where the family lived in a shack. "We would come home every summer and stay until November. He had about 50 Negroes working with him to haul in the nets...." "Daddy used to catch fish by the hundreds of barrels.... People would come from all over to buy salt fish for the winter," one of his main customers being an outfit from Wilmington (10).

Andrew Stanley (b. 1904). *This raft-builder also navigated saltwater:*
"Average of 'em was mullets and spots. Every now and then it was catfish...and a few sheepheads [the sheepshead has dark vertical markings].... They wasn't saving anything but the mullets. The other, the hogs eat 'em...and buzzards eat 'em." "I believe there was six in the boat pulling the boat 'round, and then there was fifteen, or seventeen, or eighteen sometime on the hill pulling the net out." (Int. April 1991: 17-18. See Plate 11 for Ms. Wooten's dramatic photograph.)

Louise C. Squires (b. 1916). *When Sabe Rutledge operated the fishery where the pier was later built in Surfside Beach,*
"I rode the boat sometimes when the crew went out to make a haul. The crew used large oars to paddle the boat in a semi-circle. The net was laid out as they made the run. People on the beach would get both ends of the net and drag it onto the beach. It was so exciting to me to explore the strange things that came in with the fish. (14)

•Divide the catch

Sometimes the fish were then split, gilled, and washed before they were distributed: "Take 'em in the sea and wash 'em in a big basket. They'd take 'em back onto the hill and put 'em on a scaffol' and let them dry and drain" (Katie B. Randall, b. approx. 1900). Then they were divided among the crew. (See Fig. 8.4.)

Sanford D. Cox, Jr. (b. 1916). *The catch was dealt out like playing cards:*
"People would bring the fish in baskets up to a spot on the strand. [If] there were a hundred people helping with that net, then they'd make a hundred piles of fish. It might be five pounds or it might be fifty. Then somebody would point at a pile of fish and the man with his back turned would say 'Give that to John Smith' and that was his. No argument, no nothing, nobody would pick up one of those fish, either" (Int: 23). White-bearded Mr. Nicholas Nixon owned a house behind the marsh in Cherry Grove; from a crow's nest he would watch his fishery through a spyglass salvaged from a wrecked ship. "He had a horse and a road cart parked down in the yard, and so if they had a big haul—the net gets a share—he would get in the road cart and head for that fishery" [*laughter*]. (Int: 21)

Fig. 8.4. Fishermen dividing their catch in North Carolina. Photo by Bayard Wootten, 1930s. North Carolina Collection, University of North Carolina Library at Chapel Hill.

Andrew Stanley (b. 1904): *Don't cheat at the game:*
"Don't put one in your pocket or something, or let its tail be sticking out—they'd put a fine on you. Give you ten licks for that, or eight licks, or four." The owner got a third of the catch. (Int. April 1991: 18-19)

•Split, gut, and salt the fish

According to what Grandmother told Barney Dawsey (b. 1912), "They just split them and left the scales and [head] on them, and put them in brine, a layer of fish, and a layer of salt" (Int: 17).

J.P. Cartrette (b. 1898). *On the same day that mules caught fish,*
"salt gave out at the company store, and Mr. Singleton at Enterprise gave us all he had in stock. The train was dispatched on a special trip to Conway, Aynor, and Galivants Ferry to get salt." ("Good" 22)

Claudia A. Brown (b. 1901). *Daddy would go in September in an old Ford and bring back winter meals:*
Salt 'em down, put 'em in a barrel, keep 'em cool with ice. Used "hard salt." People would keep the fish in "kags" (kegs or barrels), weighing the catch down with lead weights. (Int. 24 June: 1)

•Fry, sell, carry off, salt, and soak the fish

"It was a picnic on Thanksgivin'—for the children," declared Georgia Small Lance, whose job was to mind the usual fare of turkeys and guinea fowl (Int. Peterkin: 35).

J.P. Cartrette (b. 1898). "That night we gathered after dark in a shed covered with pine boughs located on the strand to cook our supper, which consisted of hot fried mullet and baked corn bread." They were eating by lantern light, but the fishermen came and took the lantern so that they could continue to gather fish.

Next morning the fish were piled on the strand a foot high and several yards long. "Negroes with their oxcarts were hauling the fish off like sticks of wood for eating and for fertilizer." ("Good" 22)

Florence Epps (b. 1907). *Jennie, a strong woman, probably an African American,*
stood on the beach and held an apron full of money belonging to the men—"$1400, she told me one day." She fed all those hands: "After the heavy nets had been flipped over, she would take a bucket full of fat mullet to the shack where coffee was boiling in an enamel pot, put on the hominy and cornbread, and fry the fish." (Hobeika 10)

W. Irving Jones (b. 1895). *"Joe Sarkis, he was a fish market man in Conway":*
People would trade him fur for fish. "Mr. Kirton would come along and buy all [the fur] that Joe had." All winter he bought coonskin, possum hides, minks, and so forth. "He was the only furrier in this county—out of the county, too, 'cause he went all the way down to the Everglades." (Int. Aug. 18, 1977: 3)

Clarke A. Willcox (b. 1896). "While some of the [catch was] sold fresh, transportation was so slow that most of the fish were split, salted down, and later peddled over the countryside. These would keep for months and almost every store had a keg of salt mullet which, when soaked overnight and fried crisp and served with hominy grits for breakfast, was a gourmet's delight." (viii)

Nellie H. Johnson (b. 1918). *The preserving brine was called "pickle":*
"They'd turn around and get some more sal' and pickle it. And when they take the fish outta the barrel [*illustrates*] the water be drippin', the pickle be drippin'." (Int. Peterkin: 17)

Andrew Stanley (b. 1904). *How was the fish reconstituted?*
"Took 'em out and put 'em in a tub, and pour water on 'em and soak 'em out. [Back] then I had to go way down to the branch, to a spring to get water...." "We cooked 'em and ate them; and then if I had too many, my mother sent a neighbor some over—they didn't have none" (Int. April 1991: 18-19)

Henry Small (b. 1897). *To make mullet stew in an iron pot:*
"You lay a layer of [sweet] potato, lay a layer of fish on top of that potato," and you can lay another layer of each. Then you cover it with a lid, and it's best steamed slowly on the fire, not on the stove. (Int: 19. See Plate 12.)

Doug Smith (b. 1938). *Smith's father would drive from the Aynor area to Myrtle Beach to exchange farm products for a barrel of mullet and a*

Fig. 8.5. These "blackfish," the S.C. name, started the day in North Carolina, landed at Little River, and ended up at the Ocean Fish Market in Conway, 2003. Photo by Paul Olsen.

barrel of spot:
The catch was piled on the shore by black fishermen such as Mr. Moss, who had white hair and a white beard and wore overalls all the time—"big man." "And when we pulled in there, boy, they'd gather around that trailer—they wanted that syrup and sweet potatoes" (Int: 3). In Fig. 8.5, Doug Smith unloads sea bass.

"We didn't know what a cricket was": Other fishing

Besides the seine, fishermen used whatever it took to separate fish from ocean, marsh, lake, pond, stream, swamp, or river. J. Marcus Smith (b. 1925) writes that in the mid-thirties, pilings were extended off the Ocean Plaza Hotel in Myrtle Beach, formerly a yacht club. "The 30-foot pier offered the best fishing along the coast. When the spots and whitings were running, news spread like wildfire, and locals scampered to join other fishermen" (*SN* 23 July 1994). (See Fig. 8.6.)

Fig. 8.6. Ocean Plaza Pier the summer before it was destroyed by Hurricane Hazel. Myrtle Beach *News*, 4 June 1954: 7-C. Horry County Museum.

"You could go down to the river," remembers Susie Lewis (b. 1898) and catch more fish than you could tote in just a few minutes" (Int: 13). But the more people, the less fish. Fishing places themselves have contracted or vanished. For example, according to a legal deposition in 1886, small boats could ply Morralls Inlet (later Cherry Grove Inlet, Fig. 10.3) for three or four miles up to Little Swamp, near the later Sixth Ave. S. in Ocean Drive Beach. Only a few small lakes now hint at the course of the former creek and marsh (Berry, "History," Chap. 16; p.c.). "See all of this was woods," explained Theatus G. Garrison, who retired in Loris:

> "Wasn't a thing but just swamp and there was a little lake that run right along there. It's still there but they got built up now. We used to go fishing in there. We used to take fish hooks and get us some raw meat…. We used to catch a lot of minnows: the ones that was big enough to eat, you eat; the ones that wasn't, you throw them back" (Int: 14-15)

The Waccamaw was a flowing home to largemouth bass, sunfish, mudfish, crappie, chain pickerel, redfin pickerel, sunfish, and shortnose sturgeon. As for the Little Pee Dee, Bill Davis (b. 1914) remembers that people within two miles of it were pretty self-sufficient: what they didn't grow, they hunted or hooked, and if they wanted a mess of fish, "they just went and got it" (Int: 4). In *Wading South*, Donald Millus names a dozen that cast shadows on the sandy-bottomed Little Pee Dee: "Hardhead, bream, redbreast,/Mollies-warmouth (mormouth)/mudfish-bowfin (good for stew)/trout or green trout (really bass)/jackfish, flatheads, and stripers" (135).

Raised in Galivants Ferry, Rilla McCrackin (b. 1941) counts a fishing trip among her earliest memories:

> "I was walking on a dirt road with Mother and I was holding onto a stick with my dress on. The sun was shining bright and there was dog fennels [weeds] in the field beside us. That's when we stayed on the Holliday farms. I can remember riding on the mule and wagon between my mama and daddy and going through a swamp and going to the river fishing." (Int: 1)

"In later years," she added, "loggers went into Gunters Island and really made a mess of the woods and wagon trails; you could hardly get to the river" (Int: 6). When Eugene Carmichael (b. 1905) was in high school, his attendance depended upon the chance for an outing with Daddy:

> I'd ask him to let me go fishing, and he'd tell me the only way [was if] I didn't have anything special at school that day…. But if he wasn't going fishing and had something he wanted me to do, why I [told him I] had a test or something or other at school. I needed to be there!" (Int: 4)[2]

William Oliver, who spent his boyhood on the Oliver plantation just north of Bucksport, remembers that fish supplemented the diet of slaves: "Could get pike out the lakes. Go fishing Sabbath. That was day off" (Chandler, "Recollections," 219). "I have given a lot of my fish to a lot of the blacks," said J.C. Bennett (b. 1928), "because some of them are fishing for a pastime and some of them unfortunately are fishing to fill their bellies. Oftentimes they don't catch them" (Int: 13).

Fish could be used as barter. Oscar Bellamy (b. 1897), from Little River, remembered an African American by the name of Odrick Vaught, barefoot, a familiar sight, who lived 112 years:

Over his shoulder hung a pole with a string of flounder tied to it by a grapevine. He walked the three miles from Little River Neck and crossed the inlet to sell fish. One day he knocked on the back door. Mrs. Bellamy said she'd like the fish but had no money. "Miss 'Missy,' you has de best garden in de country. I don't have time to garden." From that time on, it was an exchange of vegetables for fish. Vaught never ate pork, only fish and seafood from the inlet and ocean. (W. Thomas, "Little River")

Here is an inventory of fishing undertaken by hook, sewing thread, worm, cockroach, shad net, gig, snare, tobacco canvas, hand, balloon, and trap.

John C. Spivey (b. 1871). *"He can preach, teach, fish, or farm," declared Rev. S. George Lovell, Jr., in his Foreword to Mr. Spivey's autobiography:*
"When a small boy, I did what I now call Negro fishing. I did it with a twenty-five cents pole, a five-cents line, a one-cent hook with sinker and cork. I have fished with a green pole out of the swamp, and a piece of sewing thread with a wire crooked in the shape of a hook, but I would lose more fish off my hook than I would catch. I have fished in McCracken Mill Pond, Hunting Swamp, Darlings Lake, Grind Stone Lake, Pee Dee and Waccamaw Rivers and other places wherever I could find fish large enough to take my hook. At one time I had seven boats and would move them about, but people stole them so badly I had to cut my number down to one." "I have caught all kinds of fish from a spot to a shark, but I find more sport in the pull of a trout, whiting, or a bluefish—either of these will tell you when they bite and will give you a good pull while reeling them in." (8-9. See Fig. 8.7)

Charles Mack Todd. *Although land-hunters had guns, axes, and dogs, water-hunters had different tools:*
"They used a pole, line, hook, sinker, and cork when fishing in small streams, and gill nets when they fished in the lakes and rivers." With the pole method "they used earthworms, grub worms, and sap worms for bait…. They never fished merely for pastime, but for the meat.

Fig. 8.7. A pair of "fighting beauties"–winter trout. Myrtle Beach *News*, 4 June 1954. Horry County Museum.[3]

"Big Pete, Willie, and Boy Jake spent many happy afternoons fishing in the deep black holes down in Brown Swamp, catching blue brem [bream], red bellies, waw mouths, pikes, and jacks. Coming home about sundown with a big catch, these big friendly families would assemble at one of their homes and go in for a real fish-fry supper that always kept them up much later than their usual bed-time hour." (3: 25)

Rilla C. McCrackin (b. 1941). *The girl who slept outside by the curing barn did the same thing by the fishing spot:*
"Daddy would gear the mule up to the wagon with poles and dig some bait, enough for me and Mama. Maybe a bat of hay for the mule and maybe a few ears of corn, a few tow sacks [i.e., coarse-fibered], a quilt, and head to the river. We would head to Sandy Island or the Joe Patch or the Ferry. We would go to Canoe Lake and Nancy's Island. Sometimes he took the one-man boat and sometimes not. If the water was high we couldn't camp. Me and Mama could fish on the hills and wade in the sloughs; that is where I learned to paddle a boat. Daddy was afraid I would get drownded. We would catch morgans, hardheads, and little catfish. Daddy would catch bigger fish because he would fish deeper. We would go prepared to spend the night. We would cook and eat 'em and go gather some moss out of the trees, then pile it under the wagon. Daddy would take the bits out of the mule's mouth and hitch 'em to a tree. He would put the tow sacks on the moss under the wagon and put the quilt on that, with an ol' spread on top of us. Sometimes I would think about the snakes that might be crawlin' out there; I would listen to the mule stompin' his feet. Daddy would rake a clean spot on the white sand and pile some leaves on it and light it to run the mosquitoes off." (Int: 5)

J.C. Bennett (b. 1928). *What else could be used as bait or hook?*
"In the glue room of the box-mill, where the soybean bags were, there were big old cockroaches running around. I would get me a Pepsi-Cola bottle and catch me about two or three dozen and put a little paper in the bottle where they couldn't get out. We didn't know what a cricket was back then. You could throw that thing out on a light hook with no lead and that cockroach would run on the water. One of those big old morgans would swallow him."

Down behind Jerry Cox Company in Conway, a row of outhouses stood on the river, where "catfish would splash up and wet you." "I would get me some of them little wire tags off the edge of the soybean meal bag, wire them together and put me a hook on it. I would hang me a piece of fatback meat down there beside of me and catch about half a dozen big catfish during a sitting. The bad part is, I would sell them to people" [*laughter*]. (Int: 3, 8)

Henry Small (b. 1897). *"Lotta fish, lotta fish."* One was the shad, which swims upriver from marine waters to spawn: "We'd take a boat and a shad net to the Waccamaw River, and put your net across, shad." "My mother, she'd go fishing—I don't know how much a week. Sometime she'd come up with a long string of fish like that, different kind of fish." Bream or sometimes a mudfish—makes good stew. "And a lot of times the river would flood…and it would go down and leave pools and ponds in there [with stranded fish]. One kind was really long: "It's a sweet meat and fish juice…. We call it yemen carp" [i.e., European carp, *Cyprinus carpio*]. (Int: 13, 23-24)

Cad Holmes (b. 1945). *Holmes caught mudfish and carp in a big pond in the middle of Dark Swamp, the source of Collins Creek Branch:*
The German carp? "It's a bottom fish, it's a big fish. Most folks didn't eat it. But it was easy to catch, and you could catch one and feed a whole family. A German carp and a mudfish—you only have to catch one—and I mean you'd have a feast. They'd grow in a swampy area, didn't have to go to the river to catch one either." (Int. Peterkin: 33)

Carl B. Bessent (b. approx. 1891). *As a boy he was having bad luck at gigging flounder:*
Angry, he "stuck his fork in the hock of a pig. The animal, squealing, ran under the house with the fork in his hind quarter." ("Early" 3)

Fred W. Hucks (b. 1883) and **Lacy Hucks** (b. 1921). *Big and Little Chinesee Swamps were good places to hunt wild turkeys and to fish. You'd go in there and catch pike "this long" [a foot and a half as measured by outstretched hands]. Uncle and nephew explain what they called "mudding":*
Fred: "You'd find a deep hole in the swamp where no water was runnin' out either end; you'd muddy up—stir up the water, get the hair of the horse's tail, put it on the end of a pole, and snare the fish!"
Lacy: "You'd tie the hair around the pole and loop the hair around the fish—the hair would tighten as you pulled up…. Sometimes there's so many fish, you could seine them with a tobacco bed canvas." (Epps, "Mr. Hucks," 18)

John P. Cartrette (b. 1898). *Another boy had a close call with this kind of fishing:*
"On the west side [of the road] at perhaps an old ford, the channel was deeper and my father and some men dammed up the stream and were muddying for pike. When the water was muddied, the fish would come to the surface for air. Then with hands or boards, they would be lifted out of the water to the bank. I was in the edge throwing them out with my hands and lifted a water moccasin. Then I got out of the water." ("Good" 24. See also Millus, 67-69.)[4]

J.C. Bennett (b. 1928). *"Jigger fishing: you get a good cane pole that had a thick end and also a limber end:*
"You would take, oh, about a 60-pound test line, black line, and come back about two or three feet on the pole from the tip and wind it up to the tip, leaving yourself about a foot to 18 inches of line. The line was short. "You would take some sewing thread and kind of tie that thick line where it wouldn't fall off, so you could knot it real good. You would use two hooks sometimes and one little piece of lead that you would put a piece of fat meat on, or a piece of red rubber balloon. By tap, tap, tapping that thing on top of the water with the end of your pole, it created noise attracting the fish. "This black man, Lawrence DeWitt, would take off from the commissary store at the mill and look at the moon. He would go out and sometimes come back with four or five 6- and 8-pounders. He would sit right in the front of the boat, semi-sculling, and shake that jigger. I would sit in the back and watch him." (Int: 4, 12)

Claudia A. Brown (b. 1901). *Downstream from the box mill there was a good place to fish on the Waccamaw:*
"I heared something that keeps moving in the water and then there was a string of grass up around there. I kept looking and I said 'What is that making that fuss every minute?' My brother said 'Oh, it ain't nothin' but an old snake or somethin.' I said, 'Well, let's get out of here and go home because that thing is a-makin' a fuss back there. I happened to look along and an old big alligator was laying out there in those bushes flopping his tail. He was trying to get back in the water." (Int. 24 June: 12)

J. Harry Lee (b. 1908). *Absentee angling was a tradition (see Bishop 234):*
"I remember one Sunday evenin', I had me a trap on the Waccamaw river right down there. My wife told me we had a couple little fish in the refrigerator, and she said, 'If I had enough of them fish I'd cook 'em for supper.' I didn't say nothin', I went down to the fish trap thinkin' maybe I'd have one or two, and I opened the trap up and the fish was just like that [*moves hands back and forth, smiling*]. Most fish I ever caught at one time…. Had more'n she could cook." (Int: 20-21)

Marion Moore (b. 1931). *"Back then it was legal to set traps from Wednesday 12 to Saturday 12 in muddy water:*
"And you could set traps to catch game fish but it was illegal to sell them. They got sold—the ones we caught…. We carried them to the Sarkis Fish Market and he could sell them. He could import bream out of Florida and sell them in his market but he couldn't sell local fish. But once you got him [the fish] on ice, you couldn't tell a bluegill—whether he was caught in Florida or out of Broad Creek" [*laughter*]. "You'd set traps and hang them on the bank of the river—when the

freshet was up and the fish would run. Now if the freshet weren't up, we had a square basket that you'd take in them small creeks or the small ditches. You'd sink it down and lay a piece of railroad iron across it where it wouldn't float because it was a wood frame with a wire attached to it.   Then you had webbing—mesh webbing that Grandpa used to get off the shrimp boats they used to make for trolling shrimp nets—and you put out what he called 'wings.' You'd tie them to the trap and carry them all the way out to the bank—to the edge of the bank and he'd pull off his clothes and stomp that net down in the mud and prop it up with a form and sticks when the water was high. And when the tide fell out, you strained the creek—whatever was in there was yours…. You'd catch regular panfish—warmouth, speckled bream, blue bream and bass, mudfish." (Int: 9-10)

Gary Mincey (b. 1907). *This kind of fishing was finally outlawed. Mincey started working as a game warden around 1950:*
A fellow over here in Causey Community wrote to an official to ask if it was legal to set a fish trap on his own land…. "And Mr. Richardson wrote him back and told him 'No, it wasn't against the law to set fish traps on his own land—but make sure he didn't put none in the *water*'" [*laughter*]. (Int: 6)

"Way out of sight in an old row boat"

Boats belonging to the hotel in Myrtle Beach (as reported in a pamphlet of 1922) spend the day fishing for "hundreds of rock and black fish and other edible species" "on the rock-like formations ten or twelve miles off shore." The surplus is sold to people in cottages ("Conway," n.p.). The little summer-community of Myrtle Beach lived on finned calories. (See Fig. 8.8.)

About 4:30 in the afternoon the fish boats came in," recalls Annette Reesor (b. 1909):

"It was my great pleasure and responsibility to buy the large string of blackfish (about twelve) from Sump. The fish cost a quarter, and I shined my coin in the wet sand to make it exceedingly bright. The Negro fishermen's safe return from the rocks beyond the horizon was a joyous benediction to the day's toil. Frequently the haul included a spray of bright yellow seaweed, or a strange fish— once an octopus, which they gave to some lucky child." ("Sand" 9).

Fig. 8.8. Sailing upon food source. Horry County Museum.

Geraldine B. Burroughs, sitting next to Franklin in 1991, remembered that there were no markets, just the commissary, but people could buy a string of fish:

The most excitement was to see the fishing boats going out to sea. There were several of them, filled with colored men, who would go "way out of sight in an old row boat." They'd go out at daybreak and come back in at dark. If there were wind, they'd sail out to sea. "The one thing I remember vividly was that one of the boats didn't come in at dark. There were not electric lights. There was nothing to guide them but the sun and the moon. The boat got in I reckon about 11 o'clock, but I can remember people riding up and down the strand on horseback with lanterns to show them where land was." (Int. F.G. and G. Burroughs: 19, 21)

Not only darkness but weather could endanger these fishermen. Florence Epps (b. 1907) remembers that one time Shiney, the maid for the Epps family, assuaged the children's fears for themselves as well as for Sump and the crew:

"One stormy day as we watched the fishing boats headed for home, they suddenly disappeared. Sarah Sherwood's Mammy gathered all of the children into the Sherwoods' living room and materialized for us in each corner 'de angel' to whom she spoke demanding the safe return of the fishermen. Sure enough, when the rains subsided, the sails hove into sight and safety." (Epps, "Have," *IRQ* 1.2: 14).

In "The Fishing Boat Goes Out," Marie Gilbert (b. 1924) celebrates the importance of such laborers, whose collaboration was both athletic and esthetic:

"Eight fishermen come silently
working to mellow command
to muscle the weathered boat part way on logs
drag it over the sand
leaving keel track into the sea,
they row through the breakers and beyond.
Rhythm flows a chain from oar to oar
from shoulder to shoulder.
Forearms gleam strong black
in early glisten.
Men and boat become
a speck in dawn's pink
and disappear.

"The cry moves from cottage to cottage,
the fishermen are out!
Housewives plan for fish by noon.

"Through the morning, swimmers watch
wonder if the fishermen found the rock reef
hidden fifty feet below,
the place where fish come hungry.
And then–
the speck reappears
grows larger on blue sky.

"Some off porches, out of houses
some in wet swim suits come out of the water,
folks stroll along the strand guessing
where the boat will beach,
run forward when it shoots the breakers.

"Give the money to the cook.
She knows just what she wants.
Blue uniform dresses, white aprons
with wide straps, barefeet enjoying
the excuse to wade, rush to the fishermen
who jump out holding strings of bass, trout
black fish, make quick deals
even as they reach the boat (61)

Fish helped to power the oar, the hack, the shingle-splitting froe, the crosscut saw, and the tobacco string.
    Fishing could mean solitude or company. As with 'bacca, it was often done communally, with family, friends, or neighbors; seining required teamwork. Like turpentining, logging, and tobacco-growing, fishing had its full-time and part-time wage-earners, but most were paid by the tug, the taste, and the leisure. Although perhaps a slave, tenant, or millhand, an angler had no owner.

Notes

[1] The caption: "Fishing is a sport for any age at Myrtle Beach and Coastal Carolina. Mr. and Mrs. T.H. King, of Hartsville [S.C.], pictured here, celebrated their marriage, at ages over 90 and 60 respectively, with a round of fishing at the Ocean Plaza Pier. And, in order that our out-of-town readers may know the stories about Myrtle Beach are truthful, note that ALL the fish don't come big."

[2] Father and fishing are inseparable themes in Chapter 3 of *Billy Watson's Croker Sack*, by Franklin Burroughs. As a lad himself, Franklin G. used his mother's sewing thread for a line.

[3] Caption: "Winter trout are a big feature at Myrtle Beach during the winter months when fishing is at a standstill in many parts of the country. Here are a couple of fighting beauties, lured from the masses which lurk along the shoreline and in the coastal inlets. These two, with the smile of triumph, are being displayed at the Second Avenue pier, a trout fisherman headquarters in the heart of Myrtle Beach. These trout are caught from October to the end of May. Last week saw some fine catches."

[4] One unfortunate youngster became the catch: "A boy drown right here," said Mundy Holmes. "Have the line 'round he hand. Shark in the net. Take right on out to sea. Find the boy way up yonder to Little River. Piece of rope still tie to he hand" (Chandler, "Ex-Slave Talks," 1).

CHAPTER 9
THE DANCE

"Tuesday, January 1, 1740…. [B]eing in haste, we passed over a half-mile ferry. About sunset, we came to a tavern, five miles within the province of South Carolina. Here I immediately perceived the people were more polite than those we generally met with; but I believe the people of the house wished I had not come to be their guest that night; for, it being New Year's Day, several of the neighbours were met together to divert themselves by dancing country dances. By the advice of my companions, I went in amongst them whilst a woman was dancing a jig. At my first entrance I endeavoured to shew the folly of such entertainments, and to convince her how well pleased the devil was at every step she took. For some time she endeavoured to outbrave me; neither the fiddler nor she desisted; but at last she gave over, and the musician laid aside his instrument."
Rev. George Whitefield (b. 1714), 381-82.

Fig. 9.1. "Grandaddy [Thomas Beaty Cooper, 1863-1928] played this violin for the first dance held in the first little pavilion at Myrtle Beach" (Prather). Horry County Museum.

Whitefield was a celebrated evangelist of the "Great Awakening," a religious movement in the American colonies in the 1730s and '40s. On one of his missions from England he made his way from Philadelphia to Savannah, Georgia, six years after the anonymous explorers had dared the Waccamaw from their base in Georgetown. Like them, he was paddling against the current, for after he rebuked the revelers, performed a baptism, and led a prayer, he retired only to hear the music and dancing resume.

Of course to the faithful, Christianity itself is the highest form of recreation. It offers a sense of well being both spiritual and communal, and it offers hope for both this world and the next. Countless ascetics like Whitefield have found these sublime pleasures incompatible with worldly ones. In a letter dated 1890, the original F.G. Burroughs warned his son against going for a night of revelry, "Then to a danse or a Play":

"A nother grate eveal is whisky and gambling. Wimen will most be certan to cary you to a bar room, and from there, to the card table, and from there, to the Lawers office, and from there, to the corte House, and from there, to the jale, and the jale, to the gallos." (Kearns 112-13)

Along with this aversion to worldly entertainment, Burroughs displayed other links with the Puritans, who valued "qualities that made for economic success—self-reliance, frugality, industry, and energy" ("Puritanism"). Whitefield trod the earth as a pilgrim; Burroughs planned a railroad across it.

As everywhere, in Horry there was tension between the constraints of religion and the behavior of adherents. In 1886, for example, a terrifying earthquake caused some people to quit drinking. But salt water itself is an intoxicant. At the Pavilion in the summer of 1903, young Jessie Richardson danced to phonograph music with some other girls and,

unrepentant, received a letter of expulsion from Conway Baptist Church (Spivey, letter). In 1911 the same church protested excursions to Myrtle Beach scheduled for each Sunday. These jaunts took pupils from Sunday schools in Conway and the surrounding country, threatened the proper observance of the Sabbath, and encouraged improper conduct: "we believe that many a young life begins the downward career by these excursions" ("Resolutions").

As a young teacher, Rebecca Clark Snyder (b. 1899), who heard the drunken sailors in Chap. 3, would go from Little River to Cherry Grove Beach for a picnic and a swim. "One Sunday, in the little church, the pastor referred to the teachers in a very stern manner, saying we should not go swimming in bathing suits, but should wear dresses" (27). To be sure, Horry County reflected the general and official culture of the whole region. After the South Carolina General Assembly outlawed pari-mutuel betting, one Sunday the racetrack at Myrtle Beach (located on the corner of 21st Ave. N. and Oak Street) was surrounded by constables who let everybody out and padlocked the track (Int. Thompson: 2).

Fig. 9.2. Dancing to the juke box at the Pavilion. Courtesy Jack Thompson.

The nearby Pavilion, as Jack Thompson remembers, would be crowded in the evening as the jukebox blared (see Fig. 9.2). All the house-party folks and the military people would do the jitterbug. Over the seasons, some of the cool cats from Carolina Beach in North Carolina, and from other places, started slowing the tempo so that instead of jumping up and down they moved from side to side.

"But Myrtle Beach in the '40s and '50s was a very strict Baptist-Methodist community. The city fathers regularly sent the police chief down to the Pavilion with instructions that if any dancers shook their hips, they were to be arrested for indecent exposure. Night after night what we called the popular dancers were dragged off the dance floor by the nape of the neck and the seat of the pants and hauled off to jail. Young people would walk through the crowd with a milk-shake cup bumming $35 to get them out of jail." The harassment became so bad that in 1954 and 1955 that crowd of dancers, most of whom are in the Shaggers Hall of Fame, migrated to Ocean Drive (Int: 3).

Fig. 9.3. Charlie's Place. Charlie at right. Courtesy Jack Thompson.

Thompson remembers that when everything closed down at the beachfront, young people migrated to Charlie's Place in the colored section (see Fig. 9.3). Even bands would go there after closing their show at the Ocean Forest Hotel (Int: 4). According to an essay by Frank Beacham in *Oxford American Magazine*, the musicians included Billy Eckstine, Count Basie, Ray Charles, Duke Ellington, Lena Horne, and Little Richard. Whites and blacks came to Charlie's to hear what was then called "race music." A white patron, Leon Williams, carried techniques of the black dancers over to the Pavilion and into the jitterbug, a fast two-step especially popular in the 1940s:

"The colored girls danced with white boys, and the colored boys danced with white girls.... We hugged each other's neck. If you had been at the beach in that period of time, you'd have thought segregation didn't exist." (Beacham 52, 54)

Beacham theorizes that dancing itself helped to attract a posse of Klan members to Charlie's Place, where white kids used to sneak in to hear sexy rhythm and blues, and where the jitterbug evolved into the Dirty Shag, then into the

Shag (54-55).[1]

In the era covered by this book, Austerity pulled one oar and License pushed the other. But in everyday life the two impulses coexisted with less friction than it did between the New Year's revelers and the devout Rev. Whitefield. His dichotomy, however overdrawn, does offer a way to classify recreation into the Spiritual and Secular.

"The praises of Him Who hath set bounds to the sea:" The Church

Christianity, which African Americans absorbed and modified as they did the English language, was an important connection between the white and black communities. At least one slave prayed to Jesus against the Yankees (E. Collins 10) and, aboard the *Comanche*, Captain Thompson taught Joe Horry his Bible lessons. Blacks and whites originally worshiped together (see Malet 14.3: 33 and Kirke 17.3: 42), but around the beginning of the twentieth century, they were separated (as on the train by Conductor Crow).

After the initial stage of brush-arbors, little churches sprang up everywhere. Mary W. Hardee (b. 1907) remembers that in Lake Swamp, however, services were a luxury:

> "I hardly ever went to church. It'd be cold and we couldn't get out. We didn't have sufficient clothes to wear. We didn't—like they do now—pull 'em out of the closet and never miss 'em. We had two pairs of shoes, one for Sunday. Well, down there on the swamp we had one preacher for two churches. He'd preach one morning at Pleasant View and the next morning. And then that night he'd preach at Mt. Olive." (Int: 4)

Religion was less divorced from daily life than it would become in Horry and elsewhere. For instance the nostalgic poem "Peach Tree Ferry," by Clarke A. Willcox, Jr. (b. 1896), recalls the plowshare, the shout of the ferryman, and "the faces of those who, much loved, passed this way / As we lurched along in our wagons, singing songs like 'Trust and Obey…'" (23). According to family lore, Clarke's father (b. 1861) admonished his family as they crossed the river, their flat weighed down with livestock, wagons, and supplies: "Hold your breath and pray, children, for we're one inch from eternity."

A trustee of Socastee Graded School, Gib McCormick was interviewed in the late 1930s. He spoke of an unspecified Bible verse that could staunch the flow of blood from an injured animal or person:

> "Not so long after I was followin' a bunch o' timber hands sawin' trees in the woods. I was a saw filer. They had cut down a big tree and had had to turn the saw upside down and saw from the bottom and some way when they had got hit sawed clean through it flirted up when they had to change the saw and one tooth o' the saw cut through to the pult (pulse) of one of the nigger's arm. Blood stream off just like you stuck a hog. "Of course I found myself repeatin' over and over that Bible verse and at the same time a nigger went to work shavin' down bark off'n a tree and a-pastin' some shaved up bark and stuff over hit and it STOPPED. Now I didn't have too much confidence in that verse but hit stopped. We was fifteen miles up the river and more miles than that from a Doctor." (Chandler, "Method," 2)

Unlike the village of Georgetown, Horry had no Jewish cemetery, and unlike the city, no boy cleaned the Shabbos candle-wax off Grandmother's old Romanian candlesticks (Frommer 183). Christianity, furthermore, almost always meant Protestant. Figuratively speaking, one's denomination appeared on the family crest. As for Episcopalian, so typical among the plantation owners to the south—few curates among collards. (See Malet 21.) Although many people spoke in tongues, Latin was not one of them until the Air Force Base was constructed in World War II and stray Catholics attended mass at its chapel. In the early '40s, "If there were two Jews in Conway, there were more Jews than Catholics," declared one pioneer. She added that the town's first Roman Catholic church was finally constructed in 1961 because "the knots on the wall of the Boy Scout Hut weren't conducive to mass" (Holihan).

Although Christianity offered hope, the devil prowled about like the wildcat that once set its paws on Claudia Brown's shoulders as she chopped kindling (Int. 21 July: 2). And the buckle-hatted shadow of Sabbatarianism fell upon the day of rest: as late as 1954 the voters of Conway advised against movies on Sunday ("Thompson Re-elected").

Sacred recreation was both furthered and hindered by water. Harriet Beaty Cooper (b. 1807) records that the first camp meeting was held "on the camp ground up the lake near Graham's Landing in Burroughs Field" (qtd. in Eunice Thomas 9). Baptisms were conducted at many places such as Board Landing, downriver from Red Bluff (A. Todd); by the old bridge over the Waccamaw (E. Woodbury 9); and in the Little Pee Dee (Int. P. Gore: 10). Churchgoers even washed themselves up in branch-water: "We have been told by ones now gone to their reward of walking each Sunday, wearing old shoes or in the summertime [going] barefoot, until they came to the nearest small stream where they washed their feet and put on the Sunday shoes…" (S. Cooper 15).

Was Katie B. Randall scared when rowing across Little River at night to attend church? "No, no," she chuckled, "scared o' *what*?!" But John W. Gore, a circuit-riding preacher, was understandably daunted, as he explains in the 1896

Minutes of the Waccamaw Baptist Association. "Dear Brethern:

> "Pursuant to appointment I started out in the early part of December last, but owing to bad health and high water, and other inconveniences, I only made a short trip…." (W. Thomas, Pioneers, iii)

Soon after 1874, however, the Waccamaw helped one congregation to turn logs into building material. According to the oldest members of Socastee United Methodist Church, interviewed in the early 1960s, the best timber was donated, cut, hauled to Peachtree Ferry, floated across the Waccamaw to the Bucksville sawmill, and returned as boards (S. Cooper 14). In 1954, Union Methodist Church held many fish fries to raise money for a new building (King 20).

In one case fish provided not the means but the inspiration. During the fall of 1888, a group had taken their boat out for several luckless days at Ward's Fishery. According to the descendents of Isaac Parker "Handy" Edge, one member suggested they pray:

> With knees in the soft white sand, washed clean by the ocean, the group made a sincere petition. Suddenly a great commotion was heard in the water. Startled, they looked up and saw fish everywhere. They stumbled and bumped into one another in their excitement to get to the boat. Several rowed while the seine-thrower let down the net; then they towed in the net gradually so it would not tear, pulling for almost an hour. The pile of flopping mullet and spot was so high that it took the men two days to clean, salt, and barrel the fish. At one man's suggestions, because the Lord had been so good to them, they constructed a brush arbor made from a rectangular framework covered with branches, and continued praying. Eventually they founded the precursor of the First Baptist Church of Ocean Drive Beach, later called the First Baptist Church of North Myrtle Beach. (W. Thomas, "Sketches," 22)

Various Baptist churches were named for their watery locations: Pawleys Swamp, Tilly Swamp, Buck Creek, Cedar Creek Swamp, Collins Creek Swamp, Glenns Bay, Spring Branch, Simpson's Creek, and Bug Swamp (W. Thomas, p.c.; Eunice Thomas 6-7). In the 1940s, the Meher Baba Center was established on about 500 acres of what had been a duck-hunter's paradise along the ocean in the northernmost part of Myrtle Beach. Donated by Simeon Chapin, the pristine land was about half marsh and wetlands. His daughter, Elizabeth Chapin Patterson, was a key figure in developing the retreat, and in 1952, Meher Baba himself traveled from India to consecrate the tract for spiritual purposes (Oehler 7; White).

The following memories record more intersections between religion and water.

Rev. George Whitefield (b. 1714). *After rising early, singing a hymn, and giving "a sharp reproof to the dancers," Whitefield continued his mission:*
"At break of day, we mounted our horses, and, I think, never had a more pleasant journey. For nearly twenty miles we rode over a beautiful bay as plain [level] as a terrace walk, and as we passed along were wonderfully delighted to see the porpoises taking their pastime, and hear, as it were, shore resounding to shore the praises of Him Who hath set bounds to the sea that it cannot pass, and hath said, 'Here shall your proud waves be stayed.'" (382)

John C. Spivey (b. 1871). *At the age of 19, John took the* Maggie *from Conway to Peachtree Ferry and then walked to Socastee, where he lived with the Stalvey family while attending school:*
"Believe it or not, I had never seen the ocean." On his first visit his friends blindfolded him before reaching the dunes. When he asked what he was climbing, they told him a sandhill, which to him felt like a snowhill. "I could hear roaring and splashing but could see nothing but darkness. When in a few feet of water, I said, 'Archie, I can't stand this any longer. That water is coming in my face and it is soon going to cover me up….' The towel was taken off my head and I saw but could not speak. After a few minutes Archie said, 'Why don't you speak?' I said, 'There *is* a God.'" (3-4)

William J. Rowe (b. 1886). *At least two lay preachers worked in the Burroughs & Collins Company, one of them W.M. Goldfinch and the other, B.G. Collins himself:*
He preached in Methodist churches almost all over the county. "I think he must have appreciated the years of his good health, the extent of his prosperity, and his fine family," and wanted to make some recompense for the Lord's blessings. When he heard that the *Maggie*, his investment, was burning up, he began to sing the old gospel hymn, "My hope is built on nothing less / Than Jesus' blood and righteousness." ("Memories" 10)

G.C. McCormick (b. 1878). *The grandfather of Marion Moore served as ferryman at Bull Creek, Port Harrelson, and Eddy Lake. Here is his story re-told by the editor of the* IRQ:
"As the boat docked, the preacher doffed his hat and extended it to the captain, inquiring, 'What do you charge preachers?' The lusty captain replied, 'The same as I charge fiddlers!'" (Epps, "A Fair")

Lillie B. Latimer (b. 1882). *"I know they used to go to Bucksport and have big meetings:*
"They had a meeting on the other side of the campground out on—they call it Sand Ridge now. But you know they used to have a church there." [*She or her half-sister adds:*] "We didn't have a wharf. When the boats run, you'd have to tie the boat to a cypress knee…. Them passengers they'd put boards and sometimes you'd have to take off shoes and wade to get off the boat." (Int: 9)

Annette E. Reesor (b. 1909). *This artful writer remembers a group of children headed for a destination near the beach:*
"As the dark waters meandered from an inland swamp to the sea, there was a wide curve in [Withers] Swash, with a place deep enough for diving. To our amazement, about twenty or more people had gathered there before us. Furthermore, they were singing well-known hymns and lovely spirituals. Soon a dignified man, carrying a Bible, stepped into view. He was wearing his Sunday best clothing! Immediately we youngsters realized that this was no ordinary gathering, but of a sacred nature. [See Fig. 9.4.] [Our] faded black woolen jersey bathing suits and straw hats filled with seashells just didn't belong among people who, having just come from church, were

Fig. 9.4. Baptism. Horry County Museum.

dressed in their best clothes. We stood at the high-tide mark and watched with awed interest. The surf's roar prevented our hearing the words, but we could see the preacher take one white-clad convert after another and tilt him backwards under the dark water. The preacher raised his hands, fluttering like doves' wings, and the 'saved one,' assisted by two or three deacons, walked joyously up the slick bank. "As the congregation walked singing homeward, we strolled along the ocean's edge. Not the usual boisterous kids teasing each other and trying, vainly, to catch silly sandpipers, but reverently, deeply moved by the holy ceremony we had witnessed. Ever afterward, our swimming hole took on a more sanctified aspect." ("Babtizin'" 8)

Georgia S. Lance (b. 1926). *Roseanne Butler, a polio victim who lived with her cane in the Freewoods, was baptized in the Waccamaw at Oregon Plantation:*
"Afterward they said she put the stick down and began walkin'. So it might be healing in the water that caused her to be able to do this." (Int. Peterkin: 14)

Evelyn D. Missroon (b. 1913). *"Both [my Grampa] and Gramma were dedicated church-goers:*

"It was his delight to gather up neighbors to attend church when a 'protracted meeting' was announced by the minister. Grampa would dust off his old two-horse wagon and fill its body with the woven-bottomed, short-legged and squat, straight chairs. He would then help his guests join the family, gathering a group who either talked as they rode along or raised their voices in songs…. "I can still hear the singing of the metal-rimmed wheels of the wagon as it rolled through soft yellow sand underlying two separate branches of shallow brown water that ran across the road between home and church." ("Three" 23)

Lucille B. Godfrey (b. 1891). *Religion colored perception, as when a dead whale washed up near Hurl Rocks in 1900:*
"The old woman who discovered the whale had come screaming the news, saying that until now she never had believed that story in the Bible." ("Some" 25. See Fig. 9.5)

Carl B. Bessent (b. approx. 1891). *The same boy who stuck a vengeful fork into a pig went crabbing in a foot-deep creek:*
He saw something and struck it with a pitchfork. It knocked him out of the water and went to the other side of the creek. He told

Fig. 9.5. Beached whale. Courtesy Heritage Room, First Baptist Church, Conway.

his brother to run to the house and get Uncle Willie with the gun. "I am here," announced his uncle, "to kill the devil." It turned out to be something Carl had never seen before: an alligator. ("Early" 8)

Franklin G. Burroughs (b. 1908). *As a youngster on the* F.G. Burroughs,
"I was permitted to go below and watch the thrust of the large arms that ran from the steam-driven engine to the almost-two-story-high paddle wheels along each side of the boat. The wood-burning furnace in the boiler room, with its door being constantly opened for more fuel, seemed, to a small boy, to be The Inferno itself." ("Steamboat" 5)[2]

Rev. S. George Lovell, Jr. (b. 1918). *Interviewed under the First Baptist chandeliers by his longtime friend and confidant, Catherine Lewis, George recalled the days when an angler had to tie equipment to the roof of the car:*
"Every deacon in the church saw me leave town with my fishing pole. And then next meeting, some of 'em said, 'Well, there goes Preacher Lovell. All he does is fish.' You know, I'd been *one time*." (Int: 23)

"Cupid was aboard": The Dance

Typically, in the words of Mildred Prince Brown (b. 1915), "There was little time for recreation because it took all members of the family every hour of the day almost to make a living" (7). "I'd go fishing in the creek sometimes and go to the Waccamaw River at some time during the summer," reported Andrew Stanley (b. 1904), "but no gathering, no dancing, no piccolo, no nothing like that—you didn't hear of one. Didn't know what it was" (Int. April 1991: 36). Asserted Mary W. Hardee (b. 1907) of Lake Swamp: "We didn't do nothing!" Yet on the farm, at school, in town, or wherever, most people found a way to do something. For recreation that did not depend on water, see "Hollerin' in the cotton field":

"Hollerin' in the cotton field"

"Back in them time" recreation tended to be homemade, cheap or free, and less distinguished from labor and other workaday activities. Besides tobacco-barn raisings, recalls Lunette Davis Floyd (b. 1910),

> "We'd have 'wood-cutting' during the winter, mostly for stove wood. The women would parch peanuts and cook candy. After the men finished sawing and splitting the stove wood, we'd have candy-pullings and at times, square dances." (20)

"We had parties for entertainment," remembered Julia Smalls (b. 1890), who worked as a domestic in Conway "eight days a week":

> "We did the Old Plantation dance called "the reel"; eight and sixteen people would dance together (not close together), would stand off and swing each other…. Two sticks were rapped together and beat on the floor. A mouth organ was also used. In later days, the guitar was played." Railsplitting was held at Thanksgiving time. Rails were used to fence in the farms. Women quilted several quilts that day. A feast was enjoyed; there was lots of pork, a washpot full of cooked rice, and pumpkin pie. (Dozier, "Interview," 31.)

According to John C. Spivey (who did "Negro fishing"), the colored settlement of Cane Branch included Bill Gardner, who lived in white people's kitchens:

> "He had nothing but a fiddle and when it came moving time he was not bothered. He would go from place to place wherever he was needed to work. He was the fiddler for all the dancing parties held in the community. He would often fiddle all night and work all day." (16-17).

One ex-slave, Uncle Solomon Jones (perhaps from Marion), "could beat any bird whistling you ever heard"; another could imitate the way anybody could talk, including the original Joseph Holliday (Int. W. Jones, Sr., Aug. 11: 4, 9).

Other ways to enjoy life: leaving the farm for a joyride, riding up and down the Boulevard in cars, driving around with someone in a rumble seat, playing practical jokes, plucking worms, playing pool, dipping and spitting snuff, visiting relatives overnight, partying with the boys at the little neighborhood club (Int. Hemingway). Hollerin' in the cotton field, climbing the gate, climbing trees, hunting eggs, seeing who could jump the farthest, playing baseball, wrestling, riding horses or ponies, racing with bicycles, driving a goat cart, jumping onto a cow's back, hunting partridge and doves, sliding down a great hill of sawdust in Playcard Swamp, riding the train to Tabor City and back, watching the train come and go, walking down the railroad tracks, stealing a railroad pump car, greasing the tracks to watch the train labor (Int. Burroughs: 18), and throwing a snowball at the locomotive (Int. McWhite: 2).

Watching vaudeville at the Pavilion, a Punch and Judy puppet show, a dog-and-pony show, a medicine show, a hypnotist, or the annual cow-dip (which immersed the animals in disinfectant). Going to the circus, street dance, or movie (perhaps at a drive-in near Conway), listening to brass bands or stringed instruments. Singing "Oh, how proud you stood before me in your suit of gray" or "Oh, Buttermilk Sky." Gossiping, eavesdropping on the telephone, playing checkers, whittling a piece of wood or loafing downtown, checking the World Series score on the window of Platt's Pharmacy (reports provided by wire at inning's end), or watching to see who climbed the stairs to Dr. Archie Sasser's office and might be pregnant.

Going to chicken bogs, box suppers and parties, or "At Homes" (receptions by mailed invitation). Eating ice cream delivered by the train at noon on Saturday, playing with homemade toys, wrestling, making candy or fruit boxes. In the country, rocking in front of the fire and spitting into it; in town, strolling around and talking to every merchant or smooching by the well.

At the general store, grist mill, blacksmith's, or under a longleaf pine, chewing a cud of tobacco and chatting. Turpentine workers would tell stories like the one about the old man who was buried in the Little Pee Dee River with a jug full of money: afterward Bailey's Light would glow in the pine trees, once making two girls turn and run all the way home (Baker, "Turpentine," 14-15; Int. S. Lewis: 10). Belonging to a fraternal order, including the Cooks and Waiters Club at the beach (Int. Thompson: 5). Going to candy-pullings, drinking "Buck" or other liquor, fighting, square dancing, dancing the Big or Little Apple, belonging to one of three dance clubs, dancing in the one formal ballroom (at the Ocean Forest), roller skating on the second floor of a country store or on the pavement. Trying to pull the neck of greased goose hanging from a limb. Attending trials in the courthouse or a womanless wedding, running bases, playing on a flying ginny (a wagon wheel attached horizontally to a post), or playing see-saw on a rail or pole (Epps, "Gully").

At school, swinging earthward on young trees, forcing another boy into a clay hole dug for the schoolhouse chimney, attending field days, lectures, recitals, football banquets, and plays, watching children drill and do calisthenics to music.

Visiting the community Christmas tree (lit by candles) or going to the Christmas parade. Going to May parties with parade, food, speaker and games. Celebrating Fourth of July with speeches, races, and greased-pig catching, greased-pole climbing, and firecrackers—or in Loris, by the Old Soldiers Gathering (Int. Grainger 6). Going to Farmers Day with its parade of tractors. Going to jousting tournaments at the old Muster Field in Conway and watching the queen crowned (Kearns 107). Celebrating Watch Night (New Year's Eve), when just before daylight, the old people joined in on the song that Dave Carr crooned during his interview: "Lost Mosely barn key/Send them chillun to find it/Haunt 'em, chillum, haunt'm/Haunt them till you find 'em" (Int: 6).

What about watery play? Earlier chapters have touched on fishing, swimming, riding the train to the beach, camping on the sand, hunting for shells, dancing at the Pavilion, jumping onto dunes or onto rafts, rolling a turpentine wagon into the creek, watching the fishermen or the steamboat come and go, playing cards on the abandoned *Ruth*.

More examples turn up in the archives of memory. Children would bump another pupil off the footlog into the water or play on the icy swamp at lunchtime (Dorethea Long, "White Oak," 5, 9), or they would run in and out amid the lumber at the riverside mill and pretend the piles were skyscrapers (Int. Cutts 1-2). We "had fished so often for these poor things [crayfish]," recalled Sarah Burroughs Sherwood (b. 1884), "that I think we really had them trained. We could recognize each one as we pulled them out and dumped them back in all day long" (Kearns 94-95). On weekends bunches of people in Galivants Ferry "would just go off walking over the river bridge and just get together and have a good time" (Int. Doyle, 31 Oct: 34). Citizens of Conway would sit on the front porch while greeting churchgoers or counting vehicles that drove toward the beach; tourists would sit on the porch of a guest house while enjoying the ocean breeze. Beachgoers would watch sea turtles lay eggs (Int. Rust: 40) or hunt arrowheads in the swash (Epps, "Have," *IRQ* 1.3: 14).

The following memories attest to an abundance of recreation—most of it happy, some of it risky—that depended directly or indirectly on water, present or past.

• Beside the ocean

Here are a few surprising bonus recollections about the shore:

Turner Chestnut (b. 1896). *Turner traveled to Myrtle Beach when it was "about like Grahamville," his home:*
"They used to have a big Fourth of July gathering at the beach. People would come from all over the country, big crowds! They had a fight one Fourth of July. People just scattered out. They never did have any more celebrations." (W. Thomas, "Turner," 16)

Mary Emily P. Jackson (b. 1921). *Mrs. Jackson points out that when the first golf course was built in 1925, sand was not a bunker but the terrain:*
"With the help of the neighborhood children and his chauffeur [Dr. Gibbes, from Columbia] laid out four holes on the open sand hills" near 2702 N. Ocean Boulevard. Everything was sand. "He brought several old clubs and shared them with us so he would have someone to play with." ("Recollections" 4; p.c.)

Jimmy D'Angelo (b. 1909). *Marshland—not right for greens and fairways, said everyone but Robert Trent Jones, a famous designer of golf courses. He studied an aerial map and declared that 256 acres along the Atlantic had the makings for a great course, which opened in 1949 (Carter, "Jimmy" 32). D'Angelo, from Pennsylvania, became the first full-time pro at the Dunes Golf & Beach Club. (See Fig. 9.6)*

A great move by "Buster" Bryan: "It was his idea to build a golf course on the oceanfront, knowing that it would bring a lot of publicity and golfers into Myrtle Beach." But the venture almost folded four times. Jimmy would drive golfers around the course in a used DeSoto Suburban. "And these old farmers from back in Tabor City [just across the N.C. line] had plenty of money, they'd say, 'Jimmy, where's the club?' They meant, 'Where's the club where we can go and drink and play cards?'" Although a clubhouse was built in 1950, there was no money for furniture. Bryan said, "Let's go out in the woods and get some pine stumps. And go down to Myrtle Beach Lumber and get a 4x4 piece of plywood and put her on top of the stump and make that a table and we'll get some chairs." Thanks to more borrowed money, however, store-bought furniture was secured.

Fig. 9.6. Jimmy D'Angelo, left, helps to inaugurate the 1954 Sun-Fun Festival. Myrtle Beach *News*, Sun-Fun Souvenir Edition, 4 June 1954: 1. Horry County Museum.

Then in 1954, thanks again in part to Bryan, eight writers for major newspapers were invited to attend a testimonial dinner for Robert Trent Jones on their way to the Masters Tournament in Augusta, Georgia. "Here we are all over the papers, 'Dunes Golf Club, Myrtle Beach.' That was the start of it." (Int: 1, 6, 8)[3]

• Along the river

Riverbanks have always attracted the land-bound. The children of Lewis Asbury Dozier (b. 1876) reported that folks in the Mt. Calvary Community enjoyed fishing, swimming, and playing circle games generally along the Waccamaw River (Dozier, "Mount," 9). In 1897 the *Horry Herald* reported: "The people in the vicinity of Punch Bowl landing on the Pee Dee indulged in a nice pic-nic on last Friday" (Nolley, "Matters," 8 June).

This same editor also describes the first passenger coach on the Conway & Seashore Railroad, which took an excursion party halfway to the beach in 1899:

> "The crossing of the Waccamaw in the early morning, presented a novel and pretty scene; there being about twenty-five in the party and many boats of many kinds being used to transport them across the river. On the opposite side, Mr. Arthur Burroughs was waiting with a nicely arranged car and soon had us dashing along the new [rail]road. At several points on this end, where the road skirts the river, lovely views are to be seen and in imagination, we can see the private cars of the 'big men' stopping here and there to enjoy the beauties of the Waccamaw, to be found on this end of the road…. [In Fig. 2.16, railroad ties jut over the eroded bank a century later.] After luncheon, two young ladies of the party recited several pieces each for us, and the young people sang many pretty songs. The workmen…delighted us with several songs. The road will be completed in time for next season…."("Pic-Nic")

Just after the turn of the century, one party headed back from the ocean on open cars, as recalled in a celebrated passage by Lucille B. Godfrey (b. 1891):

> "To protect themselves somewhat from the cinders many ladies carried umbrellas, but they were burned full of little holes through which you could see the stars that night when *Black Maria* came puffing home. There was no railroad bridge then in Conway, so the passengers piled out of the cars and into the flat to be ferried across the river. To most of us it was the most stupendous event of our lives." ("Some" 25)

Lillie B. Latimer (b. 1882) and **Ruth C. Woodbury** (b. 1886). *"Tommy Bellamy would have fish fries"*:
"Like we gon' have a fish fry tomorrow, he'd come by tonight…. And when we'd go to the [Waccamaw], we'd go down on the other side of the big mill [Conway Lumber Co.]. We'd done have two tubs of fish caught. And we'd stay down there, crowds of us, and he'd feed us fish." He wouldn't charge anything, all you'd do is carry him a piece of ice and have some ice water. We'd make a barrel of lemonade. Oh-h, down by the river we could have the biggest time! And some of the white people'd be with us." (Int: 23-4)

Bertha P. Staley (b. 1907). *Downstream in Bucksport, before World War I, a contingent of the Ringling Brothers circus spent the winter, as Bertha Staley recalls with delight three quarters of a century later:*
The town had fewer than two dozen white families but many blacks. "And a lot of young people—young men that worked around the mill getting timber from the swamps on the river boats and barges—they would help out in every way. When spring came—I remember when they were putting up the big top, everybody went to watch. And those tremendous wagons that held so much equipment, it would bog down in mud because there were no pavings anywhere 'round there. Oh, they must've had six or eight horses hooked to it. They couldn't budge it, and so they brought out the elephants and hooked to it, and they came out with it!

"There were two little girls who were daughters of the head people, I guess. One of 'em was my age, and so we became fast friends when she wasn't involved with the acting and everything. When I would see them dressed in those glittering costumes, and riding those ponies, and doing those acrobatic stunts, right then and there, I decided I wanted to go with the circus!" (Int: 3-5)

Fig. 9.7. *What* hunters?

• Atop the river

One youngster had to paddle before he could bat. To play on the Toddville baseball team as a ninth grader, George W. Floyd (b. 1919) would get in a boat at Keysfield, navigate with or against the tide to Toddville, then walk about a mile to where somebody had a baseball field. (Int. G. Floyd: 6)

But usually the boat trip was part of the fun, and people enjoyed outings in all kinds of vessels. The tugboat *Henry P. Williams*, loaded with two weeks' supplies that included four horses, carried 40 men on a hunting trip: "The debarkation at Enterprise [Landing] resembled the unloading of a small circus" (J. Rice, b. 1868, 17). Some men brought their guns and supplies onto a "ducking boat," which according to the photograph and caption in the pamphlet "Conway, South Carolina" (1922) was a small, windowed barge afloat on the Waccamaw. (See Fig. 9.7.) In Eddy Lake, a decorated barge once took everyone to Yauhannah for a wedding-picnic (Snider, "Story," 13). In Bucksport, during oyster season. According to Kelly Paul Joyner (b. 1915),

> "the families of the community would be invited by the logging companies down the river to an
> oyster roast at the logging camps. There were large sheets of metal filled with oysters roasting
> over hot coals. The men were always right there to pick out the oysters for the women and
> young girls…. There would be sing-alongs on the boat going and coming home." ("Priceless" 8)

Even the steamboat was far from routine, notes Paul Quattlebaum (b. 1886): "The blast of the whistle down the river and the cry, 'The boat is coming,' brought many spectators to the wharf" ("Early" 26). Moonlight boat rides were enjoyed by the Do Good Club of Conway in 1917 (Epps, "Do Good"). A boat itself could sponsor entertainment: Florence Epps remembers that in the mid-1930s, a little showboat docked for a week at Conway and then at Socastee, leaving among her memorabilia a playbill of *Ten Nights in a Barroom* and a flyer for the same boat ("Among" 15).

Evelyn Snyder (b. 1907). *Evelyn shared her own memory of a showboat in a conversation with J. Marcus Smith:*
"When my parents agreed to attend the floating theater, I could not wait for the big night. I don't recall the play, but I do remember when the performance ended, they had a special show for an additional fee. We stayed. A few minutes into the program, they got up, took me by the hand, and we made a hurried exit." (J. Smith, "Showboat")

Ed Andersen (b. 1936). *As the epigraph to this book testifies, an exotic shop also lured customers to the dock:*
"It was nighttime and there were lanterns everywhere (the only source of light). I was amazed at the bound feet of the women and the bound head of one of the children. I was allowed to purchase a small junk (about two inches) with paper sails. When put in a bowl of water, the little boat would follow you around the bowl from the air currents generated by walking."

Helen S. Carswell. *Excursions aboard a steamboat were festive (Fig. 9.8). In 1899, Miss Carswell, a visiting Northerner, recounted the April excursion on the* F.G. Burroughs *held for about 120 actual or prospective members of the Homewood Colony:*
"The trees grew close to the water's edge, and the mingling of the shades of the live oaks with the trailing gray moss, which hangs from almost every branch, the glossy leaves of the magnolia, the beautiful holly, still loaded with bright berries, the bay, the gum, the tender green of the maple, elm and white birch; the purple blossoms of the wisteria, the

yellow flowers of the jessamine [jasmine vine] and the white of the dogwood afforded a picture varied enough to fill the beholder with delight…. The river is so narrow and the bends so many that the boat is kept swinging in and out among the islands and curves continually, the bow almost touching one bank, while the stern escaped the opposite bank. It took four hours to cover the distance of 35 miles." After a picnic at Laurel Hill [a former plantation in Georgetown County], the boat returned by moonlight. (Qtd. in C. Lewis, "Homewood," 25)

Florence Epps (b. 1907). *The child who loved swaying aboard rafts also enjoyed taking the steamboat to church picnics; to her first cotillion (at the Winyah Indigo Society Hall of Georgetown in 1924); and, as a beautiful young woman, on an excursion for visiting celebrities:*

Fig. 9.8. Group aboard the *Mitchelle C.* around 1910. Horry County Museum.

"My first and still favorite volume of Shakespeare is one edited by a Chautauqua lecturer [a cultural circuit-rider] and ordered for me by my father after the lecturer had paid me special attention on an excursion on the *Burroughs* in April, 1921." ("Have," *IRQ* 1.2: 17)

Anonymous. *On one such outing in 1893, "Cupid, of course, was aboard":*
"The maneuvers, strategies, charges and victualed sieges [exhortations to eat] he commanded were not less pleasing to his followers than to the spectators…." Launched from Conway under Captain Causey, the *Driver* stopped for passengers at Toddville, Bucksville, Peachtree, Enterprise, and Bucksport for a total of 150 people. Until midday, with "the lower deck railed in by benches against the guard posts," it "wandered away amid the mazes and labyrinths of the crooked Waccamaw…. The dark, mercurial stream seems held in its banks by living walls of nature's purest shades of green; the light shades of the sad cypress were outlined against the sturdier coloring of the crowding pines of the hill beyond. The hazel and huckleberry leaned over the mirror of the river and nodded their greeting as the boat's waves tapped at their trunks; while the wild rose, perched upon the great cypress stump, stared open-eyed at the passing load of gayety." At Laurel Hill, "the blessing was asked and a circle of silence was drawn around a table." After the picnic lunch, men representing opposite sides of the river played a baseball game. ("Excursion")

Mitchelle Collins (b. 1886). *The same walls of vegetation could close in:*
Every spring brought an all-day picnic on a riverboat. We went down to Wachesaw or Laurel Hill and would eat where the river bank was high and there was a place to tie the boat up. "You know the river is very narrow, especially at Peachtree, and we always used to be scared to death when the boats went around the bend. Limbs from the trees brushed against the deck. One of my aunts was brushed down steps from the second to the first deck. Another woman was once knocked overboard and they had to stop the boat to go get her…." (Epps, "Gully," 10)

Lillie B. Latimer (b. 1882) *and* **Ruth C. Woodbury** (b. 1886). *Although excursions were racially exclusive, blacks got their turn. Trips to Georgetown on a Friday night meant a job for one mother and a lark for her daughters:*
"Mmmmm, mmmm! That was the happiest night of my life! When time for the excursion. We didn't have any music and they had a band. And when the band started blowing and excursion going tomorrow…. Oooooh! "The band would dance on the head of the boat. The people would dance all the way down and all the way coming back…. All generations enjoyed the outing. Preachers would go, but they didn't dance. We used to sit in the living room upstairs. I'd have been out there, but she wouldn't let me go and I had to sit near that table where she was sitting…." They'd carry a basket, and when they arrived in Georgetown, "everybody would be running to put on their dress." The girls' mother would give them a quarter—"big money"—and they'd go up to the Candy Kitchen and get taffy. (10-11)

Henry Small (b. 1897). *"I've been to one of them," declared Henry, brother of Julia Smalls, son of Annie Glover and Toby Small (born into slavery, 1861), grandson of Sylvia and Titus Small (b. 1824):*
"When that boat leaves Georgetown and come to Longwood, you would dance, and blow the horn, and beat the drum all the way having a time." "It was a big boat to carry quite a many people." (16)

Jessie Dusenbury (b. 1889). *Mitt Pink, who kept the bathroom at Conway's Town Hall, told about taking an excursion, a summer pastime for Negroes:*

It was a very warm day and Mitt was overcome by the heat and almost passed out. Some of the folks on the boat thought she was drunk but Papa [Captain Zack] didn't, he told someone to loosen her clothes so she could breathe more freely. Mitt never forgot his kindness." (21)

"Just a wonder a alligator hadn't got us"

Such excursions could make life hot for wildlife. Writing in the *Horry Herald*, 1899, the editor describes one trip to Georgetown via Laurel Hill:

> "The air was filled with the merry cracks of the rifle and shotgun which was aimed at the numerous fish hawks or the lazy 'cooter' [turtle] which was enjoying the bright sunshine. Several alligators were surprised into motion and slid off into the water with a splash." (Nolley, "On the Waccamaw")

Like the practice of shooting bison from the Western train, shooting *Alligator mississipiensis* was sport for the men. "I have seen huge ones," wrote Lucille B. Godfrey, "with open jaws and slashing tails, slithering down the banks trying desperately to escape. I always felt sorry for them and ran to the other side" ("Some" 16). In 1897 a report in the *Horry Herald* describes a particular clash between 'gator and steamboat:

> "The passengers and crew of the *Maggie* returning from Georgetown last Friday had quite an alligator fight a few miles below town. Knowing the whereabouts of this big fellow, the steamer slowed down, and sure enough he was there. After shooting him several times and supposing him dead, he revived and renewed the fight. It took the Captain and several of his crew to subdue the old fellow. He was brought on here measuring 11 feet." ("Hazards")

The Sarvis brothers could swim "any kind of how." People would say, "You could tie one in a knot and throw him overboard and he'd come right out." One time the boys swam a mile from Brown's Landing to meet the others for a swim: "Just a wonder a alligator hadn't got us." "Put our clothes on over head 'n swim it" (Nichols 24). While hunting around the mill pond, they heard the dog bay: "We could hear a blowing—SHEEZE—and discovered a 'gator in there with her younguns. One boy brought home a hatchling as a present for his mother: "Run your hand in the bag and git it." Her response: "You ever bring another 'gator into this house, I'll get a part of your back!" (Nichols 25).

The reptile could inspire imitation. Wearing "the kind of bathing suits they were born with," wrote Charles Mack Todd, the boys in the pond "practiced swimming, diving, and playing 'gator by going to the bottom and crawling around on the belly" (26).

• In the river or creek

Swimming lessons were nonexistent or rudimentary during much of the county's existence. For example, the unofficial teacher of Robert Bellamy (b. 1917) was a relative who "would get you out there on a boat and dump you out, and then you would be fightin' that water" (Int: 6). In Conway the first swimming pool was built over Kingston Lake by the resourceful Charles H. Snider (who owned the Turtle's Nest cottage). Sometimes blacks and whites would swim together, and James R. Holbert, Jr., (b. 1917) would frolic near Bucksport with Wilford Batten. (See Fig. 9.9.)

Katie B. Randall (b. approx. 1900). *A matriarch with no children, surrounded by five generations of people she had helped raise, Katie turned sad:* [In 1945] "I went to help a man chop some cotton, and while I was gone my [adopted] son followed some boys down to a landing on the

Fig. 9.9. Diving from trestle into the Waccamaw, Conway, circa 1940. Horry County Museum.

creek. One tide comes in this-a-way, and the other tide comes the other way, and when they meet like that, it's strong. When they went and got me, he was drownded."

Mary Emma Reaves Jones (b. 1921). *Others had close calls in the Waccamaw, like one in the account paraphrased by Wyness Thomas:*
"One exciting place to visit was the 'alligator cave,' where the bank was steep and the black water went back into unknown regions…." "Oncc, Mary Emma tried to copy two of her friends by swimming under three rafts of logs. She became frightened when her head hit the bottom of the raft and switched directions, running into the bank under the raft. Finally she swam out the side. The following day a huge water moccasin came out from under the logs." (W. Thomas, "Reaves")

Willy Page (b. 1910). *Every year in the Aynor area farmhands would take the wagon to get fertilizer at Galivants Ferry. After they washed the sacks in the river as material for clothes, they'd go swimming:*
Once, about 26 years old, "I hit a lick or two out there; after a while I went to going down. I was on a sandbar and the water clipped me right along here. I hollered 'Jim, come here, Jim, come here, I got the cramp!' He come there and caught hold to me and was rubbing me legs and rubbing my hands, just pulling my fingers and he got me where that cramp was off of me." Willy made his way to the other side along a sandbar and escaped. (Int: 24)

J. Marion Vaught, Jr. (b. 1923). *Seventy years after its wheels screeched for the last time, Marion points to where the logging train came out of Jones Big Swamp off Highway 90:*
He and his cousin would swipe a handcar on a Sunday afternoon and pump it down to the Waccamaw, where his cousin stripped to his skivvies, climbed the loader, and dived off its boom into the river. (Int. March 17: 28; p.c. See Plate 14.)

• In the swimming hole and on the pond

Claudia Brown (b. 1901), who as a child stood on a box and handed leaves to her mother, asserts that if a swimming hole didn't already exist, people would dig one and take a swim after working tobacco (Int. 21 July: 2). There might be competition, however, with other people or species: John P. Cartrette (b. 1898) "ordered me some water wings and went in for a swim after chasing out a cottonmouth moccasin" ("Good" 24). Mary W. Hardee (b. 1907) remembers that children in the Wannamaker community found something fun to do instead of the noonday rest: "We'd slip away and go swimmin'—black and white—and the eels got so bad in there [in late summer] till we quit." (Int. 4)

Mrs. J. O. Cartrette (b. 1896). *The swimming pool in Green Sea was a mill pond:*
"Few (if any) of us in those days possessed swim suits. Not one swim did we miss because of that! We always found something to swim in, and it was there that I learned to swim. Boys, young men, from the area would 'go swimming' during their 12 to 2 rest period from farm work. If we girls could get there first (and we always did), it was all ours!" Then they would take their turn, no doubt naked because the girls never noticed that they carried extra clothes. (9)

Franklin G. Burroughs (b. 1908). *In northern Myrtle Beach, ponds mark the vestige of a blackbarrier flat. One Thanksgiving a large group hunted ducks at Round Pond, limit 25:*
A large bird flew in: "Someone called out 'goose' and everyone was anxious to get a shot at this bird. Finally, it came out over Walter Stilley [II] and he killed it. Nobody knew exactly what sort of bird it was, so with great pride, he brought it back to Conway," the bird tied to the top of the windshield by its neck, its feet dangling to the running board. The game warden had it sent to Columbia for identification: "Back came the word that this was a whistling swan [*Olor columbianus*] and that the person who killed it should be fined $25." ("Duck" 8)

• In the swamp

A good place to hunt or fish, a swamp also invited exploration:

William J. Rowe (b. 1886). *The fellow who later slogged to Conway on a railroad bike had grown accustomed to his malarial symptoms:*
"It was a drizzly and rather chilly day during a time when we had much rain. Sterritt Swamp was overflowed from one side to the other—a distance of approximately a half mile. I had pinned four or five logs together," and with makeshift raft and a pole "it took a good while to make the round trip because of vines, limbs, and snags…." "This was the day for my chill and fever but I had thought nothing about it. After riding about one-half way across the swamp, I felt the chill coming on. I turned my course toward home and began to shake." It was still drizzling and damp. "I shook and my teeth chattered until I could hardly push the raft to the shore. Soon after I landed, I was neither shaking nor cold. It seemed that I had an inward warmth and no fever followed. I have never had malaria or chills and fever since that day." ("Memories" 5-6)

• In or on the lake

Kingston Lake (see Fig. 9.10) used to turn solid nearly every winter, in the testimony of Mitchelle Collins (b. 1886). Either her father or his partner would send out mules hitched to a heavy wagon and roll it out to see if the ice would hold the children. Mr. Snider had a canoe drawn by a horse or mule that he'd let them ride around in like a sleigh (17).

Evelyn Snider (b. 1907). *When the lake froze over in December-January of 1917-18,* "The big part was filled with town people. It was the first time that many of them had ever remembered it freezing over solid. We didn't know how to skate, and we didn't have any sleds; so we would take rocking chairs" and push them all over the lake.

Fig. 9.10. Kingston Lake. Horry County Museum.

Her father also built a shoot-the-chute. "It was a wooden track with a boat—a flat-bottomed boat—fitted to it. It was blunt-ended, like a john boat, made of wood, and had a rope tied to the back which he attached to the back of his Ford. So when he got in the boat and slid down the hill—chuted down into the water and splashed the water on all sides"—he would then tie the rope to the back of the car and pull it back up. "He'd fill it with a second round of kids, and down it would go. One Fourth of July, he wanted to do something extra. So he got some old oil from the filling station, put it on the water, and set it afire. Then the shoot-the-chute went down in the midst of that burning oil and scattered it all over." (Int: 3)

Elbert McWhite (b. 1902). *This was the same water that had swallowed the Beaty children and their maid:*
Elbert, the nephew of Mr. and Mrs. B.G. Collins, was 14 or 15 years old when he got a job from Mr. Will Goldfinch, who operated the only funeral parlor in Conway, located on the second floor of the Jerry Cox Co. One day people were walking hurriedly toward Kingston Lake. Mr. Bryan met Mr. Woodward, who asked him, "What's happened? Where is everyone going?" Mr. Bryan said, "Haven't you heard? Some boys were in a boat and it capsized and two of them were drowned. I heard that one of them was your son, Eugene…." When the bodies were recovered, rigor mortis had set in. Mr. Will called his assistant: "Elbert, I want you to take each arm and leg and work them back and forth until they lie straight. Unless we do that, we can't fit them into a casket." McWhite reached out and took an arm but suddenly realized the full import: he could have been one of these boys. "I can't do this—I've got to get out of here!" Crying, he ran down the steps away from the undertaking business and toward a professorship at the U.S. Naval Academy. (Int: 3)

Spiritual or otherwise, refreshment beckoned that often involved water, liquid or frozen. It might be inspired by porpoises, invited by fish, abridged by eels, dangerous or safe, communal or solitary, clothed or naked. A pilgrim could kneel on the sand, gyrate at the Pavilion, or tilt backwards into the symbolic swash.

The holiday atmosphere of the seashore may have encouraged Jessie Richardson to dance on Sunday. Unrepentant, she never answered the reluctant letter of expulsion from the First Baptist Church (mailed by J.C. Spivey, who had once exclaimed "There *is* a God" upon beholding the ocean). Sabbath versus Shag: these impulses tended to coexist and even harmonize. At the first pavilion, for example, dancing on Saturday night yielded to worship the next day (B. Floyd, *SN* 18 March 2004). And George Lovell, Jr., pastor of the First Baptist Church of Conway for twenty-seven years, inveterate outdoorsman, baptized people in the ceremonial pool while wearing a white robe over green waders (Watkins).

Notes

[1] For more on beach music and dance, see Nagle and Holliday. As for Charlie's Place, in Fig. 9.3, the man in the Cooks and Waiters hat is Cadillac, a popular waiter at the Dunes Club. The man at left is Mallard Rucker, an entrepreneur at Atlantic Beach. The woman behind the cake is Queenie, a flamboyant and popular waitress (J. Thompson, p.c.).

One Saturday night in 1950, Charlie's Place drew an unwelcome following. The Ku Klux Klan had started what W. Horace Carter terms a "war of terrorism that struck the border section of the Carolinas" (*Virus* 194). To wear the Klan sheets, a "white Protestant Gentile" needed "temperate habits" (106), and the group punished immorality such as gambling, drunkenness, and loose sex. A convoy of night riders drove slowly around this noisy affront. When the owner sent a defiant message to the police, the cavalcade turned around. "More than three hundred rifle and pistol shots ripped through the dance hall, sending the blacks inside into a panic. They quickly punched out the window panes and returned the fire," although outnumbered by at least sixty Klansmen in twenty-seven cars. "Klansmen soon knocked down the door and charged onto the dance floor, overpowering the Negroes still inside." Fitzgerald was stuffed in a car trunk and taken to a sawmill road in a swamp, where he was severely beaten in revenge for the death of a Klansman; he awoke with part of his ears cut off (37-38; 40).

Klan sheets sailed into four rural churches during midweek services. Members of one "surmised that the pastor and leadership approved of the visit, believing it might scare some of the 'sinners' into repentance and a more moral lifestyle" (107). Finally, when Klan members transported a flogging victim from North Carolina, the diagonal line between Horry and Columbus Counties served as a tripwire that summoned the feds and destroyed the empire.

[2] One of the verses that motivated Bishop Asbury to proselytize in 1791 describes "The lake which burneth with fire and brimstone [sulfur]" (Revelations 21.8).

[3] His interviewer, Prof. Donald Millus, adds that Hole 9 is the only one in Myrtle Beach actually located on the Atlantic Ocean. Caption of photograph: "With a booming drive by Ben Few, of Fairfield, Conn., president of Liggett and Myers Tobacco Co., the 1954 Sun-Fun Festival officially got underway Wednesday morning at the Dunes Club."

CHAPTER 10
THE STORM

"Hazel washed it away."
Stanley Coleman (b. 1915), Int. 21 Oct: 12.

Fig. 10.1. Boardwalk in Myrtle Beach. Horry County Museum.

Bad weather has already thundered, blown, and poured in this compilation. According to other records, storms knocked down an occasional church or school, and in Conway a tornado touched down where the hospital would be built, dashed to pieces the house of a Negro family, levitated a wood-burning stove, swept away the logs of Captain Sasser's stable, and balanced his cow on a fence (J.P. Cartrette, "Good," 23).

During the flood of 1928, Gary Mincey (who taught boat-making in Chap. 3) couldn't get from Wannamaker to the train station in Loris; so he caught a ride to a place opposite Nichols where Joe Granger was taking people across the Lumber River by boat, then walked to Mullins and caught the train to Columbia (Int: 14). "We couldn't get out of the house sometimes for about two days," reports Theatus Garrison. Water would come up over the top of a well so that for a long time the family had to carry water home from the Loris pump in jugs (Int: 18). "Cookie" Stogner remembers when a freshet during World War II swelled the Little Pee Dee River and made tobacco barns look like hats floating in water (Int. G. Floyd: 19).

No doubt some of the floods began near Africa or in the Caribbean. "Hurricane," originally a Carib word, refers to a tropical depression that arises in warm water and packs sustained winds of 74 miles per hour or more. The concept was not available to John Lawson when he wrote *A New Voyage to Carolina*. His party, assisted by Indians, trekked through North and South Carolina in 1701, making their way up the Santee River and through a great swamp:

"Hereabouts the late Gust of Wind, which happen'd in September last, had torn the large
Ciprus-Trees and Timbers up by the Roots, they lying confusedly in their Branches, did block up

the Way, making the Passage very difficult." (24)

In a later section of his book called "The Natural History of Carolina," he reports that this same wind "brought a great deal of Rain" and drowned all the European coneys (rabbits) he had imported (128).

The Charleston *Courier* used the term "hurricane"—also called by one survivor a "terrible storm or tornado"—for the weather that ambushed North Inlet above Georgetown on September 28, 1822 ("The Hurricane"; "Further Particulars"). In 1862 Rev. Malet wrote: "This 11th October we have a gale of wind; the pine forests all around roar like the sea; lightning, thunder, and rain—what they call here 'battle rain'" (36). In October of 1894 the *Horry Herald* reported that the cotton crop had fallen off in North and South Carolina partly because of "the storm which occurred in the latter part of September" ("A Decline").

Marjorie Grainger (b. 1905) used to stay home from school in anticipation of such weather: "when the cotton was ready in the fall, before the storms came, it had to be picked" (Int: 3). Eatofel V.T. Arehart (b. 1913) was not afraid during Hurricane Hazel "because I remembered such bad storms as a child; Daddy always called them 'September storms.'" Once her mother was marooned in Wilmington for a month and a half because all the bridges were washed out on the way to the Cape Fear ferry (Int: 2). And in which season but autumn did the overflowing Waccamaw slide beneath the hooves of Maude?

Tom Fetters, in *Loggers of Conway and the Independent Republic*, reports that tropical rains inundated the Conway area in 1916, 1920, 1924, and 1928, putting the mill grounds and much of the track-work in the swamps "under three or four feet of murky water for up to three weeks until the sluggish river systems could drain the area" (13). In 1946 Rick McIver declined to buy the property of the old Conway Lumber Company for his lumber yard because it had recently been under the same element that had floated logs to saws.[1] According to *Flood Plain Information*, "Severe storms in the Waccamaw River Basin generally occur during the early spring and early fall as a result of tropical hurricanes and severe cyclonic disturbances." The September 1924 flood was the most severe on record. In October, according to the *Horry Herald*,

> "The lumber mills are still idle, as their log beds are under water, and white and colored residents of the lower grounds near the old shipyard across Kingston Lake and near the Veneer Manufacturing Co., and the plant of Charles Pate & Company, have all moved out to higher ground as boats could be navigated entirely through and round their home. (rept. *Flood* 10)

In the same month four years later, the newspaper reported that a hundred families had to move to high ground in Conway; some used boats to travel from the doors and windows of the first floor and lived on the second (rept. *Flood* 11).

Barney Dawsey (b. 1912) recalled floods in the 1920s:

> Now the last bad one, "When it come up in Stanford Roberts' and run the people out of Gunters Island, one fellow said he got up and wondered what was happening. He said he stuck his foot off of the bed and it was water. The current was still on in the house and it shocked him. He said no way he could get up. As long as that current was on, that thing would bite you.
>
> "I believe it was '24 when all the bridges washed out. I remember Harve Grainger. We lived near a swamp out there near Antioch and the old bridge was floating; some of the boards had lost their way and he come along to Aynor during all the big rain.... He got out and led that old horse [over two wide boards].... I was praying for him...." (Int: 25)

The 1928 flood caused the highest known water-level at Conway--a result of uneven rainfall distribution as well as backwater from the Pee Dee and Little Pee Dee rivers that kept the Waccamaw from draining (*Flood* 6, 9). That river's estimated peak discharge was 22,000 cubic feet, almost ten times the maximum recorded at the Longs station in 1954.

This final chapter preserves memories of autumn storms, especially the wickedly alliterative one.

"With a horseshoe in it": Autumn Storms

Riding his horse down Long Bay, Rev. George Whitefield praised the one "who hath set bounds to the sea that it cannot pass, and hath said, 'Here shall your proud waves be stayed.'"

One October day in 1893, however, low barometer collided with high tides and high winds, driving the water up and over the land from North Carolina to Georgetown and turning the *Freeda Wyley* into wooden ribs. At that time the coast of Horry was mainly wilderness: "There are no fishing camps left along Long Bay," reported the *Horry Herald*. Between Murrells Inlet and Conway the wind destroyed or heavily damaged five churches, mainly Negro ("Local" Oct. 19). One farm, "Mr. A.Z. Banta's place, the Ark, has not been seriously damaged. The waters washed away the fences and all over the crop" ("Sixteen Drowned").[2]

In Georgetown County this hurricane was often called by the name of a prominent family. "'Storm?' Oh, my Lord! Flagg storm?" exclaimed Rutledge: "Sea naturally climb right over that hill like it wasn't nothing. Water come to King Road. Reckon it would a come further if the wind didn't shift" (Chandler, "Uncle Sabe Rutledge," 60). Down the coast from Horry, along Magnolia Beach, were four households, and although Allard Flagg, Jr., and his Negro servant were able to reach land aboard the roof of his kitchen, only nine of thirty people survived the roaring blackness, the pounding surf, and the wind, which bore glass-like particles of sand. Some finally lost their grips on the topmost branches of cedar trees. In Georgetown the wharves were destroyed by the surge, and many were homeless. The rice crop was destroyed (Z. Wilson). The steamboat *Driver* carried money and supplies for survivors at the creek ("Local News" 9 Nov.).

Ben Horry (b. 1852). *"After Flagg storm, Colonel Ward take me and Peter Carr, us two and a horse,*
"take that shore to Little River. Search for all them what been drowned. Find a trunk to Myrtle Beach. Have all kinder thing in 'em; comb for you hair, thing you put on you wrist. Find dead horse, cow, ox, turkey, fowl–everything. Gracious God! Don't want to see no more thing like that! But no dead body find on beach outside Flagg family. Find two of them chillun way down to Dick Pond what drownded to Magnolia Beach…." (Chandler, "Uncle Ben Horry [Ex-Slave Story]," 313)[3]

Jessamine Buck Richardson (b. 1879). *About a decade before Jessie danced to the Sabbath Victrola, her family decided to stay in Murrells Inlet year-round instead of returning to Bucksport. In August a serious hurricane had damaged houses along the coast:*
In October the weather had been rainy and squally. She was alone with her older brother and sister, as well as with two servants, one of them the blind former slave of her grandfather, Henry Buck I. On the night of the twelfth, the wind was so terrifying that the girls went downstairs to their brother's room. When dawn broke, at what was supposed to be low tide, they saw the Inlet risen above its high-water mark and the marsh flooded.

The water continued to rise. "Every wave brought the water ten or fifteen feet higher, and every wave took back with it more chickens, coops, and debris." With brother George now gone to help a neighbor, she and Iola decided to strike out for higher ground. [Her sister would become the mother of Virginia Burroughs Marshall, first person interviewed by the Oral History Project.] She determinedly escorted "Uncle" Squire but could see little better than he. "The fine, misty rain was blinding and the roar of the wind demoralizing: the water was deep and the current strong." Turning back to the house, their party watched the steps of the porch float off and its foundation pillars crumble.

The shape of George materialized through the rain, struggling to steady both himself and his neighbor in the current. He pushed Jessamine to temporary safety on the porch floor, which rose and fell, then swam out to catch a panel of fencing to use as a raft if necessary. Hoping to keep the house itself from floating away, he cut a hole in the floor. "By that time the waves were breaking in the limbs of the giant oaks." She looked at her watch and realized that the tide was still due to rise for several hours. But nature held another surprise. "As quickly as the water had risen, it dropped. It was like a movie run in reverse. As chickens began to float back, we lay flat on the porch floor and grabbed them out of the water." In short time the water was back in its channel and the sun back in its realm. ("I Lived" 8-10)

Turner Chestnut (b. 1896). *Less notorious weather occasionally swept in by water, wind, and surge. In 1985, Wyness Thomas interviewed Chestnut at his home on the west side of Highway 90, about a mile from Tilly Swamp:*
"We had one or two storms. It put the Burroughs out of the turpentine business. First storm we had blowed the trees down in the woods. You could walk from here to the beach on logs. I've seen the time I could get right out there [in front of his house] and wade in water from here to the ocean. Wet! Wet! Take Bear Bone Sand Ridge [between Hwy. 90 and the Atlantic]: you would have to wade around it…. You would cross it with the wagons. That road, the Reaves Ferry Road, went right across Bear Bone [before the Waterway was built]. Water in it all the time. ("Turner" 13)

Andrew Stanley (b. 1904). *"It come a September storm and I was around six years old—I remember it good:*
"and it tore down everything and blowed it down in someplace. It cleared the earth. It brought that pine here [points at a stand of shortleaf]–it wasn't in this section, couldn't find any of it, and it come up thick everywhere in the yard…. And that storm carried this pine [longleaf] off. It was everywhere—in that road, that field, all out there." "It come up all under there into the house and everywhere in the yard. The storm blowed the longleaf pine down and Lacey & Gardner Company got the timber." (Int. April: 14; Int. Oct: 1)

In the Nixonville area "Everybody lived in a pole [log] house. You didn't lose too many through losing the top: you'd bore a hole in the corners of them and drive a peg in them and that kept the storm from taking them…. My grandmother lived around three quarters of a mile from here, and she was in the slavery. She was walking the road one day and she found a horseshoe. And she had all grades of big old chinny trees [China or chinaberry, *Melia azedarach* L.] in her yard—some of 'em big as that—but there was a ambrella chinny tree…" [umbrella, a cultivated variety]. She attached the shoe to the tree—"hung it in there when it was little and it growed and growed till [the shoe] was way down in the side of the tree."

"And that storm come, and zigzagged 'em and zigzagged 'em and pulled 'em up." The wind and water carried the trees east. "And later a company come in here and built a railroad from Conway to Little River Neck and got the timber. [People] would work in the woods and catch the train back out to here, jump off and go home.... And they would stop by my grandmother's house–everybody made a fire in the yard at night, and they stopped by there and talked and sat and tell what they found, and say 'I found a chair with a cow face in it,' 'I found a bedstead with holes bored in it....' And that man said, 'I found a cheena tree today with a horseshoe in it.' And she told him, 'That is my cheena tree.' So the next day he went back to work and took his ax and cut it out and brought it back to her." (Int. Oct: 1-2)

J. Harry Lee (b. 1908). *As a boy he woke up one morning and saw that the house had several big pine trees propped against it:* "My daddy'd been out cutting those trees trying to keep the house from going down [*laughter*]. Totin' 'em up there, draggin' 'em up there blocking the house. He knew that wind was springin' up early, and he knew the storm was comin'...." (Int: 15, 19)

Louise Chestnut Squires (b. 1916). *In the fall of 1927, "We had a deluge of rain and hard winds" in Surfside Beach,* "and the sea came up over the sand dunes higher than I had ever seen it. We put army blankets around us and headed for the hotel behind the high sand dunes. While we were standing on the porch, a twister touched down close by, twisting off some of the oak limbs and knocking down bricks from the chimney. They rolled down on the roof, making a terrible sound.... We put mattresses on the floor and camped there during the night. The next morning the waves were rolling in higher, the wind was stronger, and so my dad thought it would be safer if we moved farther from the beach. We piled in the Model T with our blankets." But we didn't get any farther than an old cabin about seven blocks in on Surfside Drive, because the road was covered in water and the bridges were gone, so we weathered what we now know as a hurricane." (16)

"That old black peat": Hurricane Hazel

On the morning of October 15, 1954, a heavy wind began to snap trees and push the high tide onto Ocean Boulevard in what would become North Myrtle Beach. The storm "swept ashore at high tide, just after full moon. The eye came in directly over the N.C.-S.C. line, devastating beaches to the north and the south" (C. Lewis, "Little River," 17). By J.O. Cartrette's clock—hands and inscription—the storm reached Conway at about eleven.

According to information gathered by Wyness Thomas from descendants of the Isaac "Handy" Edge family, four vacationers in Ocean Drive were washed out of their apartment and rescued by firemen:

> "People stood outside holding on to any stationary object within reach as the high winds blew. They watched in awe as the power of the waves broke buildings loose from their foundations and washed them out to sea. The ocean water came a block and a half down Main Street. Angry waves splashed over the traffic light that hung above the boulevard."

Mrs. Thomas records more firsthand details. Although over nine inches of rain fell within twenty hours, most of the damage was caused by the surge. On the several miles between Cherry Grove Beach to the north and Windy Hill to the south, only two front-row houses were left standing. Trees served as clotheslines, while power lines and telephone wires draped over piles of lumber and concrete blocks. Luckier was the house of Pearly Edge, once situated near the beach: after floating three blocks down the boulevard and back, then west toward Highway 17 and back, it came to rest in front of the Presbyterian Church. An apple still rested on the bar between the kitchen and dining room, no repairs were needed, and the house was moved back to a new foundation on its original site ("Sketches" 30).

"The onshore winds," C.B. Berry remembers, "coincided with the high tide":

> "They piled the ocean waters in Cherry Grove Marshlands some 16 feet above the low-tide level or 11 above the high, making a huge lake topped by giant waves. After the hurricane eye passed over, the winds blew seaward and created an unusually low tide. The pent-up waters in the marsh came pouring across the area where the old inlet had existed and created a new 1800-foot inlet." (Figs. 10.2 and 10.3)

Fig. 10.2. In October, 2004, fifty years later, Mr. Berry stands where the marsh broke through to the ocean.

Charlie Nixon, reports Berry, obtained $75,000 in emergency funds, assembled the bulldozers again, along with lumber pilings, and re-closed this opening (p.c.).

In Myrtle Beach the day afterward, "The oceanfront wooden boardwalk, which extended from 27th Avenue North to Third Avenue South, floated out to sea" (J. Smith, "Fickle"). In the words of Stanley Coleman, "Hazel washed it away" (Fig. 10.1).

"As I Saw Hurricane Hazel"

Two weeks after the storm, the first mayor of Crescent Beach, C.B. Berry, recorded his memories in the *Ocean Beach News*. (See Plates 15 and 17.)

On October 7, 1954, newspapers reported hurricane winds off the coast of Venezuela:

"Most of us regarded it with little interest. Even if it did come in our general direction, we were on a long bay and had many times observed that hurricanes hit the mainland far south or on the North Carolina coast. Exactly one week later we were to realize the folly of our apathy."

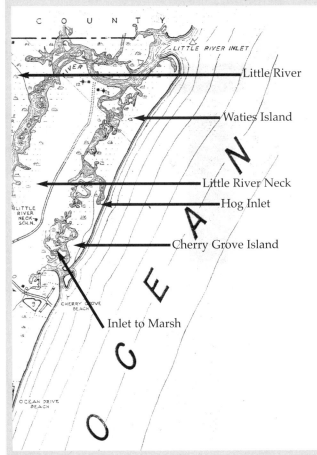

Fig. 10.3. Before Nixon and after Hazel, an inlet separated Cherry Grove Island from Little River Neck. "General, 1939."

Citizens began to pay more attention after Hazel crashed through Haiti and turned northward. Still, they expected the hurricane to strike the North Carolina capes.

At about 2 a.m. on October 15, Berry and his wife were awakened by a radio report that the hurricane was headed toward Charleston and that all persons on the beaches to the north should take precautions. Soon after they got dressed, they heard the fire siren in Ocean Drive Beach. The radio now reported that the storm was about 170 miles off Savannah and headed toward the Carolina Coast between Myrtle Beach and Wilmington. "We knew this meant us."

Even at 4 a.m. the winds were beginning to rise. Most people left their homes and assembled in the store of the Baldwin Company or at the Ocean Breeze Motor Court on Highway 17, seven blocks from the Atlantic, and at the Wampee public schools about six miles away.

The wind continued to rise and by 8:30 a.m. was gusting up to 75 miles per hour. "Rain began to pour down in great horizontal sheets. The wind now was coming directly from the east and was cutting the torrents of rain into a kind of coarse fog that gave it a white appearance. The trees would lie over at what appeared to be a 45 degree angle as the winds stripped foliage and limbs from them. Great whirlwinds formed on the windward side of our home as we peered out from the second floor window. Fearing our roof would be torn from the house, in winds that were now probably exceeding 100 miles per hour in gusts, we went downstairs….

"At about 9 a.m. the rain had stopped but the winds continued to blow with great intensity. My car would not start due to dampness so I bucked the winds and walked to Baldwin's to get assistance in starting it. I had about three blocks to go and I elected to go through the woods, which have only blackjacks (scrub oaks) because I felt this would be safer than the open roads where debris was flying. Upon reaching Baldwin's I found some forty or fifty people huddled about waiting and watching. Jimmy Baldwin told me that the whole front row of beach homes was gone—even the hotels. I thought he was only kidding…."

Fig. 10.4. Houses Hazeled. Horry County Museum.

Sometime between 9:30 and 10:30 the winds quieted for fifteen minutes as a portion of the eye passed over the refugees. Then the wind and rain came in their original intensity but from the west, indicating that the eye was now inland to the north. "Later we heard that the center of the eye had passed directly over Little River, where it lasted about 30 minutes during which time not a twig moved and birds began to sing."

Around noon Berry rode down to the waterfront. "I was dumbfounded. The hotel was off its foundation and leaning seaward at about 30 degrees. The boulevard, directly behind the first row of houses, was straddled by a continuous line of houses, parts of houses, and great piles of lumber and debris." (See Fig. 10.4.) Walking onto the strand he peered in both directions, where seemingly a great hand had pushed everything on the front back at least 100 feet. "Even the sand dunes had disappeared to uncover masses of black peat-like material that resembled paving asphalt. Scattered over the original and new-formed beach was every conceivable article of household furnishings: plates, knives, forks, electric stoves, mixers, mattresses, television sets, clothing, shoes, hammers, tools, refrigerators, and thousands of others."

Then he rode to the Tilghman Fishing Pier at Ocean Drive Beach but found no sign that it had ever existed: "Even the paved Ocean Boulevard had disappeared beneath sand." Looking north toward all the new and expensive houses, he saw only telephone poles. "Even the major part of the debris had disappeared under sand with a concrete block or a household fixture scattered here and there. The back area of Tilghman Beach is lower, for several hundred feet, than the front row and all the debris had been carried back great distances and had left the front clean. Many of the houses four or five blocks back were torn from their foundations and practically destroyed."

Harry Livingston, an alderman of Crescent Beach, and Merlin Bellamy, a policeman of Ocean Drive Beach, told Berry that at the height of the storm many houses had floated out to sea. "In some cases two houses would be driven together by the giant 30- to 40-foot waves and would then disappear into driftwood" ("As I Saw").

Four decades later, in an interview with Catherine Lewis, he added a few details: "We counted twenty-two houses sitting across the boulevard in Crescent Beach alone. We had a bulldozer go down and push out a trail around the houses so cars could go back and forth." (Int: 13-14).

Katie B. Randall (b. approx. 1900). *In Little River Neck "it tore up the beach—they had to build it over":*
"I lay down and went to sleep, and I woke up. 'Aunt Katie, let's go down to the creek'—and there weren't any houses on the creek. It took a house on the beach and brought it to the creek; then the wind shifted and took and carried it back and sot it on a hill, back on the beach."

Sanford D. Cox, Jr. (b. 1916). *Sam had made a survey for a house-owner on the beach:*
After we put our two-foot-long stakes down, he had some pump pipe in his car, five-foot sections, that he wanted driven in. "We beat the tops of off those things with a sledgehammer" trying to get them into the wet sand. I thought, Now that was a foolish thing to do. "Well, not too long after that, Hurricane Hazel hit and those pipes were the only ones standing on East Cherry Grove." The Cox family owned a house inland from the marsh: "Our beds were wood bedsteads, and the mattresses didn't get wet, even though the water went within two feet of the ceiling." The beds just floated up and then back down. (Int: 19)

Eatofel V. T. Arehart (b. 1913). *As a teacher, she was determined to get from Crescent Beach to the schoolhouse in Wampee, but her husband insisted that she wait until he brought back this report:*
"The waves are breaking over the street light at Ocean Drive. No school." "When I put my hand on the door knob to the utility room and turned it, the difference in the pressure just jerked the door out of my hand." So the couple took shelter in the Baptist Church as the eye passed. Then the wind rose up again and Eatofel stood looking out a window as big pine trees snapped. "There were many houses that were still standing, not in the place that they stood in the beginning. And others—every board was ripped apart, broken in two, some of them standing up, some of them piled up on top of each other. There was one house that I had to pass every day [which had floated upon the surge]. There were no curtains at the window and inside stood a table that had been set. The plates and cups and saucers were still sitting on the table." The ocean took the house of Pearly Edge off its [base] and set it down close to the Presbyterian Church. "They teased Mr. Pearly and said, 'Yes, you see where you wanted to go when the storm came.' He said, 'No, I was on my way to the Baptist Church and the wind gave out.'" (Int: 2-4)

Lawrence A. Parrott (b. 1898) *and Mrs. Parrott (b. 1907). In the* Ocean Beach News *of Nov. 2, 1954, C.B. Berry reports one couple's brush with drowning:*
They awoke with no inkling of an imminent hurricane. Mrs. Parrott "looked out a side window around 8:00 a.m. and was astonished to see a wave pass by on the adjacent lot." They hurried to escape. "'I looked up suddenly,' said Mr.

Parrott, 'and saw this big wave headed right for the car. What worried me was a set of steps, torn from someone's house, was in that wave and I did not want to stop lest the motor stall, and to keep moving meant being hit by the steps. The wave suddenly broke against the car and did little damage but the water drowned out the motor.' Mrs. Parrott jumped from the car and began wading through the water to get out. Luckily the car finally caught on two or three cylinders and we gradually struggled to safety.'" Their home was demolished. ("Family")

Nellie Scott Moore (b. 1939). *Even as far inland at the Pee Dee section, "Hazel was a bad woman":*
Nellie said that her father judged it too dangerous for us to leave, "so we would run from window to window watching the storm and looking. The wind was blowing a hundred miles an hour. Daddy was trying to keep us quiet. And honey [her granddaughter Kayatta], you talking 'bout scared. Hazel wouldn't sit the house down in the same spot—she would sit it down an inch or two over" [*laughing*]. (Int: 8)

Clara M. Moore. *The author of a newspaper column on Bucksport, Moore overheard a farmer declare that the storm had two positive effects:*
"One was that the rains had finally wet the ground thoroughly for the first time in over six months, and the other was he wouldn't have any trouble getting his winter firewood, for the storm had already blown up the trees or wrung them off just above the ground, and all he would have to do would be to saw it up. He said he wouldn't even have to hitch his mules to haul the wood in, since the trees were blown down right in his own yard!" ("Bucksport")

Mary Emily P. Jackson (b. 1921). *After World War II the Platts constructed a brick house to replace their log one on the once-deserted beach:*
But Hazel washed through most of it. "Mother dug her silver flatware out of the sand, and when [Ocean Lakes Campground] was built, they dug up the top of a silver vegetable dish that was buried four feet in the sand, and it was not tarnished." It took about three years for Myrtle Beach to recover. We had a bowling alley on Main Street: "I believe there were nine alleys and all of them were washed up, piled up, broken up, and each alley would weigh about 2000 pounds." A tree, at least two feet in diameter—"the whole root system and the trunk were inside the bowling alley." ("Memories" 8, 2-5. See Plate 16.)

Mark C. Garner (b. 1920). *This ill wind blew some good. Garner notes that before the Second World War, the Grand Strand was primarily a resort for North Carolinians and Conwayites:*
"Growth after World War II was steady—not rapid—and the area began to be recognized somewhat as a regional resort. Then along came Hazel. By that unfortunate natural disaster, Myrtle Beach gained a tremendous amount of fame. "I recall my wife and I were in New Hampshire and stopped into a motel, and the lady who checked us in said, 'Well, I don't know anything about South Carolina, but I know that the hurricane hit Myrtle Beach.' "That was, in a strange way, very much a benefit to the area because when they started building back the community with stronger and better structures, the little guest houses gave way to two- three- and four-story motels, which have since become twenty-story places." (Int: 6. For more accounts of this fearsome storm, see "Hurricane Hazel: 50 Years Later" and J. Wilson, "Memories.")

Eventually a "big blow" (Rutledge's term) could be predicted and people evacuated. But the sustained roar would return–as would the surge that had borne chickens, coops, and debris out to the deep, scoured the sand down to the ancient peat floor, and driven waves onto parking lots and houses onto streets. The same combination of wind and waves would arise that had stripped sand from Indian pottery, carried off the cheena, rammed the tree into the bowling alley, and left the apple on the table.

Was Hazel a catalyst for the transformation of a sleepy resort into a frenetic one? Some people believe that the area would have developed anyway, and that the real boom started with the advent of golf-hotel packages in the 1960s. In any case, New Town would become Boom Town. The bay whose porpoises were once admired by Reverend Whitefield as God's handiwork, and whose low-tide highway was commended by President Washington for its "ease and celerity," would rim what became known as the Grand Strand. Instead of vacationing in the mountains, many a tourist would walk barefoot on their surf-lulled ruins.

Old Horry distilled the longleaf into aromatic and sticky treasures and shipped them around the world. It exported trees as logs, boards, shingles, and pulpwood. The golden leaf it distributed to pockets and purses everywhere as little white cylinders. As salt it dispatched the sea. It even bid farewell to job-seeking children. But after the midpoint of the twentieth century, it would import thousands of airmen, tourists, residents (both working and retired)—and even students. The "old boot" would forfeit its emblematic status to the flip-flop or golf shoe. The chipper would come to mean a type of golf club. The ox, jam out of remembrance, would be succeeded by the duct-taped elephant, and the animal that set paws on the kindling-chopper would be memorialized by the Wildcat R.V.

And people would remember people who had listened for that boat to blow.

Notes

[1] The author recalls that Rick sometimes arrived at the Conway Lions Club with wood shavings on the shoulders of his plaid jacket.

[2] A more detailed account of the surge is handed down by Lula and S. Gordon Vereen (b. 1839). A pair of old ladies lived in a two-story frame dwelling, a former plantation house that served as a landmark to ships and to travelers on Kings Highway, "one of the few between Wilmington and Georgetown." John Vereen (the grandfather of S. Gordon) sent his oldest son, Tobe, to offer help.

> "When he arrived, the waters of the ocean were crossing the dunes and running into the first floor of the house. It was too late to get out. Quickly he grabbed an axe, chopped holes in the floor, and opened all the windows. The sea did come in, but although the house shook and trembled it held to its foundations. When the waters returned to their normal bounds, the old house still stood firm in the shelter of the mighty ancient live oak…. Someone dubbed it the Ark…"(135)

As often in oral history, this account varies from another (in Chap. 7). Since a contemporary newspaper calls Banta's place "the Ark," the origin-story makes a charming error even as it offers other valuable details.

[3] Any kinship between Peter Carr and Dave, who was six years old at the time, escaped some modest detective work. Ben Horry, like Sabe Rutledge, makes a frequent appearance in Charles Joyner's *Down by the Riverside.*

AFTERWORD

The colorful people I had sketched in *Along the Waccamaw*—how could they be portrayed more fully? I cast about for ways to do them justice in print, but to no avail. Then after videotaping speeches in class, I wondered if the same thing could be done with interviews. "I don't see why we can't," replied David Parker of the Media Center of Coastal Carolina College (later University).

So one cool November afternoon he and W. Press Courtney hauled camera, tripod, lights, and cables into the living room of Mrs. Virginia Burroughs Marshall. (See Plate 18.) Now I found myself wondering if could move the camellia flowers into the setting of the interview. While Mildred the cat wound herself about the interviewee, dogs romped outside with my daughter Katie on a bluff overlooking the Waccamaw. The experience seemed gratifying to all involved, although I was a novice in local history and (for example) blurred together F.A. and F.G., Virginia's father and grandfather.

The lights and tripod made their way to more Conway folks at places associated with them: Mary Roddey ("Rod") McCown at Kingston Presbyterian Church, Woodrow Long on his neighborhood farm, and Rick McIver at his old-time lumberyard. (A novice in audiovisuals, too, I never thought to ask Rick to operate the old machines he described.)

That spring I asked Catherine Lewis if she would interview Evelyn Snider, whom I had known since the day I couldn't keep up with her on Prof. Joe Pinson's field trip. The two friends spent a happy and productive hour beside Kingston Lake. Then at a party in a former steamboat warehouse (Fig. 2.11), I asked Charles Joyner, Burroughs Professor of History, if the Waccamaw Center for Cultural and Historical Studies would sponsor future interviews. He agreed—and conferred unexpected dignity upon the ad hoc effort by christening it the Horry County Oral History Project.

The Center began to fund the industrial-quality videotapes, the honoraria for outside interviewers, and the transcription of tapes. (See Fig. A-1.) Coastal supplied the director, the videographers, the office equipment, the postage, and sometimes a rattletrap van. Catherine supplied an understanding of the county that equaled her affection for it, as well as an acquaintanceship with promising interviewees, including those she had worked with during the Civil Rights turmoil.

Fig. A-1. Ann Glesenkamp, first transcriptionist, a student in Office Systems Technology, Horry-Georgetown Technical College.

As her silent apprentice I made a dozen runs, but over the years I served as main or co-interviewer for half the interviews sponsored by the Project. Once, because of crossed signals, I left her waiting in the July parking lot of the A&P, drove to Bucksville with Katie, and interviewed the daughter of a Civil War veteran. The videotape records a chat between the shy ten-year-old and the longtime schoolteacher, who had been a fifth grader herself in 1904. Miss Flossie tells how she used to manipulate her older sisters into carrying home her tin lunch bucket: "I wasn't spoiled," she explains, "I was just *bad*"—her stern expression breaking into wrinkled laughter.

Another time I followed an old man out of the dentist's office, introduced myself as he leaned on his cane, asked if he would consent to an interview, and got it. His name? "Donnie Grant"–the very person whom we had given up trying to contact. A high point of the project came after Mrs. Lewis and I finished the interview, when I convinced him to climb into the van, ride to Reaves Ferry, and show where he had paddled folks across the Waccamaw early in the 1900s.

Oral history clear-cuts time. As director I:

- delivered a copy of the videotape to the interviewee, with a note of thanks, often enlisting someone as courier
- had an audiotape made of the videotape
- supplied the audiotape to the transcriber, often meeting Ann Ipock at our children's dance studio in Myrtle Beach
- edited the initial transcription to correct it and make it more readable
- often dropped the transcript on Catherine's woodpile for further correction
- picked up this corrected version

- took it to the transcriber
- picked it up from the transcriber
- distributed this final transcription to the interviewee
- got a signed release form for both transcription and tape from the interviewee or a descendant
- deposited copies of the tape and transcription in Kimbel Library, Coastal Carolina University
- Retained the original transcription and release form (original videotape kept by Media Services)
- oversaw payments to the transcriber
- kept records
- re-visited a number of interviewees with Bill Edmonds, who took still photographs
- with reluctance, attended funerals

After each release was obtained, Sallie Clarkson, Head of Technical Services, Kimbel Library, catalogued the transcripts, audiocassettes, and videotapes into the library's online catalog.

The Oral History Project also transcribed earlier interviews that had been audiotaped or videotaped. And into its lucky hands fell transcriptions made of interviews audiotaped by J. William Holliday in the late 1970s; many of these were then corrected, signed off, and archived.

One year I was granted a three-course release by the Waccamaw Center and by the School of Humanities and Fine Arts, John Durrell, Dean. This gift of time allowed me, for example, to get Donnie Grant's permission to use his interview after the initial attempt failed. ("You could take my house!" he had objected when I asked him to sign, his mood little improved by the fact that a relative had pounded on his house to wake him for our appointment.)

In 1998 the Oral History Project made an appearance in my textbook, *Stretch: Explore, Explain, Persuade* (Prentice Hall) when I quoted from several interviews to help define nonverbal and verbal communication—their strengths, limitations, and interrelationships.

In 2002 the project enjoyed a windfall of interviews conducted or transcribed by students in Advanced Composition and Rhetoric. I had modified the course for the Southern Cluster, a program initiated by Lynn Franken, Dean of what had become the Thomas W. and Robin W. Edwards College of Humanities and Fine Arts. And with Dennis Reed at the camera, I returned to the lumberyard to get footage of Rick operating his noisy vintage machines–like him, sturdy and still working.

Acknowledgments

How appropriate that a book about the community was a communal effort. I gratefully acknowledge the help of many people, whether living or deceased:

I thank Charles Joyner for supporting the Oral History Project immediately and continuously; David Parker, W. Press Courtney, and Dennis Reed for providing expert videography and good company; Ann Glesenkamp and Ann M. Ipock (I smile to think of them) for providing sustained, accurate, and reliable transcription.

Just before her home office no longer cast its solitary light on Eighth Avenue, Catherine Lewis wrote this inscription in my copy of her book: "For Randall Wells, who picked me for one of the great adventures of my life." For Catherine, who accepted my invitation, I inscribe this book with praise for her knowledge of the county's history, geography, politics, and citizens–along with her lively, penetrating, appreciative, demanding, and diplomatic personality.

My warm appreciation goes to those who agreed to be interviewed or to serve as interviewers. For trying to connect me with the descendants of interviewees I thank Connie Graham, Carlisle Dawsey, Marvin Skipper, Joyce Jones (Goldfinch Funeral Home), and Conway Nursing Center.

Coastal Carolina University is a nest of experts, and I thank all the professors mentioned in the text. (Joe Pinson also helped with botany in Chapter 4.) And I thank Edgar Dyer, Vice President for University Relations, for his encouragement and assistance.

For computer hand-holding I thank Prof. Richard Collin, Jack Flanders, Terri Brown Stephenson, Matthew Morey, Vivian E. McCain, Carol Lane, Marjorie J. Metts, John England, and the Computer Lab at CCU (Abdallah Haddad, Director). For secretarial help: Stephanie Hyland and Bonnie Senser. And for library assistance: Margaret Fain, Allison Faix, Sallie Clarkson, Barbara Horner (*Sun News*), and the staff of the South Caroliniana Library. For expert transcription of the later interviews, I thank Linda Parker.

For tours of the countryside: Woodrow Long, Jeri Lynn Lovell, Rilla C. and S.T. McCrackin, C.B. Berry, Sanford Cox, Jr., J.C. Bennett, Reginald Daves, David Long, and Kenneth Inman (who spotted the log-loader in the foliage).

For sharing videotapes of earlier interviews: Rev. Dr. Carl Compton, without whom the only portrait of Dave Carr would be a photograph. For providing other materials: David Bomar Smith (who gave me that set of Holliday transcripts); Kelly Joyner (who lent me a set of *IRQs*); C.B. Berry, to whom I also owe a lot of stamps to cover postage; Wyness Thomas, who bestowed upon me the interviews she wrote for the *Coastal Courier*, itself now history; and the Myrtle Beach *Sun News*, without which many of these pages would have holes. (For example I contacted Katie Randall after reading Joanna Wilson's profile of her). For supplying an especially valuable document I express gratitude to Mary Emily Platt Jackson.

I thank J. William Holliday for giving me the leaves of his own oral history project, already cropped, strung, and dried. For other materials I thank Prof. Patricia C. Nichols, Col. Thomas Rich, Lawrence S. Earley, Greg Martin, Travis Cork III, Ellison M. Smith III, Dr. Frank A. Sanders, Genevieve C. Peterkin, Elaine A. Cartrette, Catherine H. Lewis, George N. Magrath, Sr., Blanche W. Floyd, Ann Ludlam Winfield, First Baptist Church of Conway, Mary Ann Stalvey, Lauren Ward, Carole Stegner, Martha B. Thomas, Dorethea M. Long, Virginia M. Biddle, Andy Johnson, Don Copeland, Ellen Watkins, August Dittbenner, and Ronald D. Atkinson of Eskridge, Long & Associates, Inc., Marion, S.C., who copied a large map for a total stranger. For the beach relics and Citadel ring I thank Dudley E. and Dudley C. Wells.

For her merciless proofreading I extend thanks to Marjorie J. Metts of Coastal Carolina University.

For reading one version of the manuscript or another, part or whole, over five or six years, I thank Edward Andersen, Prof. Charles Joyner, Davis Dodge, Mack Singleton, Evelyn Snider, C.B. Berry, Etrulia P. Dozier, Nancy Seeds, E.R. McIver, Jr., Jacqueline Boyce, Robin W. Edwards, Sr., Onetta H. and Norman L. Deas, Alex Moore, Woodrow and Dorethea Long, Dr. J. Marcus Smith, Prof. Eldred Prince, Jr., Janet Langston Jones, Genevieve Chandler Peterkin, Rebecca Helms, Edward M. Singleton, Prof. Donald Millus, Paula Ellis, Prof. Veronica Gerald, Prof. Lisa Warren. I especially thank Susan Hoffer McMillan for offering words of encouragement, my daughter Andrea Wells for insisting that I call it a book instead of a manuscript, and Pamela Grundy, author of *You Always Think of Home: A Portrait of Clay County, Alabama*, for endorsing the work at a critical time.

If you make it safely past the alligator, the up-rearing bear, the heavy metal door, and the fireman's suit (standing like Boston Mishoe's frozen overalls), then if you venture down the concrete stairway, you reach a crypt that an unimaginative person would call the basement of the Horry County Museum. ("And of the old post office," adds a dullard.) I thank Stewart Pabst, Director, and Robert W. Hill IV, Curator of History, for their frequent help with the ancient photographs, newspapers, tools, products, and processes.

I express gratitude to the editors of the *Independent Republic Quarterly*, and to its many contributors, for a scrapbook that is unpolished in form but priceless in content. And I thank Horry County Historical Society for launching *Steamboat*.

My appreciation goes to the amiable Sam Kinon of Sheriar Press for his help with the publication and his interest in it. And I thank Paul Olsen, Professor of Visual Arts, Captain of Quark, pal of author, for handling the design of the book, every page of which testifies to his expertise, assiduousness, and patience with yet another revision or missing image.

Writing a book enriches teaching but also competes with it, so I thank LaVerne and the late Sidney Bernard for giving me the wherewithal to skip summer school twice and thus reduce my annual number of classes to eight.

Most of all, and once again, I express deep gratitude to South Carolina's first nurse midwife in private practice, Marjory B. Wells. For years she took on far more than her share of the present while her husband tended to the past. In her ambiguous words, "I didn't really do anything except keep the house going."

WORKS CITED

Abbreviations:

Int.	interviewed by
n.d.	no date
n.p.	no page
Rpt.	reprinted in

CC	*Coastal Courier* [Horry and Brunswick Counties]
HH	*Horry Herald* [Conway, S.C.]
HN	*Horry News* [Conwayboro/Conway, S.C.]
IRQ	*Independent Republic Quarterly*
SN	*Sun News* [Myrtle Beach, S.C.]. Items without titles or page numbers refer to the weekly historical column on p. 1-C.

Berry	C. Burgin Berry
Compton	Carl Compton
Dozier	Etrulia P. Dozier
Holliday	J. William Holliday
Lewis	Catherine H. Lewis
Wells	Randall A. Wells

Interviews are documented by the name of the person interviewed, the interviewer(s), and the date:
Horton, S.F. Int. Lewis, 14 June 1990.

Within an entry, the words "Interview" and "Personal communication" occur alphabetically. The latter means one or more of the following: letter, e-mail message, annotated transcription, or conversation (face-to-face or by telephone).

Aceves, Cynthia Hucks Smith. Personal communication, 1997.

Allen, Barbara, and Lynwood Montell. *From Memory to History: Using Oral Sources in Local Historical Research.* Nashville: American Assoc. for State and Local History, 1981.

Alford, L.E. "Alford Family Data." *IRQ* 13.4 (1979): 18-19.

Altman, Mrs. P.D. [Marguerite Wideman]. "Galivants Ferry and Zion Communities." *IRQ* 1.4 (1967): 11-12.

Altman, Ryland. Int. Angie Altman Robbins, 25 Nov. 2001.

American Life Histories: Manuscripts from the Federal Writers' Project, 1936-1940. Manuscript Division, Library of Congress. <memory.loc.gov/ammem>

Andersen, Donald Edward. Personal communication, 2003.

Anderson, J.R. [Letter to editor of the *Horry Herald*.] 30 Jan. 1936. Rpt. *IRQ* 13.1 (1979): 23-24.

Anderson, O.A. "History of Wannamaker Church." *IRQ* 11.3 (1977): 22+.

Anderson, Robert. "At 88, McIver has Caught his 'Second Wind.'" *Independent Seniors*, March 2000: 4+.

Anderson, Thurmond. Int. Lewis and Wells, 1991.

Arehart, Eatofel Vereen Thompson. Int. Lewis, 16 April 1993.

Armor, Joyce. "Mickey Spillane: A Hard-Boiled Softie." *Transitions News Magazine.* March 2004: 24.

Asbury, Francis (Rev.). *Journal of Rev. Francis Asbury, Bishop of the Methodist Episcopal Church.* 3 vols. New York: Eaton & Mains, n.d.

Ausband, Jerry. "Nostalgia Nuances." *SN* 6 Aug. 2000: 5-D.

---. "Roads, Not Long Ago." *SN* 22 May 1988.

Averit, James Battle. "Turpentining with Slaves in the 30's and 40's: Pages from Life on a North Carolina Plantation." In Gamble, *Naval Stores*, 25-27.

Ayers, J.C. "History of Mt. Olive Community." *IRQ* 11.3 (1977): 14-19.

Bailey, Annie Lee Singleton. Int. Lewis, 15 Oct. 1993.

Bailey, Douglas, and Gary Mincey. Int. Lewis, 1990.

Baker, A.J. "The Fate of Maude." [Unpublished manuscript.] 13 May 1909.

---. Int. Lewis, 1967. [Tape-recorded speech followed by questions and answers.]

---. "Turpentine Industry in Horry County." *IRQ* 2.2 (1968): 13-15.

Bartram, John. *Diary of Journey through the Carolinas, Georgia, and Florida from July 1, 1765, to April 10, 1766.* Annotated by Francis Harper. Excerpt rpt. *IRQ* 6.1: (1972): 28-29.

Beacham, Frank. "Charlie's Place." *Oxford American* Nov.-Dec. 2000: 50-62.

Beaty, B.L. "The Battle of the Crater." Chapter 3 of *Sketches and Reminiscences*, by Joshua Hilary Hudson. Columbia, S.C.: *The State*, 1903. Rpt. *IRQ* 18.1 (1984): 12-19.

Bedford, A. Goff. *The Independent Republic: A Survey History of Horry County, South Carolina.* 2nd ed., revised and enlarged by members of the Horry County Historical Society. 1989.

Bell, Sylvia Lily. "A New York City Girl Became a South Carolinian." *IRQ* 27.1 (1993): 15-17.

Bellamy, James "Son Rabbit." Int. Berry, 24 March 1991.

Bellamy, Robert. Int. Wells, 6 Feb. 2001.

Benjamin, Mary Kate Jones. "Cool Springs." *IRQ* 13.3 (1979): 27-33.

Bennett, John C., Jr., Int. Donald Millus and Wells, 8 Jan. 2002.

---. Int. Wells, 14 Jan. 2003.

Benton, Billie Mae. Int. Jamie Carol Thompson and Kimberly T. Merry, 15 Feb. 2002.

Benton, E. Horry. Int. Lewis, 4 Dec. 1992.

Berry, C.B. "Area Tobacco Goes Back More than a Century." Cheraw *Chronicle* [Cheraw, S.C.] 31 Oct. 1991: 1+.

---. "As I Saw Hurricane Hazel." Ocean Beach *News* [Ocean Drive, S.C.] 26 Oct. 1954.

---. *Berry's Blue Book.* [A compilation of genealogies, surveys, interviews, and articles.] To be published.

---. "Bulldozers Help Actualize Dream." *SN* 22 Jan. 2000.

---. "C.B. Berry Speaks." *IRQ* 5.3: 11-18.

---. "Family Escapes Amidst Waves." Ocean Beach *News* [Ocean Drive, S.C.] 2 Nov. 1954. [Unattributed.]

---. "The Great Land Dispute." *IRQ* 24.4 (1990): 18-24.

---. "History of Little River." [Unpublished manuscript.]

---. "Horry County's Oldest Industry." *IRQ* 2.1 (1968): 11-15.

---. Int. Lewis, 18 March 1991.

---. "James Clyde Williamson." [Notes of interview, 25 Nov. 1995.]

---. "The Little River Bridge More Than Two Centuries Old." *SN* 7 Aug. 2003.

---. "Little River Central Spot for Pirates." *SN* 10 Aug. 2000.

---. Personal communication, 2000-04.

---. "Rambling About with Leads from Thomas Walter Livingston." *IRQ* 14.1 (1980): 15-17.

---. "River Ferries Vital to Getting Around." *SN* 15 July 1995.

---. "Tar Business Thrived in Early Horry County." *SN* 16 March 1991.

---. "Withers Families." *IRQ* 13.2 (1979): 27-32.

Bessent, Carl B. "About the Bessents." *IRQ* 5.3 (1971): 6-9.

---. "Early Little River Days." *IRQ* 10.1 (1975): 7-9.

Beverly, Silas Davis "Dock." "My Life as It Was and Is." *IRQ* 32.1 (1998): 24-26.

Bishop, Nathaniel H. *Voyage of the Paper Canoe: A Geographical Journey of 2500 Miles, from Quebec to the Gulf of Mexico, During the Years 1874-5.* Edinburgh: David Douglas, 1878.

Blanton, James P. Personal communication, 1999, 2000.

Bonnette, Henry. Int. Compton, 1985.

Boyle, Christopher C., ed. "An Interview with Ms. Ellen Godfrey, an Ex-Slave of Horry County." [An edition of an interview by G. Chandler.] *IRQ* 31.2 (1997): 14-19.

---. "An Interview with Uncle Sabe Rutledge, An Ex-Slave of Horry County." [Chandler.] *IRQ* 31.4 (1997): 5-11.

---. "An Interview with [William Oliver], an Ex-Slave of Horry County." [Chandler.] *IRQ* 31.3 (1997): 14-17.

Brickell, John. "Making Tar, Pitch and Rosin in the Province of North Carolina in 1730." Excerpt from *Natural History of*

North Carolina. Dublin: 1737. In Gamble, *Naval Stores*, 16.

"Bridge Goal after Years." *HH* 31 March 1938: 1+.

Brown, Claudia Allen. Int. Wells, 24 June 1998. See also"Happy Birthday: Centenarian," *SN* 1 Jan. 2000: 1-A.

---. Int. Wells, 21 July 1998.

Brown, Mildred Prince. "The Village of Gurley." *IRQ* 19.2 (1985): 4-8.

Bureau of Census. See "United States. Bureau of Census."

Burgess, William. "My Experience in the Late Civil War." Originally published, apparently, in the *Field* [Conway, S.C.] sometime in 1914. Rpt. *IRQ* 14.2 (1980): 4-8.

Burns, Ken. "Pardon black boxer to redeem U.S. ideals." *SN* 17 July 2004: 11-A.

Burroughs, Edward Egerton. "In My Time." *IRQ* 28.4 (1994): 21-31.

Burroughs, F.G. "Duck Hunting on the Grand Strand." *IRQ* 27.1 (1993): 6-10.

---., and Geraldine Bryan. Int. Lewis and Wells, 8 Nov. 1991.

Burroughs, Frances Coles. "Arthur Burroughs." *IRQ* 20.1 (1986): 19-21.

Burroughs, Franklin. *Billy Watson's Croker Sack: Essays by Franklin Burroughs.* New York: Norton, 1991.

---. *Horry and the Waccamaw.* New York: Norton, 1992. Reissued as *The River Home: A Return to the Carolina Low Country.* Boston: Houghton, 1992.

---. "Returning Home to Rivertown." *Preservation* Sept.-Oct. 2000: 26-33.

Burroughs, Geraldine Bryan. Int. Wells, 1993.

Butler, Carroll B. *Treasures of the Longleaf Pines Naval Stores.* 2nd ed. Shalimar, Florida: Tarkel, 1998.

Butler, Helen Gardener. See Dozier, "Interview...Smalls."

Cain, Cyril Edward. *Four Centuries on the Pascagoula* I. State College, Mississippi: 1953.

Carr, Albert. Int. Wells, 2003.

Carr, David. Int. Compton, probably 1991.

Carrison, Daniel Jordan. "A Christmas Visit of the Long Ago." *IRQ* 18.1 (1984): 20-22.

Carter, W. Horace, with Jimmy D'Angelo. *Jimmy D'Angelo and Myrtle Beach Golf.* Tabor City, N.C.: Atlantic, 1991.

---. Personal communication, 2003.

---. *Virus of Fear.* Tabor City, N.C.: Atlantic, 1991.

Cartrette, J.O. "Gleaned from *The Field* June 8, 1916." *IRQ* 8.4 (1974): 18-20.

Cartrette, Mrs. John O. "Childhood Life in Green Sea Township." *IRQ* 9.2 (1975): 8-11.

Cartrette, John P. "Allen." *IRQ* 3.4 (1969): 42-43.

---. "The Good Old Days [?]" *IRQ* 8.4 (1974): 21-25.

---. "Industrial Development in Horry County." *IRQ* 7.4 (1973): 5-10.

---. "To Bathe or Not to Bathe." *IRQ* 15.1 (1981): 26.

Catesby, Mark. *The Natural History of Carolina, Florida & the Bahamas.* 2 vols. London: Benjamin White, 1771.

Cavalli-Sforza, Luigi Luca, Paulo Menozzi, and Albert Piazza. *The History and Geography of Human Genes.* Princeton, N.J.: Princeton Univ. Press, 1994.

Chandler, Genevieve Willcox. "A Pre-World War II Travel Narrative of Horry County." In *South Carolina: A Guide to the Palmetto State, 1941.* Published by the Federal Writers Program, 1941. Rpt. *IRQ* 31.3 (1997): 34-35. Chandler is probably the author.

---. "Aunt Ellen Godfrey." In *Federal Writers'* 14, Part 2: 153-58.

---. "Conversation of Aunt Ellen Godfrey—Age 99 Years." In *Federal Writers'* 14, Part 2: 161-63.

---. "Ex-Slave Story: Uncle Willis Williams." *Federal Writers'* 14, Part 4: 208-12.

---. "Ex-Slave Talks" [Mundy Holmes]. Project 1655. Folklore. D-4-36. 3 pp. South Caroliniana Library, Columbia.

---. "Going to Windy Hill." [As told to Florence Epps.] *IRQ* 5.3 (1971): 29.

---. "Method of Stopping a Flow of Blood." Project 1655. Folklore. 3 pp. D-4-36, South Caroliniana Library, Columbia.

---. "Mom Ellen Godfrey." In *Federal Writers'* 14, Part 2: 159-60. <memory.loc.gov> Another version identifies the man as from Loris: "[Po-Buckra]," item 11 of 290.

---. ["An Old Man from Horry."] *American Life Histories: Manuscripts from the Federal Writers' Project, 1936-1940.* 1938. Folklore Collection. *American Memory: Historical Collections for the National Digital Library.*

---. "Recollections of Uncle William Oliver." In *Federal Writers'* 14, Part 3: 217-220.

---. "Uncle Ben Horry [Ex-Slave Story]." In *Federal Writers'* 14, Part 2: 308-15.

---. "Uncle Ben Horry" [Folklore]. In *Federal Writers'* 14, Part 2: 298-307.

---. "Uncle Sabe Rutledge." In *Federal Writers'* 14, Part 4: 59-64.

---. "Uncle Sabe Rutledge (Ex-Slave Story)." In *Federal Writers'* 14, Part 4: 65-70.

Clardy, W. Clyde. "Growing Up Near Wampee." As told to Marguerite Lewis and Annette Reesor. *IRQ* 19.3 (1985): 29-30.

Coan, Peter Morton. *Ellis Island Interviews in Their Own Words*. New York: Facts on File, 1977.

Coleman, Stanley, and Frances Clark Coleman. Int. Lewis and Wells, 13 Oct.1993.

---. Int. Wells, 21 Oct. 1993.

Coles, Mrs. John F. [Winnie Holliday]. "The Ferry." *IRQ* 1.4 (1967): 10-11.

Collier, Mrs. G.W. [Evangeline Wideman]. "Aynor Schools and Society of the Twenties." *IRQ* 1: 4 (1967): 3-4.

Collins, Elizabeth. *Memories of the Southern States*. Taunton: Barnicott, 1865. Excerpts in *IRQ* 11 (1977), issues 1: 4-13; 2: 9-17; 3: 37-43; 4: 39-46.

Collins, Mitchelle. Int. Lewis, 15 Feb. 1966.

Collins, O.T. "Tommy." Int. Wells, 10 August 2003.

Collins, Stanton L., M.D. Personal communication, 2002.

Columbia Encyclopedia, 6th ed. Columbia Univ. Press, 2002.

Compton, Carl, Rev. Dr. *Hearing Horry History*. Televised interviews. See Compton,"Hearing Horry History," *IRQ* 27.1 (1993): 5.

Conrad, Timothy A. "The Travels of Timothy A. Conrad from Smithville, NC, to Georgetown, SC in 1834." Harry E. Wheeler, "Timothy A. Conrad." Bulletins of American Paleontology 23.77 (1935). Rpt. Ithaca, New York, *Paleontological Research Association*, 1977: 25-27. Rpt. *IRQ* 24.1 (1990): 19.

"Conway, South Carolina." Conway Chamber of Commerce. [Probably 1922.]

Cooper, Mrs. Julian B. "Socastee." In C. Willcox 137-141.

Cooper, Sarah C. "Socastee United Methodist Church." *IRQ* 12.3 (1978): 11-22.

Copeland, Don. Personal communication, 2004.

Cox, Sanford D., Jr. Int. Lewis, 1992.

Cutts, Eugenia Buck, Belle Miller Spivey Hood, and Harriette Scoggins Stogner. Int. Lewis, 8 April 1994.

D'Angelo, Jimmy. Int. Donald Millus, Lewis, 4 Dec. 1992.

Davis, William F. Int. Lewis, 1991.

Dawsey, Barney. Int. Lewis, 9 Oct. 1992.

---, John. Int. Lewis, 26 Feb. 1993.

Dayton, Kathleen Vereen. "From Rural to Wireless." *SN* 31 March 2001: D-1+.

"A Decline in Condition." *HH* 18 Oct. 1894: 1.

"Died." *HH* 12 Jan. 1893: 3.

Doyle, Carrie Daniels. Int. Holliday, 8 Sept. 1976.

---. Int. Holliday, 31 Oct. 1976.

Dozier, Etrulia P. "Bethel African M.E. Church." *IRQ* 2.4 (1968): 7-8.

---. "The Cemetery at the Saint Paul Missionary Baptist Church Conway, S.C. (Homewood)." *IRQ* 12.2 (1978): 31-34.

---. "Eastern Carolina Junior College." *IRQ* 7.2/3 (1973): 30-31.

---. "Interview of Mrs. Julia Smalls." *IRQ* 4.3 (1970): 31-33. Based on audiotaped interview by Mrs. Helen Gardener Butler, 8 Feb. 1970.

---. "Mount Calvary #1 Baptist Church." *IRQ* 14.3 (1980): 7-9.

---. "Slave Owners in Horry in 1860." *IRQ* 9.4 (1975): 22-23.

Dusenbury, James Saye. "In Col. Dusenbury's Boyhood." *IRQ* 2.2 (1968): 4-6.

Dusenbury, Jessie. "Memories of my Father Capt. Z.W. Dusenbury." *IRQ* 5.2 (1971): 20-21.

Earley, Lawrence S. "From Cowpens to Fairways: A Cultural History of Longleaf Pines in the Carolinas." [Speech to the Longleaf Alliance, Southern Pines, N.C.] 18 Nov. 2002.

---. *Looking for Longleaf: The Fall and Rise of an American Forest.* Chapel Hill: Univ. of N.C. Press, 2004.

---. Personal communication, 2004.

"1850 Slave Schedules of Horry County South Carolina (An Addendum to the 1850 Census Report)." *IRQ* 33.2 (1999).

"1860 Slave Schedules of Horry County South Carolina (An Addendum to the 1860 Census Report)." *IRQ* 33.4 (1999).

Elliott, Manning. Int. Holliday, n.d. [c. 1977].

Encyclopedia of Southern Culture. Ed. Charles Reagan Wilson and William Ferris. Sponsored by the Center for the Study of Southern Culture at the Univ. of Mississippi. Chapel Hill: Univ. of N.C. Press, 1989.

The Epic of Gilgamesh. Trans. N.K. Sandars. Penguin Classics. New York: Penguin, 1972.

Epps, Florence Theodora. "Among Our Souvenirs." *IRQ* 1.2 (1967): 14-16.

---. "Captain Byrd." *IRQ* 4.1 (1970): 45.

---. "The Do Good Club of Conway, 1917." *IRQ* 6.1 (1972): 25.

---. "Editorial." *IRQ* 1.3 (1967): 3-4.

---. "A Fair Exchange." *IRQ* 3.2 (1969): 19.

---. "The Gully Store, Flying Ginnies, and Wooden Caskets." *IRQ* 2.1 (1968): 8-11.

---. "Have You Heard That…?" *IRQ* 1.2 (1967): 16-18.

---. "Have You Heard That…? *IRQ* 1.3 (1967): 11-15.

---. "Mildred Bedsol, 16 Year Old Teacher." *IRQ* 5.4 (Oct. 1971): 26-29.

---. "Mr. Cordie Page Recalls." *IRQ* 1.4 (1967): 4-6.

---. "Mr. Hucks of Horry." *IRQ* 3.2 (1969): 18-19.

---. "Post Offices of the Past." *IRQ* 2.1 (1968): 15.

---. "Welcome to Historic White Point." *IRQ* 4.3 (1970): 15.

"The Excursion." Anonymous. *HH* 15 June 1893: 3.

Eyton, J. Ronald, and Judith I. Parkhurst. "A Re-Evaluation of the Extraterrestrial Origin of the Carolina Bays." Geography Graduate Student Association Paper Number 9. Univ. of Illinois at Urbana-Champaign. <http://abob.libs.uga.edu/bobk/cbayint.html>

Federal Population Census. 3rd Census of the United States, 1810. South Carolina. Horry District. Microfilm.

Federal Writers' Project. *Slave Narratives: A Folk History of Slavery in the United States, from Interviews with Former Slaves.* 19 vols. St. Clair Shores, Michigan: Scholarly Press, 1976. Rpt. of the typewritten records prepared by the Federal Writers' Project, 1936-1938, assembled by the Library of Congress project, Work Progress Administration for the District.

Fetters, Tom. "Loggers of Conway and the Independent Republic." *IRQ* 20.1 (1986): 3-18.

"Final Report of Grand Jury for Fall Term of 1893." *HH* 2 Nov. 1893: 2.

Flood Plain Information: Waccamaw River, Kingston Lake Swamp, Crab Tree Swamp. City of Conway, South Carolina. Charleston, S.C.: Dept. of the Army, Charleston District, Corps of Engineers, 1973.

Floyd, Blanche. *SN* 17 July 1999.

---, *SN* 9 Jan. 2003.

---, *SN* 18 March 2004.

---. *Tales along the Grand Strand.* Bandit Books, 1996.

Floyd, George, Alice Floyd, William "Mac" Goldfinch, J.R. Holbert, Jr., Jose Holbert, and Harriette Scoggins Stogner. Int. Wells, 17 Feb. 1995.

Floyd, Lunette Davis. "The Things That I Remember." *IRQ* 31.4 (1997): 14-21.

---, Penny Gore. Int. Lewis, 2 Oct. 1992.

Fowler, John. See McCracken, Int. 26 Aug.

Frankenberg, Dirk. *The Nature of North Carolina's Southern Coast: Barrier Islands, Coastal Waters, and Wetlands.* Chapel Hill: Univ. of N.C. Press, 1997.

Fretwell, Sammy. "Bays Provide Protection to Many Species." *SN* 23 Dec. 2002: 1-C+.

Frommer, Myra Katz and Harvey Frommer. *Growing Up Jewish in America: An Oral History.* Lincoln and London: Univ. of Nebraska Press, 1995.

"Further Particulars." *Courier* [Charleston, S.C.] 4 Oct. 1822.

Gamble, Thomas. "Charleston's Story as a Naval Stores Emporium." In Gamble, *Naval Stores*, 35-36.

---. "Early History of the Naval Stores Industry in North America." In Gamble, *Naval Stores*, 17-23.

---, ed. *Naval Stores: History, Production, Distribution and Consumption*. Savannah, Georgia: Review, 1921.

Garner, Mark C. Int. Lewis, 20 Nov. 1992.

Garrison, Theatus Graham. Int. Dozier and Wells, 17 April 1995.

Gasque, Pratt. *Rum Gully Tales from Tuck 'Em Inn: Stories of Murrells Inlet and The Waccamaw Country*. Orangeburg, S.C.: Sandlapper, 1990.

Gause, Agnes Mishoe. See Scott.

---. "History of Mr. Boston Mishoe." With R. Wells. *IRQ* 29.2 (1995): 4-5.

---. Personal communication, 2001.

Gayes, Paul. Personal communication, 2002.

"The General Assembly." *HH* 18 Feb. 1897: 1.

General Highway and Transportation Map: Horry County South Carolina. S.C. State Highway Dept. in cooperation with Federal Works Agency. 1939.

Gerry, Eloise. "A Naval Stores Handbook Dealing with the Production of Pine Gum or Oleoresin." Washington, D.C. USDA. Miscellaneous Publication No. 209, January 1935.

Gibbons. See Sharitz.

Gilbert, Marie. *Myrtle Beach Back When*. Scottish Heritage Series. Laurinburg, N.C.: St. Andrews Press, 1989.

Gilland, J.D., M.D. Personal communication, 2000.

Godfrey, Lucille Burroughs. "Excerpts from the Burroughs Family." *IRQ* 4.3 (1970): 6-11.

---. "Laws Relating to Early Ferries and Roads." *IRQ* 1.2 (1967): 9-13.

---. "Some Historical Facts About the Burroughs Family, the Business, and Horry County." *IRQ* 15.1 (1981): 5-25. Pp. 18-25 duplicated in "Excerpts."

Goldfinch, James. Personal communication 2004.

Goldfinch, William McTyeire "Mac." See G. Floyd.

Gooden, Dewitt T. [Extension Agronomist, Pee Dee Research and Education Center (Clemson Univ.), Florence, S.C.] Personal communication, 2000.

Gould, Lewis P. Int. Lewis, 7 June 1990.

---. Personal communication, 2000.

Gragg, Rod. *The Illustrated History of Horry County*. Myrtle Beach, S.C.: Burroughs & Chapin, 1994.

Grainger, Marjorie. Int. Lewis, 30 April 1993.

---. Int. Lewis and Wells, 15 Sept. 1993.

Grant, Donnie. Int. Lewis and Wells, 22 Aug. 1991.

Green, John I. "The Happy Land of Horry. *News and Courier* [Charleston, S.C.], Feb. [?] 1890. Rpt. *IRQ* 24.2 (1990): 30-35.

Greene, Lisa. "Wetlands: From Marshes to Carolina Bays...." *SN* 28 April, 1991: 1-A+.

Grelen, Jay. "Water Issues Have Struck Strand Before." *SN* 30 July 2002: C-1.

Grundy, Pamela. *You Always Think of Home: A Portrait of Clay County, Alabama*. Athens: Univ. of Georgia Press, 1991.

"HCHS Fall Tour." *IRQ* 9.1 (1975): 6-8.

Hanson, Kelly. "Working Beside Their Men in the Fields, Women Do Their Share." The *Sentinel* [Loris, S.C.] 27 July 1998: Tobacco Edition, 2-E.

Hardee, Mary Williamson. Int. Wells, 1990.

"Hazards of Travel on the Waccamaw." *IRQ* 9.4 (1975): 25.

Hazel, Forest. "The Dimery Settlement: Indian Descendants in the South Carolina Low Country." *IRQ* 29.4 (1995): 32-36.

"Hazel 50 Years Later." *SN* 10 Oct., 2004. 1+.

Hemingway, Lennie. Int. Wells and Sharabia Rogers, Feb. 2002.

Hemmingway, Sally. Int. Nicole Service and Wells, Feb. 2002.

High, Bob. "Company K, 26th South Carolina Infantry." *IRQ* 23.2 (1989): 14-22.

Hill, Robert W. IV. Personal communication, 2004.

Hobeika, Mary Sarkis. "Big Joe Sarkis, First Foreign Born Citizen." Intro. Florence Epps. *IRQ* 2.3 (1968): 10-11.

Holbert, James R., Sr. [Speech to Horry County Historical Society, 11 Oct. 1971.] *IRQ* 6.1 (1972): 18-19.

Holihan, Margaret. Personal communication, 1999.

Holliday, J. William. "The Last Jitterbug." *Spectator* [Raleigh, N.C.], "Maritimes," Coastal Supplement 9-16 May 1996: 23+.

Holmes, Cad. See Peterkin.

Hopkins, Celia H. "Family's Salt Kettle Has a Long, Colorful History." *IRQ* 31.2 (1997): 26-28.

"Horry Old-Timer Fondly Remembers Six-Hour Trip from Longs to Conway." *Field and Herald* [Conway, S.C.] 28 Jan. 1980. Rpt. *IRQ* 14.4 (1980): 6-8.

"Horry Warehouse." [Advertisement.] *HH* 6 July 1899: 3.

Horton, S.F. Int. Lewis, 14 June 1990.

---. Int. Lewis, 15 May 1991.

---. Personal communication, 2000.

"The Hurricane!" *Courier* [Charleston, S.C.] 1 Oct. 1822.

Hurt, Kathryne Smith. "Some Facts About the Descendants of James Smith, Sr., of Horry County, S.C." *IRQ* 17.2 (1983): 4-11.

"Impure Blood" [Advertisement]. *HH* 18 Oct. 1894: 2.

Jackson, Mary Emily Platt, Lacy Hucks, and Catherine Lewis. "James Calhoun and Surfside Beach: Excerpts from an Interview." *IRQ* 27.1 (1993): 10-12.

---. "Memories of the Beach—Before Development." *IRQ* 24.2 (1990): 5-9.

---. Personal communication, 2004.

Johnson, Ellen Cooper. *Memoirs of Ellen Cooper Johnson*. In *Snow Hill*: 1-57. See also *IRQ* 15.2 (1981): 4-17.

Johnson, Janie Best. Int. Wells and Marjory B. Wells, 25 Oct. 1991.

Johnson, Nellie Holmes. See Peterkin.

Jones, Ruby Sasser. "My Father, the Captain." *IRQ* 4.3 (1970): 13-15.

---. "Myrtle Beach Then and Now." *IRQ* 5.3 (1970): 12-13.

---. "The Vicissitudes and Joys of a Country Schoolteacher." *IRQ* 4.4 (1970): 42-44.

Jones, W. Irving, Jr. Personal communication, 2001.

Jones, W. Irving, Sr. Int. Holliday, undated [probably 1977].

---. Int. Holliday, 11 Aug. 1977

---. Int. Holliday, 18 Aug. 1977.

"Josias Sessions (1764-1837): His Revolutionary War Record." Submitted by George Q. Sessions. *IRQ* 17.1 (1983): 10-11.

Joyner, Charles. *Down by the Riverside: A South Carolina Slave Community*. Urbana: Univ. of Illinois Press, 1984.

---. "The Far Side of the Forest: Timber and Naval Stores in the Waccamaw Region." *IRQ* 18.4 (1984): 13-17.

---. Personal communication, 2004.

Joyner, Effie Parker Todd. Int. Lewis, 16 March 1984.

Joyner, Kelly Paul. "A Priceless Heritage." *IRQ* 19.1 (1985): 6-10.

Kearns, Adalyn Sherwood. *A Collection of Memoirs of the Burroughs Family*. In *Snow Hill* 58-151. This information draws on interview notes taken by Mrs. Kearns in 1951-52. See also "A Collection…," *IRQ* 21.3 (1987): 4-6.

Keeling, William H. "Some Thoughts about the Prehistory of Horry County." *IRQ* 19.3 (1985): 23-24. See also his "The First Horryites," *IRQ* 17.4 (1983): 26-27.

King, Mrs. Hal, and Mrs. Maude Lupo King. "Union United Methodist Church." *IRQ* 11.4 (1977): 20-21.

Kirke, Edmund. [Pseudonym for J.R. Gilmore.] *Among the Pines: or, South in Secession Time*. New York: J.R. Gilmore, 1862. Excerpts rpt. *IRQ* 17 (1983) issues 1: 15-23; 2: 29-34; 3: 28.

L., S.T. [How Mullets are Caught.] *HH* 30 Nov. 1905. Rpt. *IRQ* 17.4 (1983): 23.

Lance, Georgia Smalls. See Peterkin.

Langston, Marjory Q. "Before and After 1870." *IRQ* 1.2 (1967): 13-14.

Latimer, Lillie Louise Brown, and Ruth Clay "Sabe" Woodbury. Int. Dozier and Lewis, 29 Jan. 1970.

Lawson, John. *A New Voyage to Carolina*. Ed. Hugh Talmage Lefler. Orig. publ. 1709. Chapel Hill: Univ. of N.C. Press, 1967.

Lee, J. Harry. Int. Wells, 13 July 2000.

Lewis, Catherine Heniford. "Chadbourn Railroad Brought Jobs, Hopes." *SN* 16 Dec. 1995.

---. "Cordie Page Reminisces at Age 82." *IRQ* 13.4 (1979): 20-36.

---. "History of First Baptist Church of Conway." *IRQ* 21.1 (1987): 26-39.

---. "Homewood Colony." *IRQ* 14.4 (1980): 18-29.

---. *Horry County, South Carolina 1730-1993.* Columbia: Univ. of S.C. Press, 1998.

---. Int. Wells, 13 October 1993.

---. "Little River." IRQ 24.4 (1990): 6-17.

---, Ernestine Little, and Annette Reesor. "Lakeside Cemetery." *IRQ* 9.2 (1973): 17-32.

Lewis, Susie L. Int. Holliday, 1978.

Lexington Lumber Company. Conway, S.C. [Handwritten alphabetical list of employees.]

Little, Elbert L. *National Audubon Society Field Guide to North American Trees: Eastern Region.* Borzoi. Chanticleer Press. New York: Knopf, 1980. *Swamp* draws tree names from the *Field Guide* unless noted.

"Little River Beach." *HH* 17 Nov. 1892: 2.

"Local and Personal." *HH* 26 Nov. 1936: 3.

"Local Matters." *HN* p. 3: 5 May 1871; 17 Feb. 1874; 28; April 1874; 20 June 1874; 25 July 1874.

"Local News." *HH*, p. 3: 17 Nov. 1887; 24 Nov. 1887; 8 March 1893; 23 Sept. 1893; 28 Sept. 1893; 19 Oct. 1893; 9 Nov. 1893; 28 Dec. 1893; 8 Nov. 1894.

Long, David. Personal communication, 2003.

Long, Dorethea Martin. Personal communication, 2003.

---. "White Oak School and Community as We Knew It." *IRQ* 28.1 (1994): 5-11.

Long, Woodrow. Int. Wells, March 1990.

---. Int. Wells, 13 May 1991.

Long, Woodrow and Dorethea. Int. Wells, June 2000 (uncirculated).

---. Personal communication, 2003.

"The Long Leaf Pine." [Editorial.] *HH* 16 Feb. 1893: 2.

Lovell, S. George, Rev. Dr. Int. Lewis, 1 Aug. 1990.

"Lumber." *Compton's Interactive Encyclopedia.* Compton's NewMedia, 1994.

Macklen, Julia Pryor. Int. Compton, 1992.

---. Int. Lewis, 25 March 1993. [With bracketed additions by Robert P. Macklen, 2001.]

Majar, Evelyn McCracken. "Father's Day: A Late Father Remembered in Verse." *Journal* [Aynor, S.C.]. Date unknown.

Malet, William Wyndham, Rev. *An Errand to the South in the Summer of 1862.* London: Richard Bentley, 1863. Excerpts rpt. *IRQ* 14, issues 1 (1980): 19-23; 2: 18-22; 3: 30-35; 4: 33-39. *IRQ* 15.1 (1981): 33-39.

"Map of Oregon Plantation." *IRQ* 24.1 (1990): 9. See Plat Book 4, p. 94, Record of Deeds, Horry County Courthouse.

"Market Report." *HH* 11 Oct. 1894: 3.

Marshall, Virginia Burroughs. Int. Wells, 17 Nov. 1989.

Martin, Greg. "The Ark Plantation." *IRQ* 24.2 (1990): 10-12.

"Matters Local and Otherwise." *HH* 1899, p. 3: 5 Jan.; 15 June; 22 June; 29 July; 14 Sept.

McCracken, Neal. Int. Holliday, 15 Aug. 1977.

---. Int. Holliday, 25 Aug. 1977.

--- and John Fowler. Int. Holliday, 26 Aug. 1977.

McCrackin, Rilla. Int. Amanda McCrackin, 24 Feb. 2002.

---. Personal communication, 2002.

McCrackin, Sam T. Personal communication, 2003.

McDaniel, Reginald. Personal communication, 2003.

McDowell, Gertrude ("Gertie"). "The Burgess Community." *IRQ* 12.3 (1978): 39.

McGhee, Zach. *The Dark Corner.* Washington, D.C.: Grafton, 1908. See also Catherine H. Lewis, "Education in Horry County." *IRQ* 7.2/3 (1973): 24-9.

McIver, E.R., Jr. "Conway's Practical Joker." *IRQ* 10.1 (1975): 19-20.

---. Int. Lewis, 30 Sept. 1991.

---. Int. Wells, 4 June 2002.

---. Personal communication, 2004.

---. "Water Transportation in Horry County." *IRQ* 21.1 (1987): 4-6.

McMillan, Hoyt. "A Brief History of Commercial Railroads in Horry County." [Background for the Historical Society's train excursion from Conway to Myrtle Beach.] 1985.

---. "A Brief History of Water Transportation in Horry County, S.C." *IRQ* 8.3 (1974): 42-62.

McMillan, Susan Hoffer. *Myrtle Beach and Conway in Vintage Postcards*. Postcard History Series. Charleston, S.C.: Arcadia, 2001.

---. *Myrtle Beach and the Grand Strand*. Images of America. Charleston, S.C.: Arcadia, 2004.

McWhite, Elbert. Int. Wells, 24 Jan. 1994.

Medlen, Hester Summers. Int. Lewis, 16 Oct. 1992.

Mention, Brewster. "Old Allentown and New Cochran School." *IRQ* 3.2 (1969): 24-25.

Meredith, [first name not given]. "The Life of the Naval Stores Industry as at Present Carried on in the South." [Report of Secretary of Agriculture Meredith to the United States Senate, 1920]. In Gamble, *Naval Stores*, 89-90.

Michaux, François André. "Pine Trees of the South and Their Products." In Gamble, *Naval Stores*, 8-16.

Micheaux, Dickie. "The Mystery Settlement." *IRQ* 14.1 (1980): 17-18.

Michie, James L. "The Northward Trading Post, 1716-1720: Colonial Indian Trade along the Black and Pee Dee Rivers." *IRQ* 27.3 (1993): 5-15.

Middleton, A. [Message to Lower House of Assembly.] *Journal of the Upper House of Assembly* 3 March 1732-3: 388. Rpt. *IRQ* 22.3 (1988): 29.

Mills, Jesse. Int. Patricia Causey Nichols, 16 June 1979.

Mills, Robert. *Mills' Atlas of the State of South Carolina 1825*. Rpt. Easley, S.C.: Southern Historical, 1980.

Millus, Donald. *Wading South: Fishing the 20th Century, Part II*. Tabor City, N.C.: Atlantic, 2001.

Mincey, Gary. See Bailey, D.

Mishoe, Peggy. "Woman Recalls Conway." *SN* 13 June 2002: 1+.

Missroon, Ethlyn Davis. "Three Little Spoons...A Lesson in Death." *IRQ* 23.3 (1989): 22-31.

Montaigne, de, Michel. *The Complete Essays of Montaigne*. Trans Donald M. Frame. Stanford: Stanford Univ. Press, 1958.

Montgomery, Mary D. (Bellamy). Letter to Ann Frink (Bellamy) White. 14 Nov. 1863. Intro. C.B. Berry. *IRQ* 22.2 (1998): 35-36.

Moore, Clara M. "Bucksport News." *HH* 21 Oct. 1954: 10.

Moore, Marion. Int. Ann C. Long, 15 Nov. 1993.

Moore, Nellie Scott. Int. Kayatta Scott, 25 Feb. 2002.

Moore, Richard. Personal communication, 2003.

Morris, Flossie Sarvis. "Atlantic Coast Lumber Company at Bucksville." *IRQ* 19.3 (1985): 14.

---. Int. Wells and Katie Wells, 1991.

Munnerlyn, Carlin. [County Extension Agent, Georgetown County, Clemson Univ. Extension Service.] Personal communication, 2000.

Murrell, Garland. "Memories of Days Gone by on Highway 905." *IRQ* 14.3 (1980): 5-6.

Myrtle Beach Memories. SCETV, 2003.

Nagle, Stephen J. "Beach Music." *Encyclopedia of Southern Culture*: 1043.

---. Personal communication, 2004.

Nairn, Thomas. "A Letter from South Carolina Giving an Account of That Province, Written by a Swiss Gentleman." London: 1718. Qtd. in Berry, "Horry County's," 13.

Napier, John Hawkins III. *Lower Pearl River's Piney Woods: Its Land and People*. Univ. of Mississippi Center for the Study of Southern Culture: 1985.

Nelson, Douglas. "Geology of Horry County." *IRQ* 12.1 (1978): 5-11.

---. Personal communication, 2000-2004.

New Voyage to Georgia. 1735. Rpt. *Collections of the Georgia Historical Society* 2, 1842: 39-60. Rpt. *IRQ* 23:3 (1989): 8-20.

Nichols, Patricia Causey. "Personal Memories of the Log Woods and the River: An Interview with Paul Sarvis." *IRQ*

18.4 (1984): 18-29.

Nolley, E.W.. [Editorial.] *HH* 13 July, 1899: 2.

---. "Horry and the Tobacco Industry." *HH* 9 Nov. 1899: 2.

---. "On the Waccamaw." *HH* 15 June 1899: 2.

---. "Pic-Nic at the End of the Road." *HH* 20 June 1899: 2.

Norton, J.A., M.D. "Ferries on the Waccamaw River." *IRQ* 1.2 (1967): 6-9.

Oakes, Joanie A. Interview with Fritz Sutter, 10 Feb. and 24 Feb. 1989.

Oehler, Tempe Hughes. "A Potpourri of Early Myrtle Beach Memories." *IRQ* 18.3 (1984): 6-8.

Official Atlantic Highway Association Map. From Calais, Maine, to Key West, Florida, to Cuba. Atlantic Coastal Highway Association. 1929. [The 1930 strip map appears on the reverse of the larger map, a document given to the S.C. Tobacco Museum by Dorothy Miller Dixon and Oliver Miller of Myrtle Beach.]

Ogilvie, J.W. "Horry." *IRQ* 3.1 (1969): 19-28. Rpt. of series in *HH,* 1909: 9 Sept., 16 Sept., 30 Sept., 7 Oct., 14 Oct., 21 Oct., 28 Oct., 4 Nov., 25 Nov., 2 Dec.

O'Tuel, Muriel. Personal communication, 2004.

Page, Emma. See Page, Willy and Emma.

Page, Rebecca Graham. Int. Lewis and Wells, 1990.

Page, Willy and Emma. Int. Wells, 1 Feb. 1999.

Patrides, George. *A Field Guide to Trees and Shrubs.* 2nd ed. The Peterson Field Guide Series. Boston: Houghton, 1972.

Peterkin, Genevieve Chandler, Nellie Holmes Johnson, Georgia Small Lance, and Cad Holmes. Int. Wells, 27 Jan. 2000.

"The Picnic." *HH* 11 May 1893: 3.

Pinner, T. Arthur. "A Transition in Horry." *IRQ* 5.4 (1971): 15.

Pinson, Joseph. Personal communication, 2003.

Pollard, Annette. "Peach Tree." *IRQ* 12.3 (1978): 36-37.

Porcher, Francis Peyre. *Resources of Southern Fields and Forests.* Richmond: 1863. Rpt. in Gamble, *Naval Stores,* 29-30.

Powledge, Fred. "Lawlessness in Old Horry." [Editorial.] *The Horry County News and the Sentinel* [Loris, S.C.] 28 July 1954: 4.

Prather, Frances Cooper. "Violin Notes." 1991. Horry County Museum.

Pridgen, Albert. "Turpentining in the South Atlantic Country." In Gamble, *Naval Stores,* 101-04.

Prince, Eldred E., Jr., with Robert R. Simpson. *Long Green: The Rise and Fall of Tobacco in South Carolina.* Athens: Univ. of Georgia Press, 2000.

---. Personal communication, 2003-04.

"Principal Uses of Rosins and Spirits of Turpentine." Prepared by the Bureau of Chemistry, U.S. Department of Agriculture. In Gamble, *Naval Stores,* 99-100.

"Puritanism." *The New Columbia Encyclopedia.* Ed. William H. Harris and Judith S. Levey. New York and London: Columbia Univ. Press, 1975.

Purvis, Willie Ruth. Personal communication, 2004.

Quattlebaum, Paul. "Early Conway as I Knew It." *IRQ* 24.4 (1990): 25-28.

Randall, Katie Bellamy. Int. Wells, 14 Dec. 2000. Uncirculated. See also Johanna Wilson, "Centenarian," *SN* 30 Oct. 2000: 1-C+.

Reesor, Annette Epps. "De Angel of de Lawd." *IRQ* 5.3 (1971): 21-24.

---. "Sand, Surf and Shells—A Child's Eye View." *IRQ* 1.3 (1967): 8-10.

"Resolutions." Conway Baptist Church. 1911.

Rheuark, Ella Merlene Canady. Personal communication, 2000.

Rhyne, Nancy. *Voices of Carolina Slave Children.* Orangeburg, S.C.: Sandlapper, 1999.

Rice, Carew. [Letter, n.d.] Rpt. *IRQ* 3.3 (1969): 20.

Rice, James Henry, Jr. [Letter to Sarah Cooper.] 27 July 1933. *IRQ* 11.1 (1977): 14-19.

Rich, Thomas, Jr. (Col.). Int. Wells, 7 Aug. 2002. Untranscribed.

Richardson, Jessamine Buck, as told to Janet Langston [Mrs. John A. Jones]. "I Lived to Tell the Tale." *IRQ* 13.4 (1979): 7-10.

"Robber Gang Camped Out." *HH* 19 Nov. 1936: 1.

Roberts, Chris. "S.C.'s Blacks Finding Opportunity Elsewhere." *SN* 27 July 2001: 7-C.

Roberts, Jessie Cornelius. Int. Robin Arnette, 1976.

Rowe, William J. Int. W.M. Goldfinch, Jr., et al., 31 Oct. 1968.

---. "Memories." *IRQ* 6.2 (1972): 4-13.

Rust, Roberta Ward. Int. Berry and Wells, 1991.

Sanders, James D. Int. Wells, 2002.

Sarvis, Moses Floyd. See F. Morris, "Early."

Sarvis, Paul. See Nichols.

Sasser, Paul, M.D. Personal communication, 2002.

Scott, Syble Young, and Agnes Mishoe Gause. Int. Lewis and Wells, 1990.

Sharitz, R.R., and J.W. Gibbons. "The Ecology of Southeastern Shrub Bogs (Pocosins) and Carolina Bays: A Community Profile." Washington, D.C.: U.S. Fish and Wildlife Service, Division of Biological Services, 1982. FWS/OBS-82/04."

"Shipments of Produce from Little River SC During the Year 1873." *IRQ* 3.4 (1969): 15.

Shuping, Hamp. "The Unique Waccamaw River and Its Keeper." Renaissance Fair Day, Coastal Carolina University. 8 March 2003.

Silverstein, Shel. *The Giving Tree.* New York: Harper, 1964.

Singleton, Elizabeth Goldfinch. "I Remember: Circa Late 1920's-1940." *IRQ* 9.2 (1975): 4-6.

"Sixteen Drowned." *HH* 19 Oct. 1893: 2.

Skipper, Timothy. [Note found in catalogue of Pisgah Methodist Church Cemetery, 1969.] *IRQ* 24.2 (1990): 35.

Small, Henry. Int. Lewis, Wells, and James L. Michie, 11 June 1990. See also Wells, "Henry Small," *Alternatives* [Myrtle Beach, S.C.] March-April 1997: 22-23.

Smith, Carrie Beach. Int. Wells, 26 May 2001. Uncirculated.

Smith, Doug. Int. Wells, 1 Aug. 2003.

Smith, J. Marcus, Dr. "Excitement Comes with First Fishing Pier." *SN* 23 July 1994.

---. "Fickle Hazel Struck Hard in Myrtle Beach." *SN* 14 Oct. 1995.

---. "Showboat Makes Visit to Conway." *SN* 6 Feb. 2003.

Smith, R. Cathcart, M.D. Personal communication, 2000.

Smith, Shirley. "Family History of Dicey Cox Beginning with George M. Cox and Sarah Elizabeth Dewitt-Cox." 2004. Appended to Int. J.M. Vaught, Jr., 17 March.

Snider, Evelyn. Int. Lewis, 1990.

Snow Hill: Horry County, S.C. Memoirs of Ellen Cooper Johnson (1844-1925). A Collection of Memoirs of the Burroughs Family...by Adalyn Sherwood Kearns. Privately printed, n.d.

Snyder, Rebecca Clark. "Teaching Days, Little River, SC...." *IRQ* 29.4 (1995): 25-30.

South Carolina, State of. "A Plantation or Tract of Land." [Deed.]

Spirakis, Anastasia N. "The Greek Community of Myrtle Beach." *IRQ* 32.1 (1998): 6-15.

Spivey, John C. [Letter to Miss Jessie Richardson from Clerk of Conway Baptist Church.] 20 Jan. 1904.

---. "Life History of John C. Spivey." [Typed manuscript.] 1959.

Squires, Louise Chestnut. "How I Remember It." *IRQ* 24.2 (1990): 13-17.

Staley, Bertha Paul. Int. Lewis, 21 Aug. 1991.

Stanley, Andrew. Int. Berry and Wells, April 1991.

---. Int. Wells, 3 Oct. 1993.

"State of South Carolina, Horry County." [Contract.] 21 April 1910.

Stevens, J.G. "Advent of Wood-Burning Locomotive." *News and Courier* [Charleston, S.C.], 3 June 1956. Rpt. *IRQ* 2.1 (1968): 15-16.

---. "Tales of the Waccamaw: The Rafting of Logs Has Become a Lost Art." *News and Courier* [Charleston, S.C.], n.d. Rpt. *IRQ* 3.2 (1969): 5-6.

Stevens, James P. Int. Lewis, 25 Sept. 1992.

Stevenson, Foy [Peurifoy]. "Childhood on an Horry Farm." *IRQ* 6 (1972): 8-11. See also *The Stevenson Reference Book,* Columbia, S.C.: R.L. Bryan, 1960.

156

Stilley, Barbara W. Personal communication, 2004.

Stilley, Walter A. III "Sonny." Int. Wells, 26 March 1999.

Stone, Louise. Int. Lewis, 24 Sept. 1993.

Storter, Rob. *Crackers in the Glade: Life and Times in the Old Everglades.* Ed. and compiled by Betty Savidge Briggs. Athens: Univ. of Georgia Press, 2000.

Talbert, Roy, Jr. *So Much to Be Thankful For: The Conway National Bank & The Economic History of Horry County.* Conway, S.C.: Conway National Bank, 2003.

"Tapping for Turpentine." U.S. Dept. of Agriculture. Rpt. *HH* 16 Feb. 1893: 3.

"Tar." *Encyclopaedia Britannica*, 11th ed.

Taylor, Dennis S. *Rural Life in the Lowcountry of South Carolina.* Images of America. Charleston, S.C.: Arcadia-Tempus, 2002.

Thom, Bruce G. *Coastal and Fluvial Landforms: Horry and Marion Counties, South Carolina.* Louisiana State Univ. Studies, Coastal Studies Series (ed. W.G. McIntire) 19. Baton Rouge: Louisiana State Univ. Press, 1967.

Thomas, Eulee. "Prayer Was the Key to Her Medication." *IRQ* 8.1 (1974): 36.

Thomas, Eunice McMillan. "Evolvement of Religions in Horry County." *IRQ* 8.1 (1974): 4-9.

Thomas, John. "Slavery in Horry District in the Mid-Ninteteenth Century." *IRQ* 16.4 (1982): 22-30.

Thomas, Wyness. "Elting Holliday at Rose Lake." *CC* 31 Aug. 1989.

---. "An Interview with Leola Hicks Burroughs, 1993 with References from the *Sun News,* May 10, 1992, & Feb. 7, 1993, and Muriel Cox, Horry-Georgetown Technical College." *IRQ* 32.1 (1998): 16-19.

---. "Little River." *CC* 27 Oct. 1998.

---. Personal communication, 2000.

---. "Reaves Ferry and Vina." *CC* 24 Aug. 1989.

---. "Sketches of Horry County People." *IRQ* 34.3 (2000): 3-32.

---. "Turner Chestnut Interview." *IRQ* 26.4 (1992): 13-16.

---. "Watts Family Keeps Star Bluff Alive." *CC* 9 June 1988.

Thompson, Dino. *Greek Boy: Growing Up Southern. A Myrtle Beach Memoir.* Myrtle Beach, S.C.: Snug Press, 2000.

Thompson, F.A. "Horry Found Leaf by Chance." *IRQ* 3.2 (1969): 20-21.

Thompson, Jack. Int. Wells, 25 October 2002.

---. *Memories of Myrtle Beach.* 2004.

---. Personal communication, 2004.

---. *Reflections in Time: A Half-Century Pictorial History of Horry County.* Myrtle Beach, S.C.: Coastal Federal Bank, 2004.

"Thompson Re-elected…." *HH* 28 Oct. 1954: 1.

Todd, Austin. "Board Landing." *IRQ* 14.3 (1980): 7.

Todd, Charles Mack. *When Southern Hospitality Was in Flower.* Dallas: Triangle Press, 1959. Excerpts in *IRQ* 16 (1982), issues 1: 4-15; 2: 24-40; 3: 23-34; 4: 31-42.

Tolar, J.R. "F.G. Burroughs." [Obituary.] *HH* 11 March 1897: 3.

"To Loggers of hreato Pine." [Advertisement.]. *HH* 5 Jan. 1898: 2.

"Trend Shows Fewer, but Larger Tobacco Farms." *Horry Independent* [Conway, S.C.]. Farm Edition. 10 Aug. 2000: 10.

United States. Bureau of Census. DP-1. *Profile of General Demographic Characteristics: 2000.* <http://factfinder.census.gov/bf/>

---. Bureau of Census. "Table 41—Age by Color and Sex for Counties, 1950 (S.C.)." *Census of Population, 1950.* Washington, GPO, 1952. See also *Federal Pop. Census.*

---. Department of Agriculture. Soil Conservation Service. *Soil Survey of Horry County, South Carolina.* 1986.

---. Geological Survey. "HCDN: Streamflow Data Set, 1874-1988." By J.R. Slack, Alan M. Lumb, and Jurate Maciunas Landwehr. USGS Water-Resources Investigations Report 93-4076.

United States Air Force Historical Division. "Brief History of Myrtle Beach Air Force Base 1940-1956." Rpt. *IRQ* 13.2 (1979): 8-10.

Upperman, Leroy, M.D. Int. Wells, 11 Aug. 1995. See also Yolanda Jones, "$10,000 Started Atlantic Beach," *SN* 20 Feb. 1994: 1A+.

Vaught, Elsie Collins. Personal communication, 2004.

Vaught, J. Marion, Jr. Int. Wells. 17 March [supplemented by 7 and 12 July] 2004.

--- and Elsie Collins Vaught. Int. Wells, 13 July 2004.

Vaught, Thomas Clyde. "The Snowfall: A Childhood Experience." *IRQ* 9.3 (1975): 24-30.

Vereen, Lula and S. Gordon. "Surfside Beach, Inc.—Today and Yesteryear." In C. Willcox 135-36.

"Waccamaw Line Steamers." *HH* 20 Sept. 1894: 4.

"Waccamaw Line of Steamers Rates of Freight…." [Advertisement, source unknown.] 1885.

Wachtman, Sara. "L.D. Magrath Stands as an Institution…." *Daily News* [Myrtle Beach, S.C.], 20 July 1956: 5.

Walls, Dwayne E. *The Chickenbone Special.* New York: Harcourt, 1971.

"Want Ads." *HH* 4 Nov. 1954: 5.

Ward, Dalton L. (Rev.). [Address at the funeral of Woodrow Long.] Maple Baptist Church, Conway, S.C., 8 Aug. 2004.

Warwick, Elsie Cushman, et al. "Mary Elizabeth Brookman Beaty." *IRQ* 20.4 (1986): 13.

Watkins, Ellen W. Personal communication, 2002.

Watson, D.B. "Tobacco Again." *HH* 5 Jan. 1898: 3.

Wells, Randall. *Along the Waccamaw: A Yankee Discovers a Home by the River.* American Places of the Heart.
        Chapel Hill: Algonquin, 1990.

---. *Horry Stories.* 1992.

---. "Let's call it 'The Horry County Oral History Project.'" *The Oral History Review* 29.2 (Summer/Fall 2002): 127-30.

---. *"No Match for Our Dad."* 1992.

---. *Stretch: Explore, Explain, Persuade.* Upper Saddle River, N.J.: Prentice, 1998.

---. *Wood & Water.* 1992.

White, Coyte. "A Quiet Haven for the Spirit." *SN* 6 March, 1983: 1-D.

Whitefield, George (Rev.). *George Whitefield's Journals.* Edinburgh: Banner of Truth Trust, 1960.

Wiegand, Joann Gibson. "Indian Mounds of [Waties] Island." *IRQ* 13.1 (1979): 16-22.

Willcox, Clarke A. *Musings of a Hermit at Three Score and Ten.* 4th ed. Charleston, S.C.: Walker, Evans, &
        Cogswell, 1973.

Willcox, Henry Trezevant. "Growing up with Myrtle Beach, South Carolina." In C. Willcox 142-49.

Williamson, Ruby. "Pleasant View Community." *IRQ* 11.3 (1977): 12-14.

Wilson, Joanna D. "Legacy of Learning." *SN* 14 Dec. 2003: 1-A+.

---. "Memories Made in Midst of Hurricane." <myrtlebeach.online.com> 13 Oct. 2004.

---. "Preserving Culture." *SN* 11 March 2002: 1+.

Wilson, Zane. "The Flagg Flood of 1893." *SN* 10 Oct. 1993: 1, 8-A.

Winfield, Robert. Int. Wells, 10 July 2001.

"Wonderful Air Ship." *HH* 15 April 1897: 3.

Woodall, Ione. "1850 Mortality Schedule for Horry District." *IRQ* 19.2 (1985): 9-11.

Woodbury, Edith Proctor D. "First Mail Carrier in Horry County." *IRQ* 5.5 (1971): 8-10.

Woodbury, Ruth Clay. See Latimer.

Wright, Eric. Personal communication, 2003.

Zinman, David. "Green Grass Blowing Looked Like a Sea." *Horry Independent* [Conway, S.C.] 28 April 1994: 4-A.

INDEX

Key:

passim = throughout

G3 (etc.): location on grid of 1954 map

See "first names" for individuals with no surname
  recorded

AVX Corporation, 70

Aceves, Cynthia H.S., 17

Africa, 7, 29, 133; see also Gullah, Madagascar, Morocco

air ship, 6

Allen, Barbara, ii

All Saints Parish, 7

alligator, 99, 108, 114, 124, 128, 130

Altman, Marguerite W. (Mrs. P.D.), 32, 99

---, Purdy, 99

---, Ryland, 15

Andersen (family), 63

---, Donald E., 70, 127

---, Ole, 70

---, Oscar, 70

Anderson, Robert, 20

---, Thurman, ii, 8

Anopheles, iii, 12

Appalachians, 77

Arehart, Eatofel V.T., 42, 95

Armor, Joyce, 97

Asbury, Francis (Rev.), 22, 132

Atlantic Beach G6, 94, 95

Ausband, Jerry, 20, 21, 79, 88

Averit, James B., 50

Ayers, J.C. "Don," 6, 55, 58, 59, 77

Aynor, 2, 9, 15, 17, 20, 24, 32, 62, 70, 88, 98, 103, 108, 111,
  112, 130, 134

Bailey, Annie L.S., 25, 31, 95

Bailey's Light, 125

Baker, A.J., 23, 34, 53, 55, 56, 59, 94, 125

Baldwin, Jimmy, 137

Baldwin Co., 137,

Banner (family), 7

Banta, A.Z., 134, 140

Barrett (family), 100

barrier islands: Conway, 2, 31; Horry, 2, 5, 9, 78; Jaluco,
  2, 20; Myrtle, 2, 3, 36; Recent, 2, 93; see also Round
  Pond

Barron, Charlie, 98

Bartram, John, 26, 28, 77

Bartram, William, 26

Batten, Wilford, 129

bays, bogs and trees: Plate 1, 5, 6, 17, 20, 22 and *passim*;
  see also Cotton Patch

beach, 93-105 and *passim*

Beacham, Frank, 120

Bear Bluff E5, Plate 14, 7, 69, 130

Beaty, B.L., 7

---, Brookie, 11, 12, 13, 131

---, Cora, 12, 13

---, Mary B., 8, 12, 56

---, Thomas, 8

---, maid, 12, 131

Beck (family), 63,

Bedford, A. Goff, 42, 48, 52, 54, 60

Bedsol, Mildred, 51

Bell (families), 97

---, Sylvia L., 8

Bellamy, James "Son Rabbit," 29, 80

---, John D. (Dr.), 3

---, Mary, 94

---, Merlin, 138

---, Oscar, 65, 112

---, Oscar, Mrs., 113

---, Robert, Plate 7, 84, 94, 108, 110, 129

---, Sam, 94

---, Tommy, 126

---, William, 66

Beneke, Tex, 101

Benjamin, Mary Kate J., 22

Bennett, J.C., Jr., 38, 40, 73, 89, 90, 112, 113

---, J.C., Sr., 38

Benton, E.H., 98, 100

---, Billie Mae, 103

Berry, C. Burgin, Plate 15, 4, 16, 26, 28, 41, 43, 56, 57, 58,
  59, 63, 66, 72, 86, 105, 109, 112, 136, 137, 138

Berry's Seafood, 108

Bessant, Henrietta, 29

Bessent, Carl B., 12, 21, 26, 47, 99, 114, 123

Beverly, Silas "Dock," 55

Bingham Freshet, 38

birds and fowl: duck, 127, 130; fish hawk, 129; goose,
  125; Guinea fowl, 5; ivory-billed woodpecker, 26;
  owl, 25; pileated woodpecker, 26; turkey, 5; whistling
  swan, 130; wild turkey, 50

Bishop, Nathaniel, 5, 39, 56, 57, 114

Black River, 21, 27, 31

Blanton, James P., ii, 9

---, Newton, 55

---, Olin I., 7, 9

boats and other vessels, 12, 35-48, 49-50, 51, 57, 65, 69,
  72, 96, 107-17, 122, 127-29, and *passim*; Chinese shop-
  boat, Epigraph, 127; showboat, 127; snagboat, 37;
  individual boats by name: *Altamont*, 42, *Atlantic City*,
  72; *Bicford*, 35; *Bull River*, 42; *Cassie F. Bronson*, 41;
  Comanche, ii, 40, 42, 45, 46, 47, 121; *Driver*, 42, 96, 128,
  135; *F.G. Burroughs*, 35, 42, 43, 44, 45, 46, 57, 62, 70,
  124, 127, 128; *Francis Marion*, 42; *Freeda A. Wyley*, 41,
  134; *George Elliott*, 42; *Henry P. Williams*, 127; *Juniper*,

42; *Kitty Hawk*, 72; *Louisa*, 72; *Lucy V.*, 42; *Maggie(s)*, 42, 45, 122, 129; *Menhaden*, 42; *Mitchelle C.*, 42, 45, 128; *Pathfinder*, 40; *Pender*, 40; *Planter*, 42; *Ridgewood*, 37; *Robert E. Lee*, 65; *Ruth*, 42, 43, 45, 59, 98, 125; *Samson I, II*, 40, 48; *Sessoms*, 42, 45

Bonnette, Henry, 40

Boyle, Christopher, 14, 53, 93

Branford, E.O., 88

Bratcher, George "Babe," a.k.a. George M. Cox, 52, 105

Brickel, John, 50

bridges, 1, 19, 29-31, 32, 34, 134 and *passim*; see also Lafayette, 27; Socastee, 39, 71

Broad Creek, 115

Brown, Braxton, 56

---, Claudia A., 7, 16, 80, 85, 99, 109, 111, 114, 121, 130, 139

---, Martha Ann, 15

---, Mildred P., 79, 124

---, Sammy, 46

Brown's Bay C5, 53

Bryan (family, Little River), 95

---, G.W. "Buster," 104, 126

---, James, 97-98, 99

---, Mr., 131

---, Will, 99

Buck, Edith Ella B., 12, 43

---, George, 135

---, Henry L. (I, b. 1800), 8, 16, 57, 135

---, Henry L. (II), Capt., 7, 77

---, Henry L. "Hal" (III, b. 1872), 9, 68, 77

---, Henry L. (IV, b. 1935), 41, 65

---, Iola, see Burroughs, I.

Buck Creek, 31

Bucksport C7-C8, 13, 25, 36, 38, 39, 40, 41, 43, 45, 53, 63, 67, 69, 72, 75, 83, 112, 123, 127, 128, 135

Bucksville D7, Plate 9, 27, 39, 41, 65, 122, 128, 141

Bull Creek C8, 3, 25, 27, 36, 122

Bullard, Boss, 38

Burges, Widow, 11

Burgess, William, 31

Burgess Community, Plate 12; see also Freewoods

Burns, Ken, 105

---, Tommy, 105

Burroughs (family), 8, 12, 34, 74, and *passim*

---, Adeline C., 12, 44, 56, 97, 98

---, Anthony, 53

---, Arthur M., 12, 43, 59, 62, 74, 98, 126

---, Donald M., 12, 57, 96, 98

---, Edith E., see Buck, E.

---, Edward E., ii, 17, 24, 39, 97, 99, 100

---, Effie T., see Egerton, E.

---, F.A. [Franklin Augustus], 12, 42, 44, 68, 98, 99, 141

---, F.G. [Franklin Gorham (b. 1834)], 5, 11, 12, 13, 15, 17, 53, 57, 96, 97, 119-20, 141; see also *F.G. Burroughs*

---, Frances C., 12, 59, 72

---, Franklin (b. 1942), 12, 48, 88, 116

---, Franklin G. (b. 1908), 12, 13, 40, 41, 42, 43, 46, 59, 62, 69, 115, 116, 124, 130

---, Geraldine B., 12, 33, 47, 115

---, Henry, 100

---, Homer H. (Dr.), 13, 33, 44

---, Iola. B., 12, 98, 99

---, Leola H., 72

---, Lucille, see Godfrey, Lucille, B.

---, Ruth A., 12, 43, 98

---, Sarah B., see Sherwood, Sarah B.

Burroughs & Collins Co., 25, 32, 33, 37, 42, 45, 49, 55, 56, 59, 61, 62, 69, 70, 74, 78, 95, 96, 97, 98, 103, 104, 122, 135

Burroughs Field, 121

Butler, Carroll B., 49

---, Roseanne, 123

Byrd, George, 69, 70

Cain, Cyril E., 62

Calhoun, James, 104

Camp Mfg. Co., 68

Candy Kitchen, 128

Canoe Lake A5, 113

Cape Fear, 3, 134

Cape Fear Arch, 16

Carmichael, Eugene, 112

Carolina bay, see bays

Carr, Albert, 30, 68, 72

---, David, Plate 2, i, 7, 11, 24, 52, 61, 68, 70, 93, 103-04, 125, 140

---, Peter, 135, 140

Carrison, Daniel J., 31, 48

Carswell, Helen S., 127

Carter, J. Robert, Sr., 7

Carter, W. Horace, 90, 126, 131-32

Cartrette, J.O., 31, 99, 136

---, J.O., Mrs., 130

---, John P., 8, 13, 31, 78, 81 ff, 98, 108, 110, 111, 130, 133

Catholics, see Churches

Cavalli-Sforza, Luigi L., et al., iii

Causey, Capt., 128

Ceiley, J.N., 14

cemeteries: Georgetown (Jewish), 121; Lakeside, 11; Longwood, 40; St. Paul Missionary Baptist, 11; Zion, 11

Chadbourn brothers, 32

Chandler, Genevieve W., 3, 7, 8, 9, 40, 41, 46, 53, 93, 103, 105, 108, 109, 112, 121, 135

Chapin, Simeon, 8, 122

Charles, Ray, 120

Charlie's Place, 120, 121, 131

Chautauqua, 128

Cherry Grove Beach/Inlet/Island G6, 2, 3, 4, 41, 94, 95, 96, 107, 110, 112, 120, 136, 137, 138

Chestnut, Turner, 5, 125, 135

churches: 44, 51, 79, 103, 120, 121, 125, 132, 134 and *passim*; denominations: Episcopalian, 121; Methodist, 122; Methodist Episcopal, 22; Roman Catholic, 8, 121; individual churches: Bethel African Methodist Episcopal, 17; Brown Swamp, 20; Buck Creek, 122; Bug Swamp, 122; Cedar Creek, 122; Collins Creek Baptist, 80; First

Baptist, Conway, 12, 19, 38, 120, 123, 124, 131; First Baptist, Ocean Drive, 122; First Baptist, Statesboro, Georgia, 19; Glenns Bay, 122; Kingston Presbyterian, 30, 36, 45, 141; Methodist Rehobeth, 81, 86; Mt. Calvary, 35, 36; Ocean Drive Baptist, 138; Ocean Drive Presbyterian, 136, 138; Pawleys Swamp, 122; Simpson's Creek, 122; Socastee United Methodist, 27, 122; Spring Branch, 122; St. Paul Missionary Baptist, 11; Tilly Swamp, 122; Waccamaw Association, Baptist, 79, 122; see also communities

circus, 125, 127

Civil War, see wars

Civilian Conservation Corps, 8

Clardy, W. Clyde, 59

Clarkson, Sallie, 142

Clay, Sara, 46

Coan, Peter M., 61

Coastal Carolina College/University, see higher education

Cole, Emma, 98

Coleman, Frances C., 13

---, Preston M., 45, 80,

---, Stanley, 9, 45, 95, 101, 133, 137

Coles, J.E., 78

---, Winnie H., 30

Collier, Evangeline W.P., 9, 30

Collins, Benjamin G., 31, 51, 122, 131

---, Benjamin G., Mrs., 131

---, Elizabeth, 10, 22, 30, 121

---, Mitchelle, 13, 38, 42, 57, 128, 131

---, O.T. "Tommy," 103

---, Stanton L. (Dr.), 8

Collins Creek, 114

Colored Café, Plate 3

communities/sections: Adrian D4, 4, 94; Allen D5, 71; Allsbrook E4, 54, 80; Anderson Woods, 56; Antioch, 134; Baker's Chapel D4, 53; Bayboro D4, Plate 8, 55, 59; Bear Bluff E5, 7, 69; Brittons Neck, 30; Burgess D8, 7, 24, 38, 43, 58 (see also Freewoods); Cane Branch E4, 80, 124; Carolina Forest E6, 16; Causey C1, 115; Cedar Branch F4, 1, 89; Chestnut's Crossroads F5, 28; Cool Spring(s) C4, 1, 3, 5, 13, 17, 20, 24, 57, 80, 81, 85, 93; Evergreen C5, 87; Finklea, D3, 9; Floyds C2, 14; Freemont, 25; Freewoods D8, 5, 38, 82, 109, 123 (see also Burgess); Glass Hill, D5, 19, 21, 25, 38; Grahamville E6, Plate 18, 25, 37, 66, 96, 125; Green Sea D3, 9, 14, 130; Gunters Island A4, 9, 112, 134; Gurley D4, 54, 55, 79; Hemmingway F4, 25; High Point B5, 80; Holmestown D8, 108; Homewood D5, 11, 99, 108, 110; Jordanville B5, 7, 15, 80; Ketchuptown B3, 68; Keysfield C7, 89, 127; Lewisville, 54; Longs F5, 7, 28, 36, 134; Maple D5, 54, 58, 60; Mineral Springs, 13, 18; Moore's Mill, C1, 84; Mt. Calvary E5, 35, 126; Mt. Olive D2, 6, 7, 77, 121; Nixonville E6, 56, 70, 72, 74, 94, 108, 135; Pawley Swamp B7, 86; Pee Dee B6, 78, 139; Pleasant View D3, 76, 121; Poplar F5, 54; Port Harrelson C7, 42, 70, 122; Quail Creek D6, 17; Stephens Crossroads, 11; Toddville C7, ii, 37, 55, 79,

89, 127, 128; Wampee G5, 11, 24, 27, 45, 84, 97; Wannamaker C2, 37, 130, 133; Wild Horse E6, 37; Zoan D3, 81; see also names of individual towns

Compton, Carl (Rev. Dr.), 24

Conrad, T.A., 26, 50

Conway Lions Club, 140

Conway Lumber Co., see lumber companies

Conwayborough, 4, 5, 10, 22, 28, 39, 54, 57

Cook, Pincey, 80, 112, 113

---, Walt, 80, 88, 112, 113

Cooke, Kemp, 30

Cooks & Waiters Club, 120, 125

Cooper, Harriet B., 121

---, Jule, 99

---, Julian B., Mrs., 4

---, Sarah C., 27, 121, 122

---, Thomas Beaty, 119

---, Tom, 44-45

Copeland, Don, 76

Cotton Patch Bay E6, 6

Count Basie, 120

countries and regions: Africa, 7, 29, 93; Baltic, 52; Canada, 39, 59; Caribbean, 133; England and Britain, 8, 10, 22, 43, 50, 52, 119; Finland, 63; France, 68, 96; Germany, 61; Haiti, 137; India, 122; Ireland, 7, 96; Lebanon, 110; Madagascar, 46; Morocco, 1; Netherlands, 48; Norway, 52; Orient, 83; Poland, 61; Romania, 121; Sweden, 63; Venezuela, 137; West Indies, 41

Courtney, W. Press, 141

Cox, Bill, 105

---, George M., a.k.a. George "Babe" Bratcher, 52, 105

---, Sanford D., Jr., 5, 36, 54, 97, 108, 109, 110, 138

Crawford, Will, 63

Crescent Beach G6, 94, 109, 137-38

Cutts, Eugenia B., 68, 72, 100, 125

Daggett, Thomas W. (Capt.), 37

dancing, 13, 87, 100, 103, 104, 119, 120, 121, 122, 124, 125, 128, 131-32

D'Angelo, Jimmy, 126

Dargan, Ervin, 104

Darlings Lake, 113

Daves, Reginald (Dr.), 6

Davis, Capt., 41

---, William F., ii, 15, 16, 51, 79, 112

Dawsey, Bernard, 7, 20, 30, 86, 89, 108, 111

---, John, 11

Dayton, Kathleen V., 8

Dead Line B4-B5, C4-C5, 15, 16, 70

DeLettre, Mrs., 39

Depression, Great, 8, 73, 84, 100; see also Civilian Conservation Corps, Intracoastal Waterway, Federal Writers' Project, Work Progress Administration

DeWitt, Lawrence, 114

Dick Pond E7, 109, 135

Dimery (family), 9

diseases: diphtheria, 13; fever, 11; malaria, 12, 19, 59, 95,

130; measles, 13; pneumonia, 12; polio, 13; tuberculosis, 14; typhoid fever, 17, 97; venereal, 14; see also public health
Do Good Club, 127
Dog Bluff B4, 3
Dorsey, Tommy, 101
Doyle, Carrie D., 3, 40, 56, 58, 80, 107, 125
Dozier, Etrulia, iii, 11, 17, 35, 38, 48, 72, 96, 107, 124, 126
---, Lewis A., 35, 126
Dunes Golf and Beach Club F7, 105, 126, 132; see also Singleton Swash
Dunn, T.C., 8
Durrell, John (Prof.), 142
Dusenberry [sic], R.G. (Capt.), 44
Dusenbury, James Saye, 12, 94
---, Jessie, 128
---, Ucie [Ulysses?], 67
---, Zack, 42, 44, 129
Dusenbury & Sarvis, 49, 54
"Dynamite King," 74
Dyne, Cain, 107

Earley, Lawrence S., 49, 50, 52, 54, 55, 59, 62, 63, 75
earthquake, 53, 120
Eckstine, Billy, 120
Eddy Lake C8, 3, 41, 59, 64, 67, 72, 74, 104, 122, 127
Edge, Belle, 95
---, Isaac, 122, 136
---, Pearly (Pearlie?), 136, 138
---, Spicey Ann, 13
---, Wilson, 5
Edmonds, Bill, Plates 6, 8, 9, 11, 12, 18; 2, 22, 50, 142
Edwards, Noah, 5
Egerton, Effie T. B., 12, 41
Ellington, Duke, 120
Elliott, Frostie J., 84
---, Manning, 84, 87, 90
Ellis, Jim, 72
Epps (family), 7, 115
---, Florence T., 7, 8, 23, 39, 47, 51, 67, 69, 88, 97, 99, 109, 111, 114, 115, 122, 125, 127, 128
Everglades, 16, 111
Exogyra, 2
Eyton, J. Ronald, 6

Federal Writers' Project, 8
ferries: 12, 27-29, 32, 34, 51, 63, 71, 72, 119, 121, 122, 126; Bull Creek, 25; Cape Fear River, 134 Godfrey's, 22; Potato Bed, 60; Reaves E5, Plate 4, 63, 109, 141; Reeves (N.C.), 36; Richardson's, 22; Wortham's G5, 95;
Fetters, Tom, 5, 62, 64, 68, 134
Few, Ben, 132
first names: Bart, Old Man, (turpentine hand) 57; Ben (riverboat worker), 47; Cadillac (waiter), 120, 131; Dave (turpentiner), 53; Frenchy (riverboat cook), 46; Hal (field hand), 90; Isba, Old Lady (grandmother from Ireland), 53; James (slave), 22; Jennie (cook), 111; Jim (rescuer of swimmer), 130; Joe, Grand Daddy

(from Ireland), 7; Kaleb (servant), 101; Louise (Aunt), 9; Lue (servant), 104; Maggie, Miss (teacher), 95; Mary Jane (servant), 97; Molly, Mother (slave), 40; Myrtle (servant), 101; Oscar, 33; Prince (slave), 10, 22-23, 28; Queenie (waitress), 120, 131; Sam (uncle), 7; Shiney (servant), 104, 115; Sip (old man), 68; Squire (former slave), 135; Sump (fish peddler), 115; Tom (auctioneer?), 91; Wade (driver, pianist), 98; Walter (farmer), 77; Willie (uncle), 124; Zilphy (could not talk), 7
fishing and fish, 45, 95, 99, 103, 104, 107-17, 124, 130 and passim
Fitzgerald, Charlie, 120, 131-32
Flagg (family), 135
Floral Beach, 103, 104, 105, 109; see also Surfside Beach
Floyd, Alice, 8, 9
---, Blanche, 41, 50, 63, 98, 100-01, 131
---, George, 47, 127
---, Lunette D., 16, 80, 124
---, Penny G., 88
Fore, Bud, 90-91
Fort Jackson, 102
Fowler, John, 86
Franken, Lynn (Prof.), 142
Frankenberg, Dirk, 50
Frazier, Fred, 39
Fretwell, Sammy, 4
froe, 70, 71, 72
Frommer, Myra K., and Harvey, 183
Fulton, S.W. (Capt.), 40
furs, 5, 41, 52, 111

Galivants Ferry B3, 3, 17, 19, 20, 27, 30, 40, 55, 56, 57, 76, 79, 80, 84, 88, 111, 112, 113
Gamble, Thomas, 50, 52
Garden City Beach D8, 3, 64, 94, 104
Gardner, Francis, 82
---, Bill, 124
Garner, Mark C., 103, 139
Garrison, Theatus G., 16, 29, 33, 79, 85, 95, 108, 112, 133
Gasque, Pratt, 29
Gause, Agnes M., 39, 70, 72, 74, 79, 83, 87
---, Charlie, 85
---, Mansey, 85
---, Mary S., 72
---, Paul, 85
---, Wheeler, 72
Gayes, Paul (Prof.), 16, 22, 34, 75
Geechee, see Gullah-Geechee
George II (King), 4, 100
Georgetown (town), 14, 21, 24, 26, 29, 31, 35, 37, 38, 39, 40, 41, 42, 43, 44, 46, 52, 57, 58, 64, 65, 69, 102, 119, 121, 128, 129, 134, 135, 140; see also All Saints Parish, Candy Kitchen, cemeteries, Georgetown County, lumber companies, Sampit River, Winyah Indigo Society
Georgetown County (or District) C8-D8, 1, 2, 3, 5, 14, 15, 16, 19, 27, 28, 70, 72, 71, 78, 81, 100, 135; see also Black River, Garden City Beach, Hagley, Georgetown

(town), landings, Lafayette Bridge, lumber companies, Murrells Inlet, North Inlet/Island, Pauley (Mr.), Pawley's Island, Pee Dee River, plantations, Sandy Island, Santee Rivers, Waccamaw Neck, Winyah Bay, Yauhanna

Georgetown *Times*, 57

Gerrald Lakes B3, 76

Gerry, Eloise, 75

Gibbes, Dr., 125

Gibbons, J.W., 6

Gilbert, Marie, 101, 115

Gilgamesh, 61

Gilland, J.D. (Dr.), 10

Glesenkamp, Ann, 141

Godfrey, Ellen, see slavery and slaves

---, Lucille B., 7, 11, 12, 32, 37, 41, 42, 44, 45, 46, 52, 74, 78, 94, 96, 97, 98, 99, 105, 123, 126, 129

Goldfinch, James, 32, 34

---, W.M. "Will," 122, 131

---, William McTyeire "Mac," 17, 30, 32

golf, 58, 98, 126, 139; miniature, i

Gooden, Dewitt T., 77

Gore, John W. (Rev.), 121

---, Penny F., 121

Gould, Lewis P., 81, 88

Gragg, Rod, 14, 105

Graham, E.F., 54

---, Rufus, 29

Grainger, Harve, 134

---, Marjorie, 16, 25, 125, 134

Granger, Joe, 133

Grant, Donnie, Plate 4, 27, 37, 61, 69, 71, 74, 141, 142

Gravelly Gully D7, 20, 39

Gray, Esther N., 21

Great Awakening, 119

Greek community, 98

Green, Joe, 45

---, John I., 6, 10

Greene, Lisa, 4, 6

Grind Stone Lake, 113

Gullah-Geechee, 45, 48, 72

gumbo clay, 3

Gunters Island A4, 9, 112, 134

Ham, Ruth, 68

Hanson, Kelly, 80

Hardee, Eunice W., 28

---, Mary W., 5, 11, 13, 121, 124, 130

Hardwick, Dan, 96

---, H.B., 89

---, Noah S., 94

Harlee Map, 6

Hawley, Jack, 89

Hazzard, Mr., 57

Hemingway, Lennie, 124

Hemmingway, Sally, 1, 51, 52, 83, 89

higher education: the Citadel, 2; Coastal Carolina College/University, i, ii, 16, 141, 142; College of

Charleston, 27, 31, 37, 41, 57, 68, 89, 95, 102, 137; Eastern Carolina Junior College, iii; Greensboro College, 41; Horry-Georgetown Technical College, 141; S.C. State College, 84; U.S. Naval Academy, 131

highways and roads: *Hwy. 9* (C1-G5): 25, 36, 89; *Hwy. 17* (D8-H5), Plate 7, 1, 27, 98, 103, 104, 108, 136, 137; *Hwy. 90* (D6-G5), Plate 7, 4, 7, 69, 108; *Hwy. 319* (D5-B3), 20; *Hwy. 378* (D6-B6) 27, 30, 31; *Hwy. 501* (B3-E7) 3, 4, 9, 20, 21, 30; *Hwy. 544* (D6-E8) 21; *Hwy. 701* (E2-C8), Plate 10, 27, 31; *Hwy. 707* (D7-D8), 21; *Hwy. 905* (D6-G4) (Pireway Rd.), 2, 20, 21, 29, 39; *Kings Highway* (D8-H5), Plate 10, i, 1, 2, 26, 94, 95, 97, 102, 105, 135; Bear Bone Rd. E6-F6, 135; Holmestown Rd. D8, 58; Pee Dee Rd./Highway B3-C7, 11, 20, 30, 78, 88; Reaves Ferry Rd, 135; Sand Hill Rd, 24; Socastee Rd., 22-23, 24; Thomas Rd. E5-E6, 72

Hill, Robert W., IV, 66

Hobeika, Mary S., 109, 110

Hoffer, Jerry (Dr.), Plate 17

Hog Inlet H5, 3

Hog Island, 110

Holbert, James R., Jr., 41, 90, 129

---, James R., Sr., 69

---, Jose, 8

Holihan, Margaret, 121

Holliday, Elting, 38

---, Floramae, 103

---, George, 77, 79, 89, 90, 103, 124

---, J. William, 131, 141

---, Joseph W., 40; see also Pee Dee Farms, W.F. Davis

Holliday Farms, 45, 80, 84, 112; see also Pee Dee Farms

Holmes, Cad, 3, 58, 60, 93, 114

---, London, 60

---, Mundy, 108, 117

Homewood Colony, see Sunny South Colony

Hood, Belle Miller S., Epigraph, 103

Hopkins, Celia, 94

Horne, Lena, 120

Horry, Ben, see slaves and slavery

---, Joe, 40, 46, 121

---, Peter, i

Horry County Historical Society, ii

Horry County Oral History Project, i, ii, 141, and *passim*

Horry District, 1, 2, 5, 6, 14, 22

Horry Electric Cooperative, 8

Horry Telephone Cooperative, 8

Horton, S.F., 1, 14, 88

Howell, Mr., 62

Hucks, Fred W., 4, 20, 114

---, James M., 17

---, Lacy, 114

Hughes, Howard, 72,

Huggins, Lawton, 38

Huguenot, i

Hurl [Hearl] Rocks, 34, 123

hurricanes, 133-40; David, 16; Hazel, Plates 16 and 17, ii, iii, 104, 112, 133, 136-39; Hugo, 35; of 1893, 104, 134-36

Hurt, Kathryne S., 7, 10

Independent Republic Quarterly, ii, *passim*
Indians, see Native Americans
Intracoastal Waterway, 3, 8, 17, 21, 30, 31, 35, 39, 40, 47, 51, 73-74, 76
Ipock, Ann M., 141

Jackson, Mary Emily P., 49, 93, 104, 105, 109, 125, 139
Jaluco (spot on railroad) E6, 2, 36
Jamb [or Jam], the, D2-E2, 9, 90
James, Jesse B., 17
Jenerette, Chester, 66
Jerdon, Jim, 90
Jerry Cox Co., 8, 32, 34, 37, 105, 113, 131
Jews, 7, 121
Jim Crow laws, 32, 33, 104, 121
Joe Patch, the, 113
Johnson, Charles E., ii
---, Charlie, 39
---, Ellen C., 5, 53, 56, 93
---, Jack, 99, 105
---, Janie B., Plate 8, 84
---, Nellie H., 3, 43, 58, 61, 93, 94, 111
---, W.P. and Mrs., 81
Jones, Henry, 17
---, Joe, 25
---, Robert T., 126
---, Ruby S., 13, 14, 32, 98, 104
---, Solomon, see slavery and slaves
---, W. Irving, Jr., 80
---, W. Irving, Sr., 1, 5, 15, 40, 52, 55, 56, 63, 65, 80, 88, 90, 91, 95, 111, 124
Joyner, Charles, Plate 10, 14, 52, 81, 140, 141
---, Effie P.T., 21
---, Kelly P., 11, 32, 45, 127
---, Winston G., Plate 10

Kearns, Adalyn S., 46, 53, 58, 96, 98, 119, 125
Keel, Frank, 94
Kelly, Peter (Dr.), 96
King (family), 96
---, Kirby, 9
---, Mrs. Hal and Mrs. Maude Lupo, 122
---, T.H. and Mrs., 116
Kingston, 4, 22, 39
Kingston Lake/Kingston Lake Swamp E4-E5-D5-D6, 4, 5, 10, 12, 20, 25, 30, 34, 37, 38, 40, 42, 59, 64, 67, 74, 103, 129, 131, 134, 141
Kirke, Edmund, 15, 56, 57, 121
Kirton, Mr., 111
Korean War; see wars
Ku Klux Klan, 9, 10, 16, 90, 120-21, 131-32

L., S.T., 109
Lakewood Family Campground E8, 104
Lamb, Dwight, 102
Lance, Georgia S., 5, 25, 93, 116, 123
landings: Board E5, 43, 121; Brookgreen, 46; Brown('s), 31, 129; Enterprise D7, 27, 36, 64, 111, 127, 128;

Graham's, 121; Hagley, 44, 45; Longwood C8, 15, 41, 42, 43, 45, 128; Peachtree D7, 29, 39, 41, 121, 122, 128; Punch Bowl B7, 60, 126; Wachesaw, 74, 128; see also ferries
Lane, Jack, 9
Langston, Marjory Q., 12
Latimer, Lillie B., 56, 123, 126, 128
Lawson, John, 75, 133-34
Lee, J. Harry, 5, 66, 97, 109, 114, 136
Lehto (family), 63
Lewis, Catherine H., i, 1, 4, 6, 8, 9, 11, 13, 14, 32, 36, 41, 48, 52, 59, 78, 85, 95, 99, 109, 124, 128, 136, 141
---, Minta, 11
---, Susie L., 25, 55, 57, 60, 78, 82, 112, 125
---, William D., 54
Lewis Ocean Bay Heritage Preserve E6-F6, 2, 4, 6, 50
Libes, Susan (Prof.), 16
Liggett & Myers Co., 132
Little, Elbert, 50
---, John W., 72
Little Pee Dee River B2-B-7, 2, 3, 7, 9, 15, 22, 29, 30, 42, 45, 58, 70, 76, 78, 107, 112, 121, 125, 130, 133, 134
Little Richard, 120
Little River/town/River/Neck G5-H5, 4, 8, 12, 13, 14, 21, 26, 35, 38, 40, 41, 43, 45, 47, 52, 56, 57, 58, 62, 66, 69, 94, 95, 99, 111, 112, 113, 117, 135, 136, 137, 138, 120
Livingston, Harry, 138
---, Thomas Walter, 13, 44
Livshein, Abraham, 6
logging, 61-76, 80, 95, 97, 116, 121, 124, 125, 127, 135, 139
Long, David, 16, 58
---, Dorethea M., 51, 54, 55, 59, 80, 125
---, Joshua, 7
---, William M., 49, 54, 60, 61, 65, 66
---, Woodrow W., 16, 49, 54, 55, 62, 64, 65, 67, 76, 94, 141
Loris, i, 1, 2, 7, 14, 16, 28, 29, 31, 33, 79, 80, 84, 88, 90, 95, 96, 100, 109, 112, 125, 133
--- *Sentinel*, 80
Lovell, S. George (Rev.), 19, 21, 27, 75, 113, 124, 131
Luken, Jim (Prof.), 16
lumber companies and sawmills: Atlantic Coast, 65, 70, 71; Buck, 41; Burroughs, 34, 40, 63, 67; Conway 32, 62, 63, 64, 65, 66, 68, 70, 71, 75, 126, 134; Dargan, 70; Eddy Lake Cypress, 72; Gardner & Lacy, 41, 69, 135; Georgetown, 70; Hammer, 62, 66, 72; Jackson, 16; Lexington 63; Richardson, 72; Schoolfield, 68; Trexler, 69, 70; Winborne, W.H., 63; Winyah, 64
Lumber River C1, 3, 4, 133
Lynn (family), 63

M., V.I., 44
Macklen, Julia P., 102
---, H. Lloyd, 102
---, Maude, 29
Macklin, Mr., 22
Magnolia [Huntington] Beach, 105
Magrath, Dorothy O., 64, 74
---, George N., Jr., 68

---, L.D., 59
Majar, Evelyn M., 88
malaria, see diseases
Malet, William W. (Rev.), 22, 28, 39, 54, 121
Mammy (Sherwoods'), 115
Marine Patio, 101
Marine Room, 102
Marlowe, Will, Mrs., 58
Marshall, Virginia B., Plate 18, 5, 12, 30, 135, 141
Martin, Hallie P., 55
---, Greg, 104
---, Mary Elizabeth C., 13
Maude (horse), 23, 34, 53, 134
Mayo, Lucy B., 12
Mcalroy, Widow, 11
McCown, Mary R., 141
McCracken, Neal, 21, 24, 77, 88
---, Amanda
---, Rilla C., 16, 62, 80, 81 ff, 112, 113
McCracken Mill Pond, 113
McCrackin, Sam T., 81
McDaniel, Reginald, 83, 86
McDowell, Gertrude, 43, 80
McGhee, Zach, 7, 10, 13, 64
McIver, E.R., Jr., ii, 14, 20, 29, 35, 47, 63, 100, 134, 140, 141
McMillan, Hoyt, 31, 32, 42, 65
---, Joe, 40, 47
---, Susan H., Plate 17, iii, 96, 98, 99
McNeil, Henry, 8
McNeill, D.T., 43, 97
---, Fred, 3
---, W.H., Mrs., 68, 70
McWhite, Elbert, 124, 131
Medlen, Hester S., 79
Meher Baba 122
--- Center F6, 122
Meredith [no first name], 75
Merrill, Adeline G., 98
Meyers, Jimmy, 101
Micheaux, Andre, 50
---, Dickie, 13
Michie, James L. (Prof.), 27
Middleton, A., 4
midwives, 53, 84
Mills, Jesse, 29
---, Robert, 6, 14, 35
Millus, Donald (Prof.), 108, 112, 114, 132
Mincey (family), 77
---, Gary, 37-38, 115, 133
Mishoe, Boston, 38, 72, 74, 79
---, John, 38
---, Peggy, 7
Missroon, Ethlyn D., 86, 123
Montaigne, de, Michel, iii
Montell, Lynwood, ii
Montgomery, Mary D., 11
moonshine whiskey, 9, 87, 125

Moore, Carolyn, Plate 13
---, Clara M., 139
---, Collins, 56
---, Marion, Plate 13, 25, 31, 67, 79, 114, 122
---, Nellie S., 17, 84, 139
---, Victoria J., 17
Morralls Inlet G6, 112
Morris, Flossie S., Plate 9, 43, 52, 65, 70, 94, 141
---, Samuel C., 22
Moss, Mr., 112
Munnerlyn, B.A., 43
---, Carlin, 77
Murcek, Lillian M., 17
Murdock, Widow, 11
Murrell, Daniel (Capt.), 7
---, Garland, 21, 29
Murrells Inlet, 2, 3, 21, 29, 42, 46, 97, 98, 107, 134
Myrtle Beach: Air Force Base E7, ii , 20, 102, 121; Farms, 8, 20, 32, 61, 71, 97, 99; Lumber Co., 126; Municipal Airport, 8; pavilions, 100, 101, 103, 104, 105, 119, 120, 124; racetrack, 120; State Park E8, 8, 102, 105;
--- News, 103
--- Sun, 103

Nagle, Stephen, i, 131
Nancy's Island, 113
Napier, John H. III, 62
Native Americans, ii, 3, 4, 8, 9, 27, 35, 36, 38, 39, 40, 50, 60, 95, 99, 103, 104, 107, 133, 139; see also Dimery, Waccamaw Indians
naval stores, Plate 5, 37, 43, 49-60, 64, 79, 80, 96, 97, 116, 125, 135, 139 and passim
Nelson, Douglas (Prof.), 2, 3, 16
Nettles, Jamie, 104
New Voyage to Georgia, 26, 38, 52
Nichols, Patricia C. (Prof.), 41, 129
---, Robert T., 4
Nicolson, Widow, 11
Nixon, Charlie, 137
---, Nicholas, 96, 110
Noah (Bible), 59
Nolley, E.W., 40, 78, 79, 126, 129
Norris, Frank, 125
North Carolina, 2, 4, 5, 7, 13, 16, 22, 26, 36, 40, 47, 50, 52, 53, 54, 55, 58, 59, 68, 69, 75, 78, 95, 97, 108, 111, 119, 131, 132, 133, 134, 136, 137, 139 and passim; air ship, 6; Camp Lejeune, 102; Cape Fear River, 3, 134; Lake Waccamaw, 6, 36
North Carolina, counties: Brunswick G5-H5, 4; Columbus C1-G4, 4; Robeson, 77
North Carolina, towns: Carolina Beach, 120; Chadbourn, 31, 41; Fairmont, 88; Greensboro, 41; Jacksonville, 102; Monroe, 103; Pinehurst, 50; Pireway, 29, 66, 69; Raleigh, 78; Salem, 78; Sea Breeze, 95; Smithfield, 26; Southern Pines, 50; Tabor City E2 9, 88, 90, 124, 126; Whiteville, 32, 88; Wilmington, 6, 35, 37, 39, 40, 43, 45, 47, 57, 94, 95, 96, 101, 108, 134, 140; Winston, 78
North Inlet, 134

North Island, 2
North Myrtle Beach G6, 30, 94, 95, 108; see also Cherry Grove, Crescent Beach, Ocean Drive, Windy Hill Beach
Norton, Arthur, 47, 48
---, Edward, 47, 48
---, Evan, 41
---, James A. (Dr.), 17, 27, 28, 47
---, William, Sr., 4

Oakes, Joanie, 62
O'Brien (boxer), 99
Ocean Breeze Motor Court, 137
Ocean Drive Beach G6, Plate 11, Plate 17, 21, 27, 58, 94, 96, 105, 108, 112, 120
Ocean Fish Market, 111
Ocean Forest Hotel F7, 100, 101, 105, 120, 125
Ocean Lakes Campground E8, 35, 139
Ocean Plaza Hotel/Pier, 112, 116
Oehler, Tempe H., 122
Officer, George, 59, 72
Ogilvie, J.W., 11, 58
Oliver, Daniel W., 53
---, William, 53, 112
Oral History Review, i
Owens, Ben, 9

Pabst, Stewart, 35
Page, Cordie, 8, 11, 23, 88, 99
---, Emma, 89
---, Rebecca G., i, 14, 16, 25
---, Willie, 68, 85, 130
Parker, David, Plate 4, i, 27, 141
Parkhurst, Judith I., 6
Parrott, Lawrence A., and Mrs., 138-39
Pate, Charles, Co. 134
Patrides, George, 64
Patterson, Elizabeth C., 122
Pauley, Mr., 26
Pawleys Island, 2, 22, 95
Pee Dee Farms, 79; see also Holliday Farms
Pee Dee River (Great) B7-C8, 3, 21, 22, 27, 36, 40, 42, 72, 74, 78, 113, 134
Peterkin, Genevieve C., 94, 109
Philadelphia, 26, 119
Piedmont-Blue Ridge, 3, 77
Pine Island E7, 2, 21, 32
Pink, Mitt, 128-29
Pinner, T. Arthur, 78
Pino, Bob, 39
Pinson, Joseph (Prof.), 6, 141
Pitch Landing C6, 59
pitcher plant, 6
Pitman, Uncle, 9
plantations, 3, 15, 36, 53; Ark, 41, 93, 104, 134, 140; Hagley, 10, 22, 39, 44, 45; Keyes Field, D7, 89; Laurel Hill, 128; Longwood C8, 15, 41, 42, 43, 45, 128; Oliver C7, 112; Oregon C8, 15, 123; Tip Top (Woodbourne)

C8, 15, 39, 40; see also landings
Plato, ii
Platt, Mary C. D., 105
---, Vivian F. (Dr.), 104
Platt's Pharmacy, 32, 125
Plymouth Locomotive Co., 76
plywood, 72-73
Pollard, Annette, 29
Pot [Pott, Pott's] Bluff, Plate 5, 37, 57
Potter, Widow, 11
Powell, Sally, 15
Powledge, Fred, 9
Prather, Frances C., 119
Pridgin, Albert, 53, 54, 55, 60
Prince, Eldred E. Jr. (Prof.), 8, 77, 78, 83, 87, 90, 91
---, R.M., 55
Prohibition, 8, 39, 63
public health, 2, 11-14; see also diseases
Puritans, 119

Quattlebaum, C.P. (Col.), 12
---, Paul, 42, 44, 127
Quattlebaum Light & Ice Co., 32

rafts, 64-67, 130
railroad, see train
Rainbow, Billy, 99
Randall, Katie B., 38, 94, 107, 110, 121, 129, 138
---, Thomas (Capt.), 8
Reaves, Ben, 80
---, Bill, 27
---, Ella, 80
---, Mary Emma, 80, 130
recreation, 119-32; see also fishing
Red Bluff F5, 13, 21, 37, 43, 121
Red Cross, 14
Red Hill D6, 2, 20, 38, 69, 98
Reed, Dennis, 142
Reesor, Annette E., 16, 97, 98, 99-100, 104-05, 115, 123
Revolutionary War, see wars
Rheuark, Ella M. C., 80, 85, 88, 89
Rhyne, Nancy, 93
rice, 3, 4, 14, 15, 16, 36, 39, 40, 43, 45, 72, 81, 86, 93, 99, 109, 124
Rice, Carew, 44
---, James H., Jr., 127
Rich, Thomas W., Jr. (Col.), 1, 37, 40, 65, 69, 70
---, Thomas W., Sr., 37, 69, 75
Richardson, Donald V., 47, 68
---, Jessamine B., 47, 68, 131, 135
---, Mr. (Columbia), 115
Rise, Cad, 23
rivers: see Black, Cape Fear, Little, Little Pee Dee, Lumber, Pee Dee, Sampit, Santee
roads, see highways and roads
Roberts, Agnes N., 85
---, J.C., 84
---, Stanford, 134

Rogers, Wilbur (Dr.), 16
Roman Catholics, see churches
Round Pond F6, 130
Rowe, William J., 13, 25, 33, 38, 42, 44, 62, 69, 122, 130
Rucker, Mallard, 120, 131
Rural Electrification Administration, 8
Rust, Roberta W., 7, 8, 13, 84, 85, 86, 108
Rutledge, Sabe, see slavery and slaves

SCETV, 94
Sampit River, 48
Sanders, James D., ii, 16, 20, 21, 37, 63, 103
Sandy Island C8, 113
Santee River, 3, 42, 68, 69, 133
Sarkis, Joe, 103, 109, 110, 111
Sarkis Fish Market, 114
Sarvis, Capt., 45
---, Louis F., 94
---, Moses F., 39, 48
---, Paul, 30, 41, 71, 129
---, Reuben, 30, 129
Sasser, Archie (Dr.), 8, 125
---, Paul (Dr.), 3
---, Phillip (Capt.), 32, 51, 98, 133
Savage, Jacob, 65
Savannah, Georgia, 119, 137
Savannah Bluff D6, 45
schools, public, 13, 14, 29, 51, 78, 79, 81, 125; Burroughs
    High School, 69; Conway High School, ii, 25, 103;
    Inland C7, 79; Maple D5, 79; Rehobeth B4, 62; St.
    James Rosenwald D8, 25; Sandy Plains B3, 30;
    Socastee Graded, 121; Wampee, 137; White Oak No. 2
    D4, 80, 125; see also higher education
schoolteachers, see E. Arehart, M. Bedsol, F. Coleman,
    M. Jones, Maggie (Miss), H. Medlen, F. Morris, A.
    Roberts, R. Rust
Scott, Kayatta, 139
Seaside Inn, 97, 98
seining (ocean), Plate 11, 70, 108-112, 122
Sessions, Josias, 7
shag (dance), i, 120, 121, 131
Shakespeare, 128
Sharitz, R.R., 6
Sherwood, E.J., 104
---, Sarah B., 12, 46, 98, 115, 125
shingles (roofing), 43, 70, 72, 85
Shuping, Hamp, 36
Silverstein, Shel, 50
Simpson Creek F4-F5, 76
Singleton, Elizabeth G., 101
---, Mr., 111
---, Widow, 11
skidder, 69, 71, 75
Skipper, Timothy, 12, 17
slavery, slaves, ex-slaves: 11, 13, 16, 39, 40, 50, 51, 56, 80,
    81, 121, 124, 128, 135; specific individuals: Ellen
    Godfrey, 40; Ben Horry, 46-47, 140; Solomon Jones,
    124; Sabe Rutledge, 3, 41, 68, 93, 94, 103, 105, 108, 109,

135, 139, 140; Willis Williams, 53; William Oliver, 53,
    112; see also first names
Small, Annie G., 128
---, Henry, Plate 12, 4, 37, 42, 108, 111, 114, 128
---, Sylvia, 128
---, Titus, 128
---, Toby, 128
Smalls, Julia, 39, 107, 124, 128
Smith, Carrie B., 81
---, Doug, 37, 86, 111, 112
---, J. Marcus (Dr.), 112, 127
---, Kathryne, 7, 10
---, R. Cathcart (Dr.), ii, 83, 84, 91
---, Shirley, 105
---, Tom, 7
---, William A., 7
Smith Lake D6, 67
Snider, Charles H., 67, 99, 127, 129, 131
---, Evelyn, 12, 15, 64, 67, 74, 127, 141
Snyder, Rebecca C., 43, 120
Socastee D7, 4, 5, 7, 19, 20, 22, 30, 31, 39, 40, 47, 71, 127
South Carolina, counties: Berkeley, 70; Charleston, 70;
    Darlington, 78; Dillon C1, 3, 78; Florence, 29, 78, 90;
    Georgetown C8-D8, 2, 3, 5, 14, 16, 19, 27, 28, 70, 71, 72,
    78, 81, 100, 135; Marion B1-B7, 2, 3, 7, 27, 78, 95;
    Marlboro, 78; Williamsburg, 14, 78, 95
---, towns: Andrews, 71; Charleston, 27, 31, 37, 41, 57, 68,
    89, 95, 102, 137; Chester, 42; Chesterfield, 78;
    Columbia, 8, 9, 31, 47, 97, 98, 103, 104, 130, 133;
    Florence, 31, 80, 95, 97, 101, 104; Folly Beach, 102; Fort
    Mill, 103; Georgetown, 14, 21, 24, 26, 29, 31, 35, 35, 37,
    38, 39, 40, 41, 42, 43, 44, 46, 48, 52, 57, 58, 64, 65, 69,
    102, 119, 121, 128, 129, 134, 134, 140; Greenville, 98,
    102, 103; Hartsville, 107, 116; Hemingway, 31;
    Kingsburg, 22; Kingstree, 31, 50; Lamar, 80; Lanes, 31;
    Marion, 2, 15, 23, 29, 30, 55, 80, 95, 96, 124; Mars Bluff,
    42; Mullins, 68, 77, 88, 89, 90, 133; Nichols, 133;
    Orangeburg, 80, 84; St. Stephens, 63; Santee, 80;
    Society Hill, 102; Spartanburg, 103; Sumter, 104;
    Turbeville, 90; see also Fort Jackson
South Carolina Humanities Council, i
Southern Workman, 10
Spillane, Mickey, 97
Spirakis, Anastasia N., 98
Spivey, Collins, 100, 104
---, D.A., 89, 103
---, Dock, 98
---, John C., 79, 98, 99, 113, 120, 122, 124, 131
Spivey Beach E7, 99, 103
Springmaid Beach E8, 103
Springs, Holmes B. (Col.), 47
Springs Cotton Mills, 103
Squires, Louise C., 104, 109, 110, 136
Staley, Bertha P., 45, 101, 127
Stalvey, Archie, 122
---, Shed, 30
Stanley, Andrew, Plate 6, 16, 21, 26, 27, 41, 43, 56, 66, 69,
    74, 87, 88, 94, 96, 110, 111, 124, 135

Star Bluff F5, 28

states, U.S.A. (or their cities), Alabama, 60; Arkansas, 94; Connecticut, 132; Florida, 6, 26, 44, 47, 50, 60, 100, 101, 104, 105, 111, 114-15; Georgia, 19, 26, 50, 54, 56, 60, 95, 119, 126, 137; Illinois, 1, 8, 13, 17; Kentucky, 63; Louisiana, 35, 94; Maine, 8; Massachusetts, 8, 17, 37; Mississippi, 35, 94; New Hampshire, 139; New Jersey, 59, 100; New York, 1, 8, 32, 34, 37, 41, 52, 55, 57, 59, 74, 85, 95, 101, 105; Ohio, 76; Pennsylvania, 5, 26, 119, 126; Tennessee, 35; Utah, 31; Vermont, 7; Virginia, 11, 37, 45, 50, 78; Washington, 62; see also North Carolina, South Carolina

Stevens, J.G., 67

---, James, 96

Stevenson, Charlotte, 81

---, Foy, 81, 83

---, James E., 81

Stilley, Barbara W., 73

---, Walter A. I, 40, 73

---, Walter A. II, 73, 130

---, Walter A. "Sonny" III, 40, 46, 64

Stilley Plywood Co. D6, 48, 59, 66, 67, 73, 76

Stogner, Harriette S., 8, 41, 133

Stone, Louise, 95

---, Will, 28

Stone Brothers, 56

Storter, Rob, 16

Stroud, Mr., 94

Sumpter, Keeler, 39, 74

Sun-Fun Festival, 126, 132

Sunny South Colony, 8

Surfside Beach D8-E8, 3, 89, 93, 103, 105, 136; see also Ark Plantation, Floral Beach

Sutter, Fritz, 62

swamps: 2, 4-5, 22, 23, 31, 36, 39, 61, 63, 67, 68, 69, 70, 74, 76, and passim; individual swamps: Big (doomed settlement) E6-F6, 13; Big (near Enterprise Landing) C7, 36; Brown B5-C5, 5, 20, 25; Chinners B4-C4, 15; Chinesee [probably Chinners] 20, 114; Crabtree C5-C6-C7, 20, 31, 64; Dark, 114; Dawsey C1, 25; Grier D4, 69; Hunting B6, 113; Jones Big E5-F5-F6, 69, 72, 130; Lake B3-C3-D3-D2, 5, 9, 68, 76, 121, 124; Little, 112; Maple C4-D4-D5, 4, 67, 69; Niggerfield, 20; Playcard D3, 124; Poplar D5, 24; Singleton Swash F7, 26; Spring, 20; Sterritt D6-E6, 5, 97, 130; Tilly E6, 45, 135; Waccamaw River, 4, 20, 36; White Oak C5-D5, 24; see also Kingston Lake/Kingston Lake Swamp

swashes: Singleton F6, 3, 13, 26, 41, 94, 96, 97, 98, 105; White Point F6, 3; Withers (Spivey's) E7, 3, 13, 97, 110, 123

Tabor City, 124, 126

--- Tribune, 90

Talbert, Roy (Prof.), 20, 30

Taylor, Dennis S., 1, 77

Ten Nights in a Bar Room, 127

Thom, Bruce G., 1, 2, 3, 5, 36

Thomas, Eulee, 13

---, Eunice M., 121

---, John, 14

---, Wyness, 3, 5, 28, 38, 62, 65, 66, 72, 80, 113, 122, 130

Thompson, Capt., 45, 46, 121

---, Dino, 98

---, F.A., 79

---, Jack, Plate 16, 41, 94, 98, 99, 101, 102, 103, 120, 125

Tilghman (family), 8

Tilghman Pier/Beach G6, 138

Tillman, John M., 93, 105

Tindal, Joseph, and Mrs., 86

tobacco, 1, 3, 8, 10, 24, 50, 51, 59, 66, 77-91, 94, 103, 110, 113, 114, 116, 124, 132, 133, 139 and passim

Todd, Austin, 43, 121

---, Charles M., 5, 25, 113, 129

---, Mrs. ("Granny"), 10, 59

Toddville C6, ii

Tolar, J.R., 15

trains and railroads, Plate 14, ii, 1, 2, 3, 5, 13, 15, 17, 20, 24, 28, 34, 50, 51, 52, 56, 58, 62, 67-70, 78, 98-99, 102, 105, 110, 111, 120, 124, 125, 126, 130, 136; individual trains: Black Maria, 32, 62, 64, 68, 75; Chickenbone Special, 11; Shoo-Fly, 11, 31, 32, 41; individual railroads: Atlantic Coast Line, 2, 31; Conway & Seashore, 32, 34; Conway, Coast & Western, 95; South Carolina, 31; Wilmington, Chadbourn & Conway, 31; Wilmington-Columbia line, 31

Trestle Restaurant, 43

Tyson, George, 94

United States of America, states: see states, U.S.A

Upperman, Leroy (Dr.), 94, 96

Vaught, Elsie C., 17, 51

---, J. Marion, Jr., ii, 51, 52, 62, 63, 64, 67, 69, 72, 73, 74, 86, 90, 107, 130

---, J. Marion, Sr., 63, 74

---, Odrick, 112-13

---, Thomas C., 25, 107

---, Widow

Veneer Mfg. Co. D6, 38, 40, 67, 73, 113, 134

Venus flytrap, 6

Vereen, Heck, 90

---, John, 28, 42

---, Link, see Grant, Donnie

---, Lula, 140

---, S. Gordon, 140

---, Toby, 140

Waccamaw (pen name), 8, 41

Waccamaw Indians, 2

Waccamaw Neck C8-D8, 3

Waccamaw Pottery E7, 3

Walker Chemical Works D6, 59

Wall, E. Craig, Sr., 104

Walls, Dwayne, 11

Ward (planter family), 40, 135

--- Dalton (Rev.), 65

Ward's Fishery, 122
wars: Civil, 5, 7, 8, 10, 11, 15, 22, 25, 28, 31, 37, 40, 42,
  44-45, 49, 52, 55, 56, 57, 81, 93, 102, 105, 108, 125 (Old
  Soldiers), 141; Korean, 7; Revolutionary, i, 7; World
  War I, 7, 30, 41, 70, 90, 127; World War II, Epigraph, ii,
  7, 8, 17, 21, 29, 30, 37, 58, 85, 90, 97, 121, 133, 139
Warwick, Elsie C., 13
Washington, George (President), i, 26, 93, 95, 96, 139
Waties Island H5, 3, 95
Watkins, Ellen W., 131
Watson, D.B., 78
Watts, Bertha, 28
---, Duke, 28
---, G.W., 40
Wells, Andrea E., 33
---, Katie V., 141
---, Randall A.: *Along the Waccamaw* i, 141; *Horry
  Stories*, i; *"Let's Call It,'"* i; *"No Match for our Dad,"* i;
  Stretch, 142; *Wood & Water*, i
Welsford, David C., Plate 14
Weston, Plowden C., 10
---, Mrs. Plowden C., 22
White, Coyte, 122
---, Julius "Joe," 41
Whitefield, George (Rev.), i, 119, 121, 122, 134, 139
Whitson, Alice L., 72, 74
Wiegand, Joann G., 3
Williams Box Mill, see Veneer Mfg. Co.
Willcox, Clarke A., 109, 111, 121
---, H.T., 103
Williams, Capt., 42
---, Leon, 120
Wilkins, Green, 96
Williams, John A., 53
---, Willis, 53
Williamson, James C., 56, 72
---, Ruby, 76
Wilson, Joanna D., 25, 82, 139
---, Zane, 135
Winburn, Aubrey, 85
---, J.L., 89
---, Jimmy, 85
Windy Hill Beach G6, i, 21, 26, 94, 95, 96, 109
Winfield, Ann L., 79
---, Robert, 9, 21, 30, 31
Winyah Bay, 26, 36
Winyah Indigo Society, 128
Woodall, Ione, 11
Woodbury, Edith P. D., 44, 121
---, Ruth C., 15, 46, 126, 128
Woodside (family), 98
Woodward, Eugene, 131
---, Mr., 131
Wootten, Bayard, Plate 11, 94, 110
Work Progress Administration, 8
World War I, II, see wars
Wright, Eric (Prof.), 16